George Washington
Dealmaker-In-Chief

The Story of
How the Father of Our Country
Unleashed The Entrepreneurial
Spirit in America

Cyrus A. Ansary

Washington, D.C.

Includes bibliographical references and index.

Hardcover ISBN 978-1-7326879-6-7
Paperback ISBN 978-1-7326879-0-5
ebook ISBN 978-1-7326879-1-2 (epub)
ebook ISBN 978-1-7326879-2-9 (Kindle)

Interior design by booknook.biz

Cover: *The Washington Family* (detail), Edward Savage,
courtesy National Gallery of Art, Washington, DC

DEDICATION

To Jan
Who is a fountain of joy

To Doug, ParyAnn, Jeff, and Brad
Who make a parent proud

ALSO BY CYRUS A. ANSARY

Odyssey of High Hopes

A Memoir of Adversity and Triumph

ACKNOWLEDGEMENTS

To my longtime friend and colleague, the late Steve Hartwell, whom I succeeded as chair of a series of funds, I owe the inspiration for the writing of this book. A passionate believer in the many benefits of studying history, he encouraged my interest in the life of George Washington and other Founding Fathers. The late Jim Rees, the incomparable president of Mount Vernon Ladies' Association for nearly three decades, was equally encouraging and offered the full resources of his organization once I began my research.

The main credit for this work goes to my capable executive assistant of many years, Jennifer A. Krieg. Without her tireless devotion, this project would have never seen the light of day. The first draft of this book was more than 1,200 pages; it was Jenny's grasp of the myriad details of George Washington's life, career, and Presidential accomplishments that made possible the huge task of condensing the work, while maintaining the integrity of its theme.

My thanks also to my researchers, many of whom held PhDs in American history; several had law degrees. All did careful and thorough research for discrete segments of the book. They were Erika Ban, Jennifer Copeland, John Gardner, Jason Guthrie, Mary Lee Kingsley, Helen LaCroix, Heather McHale, Mary McPartland, Sonia Merzon, Taki Miyamoto, Kathryn Moss, Jeff Pierce, Laura Robotham, Dana Stefanelli, and Brooke Stoddard. Thanks also to my editors Peter Kilborn, Jeff Alexander, and Ed Breslin for their substantial contributions at various stages of the work.

I am indebted to my son Bradley C. Ansary for his invaluable help. In the face of a changed and difficult publishing landscape for first-time authors, he took a deep interest in ensuring the publication of this book. He shepherded the manuscript through several stages of selection and negotiation to complete the process.

I could not end these acknowledgements without mentioning the contribution of my wife, Janet H. Ansary, for her love and devotion in all things, but specifically for her patience through the years the project was in development, and her willingness to read the multiple drafts of every chapter and offer her insights, critique, and suggestions.

TABLE OF CONTENTS

AUTHOR'S INTRODUCTION

First-time visitors to the City of Washington are often awed by the majesty of its many and varied monuments, the vastness of its impressive museums and galleries, the broad avenues radiating from the Capitol like the rays of the sun, and the natural panorama of the shimmering Potomac defining the city's western boundary. Americans are proud of their capital city, and foreign travelers generally rank it on a par with the capitals of other great nations.

What is mostly forgotten, however, is that the city's gestation and birth were embroiled in the highly divisive regional squabbles of the last decade of the eighteenth century. Several cities – including Baltimore, New York, Philadelphia, Richmond, and Charleston – had bitterly fought over where the capital of the new nation would be located. Finally, after a controversial backroom deal, a stretch of land along the Potomac River was selected as the future home of the national government.

Congress passed a resolution in July 1790 that directed President Washington to erect an entire city from scratch. The resolution also mandated an impossible ten-year deadline for its completion. If that was not enough, Congress also refused to allocate any funds for this immense enterprise. Yes, not a cent. It is almost as if, amid the heat of the tensions and politics of the time, the resolution was designed to ensure that the project would fail ignominiously.[1]

Washington immediately began planning how he would fulfill his congressional assignment. He carefully orchestrated a series of meetings with various town leaders in the region and permitted the rumor mill and speculation about his intentions to run free. He met with his engineering, surveying, and architectural teams to ensure that his program stayed on track. He then prepared for the inevitable negotiations – perhaps even confrontations – with the owners of the large tracts of land in and around the proposed city. No mere farmers, these men were sophisticated about their real estate. They had already started squabbling among themselves, jockeying for position.

The initial meeting took place at Suter's Tavern in George Town, a small village near the Potomac. To the assembled, Washington described what the new and opulent American capital would look like when completed; how it would include the two houses of Congress, the President's mansion, and dozens of other buildings and commercial sites in addition to roads, bridges, parks, and walkways. Washington did not need to belabor the point. The hardboiled landlords could see for themselves what those plans would do for the region. The scrub land and marshy terrain they now owned would skyrocket in value.

That realization was what Washington had been leading up to. It was the right moment to launch into serious negotiation. The session carried over into the next day. When the smoke cleared, Washington had managed to acquire outright half of the land needed for the project at no cost. Likewise, for the roadways and streets he would pay nothing. He had also secured the owners' consent to his plans for subdividing into lots the parcels for which he had paid nothing and selling them to raise the construction money for the project. He also worked out a highly advantageous arrangement for the purchase of additional land as needed.

Armed with contracts drafted by Thomas Jefferson and James Madison, Washington sealed the deal in the second day's session before leaving on a prolonged tour of the southern part of the country.

This was George Washington in rare form. Some writers—perhaps unmindful of the nuances of dealmaking or of negotiating technique—have found nothing extraordinary in what Washington accomplished. They are not to be blamed; Washington did make it look easy. Driven by the imperative of building a potent symbol to enshrine the union of the states, he had resorted to a creative and novel dealmaking technique to fulfill his congressional assignment. His use of this buyout formula was probably the first in U.S. recorded history. In today's private equity world, it is not entirely unknown to acquire a company essentially by the use of its own assets and its own credit to fund the transaction. Perhaps it was *his* approach that has become a template for modern entrepreneurs and dealmakers.

* * *

In his civilian life, George Washington was a serial entrepreneur and dealmaker at a time when the private equity world was not even a gleam in the eye of the most farsighted financier. In the vernacular of finance (as distinct from the jargon of backroom politics), a dealmaker is one whose expertise lies in the art of structuring and negotiating complex transactions. This book, however, is not merely the chronicle of Washington's forays into dealmaking, fascinating and colorful as they would be even to a modern reader. Rather, his entrepreneurial ventures are covered here because they served as the chrysalis of the astonishingly prescient economic policies he put in place as the first President of the United States. His carefully crafted economic blueprint for the country and his determined execution of its ingredients during his two terms in office are the least well understood facets of Washington's busy and productive life. They enlarged the dreams and opportunities of Americans, led to a flourishing entrepreneurial climate, and made an inspiring tale for our time.

The plethora of books in existence about George Washington would lead one to believe that the last word on his life has been written. And yet, in all these biographies, one searches in vain for any reference to Washington's long-term economic vision for the United States. The entrepreneurial society which encouraged and nurtured the successes of America's great inventors and industrialists did not sprout by sheer happenstance. It was put in place by our first President. Ironically, the throw-away line by many writers is that Washington knew little or nothing about economics.[2] Even the rare presidential scholar who ventures into the unfamiliar realm of early American economic policy inevitably becomes mired in Alexander Hamilton's fiscal initiatives. Hamilton did indeed make valuable contributions, but Washington's strategic economic plan for the country was far broader in scope. It was our first

President who painstakingly laid the foundation for the entrepreneurial society to take root in America, and it did not come without a struggle. Washington needed superhuman tenacity to overcome fierce opposition to his program.

I first became interested in Washington's role in the economic development of the United States in the latter half of the twentieth century. As a corporate lawyer with a lifetime of immersion in international finance and economics, I had the opportunity in the course of my work to observe and study the economies of various countries in Europe, Asia, Latin America, and Africa. I found much to admire in the lives and work of the members of those societies, but when I compared their commercial sectors with the American model, the differences were striking. Other countries had experimented with various forms of command-and-control economies and political structures, including fascism, Nazism, and communism, but no enduring benefit had resulted from them, while the American economy had survived repeated shocks and grown ever stronger. One could only marvel at the impressive national statistics continually coming out of the United States, and at the ability of the American economy to outpace and outperform all others.

Despite the inevitable ebbs and flows in prosperity, by the end of the last century the U.S. model accounted for a disproportionate share of global output and was the engine of an awesome standard of living at home. The dollar had achieved the status of the pre-eminent currency for trade and finance, US Treasury securities were the safe-haven financial instruments of choice for surplus funds of governments from around the world, and many flocked to the U.S. from other lands to invest in the equities markets. Even aside from the resilience and strength of the American economy, its propensity to produce life-changing innovations and technological breakthroughs was already garnering curious and excited attention abroad. Clearly, these developments were crucial elements in the metamorphosis of the United States into a superpower.

Since that time, American-style economic activity in a variety of permutations has been emulated by other nations. The result is a collective raising of living standards and national output in many countries. Some have adopted our economic approach without accepting the American-style democratic self-government, thus ushering in state-controlled capitalism. Nevertheless, it should be a matter of pride for the United States that these other nations have come so far and so fast by learning our commercial methods and our economic culture, successfully transforming themselves into economic powerhouses as well.

How did the U.S. achieve such amazing results? How could we account for our advanced standard of living? Was it pure chance? Was it something in the water? Could there be some truth to the old saying that the Almighty favors the infirm, the handicapped, and the Americans? Or was it because Americans were simply smarter, harder-working, and better educated than other nationalities? There is, of course, no evidence to substantiate such simplistic generalizations. Smart and industrious people are part of the population of *every* country, and even though an American education is highly prized all over the world, the U.S. does not have a patent on good schools. The United States is blessed with land and natural resources, but so are many other countries whose economic development has not matched ours. What was the formula for this economic success, and where did it come from? Was the model thoughtfully chosen, or did it evolve purely by chance?

The quest to unravel the origins of the special American economic model took me on an intriguing journey of discovery into the earliest days of the republic and led me unerringly to one man: the first President of the United States. As I immersed myself in the country's business and financial history, it quickly became clear that the last thing on Washington's mind was to devise a new economic theory. Forming such hypotheses, then and now, has generally been the exclusive province of theoretical academicians. Washington needed to be more pragmatic. He sought to create a work environment in America that was the antithesis of what had existed in the formative years of his own life under the British colonial rule. A description of these experiences and how they influenced his vision for the strategic economic development of the United States, as well as the step-by-step process he put in place to fulfill it, is the story of this book.

George Washington passed through life like a gale-force wind blowing across the early American landscape. Possessed as he was of boundless energy and a voracious hunger for knowledge, scarcely an area of contemporary human endeavor escaped his interest and scrutiny. (One biographer described him as a man who operated as though he had twenty hands!) Standing at the epicenter of political, military, and economic developments in America for almost half a century, Washington successfully led two campaigns that changed forever the life of all Americans. His first campaign is well-known. It gained freedom from British rule for the American colonies, making it possible to establish a system of political democracy in the United States under a new constitution. Washington then waged yet another campaign, one which laid the foundation for a unique economic system for the country and which remains largely unheralded even to this day.

The first campaign was led by *General* Washington, the second by *President* Washington. The first was bloody and dramatic, and had a finite beginning and end. The General received well-deserved public recognition for its outcome. The second was mostly quiet and subtle, consisting of a series of carefully crafted steps designed to create the ingredients of a viable economy which in time would be dubbed by theoreticians the "entrepreneurial economy." Without the economic infrastructure Washington put in place during his Presidency, the great experiment in the republican form of government might well have had a different outcome. Probably only an authoritarian government could survive prolonged dismal economic conditions. A leader of another nation in a later era articulated this concept well when he asserted that "political and military victories cannot endure unless they are crowned by economic triumphs."[3]

Upon becoming President, Washington translated his own early experiences as a colonist in British America into a mosaic of laws, policies, and practices meant to create a flourishing entrepreneurial society. Not unlike our political form of government, the economic transformation Washington put in place was neither preordained nor inevitable. To achieve it, he had to overcome formidable political opposition from many quarters, including members of his own administration, as well as personal attacks on himself. In the process, he also had to deal with substantial obstacles placed in his path by foreign adversaries. He persevered because he was keenly aware of the unfairness of the previous system, characterized as it was by graft, inequality, and central control of the colonial economies. He knew why and how it had to be changed.

As our story unfolds, the reader will see that many other bright, patriotic, and dedicated Americans participated in the creation of this economic revolution. Some are well-known, others less so. This group included John Adams, Benjamin Franklin, Alexander Hamilton, John Jay, Thomas Jefferson, James Madison, Gouverneur Morris, Robert Morris, Thomas Pinckney, and a host of others. As already mentioned, some writers have attributed this economic revolution solely to one of its participants, namely Alexander Hamilton. His work in the administration is well documented in this book. He performed brilliantly under the President's auspices, and most of his actions meshed well with Washington's overall economic design for the nation. However, the creation of the credit markets and other fiscal measures undertaken by Hamilton as Washington's Treasury Secretary were only part of the President's overall strategic plan. Washington was like the impresario of an artistic production: the one who conceives of a project, organizes the effort, painstakingly recruits the requisite talent, prepares the budget, arranges for the financing, pulls all the disparate elements together, and then oversees and approves each step in the process of bringing the production into being.

Before delving into the substance of this undertaking, let us first look at the influences that qualified George Washington for this vital initiative.

Washington spent eight years as a Revolutionary War general, and the same number of years as President of the United States. Yet what has captured people's imagination is his extraordinary valor in the face of superior British forces. His other contributions in the public sector have not received the same level of recognition as his wartime achievements. Perhaps this is understandable, as we are all fascinated by the extraordinary circumstances of wars and crises, catastrophes and controversies. Washington's military achievements have been clothed in glory by writers, but from an economic perspective, his civilian life was equally colorful, adventurous, and risk-taking. It also provides vital clues to many of his Presidential actions. In reality, biographers have perceived Washington's activities in the private sector as mere intermissions within his highly productive stints in the government. Washington himself, however, saw his government service as interruptions in his private life – obligatory service and his patriotic duty, but nevertheless temporary interludes – quite different from modern politicians who mark time between periods spent in the public sector by consulting, practicing law, lobbying, and serving on corporate boards while preparing for the next opportunity to get back into government service. Washington was definitely not of that ilk.

Washington's private involvements have gradually faded from public awareness. His running of Mount Vernon has received vivid treatment by biographers, but his dealmaking has been viewed more as a sideshow, inspiring little original research. In the chapters that follow, it is my purpose to provide a picture of those kaleidoscopic experiences as a backdrop for the influences that shaped his economic decisions as President. Scholars have not linked Washington the capitalist with Washington the President. Occasional attempts by writers to probe into this aspect of Washington's life suffer from the natural absence among historians of an intuitive grasp of the entrepreneurial dealmaking that characterized so much of Washington's endeavors. While the focus here is on his service as the country's first chief executive, this book will demonstrate how his civilian activities influenced the design of his economic agenda as President. It is my hope to encourage a new understanding of this aspect of the Washington persona, to show that his life comprised a series of interconnected influences, and to argue for the importance of his earlier commercial experiences as crucial contributions to his enduring economic legacy.

In chronicling the life of major historical figures, biographers naturally follow the written records, the paper trail. The leader who produces impressive writing or delivers memorable oratory is often embraced by his or her profilers. George Washington brought an unerring sense of purpose to every undertaking and had an extraordinary capacity to engage the hearts and minds of Americans, yet he rarely employed flowery rhetoric or lurid prose to persuade or proselytize. Perhaps he believed that when you have elegant purpose, there is no need for elegant prose.

When he took over as Commander of the Continental Army against a seemingly invincible foe, for example, he did not mark the occasion with an impassioned speech like "We shall fight on the beaches.... We shall fight in the fields and in the streets.... We shall never surrender" as did a later wartime leader.[4] Washington did not say the words; rather, he let his actions speak for him. Those actions indeed left no doubt in anyone's mind of his grim do-or-die determination in pursuit of the cause of American independence.

To Washington, it was not the words but the acts of a leader by which posterity would judge. In the public arena, talent was not what one *said*, but what one *did*. He had a passionate conviction that America would have a prominent place in the theater of history, and he was fully prepared to do all he could in aid of the realization of that prospect. Even so, he disdained grand evocations of national destiny and other self-intoxicating oratory about it. Likewise, when he initiated his trail-blazing economic and societal agendas which are the subject of this book, he delivered no inspiring speeches to commemorate the events. He acted – quietly, methodically, and confidently – to put his program in place. He had no stagecraft in his public arsenal, nor would he subscribe to a modern politician's trust in the power of hype and sloganeering. Perhaps he found flowery prose and imagery more abstract and less precise in articulating concrete thoughts and data than he wished to convey. And so he chose to account for his life through his achievements rather than through an impressive display of communication skills. Another Founder, Benjamin Franklin, said it best: "Well done is better than well said." Or, to use a modern aphorism, "Words are words... promises are promises, but only performance is reality."[5]

Washington's understated style has also created some interesting but odd wrinkles in the recounting of his life. To satisfy what a commentator called the "human thirst for a ripping good story,"[6] writers have at times created mythical tales that often endure far longer than any truths. Sometimes, as Chief Justice John Jay observed, "truth and error imperceptibly become and remain mixed and blended."[7] George Washington's life stories thus include many pithy, colorful, and catchy myths. They have in fact dogged his biographers throughout the intervening centuries, so much so that even historians have not always been immune to them.

The mischievous fable about a youthful Washington cutting down a cherry tree is perhaps inspirational for children and has value. Other myths, however, have negative connotations that tend to reflect adversely on Washington's character, his qualification for office, and his legacy. Or perhaps, as a respected historian stated, there is a drive in academia to present the Founders as highly flawed individuals, giving rise to "the mythology of founding."

In the course of this book, I will deal with three such myths, namely, that Washington knew nothing about economics, that he was a rash speculator in business, and that the source of his wealth was his marriage to Martha.

History, of course, unfolds chronologically. To be true to the subject matter, however, I have arranged the material mostly in a thematic format. The presentation comprises Parts I through IV. The chapters range across a variety of broad topics; taken together, they are designed to supply the reader with a cohesive view of Washington's strategic economic blueprint for the country. Part I begins with the Prologue and provides a glimpse into the formidable perils which he faced as the first President, and the events that had brought the country to its deeply troubled posture after the Revolution. Chapters One and Two are composed of flashbacks to Washington's youth and the projects he handled as an adult in the private sector. Their financial rewards are described in Chapter Three. Part II describes the real-life experiences of a colonist operating under British rule, both culturally and commercially. These were the influences that shaped Washington's perspective on life, society, and economics. His exposure to the Scottish and English political philosophers of that era is detailed in Part III, as are his formulae for the entrepreneurial society he would bequeath to posterity. Part IV provides a description of the President's actions, policies, and initiatives. For ease of reference by the reader, each chapter in Part IV will receive stand-alone treatment. To lay the foundation for a fully functioning economic system, President Washington had to attend to the entire range of the needs and challenges of the nation, both short and long-term, domestic and international.

Some readers may notice I do not discuss in detail an event of earthshaking impact for every aspect of life in the United States. This was the mutiny-in-the-making by the Continental Army in Newburgh, N.Y., on March 15, 1783, possibly an attempt at the takeover of the U.S. government by the military. Washington successfully defused and derailed the threat by the sheer force of his personality and by taking advantage of the deep respect and devotion accorded him by the officers under his command. This dramatic crisis occurred, while Washington was still in uniform, thus predating his Presidency and the span of time covered by this book. I mention it because the increasing incidence of military takeovers of governments around the world today brings the focus back to George Washington's monumental contribution to our constitutional government, the firm establishment of the principle of oversight of the military by civilian authority in the United States. Without his determined intervention in that potentially calamitous episode, life in this country could well have turned out differently.

A word about the historiography of this work. While much of the research for the book involved original sources, I wish to acknowledge my deep debt to the distinguished historians and biographers cited here, without whose brilliant scholarship I could not have built my case for the unique contribution of our first President to the economic edifice that we know as the American entrepreneurial society. Any errors of fact or judgment are, of course, entirely my own responsibility. Incidentally, in the process of preparing this study, I have taken the liberty of modernizing the spelling and punctuation of some of the original quotes in the text.

Cyrus A. Ansary
Washington, D.C., 2019

Prologue

AN UNFOLDING DRAMA

George Washington was nervous.

The man who would face a bayonet charge with unflinching courage; the man who would stand amid the blood and chaos of combat as if chiseled in granite, calmly directing his troops in tactical formations against vastly superior enemy forces; the man about whom Thomas Jefferson said, "He was incapable of fear, meeting personal dangers with the calmest unconcern," this same steely-eyed and iron-willed general now stood with hands so shaky he had trouble holding the paper he was reading. His voice was tremulous and barely audible, and he seemed unable to make eye contact with his audience.[8]

No man had ever seen the invincible general so moved.

The date was Thursday, April 30, 1789, and the occasion the inauguration of the first President of the United States in Federal Hall, a two-story brick-and-stone building at the corner of Broad and Wall Streets in New York City. The structure had been undergoing extensive renovation designed especially for this day's ceremonies by the young French engineer, Pierre Charles L'Enfant. He had been laboring frantically for months to ensure that the run-down eighty-year-old building was transformed into an architectural masterpiece in time for the inaugural ceremonies. In the main chamber, twelve-foot-high paintings of Their Majesties the King and Queen of France adorned an entire wall, honoring them for their crucial help during the Revolutionary War. Four heavy Tuscan columns in the center of the building extended up to the grand balcony on the second floor, topped by a pediment projecting a brilliant image of the American eagle amid the shining rays of the early morning sun, symbolizing the new national beginning. An ornate octagonal chamber for use by Congress extended to the height of both floors. Beneath the elegant cupola and dome of this structure, Vice President-elect John Adams, other members of the government, representatives of the diplomatic corps, governors, and other dignitaries had all gathered to witness the President-elect take the oath of office.[9]

It was the greatest assemblage of notables and rank from the new nation ever gathered in one place.

Washington's trip to New York had begun seventeen days earlier, when he had reluctantly departed Mount Vernon. (Martha, unhappy that George's retirement had been cut short, did not accompany her husband.) The last leg of the trip was on open water. He traversed the fifteen miles from Elizabethtown, New Jersey, to Manhattan Island aboard a splendid fifty-foot barge built especially for the occasion. Thirteen elite Naval Masters of Vessel, dressed in white uniforms and black caps, manned the oars with no less a personage in the stern calling their strokes than the President of the Common Council of New York. Musicians aboard played during the ride, interrupted only by the roar of the cannons onshore and cheers from spectators riding in the small boats accompanying the official procession.

Passing the Battery and heading into the inner harbor, Washington arrived at Murray's Wharf at the bottom of Wall Street, where he was greeted by the Governor of the State and the Mayor of New York City. They escorted him through a throng of thousands who jammed the streets, described by one writer as comprising almost everyone who lived in the City of New York, jostling to get a glimpse of the nation's new leader.

Profoundly affected by his well-wishers' reception, Washington responded in kind: waving, doffing his hat, and bowing. To all appearances, the occasion was one of a popular leader enjoying his people's adulation.

On this particular day, however, a close observer would detect an edge of tension in his manner, stiffness in his movement, even a pallor in his countenance.[10]

Inside, Washington was in deep gloom. Before leaving for New York, he had confided in Henry Knox, his former general during the Revolution and his future Secretary of War, "My movement to the chair of government will be accompanied by feelings not unlike those of a culprit who is going to the place of his execution. So unwilling am I, in the evening of a life nearly consumed in public cares, to quit a peaceful abode for an ocean of difficulties." To his friend Edward Rutledge he wrote, "I gave up all expectation of private happiness in this world." And to himself, in the privacy of his diary, he wrote, "About ten o'clock, I bade adieu to Mount Vernon, to private life and domestic felicity; and with a mind oppressed with more anxious and painful sensations than I have words to express, I set out for New York."[11]

On inauguration day, April 30, the people filled the streets leading to Federal Hall. The crowd's enthusiasm was in no way lessened by the absence of pageantry common to similar celebrations for the Crown of England and other heads of state in the Old World: No purple sashes, gold braids, or plumed helmets appeared anywhere in the President-elect's entourage. He himself wore a simple dark-brown suit made of broadcloth sent to him as a gift by a mill in Hartford, a pointed demonstration of America's newfound industrial capability after years of British-imposed prohibition on domestic manufacture. His jacket had steel buttons embossed with eagles, and his only concession to the occasion was a ceremonial steel-hilted sword which hung by his side.[12] Missing from his suit was the diamond eagle pin awarded to him by the French Navy.[13]

Washington took the oath of office on Federal Hall's grand second-story balcony overlooking the entrance. Acknowledging the crowd's clapping and huzzahs by repeatedly bowing to them, he read a short inaugural address. Senator William Maclay of Pennsylvania wrote: "The great man was agitated and embarrassed more than he ever was by the leveled cannon or pointed musket. He trembled, and several times could scarce make out to read ..., without ever taking his eyes from the paper." Fisher Ames, Congressman from Massachusetts, wrote: "It was a very touching scene, and quite of the solemn kind. His aspect grave, almost to sadness; his modesty, actually shaking; his voice deep, a little tremulous, and so low as to call for close attention."[14]

It is true, of course, that Washington at fifty-seven was fourteen tumultuous years older than the superman at the top of his game who had assumed command of the Continental Army, and the physical demands and emotional stresses of that job had taken their toll. Nevertheless, for him the performance of one's duty was a sacred charge, a matter of personal honor.[15] What he dreaded most was the prospect of being unable to fulfill the demands of the office of President, thus failing in his duty. For, in spite of his repeated successes at every level of life, his deep and practical knowledge of business and finance, history and warfare, and his personal study of the great classical works, Washington still felt keenly his lack of a formal education. How could he live up to the demands of the Presidency? "I greatly apprehend," he wrote, "that my countrymen will expect too much from me."[16]

His misgivings notwithstanding, Washington knew that the Presidency of the United States was no mere ceremonial job such as the ones enjoyed by some crowns of Europe. He was intimately familiar with the unique challenges and dangers facing the country in the closing years of the eighteenth century, and profoundly aware of the urgency of dealing with them. Devastated by the prolonged Revolutionary War and grievously weakened economically, America was torn by internal dissension and threats to disband the Union and burdened by a crushing load of foreign and domestic debt on which the government was already in default. Hostile foreign forces encircled the new nation, which was virtually defenseless against their encroachments.

Americans saw Washington as a commanding presence and felt safe with him in charge. "There is not a king in Europe," wrote an observer, "that would not look like a *valet de chambre* by his side."[17] Washington himself, on the other hand, was deeply aware of the enormity of the task ahead – ensuring the very survival of the fledgling country he had helped create. The task was as daunting as any ever undertaken by a head of state. It was indeed against an impossibly challenging background that he would begin the first Presidency. Under the circumstances, he was right to have forebodings at his inaugural ceremonies and to experience the kind of stress that hones the senses. Were he unconcerned and placid at that occasion, his audience would have had reason to feel anxious about the fate of their country.

Looking back, Washington could well remember how the nation arrived at this juncture. In October of 1781, the fate of America was similarly poised on a knife's edge. By that time, the revolt of His Britannic Majesty's subjects in America was already half a dozen years old. Exhorted by King George III, Britain had launched the greatest military mobilization in its history to defeat the colonial rebels.[18] It also used its sea power, unrivaled on the planet, to blockade the Atlantic ports of the United States, bringing American trade to a near-halt and its economy to the edge of collapse. Heedless of domestic opposition to his belligerence toward the American dominions, George III stressed once again his resolve "to keep the Empire entire and that no troops shall be consequently withdrawn from America, nor independence ever allowed."[19] On the ground, despite some setbacks, Britain's "southern strategy" showed promise of splitting the southern states from the rest of the country. The fall of Charleston, S.C., in 1780 and Britain's capture of some 5,000 American troops there were indeed devastating for the rebellion. By the time 1781 rolled around, it became clear that the colonists were at the nadir of their revolt, and the king was increasingly sanguine. The deep national anxiety in Britain over the possible rupture with the colonies was subsiding as well, and there was general optimism throughout England that the rout of the rebels was imminent.[20]

Indeed, it was thought time to wind up the fighting. Accordingly, Lord Germain, Britain's colonial secretary in charge of the war effort, issued instructions to his field commander, General Sir Henry Clinton, to commence mop-up operations in Pennsylvania, Maryland, and Virginia, explaining, "For such is beyond all doubt the low condition of Congress's authority and finances, and so weak the state of Washington's army, that little opposition is to be expected in that quarter."[21] The officer designated to dispose of Virginia? None other than General Lord Cornwallis, who had reported an unbroken trail of successes during his march to the Virginia coast. With the war going so well and Parliament on vacation, there was even time for Lord and

Lady North to throw a celebration ball at their home in Bushey, on the outskirts of London.[22]

Then came a stunning development. Those same weakened and disorganized rebels, looking ragged, emaciated, and exhausted, surrounded and trapped the elite British troops in Yorktown, Virginia. When no reinforcements arrived, General Cornwallis ordered his entire army of 8,000 men to lay down their arms on October 19, 1781, and then surrendered his own sword through a subordinate (he himself being "indisposed") to General Washington who had General Benjamin Lincoln accept it. What had been utterly unthinkable had actually happened.[23]

News of the catastrophic defeat at Yorktown reached Londoners like a thunderbolt about five weeks later, on November 25. The Prime Minister, Frederick North, 2nd Earl of Guilford, took it like "a bullet through the heart," pacing the floor in his house on Downing Street in a state of obvious high anxiety, moaning repeatedly, "Oh God, it is all over."[24]

For the British nation, accustomed to a long string of military victories, Yorktown was an unprecedented and humiliating defeat. The loss of America was a national tragedy of immense proportions, with major consequences. Had Britain plunged from the pinnacle of world power? Would it ever rise again? What would be the price of defeat – in territorial concessions, in loss of trade and prestige, in collecting debts from the former colonies? What example would this set for the other British colonies around the globe?[25]

Few in the country had any doubt about where the blame lay for this catastrophe. Charles James Fox, a member of the opposition in Parliament during North's ministry, summed up the public sentiment when he told the House of Commons that "[t]here is one grand domestic evil from which all other evils, foreign and domestic, have sprung." Pointing the finger directly at George III, he made it abundantly clear that "to the influence of the Crown we must attribute the loss of the thirteen provinces of America." In time, others were even more candid, openly stating that George III had "inflicted more profound enduring injuries upon this country than any modern English king."[26]

As for the King himself, was he immersed in self-flagellation over his crucial role in bringing about the disaster that had befallen his nation? Was there any sign of contrition, any public or private *mea culpa*? Not exactly. In an astounding act of denial, he disclaimed any responsibility for the outcome of the war, and then did not miss the opportunity of accusing the Americans of dishonesty and deceitfulness. He expressed satisfaction at being rid of them.[27]

The glee on the American side of the Atlantic matched the despair in Britain. The surrender of Cornwallis in Yorktown thrilled and excited the new nation. As British troops and the mercenary Hessian forces fled the United States in ships of the Royal Navy, so did an estimated one hundred thousand American pro-British Loyalists, leaving behind their homes, farms, and businesses to escape the onset of the new order. With his customary literary flourish, Thomas Paine exulted: "The times that tried men's souls are over, and the greatest and completest revolution the world ever knew gloriously and happily accomplished."[28]

With meager resources but inspired military leadership, plus crucial help from France – financial, naval, and troop support on the one hand, and behind-the-scenes diplomatic cover on the other – Americans had triumphed over the world's mightiest military power. Their victory created unbridled optimism about the future of the United States. Rosy predictions abounded: The country would soon become a world-class military and economic power in its own right. There would be unlimited prosperity available to everyone, down to the lowest classes. America would be an Arcadian paradise, the shining beacon of light, and a haven for the oppressed. "A day will come," the Spanish Minister in Paris confidently asserted, when America "will be a giant... It will draw thither farmers and artisans from all nations." Others echoed Horace Walpole's earlier prediction that "[t]he next Augustan age will dawn on the other side of the Atlantic." A French nobleman who attended the celebrations at the signing of the Treaty of Paris was unabashed in his cheerful assurance that "[t]he thirteen united states would form the greatest empire in the world."[29]

Immigrants *did* flock to America's shores, causing a rapid growth in the country's population,[30] but the optimism about what awaited them in the New World was short-lived. The United States was destined to enjoy neither security nor prosperity during its first tenuous years. Americans soon realized that they had to fight many more battles before they could achieve financial and geopolitical stability for their country, battles that could last longer than the Revolutionary War itself and bring their own share of hardship.

Although war-weary Americans treated Cornwallis's surrender as the end of fighting, the conflict was far from over. Neither the votes in Parliament nor the utter weariness of the British public from incessant wars (seven years with America, four years with France, three with Spain, and one-and-a-half years with Holland) made the slightest difference to the "mindless obstinacy" of George III. Still the implacable foe of his former subjects, the monarch made it known that he "hated talk of peace without an American surrender." He remained uncompromising in his opposition to American independence. He would fight on.[31]

George Washington, acutely aware of the continuing British anger over the American Revolution, held most of his army together after Yorktown. In the meantime, Britain continued to maintain troops in New York, South Carolina, parts of Georgia, and a series of forts in the Great Lakes region.

In the meantime, the machinery for peace between Great Britain and the United States of America began slowly grinding along. As the representatives of the two governments sat together to draft a treaty, the negotiations proceeded in a tense and tumultuous atmosphere. The breakthrough came with the advent of a new British Prime Minister – William Petty, 2nd Earl of Shelburne, and a large landowner in England and Ireland. Lord Shelburne had studied at Christ Church College, Oxford, distinguished himself in the Seven Years' War, and served as president of the Board of Trade and Plantations, the government body administering colonial affairs. Shelburne believed that it was futile for Britain to try to hold on to the American colonies by force, that military action was costly, and that it was vital to drive a wedge between Britain's archenemy France and its new American allies. Whatever may have been the new Prime Minister's political motives, the Americans saw his view of them as refreshingly different from North's relentless hostility. Shelburne wanted to extricate Britain from America "without further damage," but he did not wish to stop there. His bold plan was not only conciliatory but visionary, extending to trade and economic relations, and even to an Anglo-American coordinated defense system – lofty goals indeed for the times.[32]

As soon as Shelburne formed his government in July 1782, Parliament adjourned for a long recess. Judging that he would have virtually no support in Parliament for what he was proposing, the new Prime Minister seized upon the recess to try to push the American peace negotiations toward a settlement. He hoped to finish the job without the inevitable meddling and second-guessing by the hardline faction in the House of Commons once Parliament reconvened.[33]

To represent him in the negotiations, Shelburne appointed Richard Oswald, a businessman with no prior government experience. At seventy-six, Oswald was a friend and admirer of another septuagenarian, Benjamin Franklin. Oswald was a follower of Adam Smith, a fellow Scot and the enlightened philosopher whose work explaining how nations create wealth had found much favor with America's Founders. Oswald had lived in Virginia for five years and owned property in the American south. Even though he had once urged the government to punish the American rebels, he was now committed to conciliation. In time he came to espouse the conviction that "the Americans were destined to become so powerful at sea that no European power ... could safely pretend to impose any limitations on their navigation."[34]

The American team was initially represented by Benjamin Franklin and John Jay. At seventy-six, Franklin was well-known and admired in both England and France. Firmly loyal to the British Crown before the Revolution, he was now unambiguously committed to the American cause. He had been in Paris since 1776 representing America's interests, had successfully engineered the French recognition of America's independence, and secured large financial and military aid from the royal court of King Louis XVI. He spoke French, understood French culture and society well, and had cultivated many friends in the government there.

John Jay, the other American commissioner, thirty-seven years old, was an able New York lawyer with keen intelligence and deep knowledge of foreign affairs. Jay had been President of the Continental Congress. He arrived in Paris from Madrid where he served as the chief U.S. negotiator with the Spanish court. Jay's predilection ran to the English, and he was suspicious of the French. Known to play hardball in negotiations, he enjoyed George Washington's confidence.

In the fall, Franklin and Jay were joined by the third American commissioner, John Adams, fresh from negotiating loan agreements and a commercial treaty with the Dutch government on behalf of the Continental Congress. A fourth team member was Henry Laurens, with whom the chief British negotiator Oswald was also acquainted. Laurens, fifty-eight, was a former President of the Continental Congress and minister to Holland. He had suffered greatly during the war. While crossing the Atlantic in 1780, Laurens's ship was captured by the Royal Navy off Newfoundland. He was charged with treason and taken to the Tower of London, the only American official ever jailed there. Laurens was set free after fifteen months in exchange for General Cornwallis. Laurens's imprisonment and mistreatment had taken their toll of his health. He arrived in Paris as the peace negotiations were nearing the end.[35]

The negotiations soon moved into high gear. The British agreed to withdraw their troops from American soil "with all convenient speed." On the matter of American debts to English merchants, bankers, and brokers, John Adams promptly set the stage: Americans, he asserted, were not in the habit of welshing on their honest debts. Period. John Jay drafted language to the effect that the British creditors would meet with no unlawful impediments in the collection of those debts.

The Americans dug in on another question – Britain's demand for compensation for the Loyalists' confiscated properties. Franklin parried with the toll of Britain's destruction of American properties and even their towns. If the Loyalists were entitled to compensation for their lost assets, Franklin said, then so were Americans for theirs.[36] The issue remained unresolved in the draft treaty which was signed by the parties in the Grand Hotel Muscovite in Paris on November 30, 1782, subject to ratification by the respective governments.

Although it glossed over several sensitive issues, the treaty was indeed a coup for America. Not only did it acknowledge the independence of the United States, it established the country's boundaries far beyond what the members of the American team had dared hope. The new nation stretched to the Mississippi River in the west, to Florida in the south, and to Canada in the north, more than doubling the pre-war size of the republic.

In America there was great relief and rejoicing. A member of Congress summed up the public sentiment when he said the treaty contained everything Americans could wish for.[37] In England, however, Shelburne's government paid a heavy price. Parliament had been in recess until the draft treaty was signed, but the day of reckoning finally arrived. Parliament reconvened in December and the King delivered his traditional speech from the throne. He addressed the developments in America with "ill grace" and choked on the word "independence" for Americans. When Shelburne presented the peace treaties to Parliament for ratification, pandemonium broke out. Even members who had opposed the war were stunned by the concessions he had made. North announced he would form a coalition to overthrow Shelburne.

The Parliamentary assault on Shelburne did not take long to materialize. He was forced from office in February 1783, largely over what the British considered overly generous concessions to America. It took more than six months before the pact was officially executed. The formal signing took place at Hotel d'York in Paris on September 3, 1783. David Hartley, Minister Plenipotentiary for Parliament, signed on behalf of Great Britain, and Benjamin Franklin, John Jay, and John Adams signed as the American delegation. The separate bilateral agreements with France and Spain were signed the same day at the Versailles Palace outside of Paris by the British ambassador to France, the Duke of Manchester.[38]

With the adoption of the historic accord, the American army was disbanded. Eager to return to the life he loved at Mount Vernon, George Washington resigned his command and surrendered his sword to Congress in Annapolis on December 23, 1783. As there was little precedent in history for a leader voluntarily relinquishing power, Washington's parting words, "Having finished the work assigned me, I retire from the great theater of action" electrified the world and earned universal admiration for him and for the United States in Europe.[39]

Americans began to relax, wishing to return to their normal lives and resume their pre-war commercial, cultural, and social relations with their former parent while establishing new ties with other European nations. Washington too began to relax. By 1784, his vision of his own life was clear. "I tread the paths of private life with heartfelt satisfaction…," he wrote his French friend and former comrade-in-arms, the Marquis de Lafayette. "I will move gently down the stream of life until I sleep with my fathers."[40]

With the ouster of Lord Shelburne as Prime Minister, the hardliners ascended in the House of Commons. They set out to dismantle the legacy of Shelburne, forever shattering his dream of intimate collaboration with the United States. For Shelburne's vision of close and friendly Anglo-American relations, firmly based on equality, both nations had to wait for the hard feelings and hostilities to fade.[41] Shelburne, a statesman and English patriot to the end, paid the ultimate price for his prescient vision. He was shunned politically during the remainder of his life and has been subjected to unkind treatment by British historians ever since.

For all their joy, Americans were premature in their optimism. In Britain, a grim resolve emerged that helped quell defeatist spirits.[42] In time, the ministry passed to William Pitt, 2nd Earl of Chatham, in December 1783. Pitt had been home-schooled by his father, himself a former Prime Minister and an outspoken opponent of the American war. After attending Cambridge, Pitt the Younger entered politics, and within an astonishingly short period was appointed Prime Minister. He was only twenty-four at the time, the youngest occupant of that high office on record. He was eloquent, urbane, and politically mature beyond his years.[43] Pitt served a total of twenty years in the office, in two separate ministries.

Britain quickly reverted to many of the pre-Revolutionary mercantilist measures that had frustrated commercial activity and stifled development in the American colonies. Even before the formal signing of the treaty in Paris, an order-in-council made it clear that nurturing friendly cooperation with his former subjects was not on His Majesty's agenda. The order excluded the U.S. from the important carrying trade in the British West Indies, which had been the greatest source of income for Americans before the Revolution. Other measures restricted American exports of various manufactured products to Britain and its dominions. Lord Sheffield, a leading hardliner in Parliament, minced no words on the subject of trade with the United States, openly declaring that it was imperative for Great Britain to block America's trade by every means possible, for otherwise "we are to be ruined by the independence of America."[44]

Britain's lingering resentment over its defeat, however, was not assuaged by mere economic measures, no matter how severe. It refused to remove its troops from American soil as provided in the peace treaty.[45] It justified its refusal on the grounds that outstanding invoices of British merchants to Americans remained unpaid, and that Loyalists had not been compensated for their lost property. Americans took these as clever but transparent ploys. In effect, Britain was contending that the overdue bills of certain private commercial firms in England were equal in gravity to the menacing security nightmare which the presence of hostile foreign garrisons on American soil represented to the United States.

Britain also initiated a series of steps to block America's expansion to the boundaries specified in the Treaty of Paris. It used its troops in Michigan, Ohio, and along the St. Lawrence and the Great Lakes to encourage the region's Indian tribes to resist America's western expansion. Indian incursions into American settlements increased substantially, resulting in the deaths of many settlers and the destruction of their homes and farms. A U.S. military officer bluntly identified the obstacles to the country's expansion: "The road westward would be blocked until the [British] posts were delivered up." The Continental Congress, however, with neither a standing army nor funds to rearm, lacked the power to protect its citizens.[46]

Britain's core strategy was thus clear: strangle America by encircling it on the ground, with British-held Canada to the north, British garrisons in the Appalachian west, and hostile Indians to the west and north. It also sought to cut off America's economic lifeblood by imposing draconian restrictions on its trade with England and its dominions, and interfering with America's trade with other European nations. America was labeled an unreliable trading partner and a poor credit risk. Benjamin Franklin believed that the British were actively engaged in a campaign to disparage America. Thomas Jefferson complained that the British were "more bitterly hostile to us at present than at any point of the late war." John Adams stated that the British were determined to reduce the United States to economic bondage.[47]

Still, it was disingenuous of Americans to blame Britain for all the country's economic travails. Operating as a loose confederation (1781-1789), the states retained their sovereignty. They ceded no taxing power to the national government. During this period, fiscal mismanagement, dishonored obligations, and political disorganization – of which the Europeans were fully aware – were self-inflicted wounds. Britain, of course, took full advantage of the American miscalculations and missteps. As George Washington observed in 1783, "There is an option left to the United States of America, that it is in their choice and depends upon their conduct, whether they be respectable and prosperous, or contemptible and miserable, as a nation."[48]

Spain also complicated the scene for the new nation. During the Revolutionary War, in a confluence of its own interests with those of the United States, Spain had driven the British from the Gulf Coast. Now that the war was over, it too took steps to block the new republic's expansion beyond the Appalachians and joined in thwarting the establishment of America's jurisdiction over the land to the west and south. Spain laid claim to all of Florida and closed the ports of Havana and New Orleans to American products. In a devastating blow to western commerce in 1784, Spain also barred American access to the Mississippi River. As a transportation route, the Mississippi was vital for all Americans, especially those in the western territories for whom it was their commercial lifeline. For westerners, losing access to the Mississippi meant prohibitively higher costs for shipping their perishable produce across mountains and hazardous terrain. Congress's inability to defy Spain raised the specter of the western territories separating from the United States, a prospect that Spain encouraged.[49] Like Great Britain, Spain began agitating with the Indian nations to resist America's western expansion. Soon the country faced a full-fledged Indian war across its western frontier, and the terrorized and besieged settlers under constant Indian attacks despaired of ever receiving help from Congress.

The two European powers with territorial claims bordering the United States, Spain and Britain, took every opportunity to undermine America's stability, but they did not stop with using the Indians for the purpose. They also incited fractious dissident settlers to fight the new government's authority and fomented talk of secession. Britain in the north and Spain in the south were mercilessly squeezing the new republic in a combined military and economic pincer movement that threatened the existence of the frail confederation's survival. The European powers fully expected the American republic to disintegrate.[50]

The United States found itself as stymied at sea as on land. The country was sending its ships freely into the Atlantic Ocean and the Mediterranean Sea to find new markets for its products and new sources of supply. Americans had not expected to find marauders roaming the entrances to the Mediterranean, attacking their unarmed merchant ships, and capturing and enslaving their crews. Reports of the vicious treatment of these sailors raced across the republic, engendering national outrage, but the U.S., without a navy, was powerless to retaliate.

By the time the Treaty of Paris went into effect, any remnant of revolutionary ardor had already begun to wane in America. The thirteen states, never quite sold on the idea of a national union, began reverting to their old ways of viewing themselves as sovereign jurisdictions. They erected barriers against internal trade, levied import duties on products of other states, engaged in border squabbles, issued their own currencies, and tried to conduct their own foreign affairs. The states still harbored deep suspicion of any measure that would strengthen the central government.

The Continental Congress had no coercive authority over the states and lacked the power of taxation.[51] The impotence of Congress during this period inevitably crippled the economy. Its paper currency was virtually valueless, and the government was so mired in debt there was serious doubt about its solvency. By the time the peace treaty was concluded, Congress was barely staving off financial collapse.[52] While its domestic creditors remained unpaid, Congress also went into default on its foreign loans. It had been granted a grace period by its European creditors, but after November 1782, interest payments started falling due on the loans. France, whose aid to the American Revolution had bankrupted its own treasury and resulted in serious social unrest, now pleaded with the U.S. to pay at least the interest on its loans, even if not the principal. Likewise, the Dutch, whose loans to America (in reality, loans made to the French king for the sole benefit of the Americans) had come at crucial junctures during the War, now were clamoring for repayment.

The U.S., unfortunately, had no way of complying with these demands, no matter how pressing.[53] So, in addition to being operationally strapped, the central government lacked credit in international financial markets. Congress showed little inclination to confront the dilemma or its own inadequacies. Its members' attendance became sporadic and lackadaisical, and it was often difficult to muster a quorum. Apathy at the highest level of the government rippled down through the nation. By the 1780s, the early euphoria of independence had evolved into a sense of crisis, with dire warnings that the situation was becoming critical. The country was in fact sliding into its first full-fledged depression. Although the unemployment and economic malaise struck different regions of the country unevenly, by the time of the first Presidential administration, the economy of the United States had shrunk almost by half.One estimate of America's per-capita Gross National Product showed a forty-six percent drop from 1774 to 1790. (By way of comparison, during the Great Depression years of 1929-1933, real per-capita GNP declined forty-eight percent.) "It is really mortifying," George Washington wrote to John Jay. Jay himself, in a letter to Thomas Jefferson in Paris, described the period as one of "much public and private distress." A New Jersey congressman lamented that the United States was woefully inattentive to its dangerous situation. "Like a flock of sheep [on] its way to a slaughter pen," he said, "the nation was headed toward ruin."[54]

It is hard to think of a more challenging period in U.S. history than the years immediately following the Revolutionary War. Washington was deeply aware of the whirlwind of forces buffeting the nation – its social and political turmoil, its economic hardship, and its geopolitical instability. As he had predicted early in the decade, "No morn ever dawned more favorable than ours did, and no day was ever more clouded than the present."[55]

By 1787, public dissatisfaction had reached a boiling point. That year, a convention of many of the nation's brightest minds was called to devise a proper structure for the American government. Thus was born the Constitution of the United States, followed by the election of a new chief executive for the country. Although these initiatives established the proper underpinnings for the U.S. political system, the country's financial burdens and economic difficulties did not change, nor its posture vis-a-vis the hostile foreign forces, Britain and Spain in particular.

At the end of its rope, the desperate populace turned once again to the single leader all Americans trusted. With an almost spiritual faith in George Washington's abilities, they called on him to pull off yet another miracle. His reluctance to take the helm once again was understandable. He had hoped to spend his later years tending the farm in Mount Vernon, keeping it "trim, handsome, and thriving." A modern American President at fifty-seven would be deemed youthful. Not so in the eighteenth century, when the average life expectancy was fifty-one years. Moreover, the titanic stresses of waging the Revolution, as well as the many bouts of serious illness over the course of his life, had by then taken their toll of Washington's trim and athletic physique, and his iron constitution. Being the Chief Magistrate (as Washington often referred to the Presidency) of this vulnerable and fragile new republic, with its agonizing challenges and complex problems, would be another awesome responsibility. It called for reserves of strength and stamina his advanced age might not provide, and for a mastery of multiple fields he was unsure he possessed. He had "escaped the quicksand and mires which lay in his way" during the war, but the ones in the path of the brand new republic, while of different genres, were no less deadly. Nevertheless, given his ingrained sense of duty, George Washington's eventual acceptance of the first Presidency was predictable.[56]

This, then, was the "ocean of difficulties" Washington contemplated during the first inaugural ceremony. During this critical period in the birth of the new nation, it was by no means certain that the United States would survive its infancy.[57] *Schadenfreude*, the pleasure derived from an adversary's suffering, was the dominant emotion of the heads of state in the Old World. [58] The absolute monarchs of Europe, concerned that the republican fever gripping the United States might prove contagious for their own citizens, were likewise gleeful at the misfortunes of the new nation. The noble experiment in self-government was at risk of failure.

Earlier, Thomas Paine had declared that "[t]he cause of America is in a great measure the cause of all mankind." Americans were convinced they could not fail, and that George Washington, standing athwart history, had not taken on the mantle of the Presidency to preside over the fragmentation of the republic he had labored mightily to help create.

There was indeed room for soaring idealism.

PART I

Chapter One

A FARMER'S LIFE

Who would believe that the family with the most influence in shaping the mind of young George Washington was that of an English lord whose passion in life was fox hunting, and who lived on a vast estate with a grand mansion for living quarters?

Anonymous

In a life destined to roil with wrenching hardships and soaring achievements, George Washington faced his first major loss with his father's death. Augustine Washington (whom everyone called Gus) was forty-eight years old when he died in 1743. George was eleven, and Gus's passing shattered an idyllic, fun-filled childhood of fishing in nearby creeks, riding horses, and hunting small game. He now had reason to wonder what was in store for him without the kindly blond giant whose fatherly concern for the education of his sons had always given George a sense of security about his own future. Since early childhood, George had delighted in the stories told at family gatherings about a school in England, the elite Appleby School in County Westmoreland, alma mater to his father and two older half-brothers, Lawrence and Austin. Approaching his teens, George trusted that he would be next to take the thrilling ocean voyage to the land of his forefathers and start learning Latin, Greek and French, the sciences and geometry, and the history and culture of the English-speaking people.

With Gus's untimely death, George's cherished expectation of a classical education at a fancy boarding school in England was forever dashed. There would be no room for such extravagances in the family finances. He would have to struggle along in life unschooled, like the common run of provincial men. It was a blow that haunted him all his days, even as it motivated him to compensate for his "consciousness of a defective education." George felt he would never be able to fulfill his longing to visit the country his great-grandfather John Washington had first departed in 1656 for colonial America, and its capital London, the most exciting city in the world to the colonists. "I dare not even think of such a gratification," he would write later, "than which nothing is more ardently desired."[59]

After Gus's death, George's upbringing fell to his half-brother, Lawrence, fourteen years older than George. At twenty-five, Lawrence was handsome, likable and self-assured, with a high forehead, an open countenance, and an intellectual bent. He was a captain in the colonial regiment attached to the regular British army. George would remember the day he, as a five-year-old, sat mesmerized, watching Lawrence preparing to go off to war, resplendent in his dazzling British colonial officer's uniform with its shining insignia of rank, to serve in the Battle of Cartagena against Spain. That may well have been the defining moment that drew George to a military career. Lawrence was George's role model in other ways as well, particularly in his activities in business and politics, which George tried to emulate in his own life.

Soon after returning from the war, Lawrence began courting Anne, the pretty and cheerful daughter of Colonel William Fairfax, a neighbor. The two married in July 1743, about two months after Gus's death, and moved to Epsewasson on the Potomac River. The rest of the Washington family continued to live in the modest house near Fredericksburg,

Virginia, to which they had relocated several years earlier to be near Gus's iron ore mine. Deeply attached to Lawrence, George often rode off on his horse from Fredericksburg to stay with his brother and his new bride.

The Fairfax Family: An important influence shaping the views of the youthful George Washington toward life and society was the Fairfax family, the most prominent name in Virginia. Headed by Thomas, 6th Lord Fairfax, the family lived on a vast estate with an impressive mansion for living quarters on the peninsula between Dogue Creek and Accotink Creek along the Potomac River. How Thomas Fairfax had come by his large landholdings is a story of the crucial importance of one's lineage in the English society of the time.[60]

Known for its reverence to royalty, England experienced a fateful date in its history on January 30, 1649. Seven years before the first Washington left for the New World, King Charles I was publicly tried and convicted of treason. The writ of execution was signed by Oliver Cromwell and other members of Parliament. Charles lay face down on a scaffold erected outside the Banqueting House in Whitehall, London, stretched out his arms, and was instantly beheaded.[61] His son, nineteen-year-old Prince Charles, was exiled to The Hague in the company of a group of close supporters. His banishment began a period of financial hardship for the royal entourage, some of whom resorted to selling family jewelry and heirlooms to survive. To reward them for their loyalty, on September 18, 1649, at St. Germaine-en-Laye near Paris, young Charles issued to seven of his "right trusty and well-beloved companions" in exile a grant of a tract of land in North America called the Proprietary of Northern Neck, the region between the Potomac and the Rappahannock Rivers in Virginia. The deed purported to bestow upon the grantees almost feudal powers over fourteen hundred square miles of real estate, with only minimal annual rent to be paid in perpetuity to the Crown. It is, of course, doubtful that the grant had any validity at the time, as Charles had no official position then.

Eleven years later, in 1760, monarchy was restored, and Charles, now thirty, triumphantly returned to London to be installed on the throne of England amid much pomp and celebration. Oliver Cromwell had died two years earlier, but the new king lost no time in tracking down the other signatories to his father's execution order. Charles II had them drawn and quartered, literally, their bodies cut into pieces while still alive in one of the most gruesome display of regicide punishment on record.

Restoration caused the earlier land grant to become immensely valuable overnight, sparking a spate of litigation and controversy over the ownership of this vast American domain. When the smoke cleared after several decades of political and judicial maneuvering, one man emerged as the unrivaled winner of the prize. He was Thomas, 2nd Baron Culpeper, the royal governor of Virginia, and he had achieved control of the entire property.

Lord Culpeper's enjoyment of the acquisition he had plotted so long to complete was cut short by his death in 1689. It set in motion a whole new round of conflict and lawsuits. Culpeper had a daughter, Catherine. He also had two illegitimate daughters whose paternity he had acknowledged. He had hardly been laid to rest before the two Culpeper families began fighting furiously over the estate. Sparing no expense and neither side giving an inch, they sparred for years in the English courts and in Parliament. Eventually nineteen-year-old Catherine Culpeper ended up with five-sixths of the Proprietary of Northern Neck, suddenly becoming a most marriageable prize for legions of suitors who began beating a path to her door. Among them was Thomas, 5th Lord Fairfax, thirty-three years old. With little income or property behind his noble status, he saw a way to secure some hard assets to shore up his shaky financial circumstances. He courted Catherine and won her. Through their marriage, control of Northern Neck passed from the Culpeper line to the Fairfax line. A son from that union was Thomas, 6th Lord Fairfax, who was the Proprietor of the estate when George Washington came of age.[62]

Thomas was short and portly, with an aquiline nose and an aloof and eccentric demeanor. Moody and often solitary, he bought the latest fashion in clothes but never wore them. His passion was foxhunting. As a student, he had studied English literature at Oxford and contributed articles to a learned and influential publication, *The Spectator*. Later, he kept company with an attractive young woman in London with whom he was very much taken. He proposed marriage, and she accepted. Their families negotiated property arrangements on behalf of the couple, and committed the details to a voluminous legal document signed by both parties, as was customary. Shortly before the nuptials, however, Thomas's fiancée abruptly broke off the engagement. It seemed that she had received a better offer. In the rank-conscious English society of the time, it was not every day one received a marriage proposal from a duke! She unhesitatingly canceled the nuptials with Thomas (who was a baron) and accepted the duke's offer. Who could blame her? Every woman would choose the high honor of being a duchess over the lowly station of being a mere baroness, would they not?

Taking the rejection personally, Thomas became depressed and retired into seclusion. In time, he slowly recovered, but remained embittered throughout his life. Like Professor Henry Higgins of *My Fair Lady* fame, who would rather face the Spanish Inquisition than let a woman into his life, Lord Fairfax shunned women for the rest of his days.[63]

The phlegmatic Thomas was jolted out of his seclusion when he heard that the ownership of his American property faced challenges on multiple fronts. Galvanized, he sailed to Virginia to inspect his holdings personally. Arriving in 1739, he discovered that the managers had left the estate deeply in debt. They had also conveyed many parcels to their children and other relatives at prices even less than the value of the timber on the land. To add insult to injury, the Lieutenant Governor of Virginia had not only failed to put a stop to the managers' chicanery but was in fact leading the charge against his Lordship's title to the land. Appalled, Thomas cut short his visit and hurried back to London. He filed a petition with the Privy Council to confirm his title, adjudicate the boundaries of his Proprietary, and enjoin the Lieutenant Governor from taking further action with the land. The Council referred the matter for investigation to the Lords Commissioners for Trade and Plantations, and Thomas devoted himself to pressing his case to the Crown before returning to America.[64]

Thomas's behind-the-scenes efforts were richly rewarded. On April 6, 1745, the Privy Council made its decision in the case of *Fairfax vs. Virginia*, granting Fairfax's petition, not only confirming his title to the land in Northern Neck, but so interpreting the boundaries specified in the grant from Charles II as to set the acreage at 5,282,000 acres. It was indeed a spectacular victory for Thomas. Now it was time for him to return to Virginia and take up permanent residence. He settled there in 1746.

Thomas was the first titled aristocrat with whom young George Washington became acquainted. In the Fairfax menagerie, however, it was Lord Fairfax's new property manager who influenced the teenager the most.

To run the Proprietary of Northern Neck, Thomas needed the services of someone with management skills and general commercial competence, attributes of which he had previously been openly disdainful. Deceived by his previous managers, he sought someone utterly trustworthy. He found his candidate in his cousin, William Fairfax, who until then had had quite a varied career. English law mandated that the first-born sons inherited most of the family estate, leaving little or nothing to daughters and younger sons. In the Fairfax line, William was the younger son of a younger son. He received a meager inheritance, much too small to maintain his aristocratic grooming, but private commercial and industrial work requiring sweat and grit would be unseemly and demeaning. With few suitable options, William joined the Royal Navy and later the regular Army, where he rose to the rank of colonel. He then secured a patronage appointment as a Collector of Customs for the colony of Massachusetts. At this point William came to the attention of Thomas Fairfax, who arranged to have his cousin transferred from Massachusetts to the same post in Virginia, which would also enable him to take over as the Agent for the Fairfax Proprietary.

William Fairfax was an intelligent and hardworking man of fifty-two when he settled down at Belvoir in 1748. Managing the Proprietary entailed issuing land grants in the name of Lord Fairfax, collecting rent from the planters, and otherwise overseeing the countless details of administering a vast estate. In time, Col. Fairfax became a prominent Virginian in his own right, holding office as a Justice of the Peace and a member of the House of Burgesses, while still retaining his post as Collector of Customs for the South Potomac. His young neighbor, George Washington, to whom William took an immediate liking, was sixteen. George became a frequent visitor at Belvoir, where William treated him like a son.

When the Privy Council rejected the adverse claims against the Proprietor's title, it created a great stir in the real estate community in Virginia. Now the desirable land close to the Potomac would be available for sale to the expected influx of newcomers and investors. The development of the Shenandoah Valley had already begun, and the area was generating a lively market in smaller parcels, a trend of which young Washington was a major beneficiary with William helping launch his career as a surveyor.[65]

The Agent's own son, George Fairfax, though seven years older than George Washington, also befriended him. They hunted, fished, and rode together. Later, George Fairfax married Sarah Cary, whom everyone called Sally. Only two years older than himself, Washington found her vivacious and outgoing. Years later, Washington acknowledged that the happiest memories of his youth were of the times he spent at Belvoir with George and Sally Fairfax.

Washington as Surveyor: At fifteen, George Washington looked for opportunities that might suit a boy with little formal education. Jobs were scarce, and those that paid in cash were even more so. The keen business sense which became a hallmark of his work in later life demonstrated itself early when he noticed that most of the surrounding land had not been surveyed and had no recognizable boundaries. He already had a solid grounding in math. "Without arithmetic," he would write in his diary, "the common affairs of life are not to be managed with success." Growing up, he had learned to use his father's surveying instruments, such as a theodolite to measure angles and a compass, and he had practiced map-making in the meadows near Little Hunting Creek. So he decided to take up surveying as a profession and was soon running lines for neighbors and doing simple surveys.[66] When he turned sixteen, his mother let him join a surveying party led by a veteran surveyor to the remote South Branch of the Potomac River. William's son George Fairfax went along as his father's representative.

Armed with surveying gear, Washington roamed the hills and valleys of backwoods Virginia for thirty-three days. Awed and enchanted by the wilderness, he could readily identify the trees and plants in the forests and judge the fertility of the soil of the farms he saw. He was fascinated by the outlying settlements and the Indians he came upon. He took detailed notes in a journal, the first of many he would keep all his life.

Following the river upstream through "the most beautiful groves of sugar trees," he was struck by the majesty of the land and sought to capture it all in his journal, including site measurements. Years later, a visitor to Mount Vernon would write that Washington could recite from memory "all the rivers, lakes, creeks and the means to procure a communication between these waters and Portsmouth in the province of Maine as far as the Mississippi."[67]

Roaming Virginia's Shenandoah Valley and Blue Ridge Mountains, Washington had to cultivate a hardy lifestyle. At one stop, he found the bed to be "nothing but a little straw matted together without sheets or anything else, but only one threadbare blanket with double its weight of vermin such as lice." Washington preferred to sleep "in open air before a fire." Rising early to make the most of daylight, he hacked brush to accommodate surveying sight lines, dragged heavy surveyor's chains, forded freezing rivers, and mingled with pioneers and Indians. Following what he called the "worst road that ever was trod by man or beast," the surveying crew blazed their trail west.[68]

The snows melted, Virginia's rivers swelled and rushed, and when the summer of 1749 came, George secured his first job as an assistant to the surveyor who was laying out a town on the Potomac River. It would become Alexandria, today a thriving and picturesque city of 150,000 in suburban Washington, D.C. Upon completing the assignment, he qualified for a surveyor's license from the College of William and Mary, enabling him to take assignments anywhere in the colony. Next, he took an oath of allegiance to the Crown and was then sworn in as an Official Surveyor of Culpeper County. He was eighteen.[69]

George had barely hung out his shingle when he received an enticing offer from the Fairfax estate. Would he take on an assignment as lead surveyor? He could map out a vast stretch of Lord Fairfax's land in the Shenandoah Valley into lots for small farms. Accustomed by then to staying weeks in the wilderness, living off the land, and sleeping under stars, he hit the ground running. Soon recognized for hard and meticulous work for the Fairfax family, he began building a busy and profitable practice.[70]

Before he was twenty, George had earned almost £400. Soon his annual income amounted to more than most Virginia planters earned in a year from their crops or Fredericksburg's tradesmen from their skills.[71] George could now contemplate a long and lucrative career in his chosen profession. With farming and real estate development being America's liveliest businesses for decades to come, surveying could put Washington at the forefront of the colony's economic growth. He kept a sharp eye on population trends affecting housing, farming, and road building, and learned where to look for choice sites. He studied the financing methods employed in real estate transactions, knowledge he would later use time and again in starting businesses.

When he became a military commander in combat, Washington would call upon his surveying skills to gauge enemy positions from great distances. As President, he used the same expertise to lay out government sites and oversee the development of the new city that would become the nation's capital. During his lifetime, Washington surveyed more than a hundred and ninety tracts of land.[72]

In George's formative years in Virginia, ownership of land determined one's standing in the social pecking order. Farming was how the majority of colonists made their living, but farming was not the route to riches. As his brother Lawrence was fond of telling George, wealth and social status came with buying and accumulating acreage. Washington soon began looking out for real estate to invest his earnings. It was work. He would have to put up with the conditions of primitive travel and sit through tedious negotiations to close a deal, but there was no mistaking the rewards.

In the fall of 1750, George made his first land acquisition. He took title to a Shenandoah tract of 453 acres, followed with 550 acres in Frederick County, and 456 acres on nearby Bullskin Creek. Before the year was out, he had thus succeeded in pulling off the purchase of these three choice parcels totaling 1,459 acres, enticing the sellers with down payments in scarce hard currency. And he was not yet nineteen.[73]

Early Professional Influences: When George was growing up, matters of business permeated family conversation. It is safe to say that his grounding in negotiating deals, running agricultural and commercial projects, and engaging in foreign commercial transactions first entered his precocious young mind around the family dinner table.[74] George's father Gus had shown an affinity for business at an early age. One can imagine young George exposed to a variety of business topics, such as deals Gus and his friends were making, opportunities in exporting farm products to England and bringing back finished goods, how to secure scarce financing for their various activities, and of course the frustrating topic of ever-changing British tariffs and taxes.

Later in his career, Gus had turned to a wholly different pursuit, iron ore mining, hardly a common occupation in the colonies at the time. In the early eighteenth century, England planned to push aside Sweden as its primary source of iron, in part by encouraging iron ore mining in the American colonies. By chance, Gus Washington's land along Accokeek Creek near Fredericksburg turned out to hold rich deposits of the ore. To develop the site, Gus went into partnership with Principio Company, an English firm that had already built a furnace across the river in Maryland. Gus plunged into the venture. Initially, Principio was to manage the entire facility, from building the smelter to extracting and processing the ore and shipping the finished product to England. After some years of stressful relations between the transatlantic partners, Gus achieved a significant advance in the negotiations by taking charge of the entire operation on the American side.[75] George never forgot his father's mining operation. (More on this later.)

Once into his late teens, George was a frequent visitor at the sprawling Fairfax estate, learning about the aristocratic English lifestyle, observing the operation of Virginia's biggest real estate enterprise, and occasionally tagging along on fox hunts with Lord Fairfax. The Fairfax association itself became a first-rate tutorial in administrating the affairs of a large estate, subdividing and selling land, handling title disputes, dealing in timber, and paying "quit-rents" in perpetuity to the Crown of England.

Observing his youthful visitor's quick mind and eagerness for knowledge, Lord Fairfax once remarked that George Washington would be "a man who will go to school all his life" – a remarkably discerning and prophetic observation about the eternally inquisitive teenager.[76]

George also had a front-row seat at his brother's busy real estate ventures. In 1747, Lawrence set out to join the rush for large tracts along the tributaries of the Ohio River, but the competition was fierce. To ensure favorable treatment of his petition by the Crown, he needed a star-studded cast of well-connected partners on both sides of the Atlantic. Lawrence succeeded spectacularly. He lined up the Lieutenant Governor of Virginia, Robert Dinwiddie; Thomas Lee, of a socially and politically prominent Virginia family; John Hanbury, an influential London merchant; and no less a powerful member of the English nobility than the Duke of Bedford. At the time, Britain intended to solidify its position in the unoccupied portions of North America and to promote the development of the Ohio territory. Lawrence and his partners, calling themselves the Ohio Company, were granted 500,000 acres beyond the Alleghenies on the "western waters" of Virginia. On the first portion of 200,000 acres, the partners committed to building a fort and trading post at a site on the Ohio called The Forks, where the Allegheny and Monongahela Rivers converge (the site of Pittsburgh today). They agreed to settle at least two hundred families within the grant's boundaries and invest in infrastructure projects. Upon fulfilling these conditions, the Ohio Company would acquire the grant's remaining 300,000 acres. Lawrence, as president of the company, began work to fulfill the Crown's conditions within the allotted timetable.

Securing the grant, however, was to mark the apogee of Lawrence's career and his life. He developed a bad cough and was diagnosed with tuberculosis. Hoping that a tropical climate might help, he decided to go to Barbados. George, distressed by his brother's condition, suspended his surveying practice to accompany Lawrence on the voyage, the only trip he would ever take beyond the American colonies. During the brothers' stay on the island, Lawrence's health steadily declined. He decided he might do better in Bermuda and prevailed upon George to return to Virginia.

While in Barbados, George observed the business practices on the lush island, a British colony then. During the sea voyage home, he noted in his diary the high interest rates prevailing there, the gap between the rich and the poor, the absence of a middle class, and the potential for developing the colony's natural resources.[77]

Bermuda failed Lawrence, too. He went home, and in what should have been the prime of his life, he died. He was thirty-four. He had been a loving and affectionate older brother for George and his role model.

Lawrence had become the ideal surrogate father for George – "my best friend," George had remarked earlier.[78]

George was one of five executors under Lawrence's will, but the other four left to him the practical details of administering the estate. He took on Lawrence's positions in various projects, including a meeting with Lieutenant Governor Robert Dinwiddie that would change the course of his life. Dinwiddie, a descendant of a merchant family in Glasgow, was initially appointed Collector of Customs and the Surveyor-General for several of the American colonies in 1738, and moved soon after to Virginia. A portly man with a Scottish brogue, he had a stern face, a pronounced double chin, heavily-lidded eyes, and a cool and penetrating stare. As the Crown's representative, conflict-of-interest rules did not apply to him, and he was free to use his official position to seek opportunities for personal gain.[79]

The work of the Ohio Company continued apace after Lawrence's death. With material help from Dinwiddie, it established a trading post at Wills Creek on the Potomac near present-day Cumberland, Maryland, but was having difficulty building the fort at the Forks of the Ohio. The Crown's land grant had not foreseen foreign intrusion into the company's territory. By late 1753, the western lands most familiar to Washington reverberated with the sound of French soldiers and traders felling trees and fortifying the virtually impenetrable forest. The French, who laid claim to all the land draining into the Ohio River, were thwarting the Ohio Company's development project.

Once informed, Dinwiddie intervened. As a major partner in the company, he was unabashed in his support of its corporate goals. Critics charged that the Lieutenant Governor was trying to influence official policy and "embroil all colonies in a war" to protect his personal financial interests. Dinwiddie was undaunted. "I have the success and prosperity of the Ohio Company much at heart," he admitted openly. He reported the activities of the French and their Indian allies to the authorities in London. [80] The reply instructed him to find out whether the French were encroaching on Crown lands and, if so, to demand that they depart from the region. He was also ordered to erect a fort at the Forks of the Ohio. Dinwiddie had to be most pleased with himself; King George would be footing the bill for the fort, not the Ohio Company, which had originally agreed to build it.It certainly paid to be the royal representative in an American colony.[81]

After conferring with the Governor's Council, Dinwiddie decided to select a suitable emissary to deliver the ultimatum to the French in the rough and dangerous country inhabited by hostile Indians seven hundred miles from civilization. George Washington was in Williamsburg at the time. They met, and upon one look at the strapping young man, Dinwiddie knew he had found his candidate. With his customary fearlessness, George grabbed the assignment. "I have ... resolution to face what any man dares," he summed up his qualifications for the job.[82]

Still, all Washington knew at the time was that he had been assigned the tasks of making a routine reconnaissance somewhere in the Ohio Valley and delivering a message from the British Crown to the French commandant. He set off with a guide over treacherous, snowbound terrain toward the French positions near Lake Erie. For George, the trip turned into a backbreaking, month-long grind, fending off Indians and nearly drowning in the icy Allegheny River. By the time he completed his assignment, Washington had learned that the French were digging in to occupy the territory, building fortifications for a garrison there and forming alliances with the nearby Indians. In a grisly incident involving a tribe he was trying to recruit as a British ally, the leader of the French patrol, Joseph Coulon de Villiers de Jumonville, was scalped and killed by the Indians.[83] Historians called the scalping the spark that ignited the conflict Winston Churchill later called "the first world war."

Dinwiddie reported Washington's detailed intelligence to London and was told to forcibly eject the French. As war broke out, Dinwiddie found himself dealing with military matters in which he had little experience. Gratified by his choice of Washington for the assignment, Dinwiddie offered to make him a captain in the Virginia militia. Seeing an opportunity to follow Lawrence's lead into a military career, Washington quickly accepted. Dinwiddie then tried to round up troops for Washington's command, but even after offering a £10 enlistment bonus, he found few takers. He then resorted to offering free land. He promised to set aside 200,000 acres of western land as payment for a mission against the French. The land would be allocated according to rank and conveyed to each soldier upon the successful conclusion of the mission. The promise had the desired effect, and enlistments surged.[84]

With that, Washington abandoned his promising start as a surveyor and seized on the calling that would launch him into the history books. He joined the battle with the French and the Indians, on which he dutifully submitted periodic reports to the Lieutenant Governor. Dinwiddie routed some of the reports to London, where the bare-bones but nevertheless graphic details of these adventures were published as *The Journal of Major George Washington* and were widely acclaimed. They turned the twenty-two-year-old author into a household name on both sides of the Atlantic.[85]

Surely Washington could not have surmised that his reconnaissance mission might trigger a world war. Dubbed the French and Indian War in the colonies but referred to in England as the Seven Years' War, it embroiled the day's superpowers, Britain and Prussia, against France, Austria, and Russia in a prolonged and bloody clash in Europe, Asia, Africa, and the Western Hemisphere. It took the lives of more than a million soldiers and civilians. By its end in 1763, Britain had won possession of all of North America east of the Mississippi River, buttressing its older colonies along the Atlantic seaboard.

Even though his role in lighting the fuse of war was inadvertent, Washington's army career had a meteoric rise, in the course of which he mastered the skills of organization and command. His tenure amounted to a concentrated dose of instruction in the ingredients of effective leadership, enabling him to survive in battle, politics, and business. The young officer soon leapfrogged his contemporaries and more experienced officers to be appointed commander-in-chief of the Virginia Regiment with the rank of colonel, earning a salary of "30 shillings a day, £100 yearly for his table, an allowance for batmen and a commission of two per cent on all funds he handled." With little support or supervision, Washington managed the operation personally, selecting his own staff and combat officers, and setting up the recruitment and processing of soldiers. He also served as the paymaster and procurer of food and supplies, and the keeper of all accounts.[86]

All this might have led to a lifelong commitment to the military. Not so for George Washington. As he gained maturity in the service, he realized that colonial officers had low prospects for recognition in the British army, and that British "regulars" looked with contempt upon local troops. England's ambassador to France, General Lord Albemarle, reflected the imperial turn of mind of English officers and their casual condescension toward colonial soldiers when he declared in a letter, "Washington and many such may have courage and resolution, but they have no knowledge or experience in our profession. Consequently, there can be no dependence on them." Washington was stung by the arrogance. In language similar to his later description of Britain's tax policies, he said, "We can't conceive that being Americans should deprive us of the benefits of British subjects." Eventually, he made his decision. For him, the die was cast and there was no turning back. "That laudable ambition of serving our country," he declared, "…is now no more." He resigned his commission after five years of service, to the regret of his regiment for "the loss of such an excellent commander, such a sincere friend, and so affable a companion."[87]

At twenty-seven, Washington's thoughts were already reverting to a civilian career.

Washington as Farmer and Manufacturer: The house where George spent three years of his childhood had a mesmerizing view of the Potomac River and the jaw-breaking name of Epsewasson. Gus Washington's will bequeathed the house to Lawrence, who took possession after his return from a foreign military excursion. He changed its name to Mount Vernon, in honor of English Vice Admiral Edward Vernon, under whom he had served in Britain's ill-fated amphibious campaign against Spain. When Lawrence died, his will bequeathed Mount Vernon to George, subject to a life estate in Anne, Lawrence's widow. While George was settling Lawrence's debts, Anne remarried and moved out of Mount Vernon. Under the law, control of Anne's assets passed to her new husband who also shared in them. When George offered to structure a deal to buy out Anne's life estate in Mount Vernon, her new husband intervened, objecting to the payment of any part of Lawrence's debts from Anne's inheritance. In time, a settlement was reached. George leased the property from Anne with payment of 15,000 pounds of tobacco per year or the equivalent in cash. Upon Anne's death George would come into full ownership of the estate. Until then, George was assured of "quiet possession" so long as he did not default on the delivery of cash or tobacco. Anne died six years later, and Washington became the sole owner of the property where he had many cherished childhood memories.

George returned to Mount Vernon after completing his military service, to prepare for the Big Event of his personal life. He had met Martha Dandridge Custis, who had recently lost her husband Daniel Parke Custis. Martha was a captivating young widow of twenty-seven with dark hair and hazel eyes, a warm personality, and a calm disposition. She was sought after by other men in Virginia, but she reciprocated the advances of the tall man with military bearing and impressive personality who called on her at the White House Plantation on the Pamunkey River on March 16, 1758, and on several occasions afterwards. Smitten, George proposed, and Martha accepted. He wasted no time ordering from London "the best superfine blue cotton velvet" for his wedding suit. Martha too was ordering a fine dress from London. Having been widowed only the previous July, she required that her attire be respectfully discreet. But arrayed in shimmering layers of silken white down to a pair of purple silk shoes, it fell well short of funereal. The wedding occurred on a cold and snowy afternoon on January 6, 1759. George and Martha then honeymooned at the Custis home, followed by a stay in Williamsburg for Washington to attend a session of the House of Burgesses. The couple then set out on a leisurely ride to Mount Vernon, arriving there on April 6 with Martha's children, John Parke Custis, four years old, and Martha Parke Custis, two.[88]

Undaunted by a harsh drought during his first year as the owner of Mount Vernon, George saw himself as a proud planter, as southern tobacco farmers preferred to be called. Although the house was dilapidated, the property run down, and the farm unprofitable, he intended to renovate the house, expand the land, and revitalize the farming operation. The project would be ambitious and costly, but George, venturing into the private sector for the first time since his early surveying assignments, was determined to make the farm pay for itself.

George's forays into the private sector began in earnest at Mount Vernon.

Like other Virginia farmers, Washington concentrated on growing tobacco, the colony's leading staple for generations. He made a detailed study of the plant and its labor-intensive cultivation, from sowing to cutting to curing and storing the leaves. The results of his efforts were mixed. He had to cope with poor soil conditions, erratic weather and water supply, and other natural disruptions. Worse than these agricultural challenges, however, were the commercial and political practices he found stacked against him. Americans were required to sell their products only in the English markets and therefore needed English brokers to find them buyers. The colonists were also constrained in their selection of ships that carried their tobacco to Britain. The shipping requirements were especially onerous. A transatlantic voyage might take a month in the best of times, or two or more, battling fierce seas and evading enemy ships. Tobacco being a perishable commodity, the care taken of its delicate leaves during the crossing was crucial to preserving its quality. However, a farmer dissatisfied with the shipping company had little recourse, as government regulation restricted his choice of carriers. For insurance coverage, the farmer was likewise required to turn to an English underwriter, who was often the same merchant or trader the colonist used as his broker.[89]

For the American farmer, the English broker was a vital link in marketing his tobacco. Transatlantic trade called for patience, an aptitude for risk-taking, and a mastery of onerous regulations. Between the colonial farmer and the London trader, the British system heavily favored the latter. At every stage in this transatlantic trade, each intermediary added a markup plus its own commission, all at the farmers' expense. The colonists often experienced long delays in securing payment for their produce. Beyond that, various regulations put the planters at great disadvantage. They lacked control over their choice of customers and markets, and had virtually no pricing power.

Budding tobacco farmer George Washington initially focused on the land and perfecting his tobacco crop but soon found himself ensnared in the commercial side of the business. Martha's first husband had been using the trading house of Robert Cary & Co. in London for his various transactions, so Washington gave his business to Cary. But for years, in letters to Cary, he complained about wrong sizes or defective merchandise shipped to him, packages misaddressed to wrong ports, and unfair or exorbitant fees and charges heaped on his account. It was clear to Washington, as to his fellow planters attached to other trading houses, that shoddy British merchandise was being foisted on the colonists at inflated prices, and that fraud was rampant. Often, after Washington placed an order, the product's price unexpectedly leaped, or, conversely, when he was selling his tobacco, prices plunged after his produce was already on the way to England.[90] In these and similar situations, the colonists could only seethe at the unfairness of the system and write letters of complaint, but they had no real recourse.

Upon the completion of a sale of tobacco, the proceeds, less Cary's brokerage and other charges, would be credited to Washington's account on Cary's ledger. Since the British prohibited manufacturing in the colonies, Washington ordered farm equipment and other finished goods through Cary. The cost of his purchases, together with the broker's commission and freight and other charges, would be deducted from his account. This meant that Washington was bearing the mandatory fees of his British broker at both ends of a transaction. With razor-thin profit margins characteristic of farming, the double charges for the brokers' commissions, plus freight and handling, were tough to bear. As a result, George Washington and other farmers almost invariably carried negative balances in their brokers' accounts, tantamount to having "overdraft privileges" in today's parlance. Interest on the indebtedness continually increased the amount by which the farmers were in the red. Despite being chronically in debt in this arrangement, the colonists were nevertheless satisfied with the system, under the illusion that their overdraft privileges would last forever. As long as everyone prospered and British merchants allowed the debts of their customers to grow without seeking repayment or penalties, there were few immediate consequences.[91] Regrettably, the day of reckoning arrived all too soon.

Two successive financial panics in Britain spelled disaster for the American colonies. The first occurred in 1763 with the convergence of a series of adverse economic conditions. The colonists' crops brought steeply lower prices in the English markets while the cost of manufactured goods from England soared. English merchants abruptly demanded that their American customers pay off their debts in gold, silver, or pounds sterling, all of which were severely in short supply in the colonies. Coming on top of new British taxes and tariffs, the sudden curtailment of credit was a financial body blow to the colonists. Reeling, they now recognized that they were truly not in control of their own destinies.

Washington adroitly avoided being caught in the slipstream of the Panic of 1763 through the prudent husbanding of his resources, but he learned a hard lesson in the process. He would have to live within the strictures of British control and buy British products for his farm, but he would be wise to lighten his dependence on British credit. His judgment was amply vindicated during the next financial chaos.

A second panic struck in the British Isles nine years later in 1772, with crippling repercussions in the colonies. The increasing scarcity of hard currency in America pushed many American debtors into default. As panic spread, many were forced to sell land and other assets to satisfy creditors.[92] Thomas Jefferson found himself in financial trouble even after selling portions of his holdings in an unsuccessful effort to extricate himself from debt. Washington, on the other hand, did not have to resort to liquidating assets and remained unscathed. Robert Cary & Co. made a pointed suggestion that he should demand repayment of some loans he had made to friends and other needy Virginians. The advice was not particularly well received. Washington always took pride in helping out needy friends and neighbors with loans, but he was never hard-nosed in collecting. He resolved instead to continue reducing his dependence on credit from his London broker.

The panics of 1763 and 1772 sharpened Washington's focus on his personal goals. His long-range aspirations were to accumulate choice real estate for development and to invest in promising new businesses. To use his agricultural activities as a platform from which to get into other profitable endeavors, he had to make his farm self-sustaining. For that, he needed to bring the latest farming techniques to Mount Vernon, even if it meant breaking the traditions of Tidewater Virginia. He saw that restricting himself to tobacco was not the route to the fulfillment of his other goals.

To broaden his economic base, Washington read farming books and manuals, discussed his ideas with knowledgeable contemporaries, and experimented with an array of seeds and grains under a variety of soil and water conditions. He decided to try a series of new crops. He noticed that the Royal Navy needed industrial hemp to make cords for the rigging of its ships. The primary source then was Russia, the low-cost producer, but Russian exporters chafed at the long delays in receiving payment. For strategic military reasons, Britain wanted to reduce its dependence on Russia. Washington spotted an opportunity, though in this case for naught. After experimenting, he found hemp and a similar crop, flax, unsuitable for his soil.[93]

Other choices were more promising: wheat, corn, potatoes, rye, apples, peaches, cherries, and other fruit trees, as well as scores of vegetables including broccoli, cauliflower, asparagus, and other greens. In most cases, Washington could find local customers for the produce, so he would beat the hassle of shipping to England. Cultivating these crops was also less labor-intensive than tobacco, freeing labor for other work. More importantly, the terms of sale for the new crops would be "cash on delivery," and Washington would know the price his products would command by harvest time.

Thus inspired, he began to diversify his crops. This required a major reorganization of his operations, but it began to pay off. In the case of wheat, the plant he was emphasizing most, in a little over four years he achieved more than a twenty-fold increase in its production, to 6,200 bushels. Soon he was also producing 10,000 bushels of corn annually. As he and other Virginia farmers began promoting wheat and corn, Virginia became a major exporter of grain.[94]

Once his wheat crop was established at Mount Vernon, Washington realized he was letting another opportunity slip away. There was more revenue to be derived from converting his grain to flour, work then done by local milling houses. He saw that setting up his own mill could work from both the engineering and financial standpoints. He decided to try the latest technology and build an automated milling machine. It simplified the process and required less labor. He would start grinding grain for internal use at Mount Vernon and soon for sale. The construction took a year, and in 1770 he was producing flour which he marketed under the "George Washington" brand.[95] Later, he bought an ocean-going schooner to export his finest flour to markets in Europe. With this new venture, he was one of the first in the colony to use such high-tech machinery.

Washington's flour brand

Washington's study of agricultural sources led to several inventions of his own. One was a sixteen-sided barn to separate wheat kernels from the stalk indoors. Another was a specialized plow. He developed an intricate crop rotation system, and a specially-designed open-sided structure for the production of fertilizer. He built a greenhouse at Mount Vernon where he experimented with exotic plants. He laid heating ducts underground to warm the floor in winter.[96] He experimented with types of fertilizer to find which possessed the optimum nutrient-enriching properties. Black mold, he found, was best.[97] He also conducted experiments with artificial lighting.[98]

Slowly, Washington's income from agriculture started growing handsomely – enough to let him try other ventures. He turned to manufacturing. Britain prohibited manufacturing in America but exempted goods it needed at home, such as ships built in New England for the Royal Navy. A loophole allowed the manufacture of products intended for internal home or business use. Since Washington grew all the raw materials for weaving into cloth, he set up a shop equipped with looms and spinning wheels to make fabrics for Mount Vernon. He began making woolens, broadcloth, cotton, calico and silk. He hired more weavers so he could market his fabrics beyond Mount Vernon. Then he thought, why not leather? He built a tannery and made shoes. He hired coopers to make barrels to carry his manufactured goods. He moved on to fertilizer, wagons, rope, harnesses, saddles, and bricks.[99]

He considered the Potomac River as it rolled for miles past Mount Vernon, teeming with shad and herring migrating to spawn. He built a commercial fishery. In 1770, even as the American colonists were shocked by reports of sporadic violence involving their fellow colonists and British soldiers – in the Boston Massacre and New York's Battle of Golden Hill – Washington recorded the sale of 470,000 herring and 4,000 shad. To corral them, he first used a small boat his men built and later commissioned a shipwright in Norfolk to design and build a schooner. Spreading his seines across the Potomac, he harvested 1.3 million herring in 1772 and 11,000 shad.[100] He packed the catch in salt, 800 to a barrel, then shipped them to other colonies and abroad.

Washington next turned to alcohol. He built a distillery to make whiskey and brandy. To store the raw materials – ground corn, rye, malted barley, and yeast – he built a warehouse near the flour mill. Starting small, he later expanded to house mash tubs, a boiler, and five copper stills. From an initial batch of 80 gallons of whiskey, the distillery raised the year's production to 4,500 gallons, and the following year to 10,500 gallons. Washington made brandy from cider at a ratio of one gallon of brandy for five of cider. [101]

In time, with shoes, fabrics, brandy, flour, herring, corn and tobacco rolling out of his fields and shops, Washington began marketing his products to others and even exporting to foreign buyers in violation of British rules.

At the height of his management, Mount Vernon, once a struggling tobacco farm, became a thriving industrial village of over eight thousand acres comprising five separate farms, plus a mill and a dairy and hundreds of cows, sheep, and swine. Washington oversaw a work force of several hundred including slaves, composed of tanners, blacksmiths, carpenters, coopers, weavers, fishermen, millers, laborers and farmhands.[102] The run-down house he had inherited from his brother Lawrence was now an imposing mansion with an extra floor added and a grand piazza of Washington's design running the length of the house above the banks of the Potomac.

The devotion and care Washington lavished on his estate produced remarkable results. By the time he took command of the Continental Army in 1775, he had expanded his manufacturing far beyond anything previously attempted in Virginia. He had reversed the chronic negative balance in the account with his English trading house and demonstrated to other colonial farmers that they too could control their own marketing operations – in essence, their destinies. In the process, he also made important contributions to Virginia's farming culture.[103]

Colonists' resentment against British mercantilist policies eventually cascaded into the American Revolution – ironically commanded by the same man who had earlier ignited the Seven Years' War thousands of miles away from London and Paris in the backwoods of Virginia.

One cannot discuss the economy of colonial America without acknowledging the institution of slavery. Washington was the son of a Virginia planter who owned slaves, as did many of America's Founders, including Benjamin Franklin, Benjamin Rush, Thomas Jefferson, James Madison, and Patrick Henry. When Washington bought out his sister-in-law's life estate to take possession of Mount Vernon, he became the owner of eleven slaves. That number grew to 126 as he expanded his farming operation. Slavery was particularly deep in the Virginia culture. It was what God had ordained, according to religious dogma of the time. To judge a man's standing in the community, you asked how many acres and how many slaves he owned.

Washington would not deny that he was born and grew up in the abhorrent colonial slave culture, but history would bear witness that he tried to rise above his beginnings. There is substantial evidence that, as he grew in maturity, he began developing serious doubts about the practice. This change of heart may have first germinated in a pragmatic context, when he switched from being a planter to a farmer. Tobacco was highly labor-intensive, and when Washington abandoned it in favor of other produce, he needed fewer slaves. This put him in a quandary, however. Hampered by his own humane policies at Mount Vernon, he could not simply lay off his excess labor as he would not sell a slave against his or her will, nor would he break up slave families. His pragmatic solution? To train some of his slaves to be spinners, millers, carpenters, fishermen, blacksmiths, tanners, etc. Occasionally, one showed an aptitude for management and was elevated to overseer. A few showed interest in botany, developing expertise in herbs; Washington used them as black doctors. Billy Lee, Washington's valet, was intensely loyal and insisted on staying by his side for more than 30 years.

Some writers have emphasized Washington's humane treatment of his slaves, which was indeed a far cry from the backbreaking labor in the rice fields of the Deep South. A visitor to Mount Vernon was incredulous that Washington "often works with his men himself, strips off his coat and labors like a common man." Another remarked that Washington "treats his slaves far more humanely than do his fellow citizens of Virginia." Other writers have focused on his treatment of slaves as property by insisting on recovering the runaways.[104]

Washington wished to free all his own slaves upon his death, but many of his and Martha's slaves had intermarried, and to break up any slave families gave him "the most painful sensations." So he provided for general manumission of all the slaves upon Martha's death. She chose not to wait, and actually signed the order to free them a year after he died.[105]

When it came to the *institution* of slavery, Washington had no ambivalence: *He hated it.* He said so repeatedly in his private correspondence. Washington saw that the business of slaveholding required transactions "so foul that he could no longer stomach them," as reported by one of his biographers. In fact, shortly before he took command of the Continental Army, he presided over a hearing which denounced the slave trade by "declaring our most earnest wish to see a stop forever put to such a wicked, cruel, and unnatural trade." When a young black woman sent him a poem during the Revolutionary War, Washington was quite encouraging to her, even effusive in his praise; Jefferson less so. Later, General Washington took the first steps toward integrating black and white regiments. "There is not a man living," he declared to Robert Morris, "who wishes more sincerely than I do to see a plan adopted for the abolition of [slavery]." He was also prescient when he said before his death, "I can foresee clearly that nothing but the rooting out of slavery can perpetuate the existence of our union."[106]

When Washington returned to Mount Vernon in 1783 after the Revolutionary War, he set out with renewed energy to revitalize his farm after his years of absence. He needed a highly qualified farm manager and began making inquiries to locate one. Coincidentally, he received an unexpected letter, one which rekindled old memories and would help with his search. Washington remembered George and Sally Fairfax, two friends and neighbors with whom he had spent much of his youth. Before the start of the Revolution, when colonial feelings were running high against the English, the Fairfaxes pulled up roots and, moved to England, and lost contact with their American friends. Unknown to Washington, George Fairfax had tried to reach him as the war raged. Britain, however, intercepted and confiscated his letters. George Fairfax feared being taken into custody for fraternizing with the enemy.[107]

Once the fighting ended, Fairfax resumed correspondence with George and reported finding himself a popular man in England. People who had shunned him earlier for his support of the colonies were pestering him for letters of introduction to his friend George Washington. The general was quick to respond. On July 10, 1783, he wrote telling Fairfax about his and Martha's lives and about those of American friends and neighbors George and Sally would remember. He brought Fairfax up-to-date on the fate of Belvoir, the proud Fairfax home on the Potomac near Mount Vernon, which had been destroyed by the ravages of war. In a rare glimpse into his own warm personality, Washington then offered the Fairfaxes the hospitality of Mount Vernon if they should return to America, and concluded with a rather intimate expression of his own longing to "bid adieu to public life."[108]

Washington wrote again to George Fairfax. He asked for help in finding a farm manager. He said he was looking for someone who "Midas-like" could "convert everything he touches into manure, as the first transmutation toward gold!" Fairfax obliged by putting Washington in touch with the foremost agricultural expert at the time in England, a man named Arthur Young. Washington promptly communicated with Young, who turned out to be eager to help the famous American.

During the pre-war years at Mount Vernon, Washington had worked on honing his hands-on style of management. In his business and agricultural activities, he kept close track of finances and maintained detailed records. The habit of methodical organization, delegation of authority, and formulation of a strategic plan for every project – all traits he developed early in his professional career – served him well in all his involvements. He personally supervised every aspect of the operation at Mount Vernon, rising before dawn to make the rounds of the property, which came to span more than twelve square miles. He immersed himself in reading about the science of farming, experimented with different crops, and searched for new markets.

Washington's legendary attention to detail, widely documented by Revolutionary War historians, was evident in his farming operations. He invented his own bookkeeping system to keep daily track of his income and expenses. To maximize the yield of his crops, he kept a daily log of the weather at Mount Vernon. Senator William Maclay of Pennsylvania, a contemporary of Washington's and a prodigious note-taker himself, joked that for Washington "not a day's work, but is noted what, by whom, and where done; not a cow calves or ewe drops her lamb, but is registered. Deaths, whether accidental or by the hands of the butcher, all minuted [sic]. Thus the etiquette and arrangement of an army is preserved on his farm."[109]

In his biography of the first President, Woodrow Wilson attested to Washington's careful and prudent approach to his farming and business activities. He wrote:

> "To be farmer and merchant at once, ...conduct an international correspondence; to keep the run of prices...., and know the fluctuating rates of exchange; to understand and meet all changes...in markets three thousand miles away, required an amount of information, an alertness, a steady attention to details, a sagacity in farming and a shrewdness in trade, such as made a great property a burden to idle and inefficient men. But Washington took pains to succeed."[110]

For most people, Mount Vernon would have been all they could handle. Washington, however, was accustomed to thinking in larger dimensions. Like the generations of successful entrepreneurs who followed in his footsteps, Washington relished complexity and reveled in juggling multiple projects concurrently, as chronicled in the following chapter.

Chapter Two

FARMER TURNED ENTREPRENEUR

There is a natural aristocracy among men. The grounds of this are virtue and talent.

Thomas Jefferson

The drive to amass wealth is a basic human emotion." That old saying has been attributed to America's early master of the one-liner, Benjamin Franklin, a man who became wealthy before turning to public service. In every generation, Americans have amassed staggering fortunes through activities as diverse as railroads, steel, oil and automobiles, semiconductors, biotechnology and aerospace, the internet and social networking. As a cradle for the creativity and risk-taking that lead to the generation of wealth, virtually every industry has had its day in the sun. In the mid-eighteenth century when George Washington was seeking his own path to professional fulfillment, the most seductive option was developing land. Even in the twenty-first century, playing the property market remains a favorite preoccupation of many an investor.

Washington had a consuming, lifelong interest in real estate, perhaps because financial markets had not yet taken root in the colonies. The strictures under which the colonists operated drastically limited their investment choices. The capital markets, where investors trade stocks and bonds to nurture the growth of businesses, and the commodity markets too flourished in Europe but barely existed in America. Trade regulations issued by the home government for the governance of its American colonies kept the supply of precious metals and hard currency at an ever-dwindling state, creating a shortage of capital for starting businesses and new projects. By a process of elimination, land was the great store of value. For many, it was the only game in town.

An observer of Washington's civilian life would be struck by the speed with which he evolved from a small landowner to a real estate magnate. In the span of only a dozen years, he went from the eager youth barely out of his teens, carefully husbanding his resources and surveying fees to buy small parcels of land at strategic locations, to the seasoned businessman organizing groups to handle large and complex transactions. As his talent for dealmaking began to manifest itself, he made confident forays into ever more sophisticated aspects of business and finance, and ever larger entrepreneurial projects.

The Wonder of Landholding: America in the eighteenth century teemed with British and other European immigrants lusting for land in the New World. Patrician or humble, seeking a few acres to support a family or thousands on which to build fortunes, immigrant settlers kept pouring in. The combined populations of Connecticut, Maryland, Massachusetts, New York, Pennsylvania, and Virginia soared by nearly one-third in a single decade, and land was the common denominator. Washington wrote that "emigrants are daily and hourly settling on the choice spots."[111] When cheap land along the Atlantic seaboard started running out, settlers began looking west. They came upon fertile soil and rushing rivers on prospective trade and migration routes. "It is the passion of every man to be a landholder," a contemporary observer wrote, "and the people have a natural disposition to rove in search of good lands, however distant."[112]

In the second half of the eighteenth century, George Washington was hardly alone in seeing unparalleled opportunities in western lands. Well-known figures of the age – Benjamin Franklin, Sir William Johnson, Robert Morris, Patrick Henry – all believed that immigration and natural population growth would increase land values. Their search for the most auspicious tracts led them to the foothills of the Appalachian Mountains, the regions abutting the tributaries of the Ohio River, and the watersheds of the Mississippi. In their single-minded pursuit of property ownership, these men opened up the country and spread the vision that there was a whole continent out there into which to expand.[113]

As both a farmer and a professional surveyor, Washington enjoyed a few advantages over others eyeing western lands. He was experienced in judging soil conditions, and had a thorough knowledge of the location of rivers, roads, and existing communities in many parts of North America. He also possessed insights into the strategic direction of population movements on the frontier. In a prolonged burst of energy, he used every means available to build up an inventory of much desirable acreage. "Land is the most permanent estate and the most likely to increase in value" was his strong belief and unceasing drumbeat.[114]

With an eye for the development potential of a piece of ground, Washington cast a wide net in search of desirable property. His home turf, of course, was Virginia, a huge colony at the time. It engulfed the present states of Indiana, Illinois, Kentucky, Michigan, Ohio, West Virginia, Wisconsin, and parts of Minnesota, and stretched from the Chesapeake Bay in the east, to the Mississippi River in the west, the Great Lakes in the north, and the North Carolina border in the south. Yet it never seems to have occurred to Washington to restrict his real estate activities to his home turf. In his search for land, he traveled extensively on foot and horseback into other colonies. In the end, he owned land in all of Virginia, as well as Maryland, Pennsylvania, New York, and the Northwest Territory.

A Swamp for Washington: Long before Washington became a national figure by leading America's war effort for independence, he had already established a reputation as a man with a knack for private enterprise. His deal flow – the ability to attract a steady stream of major projects

– would have been the envy of today's private equity firms. Because his own activities in farming, real estate, and manufacturing required close supervision, however, Washington was judicious in making new commitments. Not for him the temptation to swing at every pitch. On the other hand, when a business proposition piqued his interest, he spared no effort in pursuing it.

It was the Nelson brothers, William and Thomas, well-known Virginia politicians and businessmen, who tipped off Washington in early 1763 about a swamp in Southern Virginia that might merit a site inspection. With the off-putting name of the Great Dismal Swamp, it consisted of some 1,800 square miles (about half again as large as Rhode Island) sandwiched between the James River and Albemarle Sound, straddling the borders of Virginia and North Carolina. At the heart of the property was Lake Drummond, flat, glassy and eerily black, reaching five miles across at its widest. Within the dark waters and tangled vegetation of the swamp existed a spider-web network of many other lakes and rivers. An early visitor, enraptured by the wild natural beauty of the terrain, observed that as the sun sank down in the west, its last rays came at a long, low slant into the marsh through a thick stand of gum and cypress trees, "making the little green marsh glow like gold."[115]

Responding to William Nelson, George Washington took a break from a meeting of the Virginia legislature, of which he was a member, to visit the property. At thirty-one, he was already skilled at evaluating a piece of real estate. He would need to judge its location and the surrounding area, walk or ride the roads leading to it, check the soil, trees, and vegetation, make an overall assessment of its potential, and generally get a feel for its demographics. In the spring of 1763, in the company of his two brothers-in-law (Fielding Lewis and Burwell Bassett) and a cousin's husband (Dr. Thomas Walker), together with a guide, he took the ferry from Williamsburg to Norfolk, and then went by horseback to Suffolk. The land, he found, was a coastal quagmire about twenty miles long, with a sixty-five-mile perimeter.[116]

To Washington, the swamp was the last remaining large undeveloped tract in Tidewater Virginia. The local settlers, however, saw the place as nothing but wasteland unfit for farming, and at first glance it did appear to be an impassable morass of fallen trees, great stretches of reeds, dark, marshy waters, and an abundance of mosquitoes, alligators, and copperhead snakes. It would be a challenge to penetrate this primeval jungle, but Washington was a determined explorer. The vegetation was so thick and tangled he often had to lie flat in the boat to slip through. With the practiced eye of a professional surveyor, he assessed the contour of the terrain and the feasibility of digging drainage channels to serve the nearby coastal cities. He noticed something peculiar about Lake Drummond. However topographically implausible, water flowed out of Lake Drummond, rather than into it, as the lake sat above the surrounding wetland. That could facilitate draining a part of the swamp, freeing it for building, logging, and farming. The water itself was also a surprise. Amber-colored and not clear, it was highly prized on sailing ships, as its special qualities caused it to stay fresh for a long time. Washington also noticed the great diversity of trees, particularly the cypress and Atlantic white cedar that would be ideal for ships, homes, barns, and shingles. Finding the swamp's soil "excessive rich,"[117] he considered growing hemp there to sell to the Royal Navy as rigging cords for its ships.

There were, of course, countless unknowns. Did any portion of the property have the right soil for farming? Would growing rice work well in the marshy environment? Could shingles and clapboard be made in sufficient quantity to make their production worthwhile? How would anything made in a part of the swamp be transported to markets in the east and elsewhere? What about the availability of labor? He continued to ponder these questions as he went back in the fall, and again during repeated follow-up visits. One thing was clear: This vast savage terrain concealed magnificent resources near the burgeoning economic centers and the open sea. By his rough calculation, building a north-south canal would connect the waters of Chesapeake Bay in Virginia and Albemarle Sound in North Carolina. It would not only serve as a transportation artery for Norfolk but would also free up tens of thousands of acres for farming and home sites. While preserving the essential character of the terrain, a portion of it could be used for development. There was much to plan, measure, and analyze. Before lifting a shovel, he would have to recruit a competent engineer.[118]

Merely organizing the project would involve endless red tape.[119] To justify the Herculean effort needed to bring the project to fruition, Washington set his sights on 150,000 acres. He anticipated no difficulty collecting the required signatures. There was yet another obstacle: To avoid conflicts over title with other landholders, Washington needed to show what other grants had already been issued. Without a central land registry, this kind of information was not readily available.

After attending to these and a myriad of other details, Washington turned his attention to the most important decision of the project: the selection of his partners. As all grants of land originated from the Crown, it would be necessary to make the right English connections. A member of the aristocracy in London, preferably an associate of the Prime Minister or another heavy hitter, would have to be included in the group. The American colonies, of necessity schooled in the ways of the English, also operated pretty much in the same pathway. So, one or more Virginia politicians, affiliated with the royal Lieutenant Governor or with solid connections of their own in London, would have to be brought into the group. The organizers, including Washington himself, would have to share in the development costs until the project became self-sustaining.

Having given the matter careful thought, Washington prepared to finalize the composition of the group. He had three in mind to provide political cover in Virginia and another three to do the same in London. The remaining five would be Virginia businessmen.[120]

Having established the group, Washington needed to name the business. Ideally, it would evoke images of the rich stands of trees, the burbling and meandering rivers, the lush primal vegetation and ferns, and the wonderful variety of marine and land animals in this immense tract. That would be the land-sale hyperbole of today, but Washington never thought of it. Even though he often waxed rhapsodic about the shimmering waters of the Potomac flowing past the verdant rolling hills of his beautiful Mount Vernon, he normally lived in a world far removed from enticing brand names and sound bites. As his writings, his diaries, and his letters amply demonstrate, he was rarely given to mellifluous prose. Rather, he was focused on substance and results, not affect and color. He settled on the plain and dreary "Dismal Swamp Land Company" as the name.

The partners convened formally for the first time on November 3, 1763, two days after winning the grant. Rather than struggle with the red tape of securing Crown approval for a more typical joint-stock company, Washington settled on the far simpler Articles of Agreement. Each partner would own one share in the company, or a one-twelfth interest, for which he would pay £50. Each would commit to bearing a twelfth of the development costs. The company would have a right of first refusal if a member desired to sell his share. As the petition to the Council bore the signatures of one hundred and fifty-one individuals, the company would have to obtain assignments from all who were not members of the organizing group. The Council's order allowed the company only seven years to complete the survey of the property. Otherwise, it ran the risk of forfeiting the grant, opening the floodgates to other fortune hunters.[121]

In the partnership, Washington was first among equals. He would organize the development effort and monitor its progress. He appointed John Washington, a distant cousin, as the project manager. He would assess the members for their periodic contributions and could penalize those who fell behind.

Today, such ventures are at times structured as limited partnerships. The organizers assume the role of the general partner and retain control of the operation. They are compensated by a percentage of any gains, receive ongoing fees as reimbursement of expenses, and may have other rewards. Their "carried interest" was earlier taxed at a lower rate than ordinary income. The outside investors are designated as limited partners and generally have little say in how the enterprise is run. Unlike the private equity firms of the twenty-first century, however, Washington gave of his time and energies unstintingly to any project he initiated. He organized the effort, hired the personnel, and managed the operation. And yet he never sought any pay or additional percentage or gain for himself. In the Dismal Swamp Land Company, he had one share which he owned jointly with his brother-in-law Fielding Lewis, for which they had paid the same £50 as everyone else, and they met their pro-rata share of expenses.

Under Washington's personal direction, the project began moving on multiple fronts. On the plantable portion of the property, survey work was proceeding apace on nearly fifty thousand acres. A labor force of fifty was busy growing corn, raising sheep, hogs, and cattle, and producing a steady supply of shingles, clapboard, and slim slabs of juniper and cypress for schooners from Suffolk to ferry to markets in Philadelphia and New York. The company established a rice farm for local consumption and export to Antigua. It built housing, barns, and roads, and then began digging a five-mile-long drainage channel to Lake Drummond. Mules and horses helped, but lacking motorized machinery, most of the work – the clearing, earth-moving, planting, digging, and construction – was done by hand. Even so, the company was considering a more ambitious undertaking: building a channel between the rivers emptying into Albemarle Sound.[122]

Virtually overnight, a busy and active operation was springing into being. As word spread that George Washington and other prominent individuals were associated with the project, new groups began forming for the same purpose, some expecting to get a free ride by piggybacking on Washington's research and design plans. All the activity stirred up a buzz about land values in the Great Dismal Swamp. Among the founding members, some shares changed hands. Washington's new enterprise had started off strong, running and racing for the black.[123]

That is, until the American Revolution intervened.

For eight harrowing years, General Washington, commanding the Continental Army, had to neglect his entrepreneurial masterstroke, the Dismal Swamp development, and his Mount Vernon ventures in farming, milling, fisheries and distilling. In his absence, they all began "declining every day," as he later acknowledged to his chagrin."[124]

The war hammered the Dismal Swamp Land Company. It decimated the work force. Thirty-five-year-old John Washington, the project manager, left to join the fighting for the new United States. Without effective oversight, all operations floundered. The swamp became a sitting duck for intruders and thieves. Well into the war, in 1781, the fighting hit home. A Royal Navy raiding party anchored at Portsmouth and attacked the Dismal Swamp's new plantation, destroying houses and barns, and stealing equipment. It left devastation and ruin in its wake. Then, too, no laws protected the property of soldiers gone off to war. Speculators and settlers seized upon the provision in the partners' grant requiring that the developers complete their survey by a seven-year deadline. It inspired a rush for options on the Dismal Swamp acreage.[125]

In the meantime, Washington heard nothing about the company. Not one word for eight years: it might as well have been a century. After the war, he was stunned by the state of the project that he, largely alone, begat and entrusted to others. He was particularly frustrated that his partners had virtually abandoned the business in his absence. In this as in other projects, his long stint in public service had cost him dearly. Distressed by the irresponsible behavior of his fellow organizers, he stepped back somewhat from his hands-on pre-war role in the active management of the company but made certain the operation was still in good hands. He asked David Jameson, a businessman in Yorktown, Virginia, and owner of a quarter-share in the company, to look after the business and to represent him in future meetings. Nevertheless, the multitude of new investors in the swamp kept pulling Washington back into its affairs up until he assumed the Presidency.

Hugh Williamson, a politician who owned acreage in the swamp on the Carolina side and later a signer of the Constitution, urged Washington to persuade the Virginia and North Carolina legislatures to resurrect his vision of a canal for the property. Williamson too believed that a man-made waterway to Norfolk would benefit all communities in the region. He need not have asked. Washington knew that canals, like roads, would be crucial to unifying the new United States. In this he had important support. In earlier correspondence with Patrick Henry, then Governor of Virginia, Washington had advocated canals. Convinced of their promise, Henry became a landowner in the Dismal Swamp himself.[126]

Across the ocean in Paris, Thomas Jefferson was equally enthusiastic about canal-building in southern Virginia. "It is the only speculation in my life I have decidedly wished to be engaged in," he announced. He asked Hugh Williamson to buy shares in the canal on his behalf.[127]

In 1787, while Washington was busy presiding over the Constitutional Convention in a monumental effort to create a new framework for the nation's governance, the momentum for building the canal surged. With the open support of two former governors, Patrick Henry and Thomas Jefferson, Virginia passed the enabling legislation for its construction. Entitled "An Act for Cutting a Navigable Canal," it was to become effective "after the passing of a like act by the General Assembly of North

Carolina." Raleigh signed on three years later, during Washington's first term as President.[128]

To finance the project, Washington advocated a novel formula already tried in England – a public-private partnership. It worked by setting up an early version of a corporation called a joint-stock company, then having an initial offering of shares to the public while reserving a block for the state governments. Sale proceeds would be used to build the canal. The entity formed to operate it was the Dismal Swamp *Canal* Company. As planned, its ownership was split between the shares set aside for Virginia and North Carolina, and those offered to the public. The Dismal Swamp *Land* Company became the largest public shareholder in the new entity.[129] The Canal Company was then given the exclusive right to collect tolls on vessels, people, and freight transported on the canal.

The cooperative venture between the two states began work in 1793, and the first section of the canal, running ten miles north-by-northwest from Lake Drummond, opened for business in 1804. The entire twenty-two-mile project was completed in 1828. Toll collection grew briskly, not only from the vessels using the canal but also from land traffic on the flanking road. The Lake Drummond Hotel, built at the state line, opened early in the first decade of the new century, and became a popular gathering place – with activities as disparate as trysts for lovers and dueling for those less enamored of one another. The canal roused the region's sleeping economy, as Washington had predicted more than half a century earlier.[130]

Once the public-private partnership was underway, the Canal Company became a template for the financing of other canals, roads, and public works projects throughout the United States.

Washington's brother-in-law Fielding Lewis died in 1781. As he and Washington had owned their share in the Dismal Swamp Land Company jointly, Lewis's eldest son wrote his uncle after the war about the disposition of the share, but Washington felt the timing was not right for a sale and counseled patience. The correspondence continued after Washington became President. When settling the Fielding estate became urgent, Washington gave in. The stock was sold in 1795, to Washington's old comrade-in-arms, Henry "Light Horse Harry" Lee, the father of Robert E. Lee.After Washington's death in 1799, Lee defaulted on an installment, and under the terms of the original sale, the shares reverted to Washington's residuary estate.[131] His executors then transferred the shares to Washington's nephew, Bushrod, who received the company's regular annual dividends during his life. As a postscript, the company was sold in the early twentieth century, and the proceeds distributed to all the then stockholders.

Today the canal, running along the eastern edge of the Great Dismal Swamp, is the oldest continually operating man-made canal system in the United States. Listed in the Register of Historic Places and designated a National Civil Engineering Landmark, it is a link in the 3,000-mile Intracoastal Waterway which runs parallel to the east coast from Manasquan Inlet in New Jersey through Norfolk and the Florida Keys before following the Gulf Coast to Brownsville, Texas. As for the swamp itself, its core of 112,000 acres has been preserved as the Great Dismal Swamp National Wildlife Refuge, established by Act of Congress in 1974. It has become an important environmental attraction, a lush habitat sustaining a variety of wild animal and plant life.[132] It is surrounded by homes, farms, and commercial establishments for more than one-and-a-half million residents of Virginia and North Carolina.

While he was President, Washington once wistfully called his experience in the Great Dismal Swamp his "most promising" involvement before the war. Almost two decades earlier, referring to the swamp, he had predicted that those "sunken lands...will in time become... most valuable."[133] He was not far wrong. He sold his interest in the Dismal Swamp Land Company in 1795 for $20,000. As will soon become clear, this was a large sum indeed in the eighteenth century,

When the first boat sailed across the first segment of the Great Dismal Swamp Canal in 1804, and when the Dismal Swamp Land Company paid its first dividend in 1810, the man whose ideas were the springboard for the projects, and whose energies were the motive power for their success, was not there to witness the fulfillment of his vision. Even though George Washington had died before the turn of the century, his passion for conquering the early American wilderness, by building canals and waterways and his pioneering use of innovative financing methods for major projects sparked a nationwide movement in canal building and infrastructure development that has endured through the centuries.[134]

* * *

Quest for Bounty Lands: Washington's passion for land accumulation took many forms, all of which he followed up with great determination. Perhaps nothing illustrates this tenacity more than his quest to collect the rewards promised him during an early military campaign.

When Britain's Lieutenant Governor Robert Dinwiddie hired Washington to help rid the Ohio Valley of the encroaching French, he offered enticements for the dangerous mission. Dinwiddie was not authorized to draft colonists, so to recruit conscripts, he came up with the bait that would hook any young pioneer: free land. He would grant shares of a 200,000-acre tract to those who joined the militia at the start of the French and Indian War.[135] For the soldiers to collect a grant to what became known as Dinwiddie's Bounty Lands, the French had to be driven from the land they had seized. Washington's share as the commander would be between ten and fifteen thousand acres, with diminishing shares for lower-ranked officers down to the enlisted ranks.

That was the plan, but Dinwiddie's posting to Williamsburg ended in 1758, leaving his bounties undelivered and in limbo. It took Washington many years to tackle the royal bureaucracy in Williamsburg and London in a determined effort to secure the promised rewards for himself and his troops. George Mercer, a fellow veteran of the French and Indian War, echoed Washington's own resolve when he wrote, "[We] will leave no stone unturned to secure ourselves this land."[136]

The war was still raging when Dinwiddie retired back to England in 1758. The Privy Council appointed Francis Fauquier, and after his death, the king appointed Norborne Berkeley, Baron de Botetourt, as the new Governor-in-Chief of the colony. The baron was an affable and charming fifty-year-old bachelor. Starting out as a commoner, he had won election to the House of Commons from Gloucestershire before securing his peerage in 1764. When the Crown sent him off to Virginia, it was intended that the baron would deliver a tough and blunt message to Virginians that the era of passive and amiable governors was over. As it turned out, however, Botetourt's genial manner and his patience in public life soon won him many friends in the colony. Obviously, in his twenty-five years in Parliament, Lord Botetourt had learned how to deal with conflicting constituencies.[137]

Washington had to begin anew to press his case for the Bounty Lands. At his behest, Patrick Henry, the Speaker of the House of Burgesses, read into the record Dinwiddie's original proclamation, a powerful reminder of the sacrifices made by the sons of Virginia in the French and Indian War. Washington then followed up with a letter to the new Governor, in which he made a strong argument for honoring Dinwiddie's commitment. Somewhat taken aback by this firestorm about a predecessor's actions already many years old, Lord Botetourt authorized the veterans to commission twenty surveys of the land. This was a major step and the first sign of progress. The surveys, though expensive for the petitioners, would enable them to bypass other title-holders in the Monongahela and Youghiogheny regions down the Ohio River.

Washington called a meeting in Fredericksburg of all the potential beneficiaries of the awards. They decided that a surveying team should venture down the Ohio River to scout out the terrain. The trip would be both arduous and a dangerous encroachment into Indian territory. In retaliation for white atrocities, Ohio Indians were taking the scalps of settlers found invading their hunting grounds. (Washington's personal real estate agent and fellow surveyor, William Crawford, would later be tortured and burned at the stake by Ohio Indians.[138]) Washington agreed to lead the mission.[139]

In the company of several frontiersmen and Indians, Washington led his team in two canoes down the Ohio River as far as its confluence with the Great Kanawha. On the way, they did come upon Indians, but they were friendly. Kiashuta, their leader, remembered Washington from twenty years earlier. Kiashuta wished to open trade relations with Virginia, and Washington promised to speak to the Governor about it. The group then floated down the Ohio for two hundred miles, making rough surveys along the route and hacking trees to locate boundary markers.[140]

The trip took sixty-four days. When Washington returned to Virginia, he found out that Lord Botetourt had contracted fever in September, suffered severe convulsions, and died in early October 1770. He had been a most popular emissary to the colony. He was buried in the chapel at the College of William and Mary. Virginians erected a monument to his memory at Williamsburg. His statue remained undisturbed during the Revolutionary War and still stands today, albeit in some disrepair.[141]

King George III then named John Murray, 4th Earl of Dunmore, the brother-in-law of the President of the Privy Council, as Botetourt's successor. He had been serving as the Governor of New York for only three months and recoiled at leaving. He arrived in Virginia several months late, fuming. "Damn Virginia," he said. "Did I ever seek it? Why was it forced on me?" Virginia, too, recoiled. An English officer described Dunmore as "most unfit." In a letter to Catherine Macaulay, a British historian, Richard Henry Lee, wrote on November 29, 1775, that if the "administration had searched through the world for a person the best fitted to *ruin* their cause, they could not have found a more complete agent than Lord Dunmore." Once resigned to staying in Virginia, Dunmore tried to make the best of it by accumulating wealth in a hurry through the use of his official position.[142]

Clearly motivated by personal gain in regional development matters, Dunmore showed no interest in discouraging western migration. He upheld Botetourt's order for twenty surveys of the Bounty Lands. The Governor's Council then authorized the distributions to the veterans, and they were made over a two-year period between 1772 and 1774. Washington's personal share of the awards came to 33,000 acres, or more than fifty-one square miles on the Ohio and the Great Kanawha Rivers.[143]

It all happened none too soon. The American colonies were protesting the king's imposition of new taxes, and public uproar in newspapers and state legislatures was taking on a vehement tone. The king ordered the governors to suspend all grants except those to veterans, and prohibited new land surveys. Dunmore, growing edgy, declared martial law, dissolved the House of Burgesses, and threatened to annul all grants. He believed that "Americans were deluded in expecting to hold out against British power." When protests turned to bloodshed and outright rebellion by the colonies, Dunmore took flight.[144]

Eight years later, at the conclusion of the American Revolution, the new Commonwealth of Virginia confirmed the claims of the 1754 veterans.[145] Thus, through more than two decades of war and peace, against bureaucratic indifference, rival claims of English aristocrats and others, a hazardous trip through Indian country, many hours devoted to negotiating with the authorities, preparing petitions, and traveling on horseback and canoes to distant locations, Washington had steered his ship into port.

* * *

Not all of Washington's bounty claims, however, had a salutary outcome. In February 1774, Washington purchased a land warrant issued to one Captain John Rootes by the colony of Virginia in 1763 for serving in the French and Indian War. The warrant entitled Rootes to 3,000 acres of land northwest of the Ohio River.[146]

As the new holder of the warrant, Washington arranged for surveys of the property and recorded them with the official surveyor of the Virginia Military District of Ohio. He returned the warrants to the Commonwealth of Virginia in 1783, and the land grants were officially issued to him. A year later he ran into a glitch.[147]

In 1784, Virginia ceded its vast Ohio territory to the federal government, except for 4.5 million acres in southwest Ohio that had been set aside for all the veterans of the Revolutionary War (except, of course, George Washington, who had declined any rewards, either in cash or land, for his service in that engagement). His new 3,000 acres lay in this region. Recognizing that warrants awarded for service in the French and Indian War would be rendered void under the terms of the 1784 relinquishment, Virginia in January 1792 authorized the satisfaction of such claims in its Military District. To be eligible for this exception, the claimant was to have served in the 1775-1783 Revolutionary War. Washington, who satisfied all the requirements, reasonably believed that his Rootes warrant was safe.[148]

Then the glitch arose. A purely procedural requirement prevented him from claiming title to the land. A new federal statute, enacted in 1790 and ironically signed into law by President Washington himself, required that all such claims had to be filed with the U.S. Secretary of State, not with the state of Virginia.[149] Amid the demands of his Presidential duties, Washington overlooked how the new law might cloud his own title until the summer of 1798, the year before he died. Aghast, he wrote to Colonel Richard Anderson, the former surveyor of the Virginia Military District of Ohio, under whose auspices Washington had first submitted his claim.

He was assured that his lands were safe.[150] Washington then included the 3,000 acres among the bequests he made in his estate.[151]

Six years after Washington's death, a new deputy surveyor of the Military District, Joseph Kerr, took office. Kerr arranged for three separate claims to be recorded against Washington's parcels. The new owners in turn transferred title to two of the parcels to Kerr himself. With that, Washington's 3,000 acres were now irretrievably lost to his heirs.

George Washington, who made it a hallmark of his Presidency to root out corruption and leave a legacy of honest government, thus became himself the victim of corruption at the hands of a tainted official. Far from being exposed, Kerr went on to become a U.S. Senator from Ohio.[152]

* * *

In Search of Coal: *It is May 27, 1754. Lieutenant Colonel George Washington, 22 years old, has been creeping in the woods all night with his troops and Indian allies toward the French position. When he was commissioned back in March, Governor Dinwiddie instructed him to proceed toward the forks of the Ohio to complete the construction of Fort Necessity at Great Meadows, near Pittsburgh. He was authorized to use whatever force was necessary to complete his mission. After daily mishaps and misadventures en route, it has taken him more than two months to reach the vicinity of his destination.*

It is now early in the morning, and the Virginians are within 100 yards of the unsuspecting French troops. A few more steps and Washington's command would be out in the open.

Washington stands up, shouting the command to fire. Bullets begin whizzing in the air, a sound young George finds "charming." Taking heavy casualties, the French raise their arms as they run away from the Indians to surrender to the English troops. The tales of Indians taking the scalps of live prisoners have the French in terror. The battle is over within minutes. It is a rout of the French.

Washington is exhilarated. He has his hands full, however, keeping the Indians from taking the scalps they believe to be their due.[153]

Sixteen years later, in October of 1770, Washington traveled to Great Meadows, near Pittsburgh, the site of that fierce battle he had fought in his youth.[154] It was of course familiar ground, but this was no walk down Memory Lane. There was not a word in his diary about the earlier episode. Rather, it was the commercial prospects of the region that had brought him back there on this trip. But what was he scouting out at the site of old battles from his youth?

Even though he later built a commercial milling operation in the area, more than gristmills and fertile soil were on Washington's mind on this trip. What had piqued his curiosity was a report that there was a coal mine nearby, still a curious phenomenon at the time. Back in the thirteenth century, English King Edward I was informed that the emissions from burning coal were "corrupting the air with great stink and smoke." So he banned burning coal and threatened any transgressor with torture or execution. The king's energy policy, however, was ignored in the intervening centuries. When Washington was small, as already recounted, his father managed an iron ore mining project near the family farm in Virginia. George had never forgotten that the iron furnaces of his childhood used coal for smelting.[155]

On this trip, Washington with unerring instinct headed for the site of a coal mine near Pittsburgh. He wanted to see the quality of the coal, how it burned, and how dense its smoke was. The mine, he wrote, contained coal deposits "of the very best kind, burning freely and abundance of it." At the time, most Americans were unaware of coal, even though it had been imported in limited quantities from Britain as early as 1730. In an era when fossil fuels and other sources of energy were yet to be discovered, Washington saw great potential in the use of coal for industrial purposes, as well as for home heat. The public may have been oblivious of it, but Thomas Penn, the patriarch of the Penn family, the colony's largest landholders, was fully aware of the existence of coal in the vicinity of Pittsburgh as early as January 1769. *It would appear that so was George Washington.* He was one of the first in America to consider investing in a coal field.[156]

Modern oil prospectors buy or lease large tracts of land in the expectation of finding oil underneath. Those who succeed in striking oil reap rich rewards for their labors. Washington was a pioneer in using the same technique for coal. By the time he left the vicinity of Pittsburgh on this trip, he had put together several parcels for purchase: 1,644 acres in Fayette, 234 acres in Great Meadow, and 3,000 acres in Washington City, for a total of about 5,000 acres along or near the Monongahela River and Pittsburgh.

Washington's vision for the region and its resources proved accurate. Less than a half-century later, the nation would be running on coal. The entire territory surrounding Washington's tracts was layered with coal seams. In time, nearly a thousand coke ovens in the area would be going full blast. "The tract of land [Washington acquired] contains valuable seams of coal," an early writer observed, "and with some contiguous territory is valued at upward of twenty million dollars."[157]

With the signing of the 1783 Treaty of Peace ending the Revolutionary War, Washington disbanded the army, resigned his commission, and began turning his attention back to his commercial pursuits. Once again, the appeal of "western" lands loomed. He decided to visit the substantial Ohio Valley holdings he had accumulated before the war. On a wet and rainy day in September 1784, he set off on horseback on a month-long journey of nearly seven hundred miles. Washington was returning to Great Meadows.

Two weeks' travel brought him to his first stop at the site of his mill. After acquiring the 1,644-acre tract on the Youghiogheny River in 1770, he had hired one Gilbert Simpson, from Loudon County, Virginia, to move to the site at the Youghiogheny River. He was to clear the land and build and manage the mill. Over the years Simpson sent Washington occasional reports of his progress, each time apologizing for having to ask for money but did so anyway. It was £250 the first time, later it was £300, and he kept on asking until Washington had sent him a total of £1,200 sterling, a substantial sum. Now, a decade later and only a few months after the signing of the peace treaty, Washington had come to the mill to see what his manager had accomplished over the years.

He was aghast. The mill was in utter disrepair. What Washington had in abundance, instead, was an unending stream of Simpson's excuses: There were natural disasters; the dam on the river collapsed; there was an outbreak of smallpox; flies almost killed his horses; Indian uprisings disrupted the work; he caught a cold that turned to fever; his wife had refused to accompany him to the mill, and no one could expect a man to live without his wife. Washington could only fume at the man's stupidity, but there was not much he could do. As one writer commented, Simpson could not have been too stupid; he had successfully defrauded Washington not once, not twice, but multiple times over the years.[158]

Perhaps Washington should not have been surprised. As in so many of his initiatives, he was ahead of his time. He was probably the first American to set up a plant in a remote site. He already had a well-run mill on Dogue Creek at Mount Vernon. At a time when communication was dependent on horses, overseeing a business two hundred and fifty miles from Mount Vernon was a bold experiment in remote management.

Nevertheless, the crucial element in the disaster he faced in Pennsylvania was, of course, his inability to oversee his business affairs while running the Revolutionary War. For this project, therefore, the outcome was pre-ordained. Faced with the circumstances, Washington decided to bail out. He arranged to auction off the mill. Many people showed up, but they had come to ogle the celebrity general, not to buy a mill. In the end, he sold the property for payment in wheat. He would have preferred cash.[159]

Title to Land: Washington's next stop on this trip was to visit the tract of 2,828 rich meadowland acres he had purchased fourteen years earlier in 1770, near the confluence of the Monongahela and Allegheny Rivers. Again, the news was bleak, as unpleasant surprises dogged his footsteps everywhere on this inspection tour – another inevitable consequence of his enforced absence from his affairs while commanding the Continental Army.

His land, Washington found, had been expropriated.

While he had been fighting the War of Independence, thirteen families from a dissenting offshoot of the Presbyterian Church calling themselves the "Seceders" had set up housekeeping on his property. They had built houses and barns and gone into full-scale production of wheat and corn. When Washington confronted them, they were defiant and began raising questions about the validity of *his* chain of title. They said he derived his title from the King of England, and everyone knew that the Crown had no standing in America any more. Never mind that the person whose land they had seized was the one who had brought about that change. They were not impressed. They had no intention of paying rent, nor were they interested in buying the property, contending they already owned it. It was enough to raise a general's blood pressure. Faced with unrelenting stonewalling by the squatters, Washington's frustration reached the boiling point. Losing his temper, he called them trespassers and ordered them off his land. The families were unfazed. In fact, one of the squatters, who happened to be a Justice of the Peace, is reported to have fined Washington for using improper language. They then informed him that only a court of law could evict them from the land.

The die was cast. Washington would have to resort to litigation to recover his property. He began making inquiries to find a lawyer in the area. Historians have often written about Washington's well-honed instincts for selecting the right people when the need arose. His search in a nearby town led him to a lawyer named Thomas Smith, a Scottish immigrant who understood real estate. Washington had made a wise selection; Smith in time became one of the best-known trial lawyers in Pennsylvania and eventually served as a justice of the Supreme Court of the state. Washington instructed him to bring suit for ejectment. The Seceders hired a Pennsylvania attorney, Hugh Henry Brackenridge. Well-known as a playwright and newspaper publisher, Brackenridge had a reputation for flamboyance. He would go toe-to-toe with Thomas Smith before Judge Thomas McKean, the circuit judge who would preside at the trial.

Smith performed substantial research on the case, concluding that the outcome of the controversy rested on several decisive issues: Since the records of Washington's title had been destroyed by British raids during the Revolutionary War, would the jury be persuaded that he in fact had good title? Were the required surveys performed on Washington's behalf by a duly-certified Pennsylvania surveyor? Had Washington perfected his title by making improvements on the property after purchase, as the law required? And, lastly, did the squatting families take possession of the disputed tracts before Washington had recorded his warrant, giving them a prior prescriptive right to the land?

The pretrial process lasted two years, during which Washington kept up a steady barrage of letters and advice to his own lawyer, including a fourteen-page recitation of facts as he saw them. Smith, in turn, tried to caution his client about the vagaries of a jury trial in Pennsylvania, that local sentiment greatly favored the squatters, who were known to many in the area, that the jurors would feel little sympathy for an absentee landlord, and that similar cases in the state had resulted in verdicts against property owners.

Some biographers have expressed surprise, even disbelief, that Washington would engage in a protracted controversy with some Pennsylvania farmers over a piece of ground. But a greater principle was involved. Washington believed that respect for property rights was the lynchpin of a free economy. He objected to squatters – he called them *banditti* – occupying land they did not own and contributing little to the community. Having lived through the confused state of land titles during the colonial period, Washington was determined to strike a blow for property rights.[160]

Despite all the obstacles, after two days the jury came back with a verdict for George Washington. Perhaps this was one time it paid to be a national hero. The squatters still refused to pay rent or buy the land; they preferred moving out to search for another parcel of free land. As for Washington, he sold the property in 1796.[161]

*   *   *

Not all of Washington's creative energies were directed toward his own business affairs. Even in his youth, his focus oscillated between public projects and private ones. As the scale of his commercial operations grew, he also confidently undertook initiatives that rightly belonged in the public sector. The full array of his dealmaking skills found expression in two large and enduring public projects. One, relating to water transportation, is covered here. The other, his largest and most significant for the nation, is described in Chapter Twelve.

*   *   *

Inland Waterways and Canals: In July 1754, twenty-two-year-old George Washington, a lieutenant colonel in the Virginia militia, suffered a stinging defeat at the hands of French forces at Fort Necessity. He retreated to Fort Cumberland, fifty miles to the east, to ponder the recent events in broader perspective. Britain was obviously determined to wrest control of the area from the French, but Washington saw a major obstacle. The supply lines were long and difficult. As he gazed at the Potomac River, he saw in its glimmering stretches a super-fast logistical chain. A natural artery to the interior. The ideal highway between eastern commercial centers and military outposts in the west.[162]

It was an intriguing idea. He decided to test it. In August, he and several military companions took a canoe trip on the Potomac for a couple of hundred miles. They encountered daunting rapids and sheer vertical drops. Washington's canoe nearly sank. While the group was struggling with the rapids, he was busily taking notes on the location, depth, and extent of the falling water.[163]

His Potomac adventure ended the same month it had begun in 1754, but Washington's preoccupation with river improvement became a lifelong endeavor.[164] Fueling his drive was the abysmal state of overland transportation in the eighteenth century. It was a true deterrent to commerce. What roads, bridges, ferries and lodging facilities existed were few in number and poor in quality. The uncharted and dazzling expanse of western lands beyond the mountains seemed as remote to Americans of that era as what lay beyond the oceans. To Washington, inland navigation conjured up images of easy and cheap movement of people and goods, of economic growth. Further stoking his enthusiasm were excited reports from England about the brand-new technology of canal building.[165]

Virginia had an abundance of river systems. The James River flowed eastward through the Blue Ridge Mountains to Chesapeake Bay. The Potomac followed a parallel pathway from western Maryland down to the Chesapeake. Both waterways boasted long stretches of smoothly flowing water, interspersed with crushing rapids varying from a few feet to nearly eighty feet in height.[166] Pragmatic Washington recognized that clearing hundreds of miles of river would be a formidable engineering feat. Then, too, financing such a project would be a challenge. Taxpayers would not readily suffer a tax upon the whole whose benefits would primarily redound to the few. Nor would private enterprise alone be able to bear the burden of such a large undertaking. But what about a blend of public and private financing? Investors would have to be given "a kind of property in the navigation," he mused, an exclusive right to collect tolls on waterways. (In time, this would become a financing template for infrastructural projects in all the colonies.)

Once his stint as Commander of the Continental Army was over, Washington quickly launched a campaign to convert his vision of river transportation into concrete proposals. He boned up on the prevailing methods of canal construction and the pros and cons of sluice works and lock-based systems. He studied the available literature but could find no one in America knowledgeable about building them. So, he dispatched a man to England to study canal technology first-hand. Finally, he felt ready.

As he saw it, the starting point would be to create a joint-stock company for the sole purpose of extending the navigable portions of the Potomac, and another to do same for the James. In the eighteenth century, incorporation was no simple matter. He needed to line up support in the Virginia and Maryland legislatures for the endeavor. He recruited James Madison to oversee this initiative. Thomas Jefferson also echoed Washington's passion for the project; he believed canals were vital to Virginia's future.[167]

When none of his Virginia colleagues would accompany him, Washington traveled alone to Annapolis before Christmas 1784 to hammer out an agreement between Virginia and Maryland. It took some doing, but he got the Maryland legislators to go along with his project. Then in January, at his behest, Virginia passed the enabling legislation for the Potomac Company. The law creating the James River Company followed shortly thereafter. The states would grant the companies the exclusive right to collect tolls along the rivers. Each company would then have an Initial Public Offering: The Potomac Company would raise £50,000 sterling in subscriptions. The two states, Maryland and Virginia, would each purchase 50 shares. The James River Company, a strictly Virginia enterprise, would issue subscriptions for 500 shares of $200 par each. The commonwealth would buy 100 of those shares.[168]

The IPOs sold out quickly, and money poured in. Washington bought five shares of stock in the James River Company but declined to serve as its president.[169] He readily agreed, however, to serve as president of the Potomac Company. No surprise there. He had lived and played on the banks of that river since early childhood. He also splurged and bought twenty-four shares in that company.[170] He then supervised the first meeting of Potomac's board of directors, organized the recruitment of skilled engineering staff and other personnel, and devised a project timeline. He divided the workforce into two teams of fifty, each group working on a different segment of the river.

In no time, the venture was transformed from a mere business plan into an operating entity. He lectured the directors on the sluice and bypass canal options, and then led them on a three-day tour of inspection of the project.[171] He continued his oversight of the company until he was satisfied that it had "the Potomac navigation in hand."[172] He took pride that "instead of ten years which the company is allowed for opening the navigation, it will be made passable in little more than half the time."[173] He only resigned from the company to serve as President of the United States. Eventually, he was replaced by Tobias Lear, his longtime aide.

The James River Company followed a similar pathway, until the directors informed the legislature in 1790 that "the canal and improved navigation of the James River is fully completed from the first obstruction at Westham down to a place called Broad Rock."[174]

In recognition of Washington's efforts, the Virginia General Assembly voted to reward him with 100 shares of stock in the James River Company and 50 shares in its Potomac counterpart. He agonized over whether he should accept. He was concerned that his advocacy of inland navigation might then be misconstrued. But he was equally concerned he would give offense to the people of Virginia if he turned down their gift. He finally agreed to accept the shares in trust for "two charity schools, one on each river for the education and support of the children of the poor and indigent," particularly the orphans of soldiers who had died in the war. James Madison reported that of all the available options for compensating Washington, this seemed to be "the mode least injurious to his delicacy as well as the least dangerous in precedent."

Washington's James River shares were transferred to Washington and Lee University (then Liberty Hall Academy), and his Potomac stock was similarly donated.[175] As for the companies' shares he had purchased with his own money, he still owned them when he died in 1799. In his will he advised his heirs to hold on to the stock, "there being a moral certainty of a great and increasing profit arising from them in the course of a few years."[176]

The Potomac Company was reborn in 1824 as the Chesapeake and Ohio Canal Company. James River Company, too, was later reborn as the James River and Kanawha Canal Company.[177] Long after Washington departed from the scene, his fingerprints were still evident on the C&O Canal, and to a lesser extent on the James River and Kanawha Canal. He, of course, had not been alone in believing that inland navigation was essential to the success of the American experiment. Others too had spoken of "that rising world" across the mountains to the west, and of the need to "apply the cement of interest" to bind it to its eastern counterpart.[178]

What set Washington apart was his tireless advocacy of canals, and their underlying political and economic imperatives. The rise of the two canal companies and their success were testaments to Washington's passionate resolve to foster the nation's economic growth. He proved himself both a thinker and a doer. In the words of famed journalist Joel Achenbach, "any enterprise in America in 1785 would be pleased to have as its chief visionary General George Washington."[179]

Chapter Three

FRUIT OF ENTREPRENEURIAL LABORS

Wealth is an irresistible magnet. Money smells powerfully, and its odor will draw people from far and near.

David Landes
Harvard Professor

A Rash Speculator? George Washington? History books covering George Washington's military career are replete with stories of his "immunity" to injury. In scores of battles and skirmishes starting from the earliest days of his youth, he remained unscathed while others nearby were injured or killed. He even walked away unharmed when there were bullet holes in his uniform. The most colorful anecdote reported is the one about an Indian who fired several shots at Washington at close range, missed every time, and finally gave up, deeply puzzled. This young fellow, the Indian was heard to mutter, had to be under the protection of the Great Spirit![180]

Immune to battlefield injury he may have been, but Washington was certainly no less vulnerable to mishaps in his commercial activities than other businessmen. In fact, because he was involved in many more projects than most men of his time, he had his share of commercial calamities. Perhaps for this reason, some writers have tended to depict him as a rash speculator in business, and to intimate that he only made money by marrying it.

Let us see whether these are fair characterizations of him.[181]

It is, of course, the nature of the entrepreneurial temperament to be risk-taking. Entrepreneurs are often exuberant optimists and innovators, and the creative process, coupled with the effort to commercialize a new product or service, is always fraught with uncertainty of outcome. Most economists and social scientists studying entrepreneurial activity agree that risk-taking "is positively associated with pro-activeness and innovation," and that it is a distinct dimension of entrepreneurial orientation.[182] From this perspective, Washington's real estate transactions should also be assessed by examining the methodology used by many sophisticated developers throughout American history, including the present. They often strive to build an inventory of land in the expectation that they will proceed to the development phase of their work on a schedule dictated by the cycle of demand for real estate services, the availability of equity and debt financing, and a host of other factors. In the eighteenth century, the demand was primarily for housing and farm sites. Whether then or now, the process molds the developer into a "patient investor," and Washington clearly fit that description. He selected each project after carefully assessing its potential and then worked tirelessly to bring it to fruition. A study of his involvements can only lead to the conclusion that he brought a disciplined approach to risk-taking. Naturally, it did not work in every case, as no one bats a thousand in business. While contemporaries such as John Wilson, Thomas Jefferson, Robert Morris, and others ran afoul of their creditors, Washington never sailed close to the wind.

In a setting quite different from business, however, Washington actually showed a willingness to be the ultimate risk-taker. And was it not fortunate for this nation that he did? He was fully cognizant that he was assuming extreme risk when he accepted the leadership of the American insurrection against a powerful British king. "I am now embarked," he wrote his brother-in-law, Burwell Bassett, on June 19, 1775, "on a tempestuous ocean from whence perhaps no friendly harbor is to be found."[183]

If America had lost its fight for independence, the wrath of George III, the vengeful English monarch, would have been horrific. The penalty for treason against the Crown was indeed savage and inflexible:

> "The punishment of high treason in general is very solemn and terrible. (1) That the offender be drawn to the gallows.... (2) That he be hanged by the neck, and then cut down alive. (3) That his entrails be taken out and burned, while he is yet alive. (4) That his head be cut off. (5) That his body be divided into four parts. (6) That his head and quarters be at the King's disposal."[184]

Can any form of punishment devised by man be more terrible? In a famous understatement attributed to Benjamin Franklin, he summed it up well when he said, "We must all hang together, or most assuredly we shall all hang separately." Washington was, of course, the visible face of the American Revolution, but scores of other Founders would not have escaped King George's wrath. Lest we forget, they all took the ultimate risk in the defense of our freedom.

He Married Money. Or Did He? Despite Washington's deep involvement in farming, real estate, and business, and his financial savvy, the myth that Martha was the source of his wealth endures. Writers have had a field day with Washington on this issue. It is a perpetual refrain: Martha's money is what attracted George to her. It was no accident that he called on Martha, her being probably the wealthiest woman in Virginia. Her wealth made her the prize catch of the Chesapeake society. Martha's money made her husband one of Virginia's richest men. These sorts of statements perpetuate the myth of what "Martha's wealth" did for George Washington.[185]

To judge how Washington made out financially in his own enterprises, therefore, one needs first to take a close look at the frequent refrain that "Washington married money."

George was only seventeen when his future wife, Martha Dandridge, married her first husband, Daniel Parke Custis, in 1749. The couple had four children, only two of whom survived: John Parke Custis ("Jacky") and Martha Parke Custis ("Patsy"). Daniel died in 1757 after eight years of marriage, at which time Martha was twenty-six, Jacky two, and Patsy a baby.[186] Daniel left no will, and Martha had to post a bond to qualify as the administrator of her late husband's estate. The court appointed three commissioners to appraise the assets, and they did in fact come back with the oft-quoted – but, as will be seen shortly, misleading – figure of £30,000, which became the amount of bond Martha had to post. Daniel's estate also included nearly 18,000 acres of land in five local counties, but they were not a part of the probate estate. Virginia law, patterned after the English model, provided that real estate passed directly to the male heir. As the daughter, Patsy could claim no share in her father's land. It was her brother Jacky who inherited it, two-thirds to vest immediately, the last third to vest upon his mother's death. Despite this windfall, Jacky could still share in the remaining assets. They would be divided equally among Martha, Jacky, and Patsy.

What happened to the liquid portion of Daniel's estate is instructive of the hunger for hard currency sweeping the colony at the time. After Daniel died, Martha was besieged by friends and family asking for money. What they really wanted was to get their hands on the cache of sterling in the estate, perhaps hoping that the young widow was not aware of differences in value between pounds sterling and Virginia pounds. She eventually succumbed to these entreaties and over the course of the following months made a series of nine loans which practically depleted her late husband's cash reserves in sterling. Later, when the estate was being settled, the notes receivable from all these loans were passed on to the infant Patsy. Daniel had also owned stock in the Bank of England worth £1,650 sterling. This too was passed on to Patsy. These financial assets became Patsy's one-third share of her father's estate, after which she no longer shared in the inheritance.

The remaining assets were appraised by court appraisers at £23,600 Virginia money, to be divided equally between Martha and Jacky, or £11,800 each. While these divisions among the three heirs underwent several iterations in subsequent years, the basic arrangement remained the same.

The two currencies – pounds sterling and Virginia pounds – had widely divergent values. While sterling was stable and coveted everywhere in North America, the colonies' own currencies fluctuated widely against one another, as well as against sterling. Virginia pounds started depreciating almost immediately after they were first issued in 1755. The colony kept consistently running deficits in its trade with Britain, which created a scarcity of sterling and precious metals in Virginia. What made matters worse was that British merchants were refusing to accept payment for their merchandise in Virginia paper. Despite periodic efforts to set a uniform conversion ratio for Virginia paper into sterling, in practice the market rate was substantially below the "official" one. The Board of Trade in London finally lost patience and had Parliament pass the Currency Act of 1764, which banned the issuance of paper money in all the colonies. Washington, who kept a close eye on currency transactions in his own commercial affairs, often adopted an exchange rate valuing Virginia pounds at forty percent of the British pound.[187] At that rate, Martha's £11,800 share of Daniel's estate in Virginia money would convert to £4,720 sterling, from which were deducted the various probate and attorneys' costs and fees. This amount, however, was *not* in cash but consisted of clothing, linens, silverware, household furniture, chinaware, jewelry, supplies, livestock, etc., and even perishable items such as unsold crops – items that hardly lent themselves to ready conversion into cash at anything close to their appraised values.

After George and Martha married, Washington was appointed guardian of Jacky and Patsy by the General Court at Williamsburg on October 21, 1761. He was required to post a bond and to report annually to the court on the state of the children's affairs. Washington began immediately to manage the assets for the children's benefit. He set up a separate columnar book for the children's accounts. Using a double-entry bookkeeping system of his own invention, Washington kept detailed records of the daily income and outgo in each account. Despite his extraordinary personal and national preoccupations, Washington kept these accounts up-to-date and reported on them to the court during the course of his guardianship. He also set up separate accounts with three English trading houses for the consignment of the tobacco crops from Jacky's land and put the profits into income-producing financial instruments for his stepson.

Washington treated Patsy's assets similarly. He ordered Robert Cary & Company in London to transfer the Bank of England shares into Patsy's name. He collected for her the semi-annual dividends on the bank stock, and the principal and interest payments on the loans Martha had made which now belonged to Patsy. He tracked and kept a running total of the balances in her account. Although partly discolored, faded, and mutilated, the account book for Jacky and Patsy, written in Washington's own hand, is still in existence at the Virginia Historical Society in Richmond and at the Washington and Lee University in Lexington, Virginia.[188] By the time of Patsy's death in 1773, Washington's skillful management of her assets had caused her estate to soar in value to £16,000 sterling.[189]

Under the eighteenth-century doctrine of "coverture," married women were not permitted to own property in their own names, even though single women could do so. A husband had control of his wife's estate. At the time, it was common for a husband to commingle the assets of his wife with his own immediately upon marriage. As will become clear, Washington had good reason to keep Martha's assets separate from his own and maintained her "dower" records in the same meticulous manner he did for his wards.[190]

In any discussion of Martha's dower and her children's inheritance, one cannot overlook the other side of the balance sheet, namely the liabilities. To find out the value of what Martha and the children inherited from Daniel, one has to take into account any debts or obligations he may have left behind. American bankruptcy courts are replete with records of asset-rich individuals whose outsize liabilities sank them. It was precisely the liability side of Daniel's affairs that hung like a dark cloud over him in life, as it had over his father's life, and which now cast an ominous pall over the assets of Martha and even her children.

The story goes back two generations before Daniel himself and, incredible as it may seem, is a truly Shakespearean saga of adultery, murder, fraud, illegitimate children, and a lawsuit that wound its way through several judicial systems over the mind-numbing span of two-thirds of a century, long enough to eventually embroil George Washington. The bizarre histories of two eccentric Virginia families are inextricably linked to the "wealth" Martha possessed after the death of her first husband. By the time George Washington became involved, Martha's contingent liabilities inherited from Daniel had incredibly ballooned to over £150,000.

If every family has to have a rogue in its history, the one in the ancestry of Martha's first husband was his maternal grandfather. His name was Daniel Parke, and he was born in York County, Virginia, in 1669. His parents were politically savvy and well connected in the colony. As a boy, he was sent to England for his schooling, but then summarily called back to Virginia at sixteen for an arranged marriage to another teenager by the name of Jane Ludwell. Precocious and ambitious, Daniel Parke threw himself wholeheartedly into politics and business once back in the colonies. By nineteen, he was elected to the Virginia legislature, then became a vestryman, and later won a coveted seat on the Governor's Council. From the union with Jane, he had three children, of whom two daughters survived, Frances and Lucy. On the business side, he was into farming, shipbuilding, and the manufacturing of bricks. The marriage, however, was far from a happy match. Jane could be temperamental while her husband was arrogant, driven, and given to fits of violence. He was also blatantly promiscuous. By the time he reached his late twenties, he decided colonial life was too confining. He abandoned his Virginia family and returned to England in 1697, where he hoped to run for Parliament.

Settling down in Hampshire County on the southern coast of England, Daniel Parke took on a mistress, a married woman named Mrs. Berry. Her child, Julius Caesar Parke, was undoubtedly Daniel Parke's illegitimate son. Daniel Parke's career then took an abrupt turn in 1702 when he met John Churchill, the 1st Duke of Marlborough. Despite his provincial status, Parke soon became the duke's aide-de-camp with the rank of lieutenant colonel. He fought in the battle of Blenheim in Germany, which ended the War of the Spanish Succession in a decisive victory for England in 1704. Celebrating the occasion in a tavern, the duke scribbled the news of the war on the back of a bill and selected Parke to deliver the tidings to Queen Anne. Marlborough intended to honor his aide, knowing that the Queen customarily rewarded the bearer of such auspicious news £500. Parke was also aware of this, but he had other ideas. Hastening by horse and ship from the Danube to the Thames, he arrived in the imperial court. Described as a man "of fine appearance and handsome bearing," he was received in audience, knelt before the Queen, and delivered Marlborough's message. When she asked what he would like as a reward, Parke replied with a show of humility that his dearest wish was to have a portrait of Her Majesty. The Queen was delighted. Instead of a mere £500, she awarded him £1,000, a miniature portrait of her likeness set in diamonds, and an appointment as the royal governor of the Leeward Islands in the Caribbean. (The Duke of Marlborough, who was married to Queen Anne's best friend, later gently reminded his sovereign that, next time, £500 would be sufficient.)[191]

Back in Virginia, Parke's daughters grew to adulthood and married. Frances married John Custis in 1705, and produced two children, a daughter also named Frances Custis, and a son named Daniel Custis (Martha's first husband). The other daughter, Lucy, married William Byrd in 1706. Daniel Parke's wife Jane, however, did not fare so well. Attractive and vivacious before marriage, her husband's prolonged neglect of his family, his infidelity, and his fits of temper had taken their toll of her spirit. A depressed and broken woman, she died in 1708.[192]

Unmindful of what was in store for him, Daniel Parke arrived in Antigua, the largest of the Leeward Islands, to assume his post as the royal governor in 1706. In the words of the imperial historian, the island was "the hottest, the most disease-ridden...the most undesirable place imaginable to live in."[193] Its government was fractious and corrupt to the core, and its people were violent and difficult to govern. Driven by raw ambition, Parke exercised his prerogative as the Crown's representative to amass a substantial fortune there over the next four years. Once again he took a married woman for a mistress. Her name was Catherine Chester, and she was the wife of Edward Chester, the local representative of the slave-trading Royal African Company. Oblivious of the fury of Catherine's husband, Parke continued his illicit liaison and fathered a child named Lucy Chester. Nor was Catherine his only dalliance on the island. He quickly developed a reputation for having affairs with several other married women as well.

Politically, the islanders engaged in increasing conspiratorial intrigues among rival factions. Contemptuous of the local dynamics, Parke made little effort to control them. His myopic view of these societal stresses, coupled with his amorous peccadillos, eventually turned the population against him. Four years after his arrival, local outrage reached a boiling point. On December 7, 1710, there was a bloody riot in Antigua, and the governor's mansion was attacked and ransacked by a large mob. Scores of men on the governor's staff and all of his security detail were killed. Parke himself was dragged out of his quarters, repeatedly knifed and beaten, and his spine crushed. The mob ripped Queen Anne's diamond pendant from his neck, shot him in the face point blank, and mutilated his body. It was later reported that two of the mob leaders had been Catherine's cuckolded husband Edward Chester and his brother Charles.[194]

The news of the rioting and murder took nearly three months to reach London. It aroused fears that the revolt might spread to the North American colonies, and so severe punishment of the Leeward Islands perpetrators was called for to deter copycat rebellion in other royal dominions. In time, the leaders of the Antigua insurrection were fined or imprisoned, and the Crown's prerogatives and powers were restored. The Queen eventually pardoned the Antiguans, and calm returned. As for the Duke of Marlborough, the Antiguan affair resulted in a brief period of decline in his prestige as it had been one of his favorite officers who had failed in his duty.[195]

When Daniel Parke originally sailed for the Leeward Islands, he left behind substantial assets in Hampshire, England, as well as in Virginia, but there is no record that he had previously owned any property in Antigua or any of the other Caribbean islands. When he died, however, his fortune in Antigua was estimated at £30,000 sterling, at least twice the value of all his other holdings.

Parke's Virginia family received the news of his death in 1711. Amid the distress about the murder, Daniel Parke's sons-in-law, John Custis and William Byrd, began contemplating their wives' inheritance from their father's estate and calculating their respective shares. Parke's debts did not appear to be significant. Between them, Custis and Byrd entered into an agreement whereby, in return for assuming Governor Parke's debts in England, Byrd would take possession of all the English assets plus one piece of land in Virginia. Custis would keep the remaining Virginia properties. It seemed a good bargain and made the division of assets fairly straightforward.[196]

The Virginia family was also shocked to learn that Parke had left an illegitimate child, Lucy Chester, in Antigua, and another, Julius Caesar Parke, in England. In time, the family received a copy of a will made by

Parke in Antigua dated January 29, 1709, and learned that Daniel Parke had bequeathed his entire estate on the island to Lucy Chester. He gave his Virginia and English assets, however, to his daughter Frances. He then gave additional instructions to Frances: "My will is that my daughter Frances Custis pay out of my estate in Hampshire and Virginia the following legacies and *all* my debts, that is, to my daughter Lucy Bird one thousand pounds sterling, to my godson Julius Caesar Parke fifty pounds sterling each year during his life..." There was also a precondition to Parke's bequests: Anyone receiving benefits under the will, and all of such heirs' issue, were required to take the name "Parke" and use the Parke coat of arms. Separate executors were then named for Antigua and Virginia. Parke's Virginia family was informed afterward that the will had already undergone probate in Antigua.[197]

Reality soon shattered the Custis and Byrd fantasies of inherited riches. The first blow came in May. The executor in London provided Custis a list of Daniel Parke's known debts in England, which came to about £6,680. Additional debts were expected to show up, which, added to the bequests to Lucy Byrd and Julius Caesar Parke, would bring the total to about £10,000, while the Hampshire properties could bring only £4,000, leaving a shortfall of £6,000 sterling. That was a substantial amount, for which William Byrd would be responsible.[198]

At this point, John Custis must have been feeling elated about the bargain he had made with his brother-in-law, but then came the second blow. He received a letter from a man named Thomas Dunbar, who introduced himself as the husband of Lucy Chester. Under the late Governor's will, Lucy and her husband were to take over all of Parke's assets in Antigua *free of all debts*. Dunbar further stated that Daniel Parke, in the process of accumulating his properties on the Island of Antigua, had incurred liabilities of about £5,000, and that after his death the local creditors had secured judgments against his estate there and forced the sale of some assets to satisfy their claims. It was clear from the plain language of the will, Dunbar insisted, that the Governor intended to insulate Lucy from any responsibility for the debts of his estate, which was why he had provided for the payment of all his debts out of the Virginia and English assets. Dunbar was seeking reimbursement from Frances Parke Custis for the amounts by which the Antigua estate had been diminished as a result of the action of the creditors. If an amicable settlement could not be reached with Mrs. Custis, Dunbar would seek redress in the Virginia courts.[199]

(*See* the following exhibit as an aid in sorting out the quaint and confusing old custom of giving the same names to members of succeeding generations in a family.)

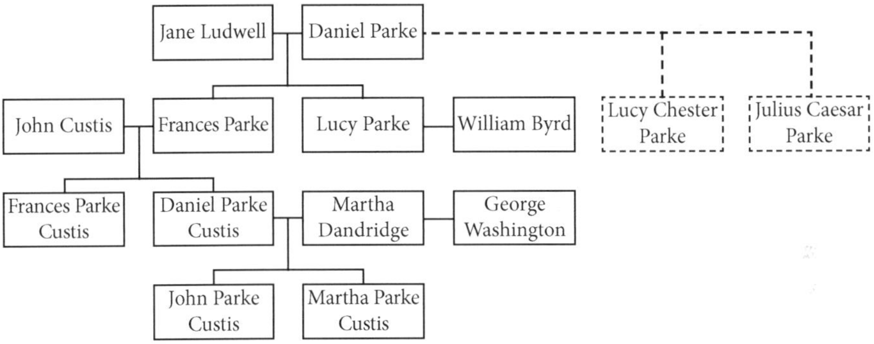

Martha's father-in-law, John Custis (who insisted on being called the Colonel) was a tyrannical and highly opinionated man who loved money above all else and looked with contempt upon anyone whose wealth did not match his own. He refused permission for his son Daniel to marry until he was thirty-seven years old. Daniel had had to employ successive intermediaries to intercede for him with his father – and catch the elder Custis in a rare receptive mood – to get his father's grudging consent to Daniel's marriage to Martha Dandridge. Even then, the Colonel loudly proclaimed that Dandridge's daughter "was much inferior to his [own] son."[200]

The demand from Thomas Dunbar made the Colonel's blood boil. Over his dead body would those Caribbean *banditti* get a farthing from him. He would fight them to the ends of the earth. His reply to Dunbar was replete with adjectives, but its essence was that there was no money left in the estate as the debts had already depleted all the assets. Custis then proceeded to line up several trial lawyers in the colony of Virginia to represent him in this matter. What he had not counted on was the tenacity of his Antiguan antagonist.[201]

Meanwhile, the English executor of Governor Parke's estate sought advice about the provisions of the will from Sir Edward Northey, the Attorney General of England. The reply gave a detailed legal opinion which confirmed Dunbar's claim in every respect. Dunbar himself also sought counsel on the will. He turned to no less an expert in the law than the Lord Chief Justice of England, Sir Robert Raymond, who presumably reached similar conclusions.[202] Thus bolstered in his position, Dunbar wasted no time in filing a lawsuit in Virginia claiming that under Daniel Parke's will, his heirs in the colony were responsible for the debts incurred on the islands, and that any amounts already paid out by them could *not* be used to reduce their obligation to the Antiguan creditors. The litigation (which became known in history as the "Dunbar suit") asked for judgment in the amount of £6,000, plus interest and costs. More than four decades after Daniel Parke's death, on April 10, 1754, the Virginia court summarily dismissed the case on technical grounds.[203]

Disappointed but undaunted, Dunbar filed an appeal with the Privy Council in London, and both sides filed lengthy briefs in support of their positions.[204]

In London on April 3, 1755, the Lords of the Council referred the case for a hearing by a committee of the Board of Trade which took place on Friday, June 24, 1757. The judgment of the Virginia court was reversed, and the case was remanded for a trial on the merits.[205]

By this time, all the original parties to the Dunbar lawsuit had died. Martha's husband Daniel Custis was now the defendant in the case. The litigation was already several decades old, and Daniel was resigned that it would be a permanent overhang on his assets.

> "I would never meddle with one farthing I have in England until my lawsuit there was over," he wrote, "which, if it should go against me, all I have in the whole world would scarcely do."[206]

Martha was witness to the emotional toll on her husband from the pendency of the suit. The accumulated interest and costs over several decades, together with the burgeoning legal fees, and the potential of being wiped out if he lost the case were the sword of Damocles hanging over Daniel's head, affecting his health. It is a reasonable surmise that the various pressures on him contributed to his premature death on July 8, 1757.

Over the following months, even as Martha was mourning Daniel, making the necessary funeral and other arrangements, and protecting and caring for her small children, she knew that all the responsibilities with which her late husband had been burdened now rested on her shoulders. Level-headed and capable, she was aware of the multiple spheres of activity to be supervised. She needed a man of demonstrable toughness to take charge of managing the estate of her children, oversee the defense of the devastating claims of the Antigua heirs, and collect the money she had lent to several borrowers after Daniel's death. In Virginia, the go-to individual for the handling of such difficult matters was John Robinson, the Secretary of the colony and the most influential politician there. He had the heft -and -clout to deal effectively with the kinds of problems Martha faced, particularly the highly troubling litigation with the illegitimate issue of Daniel's grandfather. Through her lawyer, Martha inquired whether Robinson would be willing to help. He replied that he would agree to serve as the nominal legal guardian of the children, but that is where he drew the line. He had too much on his plate to take on new and demanding duties. That was disappointing. Bogged down with all the major responsibilities left from Daniel's death while raising her small children, Martha was almost at her wits' end. What was a grieving widow with two small children to do in an era when women had few rights?[207]

When tall and trim George Washington, exuding confidence and competence, unexpectedly appeared at her house on the Pamunkey River on March 16, 1758, Martha had to have been pleased. She agreed that he could come again. Aside from his many other attributes, he was, in her assessment, more than a match for those buccaneers from the Leeward Islands. When he proposed, she did not hesitate. The rest, of course, is history – and confirmation that Martha Washington, in addition to being possessed of a comely appearance and a warm personality and "everything that is benevolent and good,"[208] was a woman of unerring judgment in men.

After his marriage, it was George Washington's turn to become concerned about the Dunbar litigation, and particularly about its effect on Martha's dower and the inheritance of Jacky and Patsy. Wasting little time, he came right to the point and inquired of his lawyer, John Mercer, on April 20, 1759: "If Dunbar obtains his suit at law against Col. Custis's estate, how far will Mrs. Washington's dower be liable?" He also asked Mercer to what extent any asset Washington used from the Custis estate would be liable under the Dunbar claim. Mercer minced no words: *any assets that could be traced back to Governor Parke's estate would be liable under the suit.*[209]

As the case dragged on interminably, both sides continued to hire the best lawyers in the colony of Virginia and to run up substantial legal fees and costs. Washington was aghast that he was still incurring such expenses fifty years after Governor Parke's death. It was, in Washington's characteristic understatement, "a heavy and expensive chancery suit." To lose the case would be catastrophic for generations of the Parke-Custis heirs. When it was remanded by the Privy Council to Virginia for a trial on the merits, the heirs of Thomas Dunbar were required to obtain proper documentation of their claim from Antigua. The lawyers hired by Washington, being on the defense side, made full use of delaying tactics, demanding proper authentication of every single document relating to the successive plaintiffs and their heirs. Through several substitutions of parties and changes of counsel, Washington was as determined to fight the Dunbar claim as had been the original named defendant, the late Colonel Custis. By then, the Dunbar claim, with interest compounded at five percent per year, had already reached the astronomical sum in sterling of £150,191![210] Washington had no choice but to continue his focus on litigation strategy – and paying legal bills – until the day he was named Commander of the Continental Army of the United States.[211]

As it turned out, there was never a judicial resolution of the Dunbar claim. The delays and postponements in the proceedings engineered by the lawyers hired by Washington on behalf of Martha and her children finally bore fruit. When the United States declared its independence from Britain in 1775, it rendered the decision of the Privy Council moot, i.e., non-binding on the Virginia state courts. After that, the Antigua litigators, presumably discouraged by the geopolitical turn of events, as well as by the expense of fighting a determined adversary in the American judicial system, no longer pursued their cause of action.

* * *

Having provided a description of the assets and liabilities of Martha's inheritance from her first husband, we now turn to a retrospective on Washington's own estate.

The last seventeen years before the start of the Revolutionary War were the longest continuous period Washington had spent in the private sector in his adult life, enabling him to accomplish much. At Mount Vernon, he rebuilt the small house badly in need of repair into a magnificent mansion exquisitely furnished in a symphony of appealing green hues with stylish furniture and a round banquet hall capable of handling dozens of guests seven days a week.

As the revenue stream and cash flow from his activities began to grow, Washington was able to transform the rundown farm with poor soil hemorrhaging red ink he had inherited from Lawrence into a large and bustling agricultural and manufacturing center producing a diversified product line and operating in multiple markets. He also amassed a substantial inventory of land, was engaged in several notable projects in various stages of development, and was the prime mover in a series of initiatives involving a mixture of both public and private funding. At every step along the way, he was prepared to get his own fingernails dirty. The operating style of sitting back and letting others do the heavy lifting never applied to George Washington.Equally successful on the civic and political side, Washington was a member of the state legislature, a justice of the County Court of Fairfax, a member of the Court of Oyer and Terminer of the County, and a vestryman in his church. His reputation for good judgment and followthrough was such that he was frequently named as executor or trustee of others' estates, and was sought after as the lead partner in more business ventures than he could possibly handle.[212]

What had been a highly gratifying life for Washington was brought to an abrupt halt with the onset of the American Revolution, but once the war ended, he went back to his farming and other business activities with a vengeance. To make up for lost time, he began operating at hyperspeed, and when all was said and done, his love for accumulating and developing land had led him in his lifetime to become one of America's major landholders. Those who owned millions of acres, such as the Fairfaxes in Virginia, the Baltimores in Maryland, and the Penns in Pennsylvania, had their forefathers and the Crown of England to thank for their good fortune. Several others who tried their hands at building real estate empires in the eighteenth century, such as George Croghan, John Wilson, Robert Morris, and others, ended up broke when the market turned against them. Washington, on the other hand, was able to hold on to his holdings and continue to prosper.[213]

The elements of Washington's strategic plan – of colorful entrepreneurial adventures and bold forays into dealmaking – constitute fascinating case studies for succeeding generations of self-starters similarly inclined in the business world. Clearly, he had a passion for the entrepreneurial life, and like scores of dealmakers that came after him, he had the capacity to handle multiple projects concurrently. A nose for the deal, thorough research and investigation, tenacity in negotiation, and detail orientation were the qualities that made Washington a success in the early and as-yet-unorganized American business environment.

When George Washington was appointed commander-in-chief of the Continental Army, Congress had already established the salary for that position at $500 a month. With a declaration that "as no pecuniary consideration could have tempted me to accept this arduous employment at the expense of my domestic ease and happiness, I do not wish to make any profit out of it," he rejected all compensation for fighting the Revolutionary War. He even turned down his share of the bounty land, which would have come to over 23,000 acres – a substantial addition to his other holdings – had he accepted. (By way of comparison, the Marquis de Lafayette, who served under George Washington during the Revolutionary War, was paid $24,400 by Congress, and awarded 11,520 acres of land valued at $115,200 and a cash bonus of $200,000.[214])

Washington only asked for a reimbursement of his actual expenses, of which he kept meticulous records. Writers have cited widely divergent figures for those expenses, from $160,000 in Continental dollars to £6,114 sterling. The most reliable figure is probably the one quoted by

James Thomas Flexner, a respected Washington biographer. He listed Washington's wartime expenses for eight years at £8,422 sterling for household expenses and £1,982 for "secret intelligence."[215]

Despite being taken away from his highly absorbing business activities for long periods of government service, George Washington nonetheless became one of the most successful businessmen in early America. To put his real estate holdings in the context of today's geography, by the time of his death he had painstakingly accumulated 18,287 acres in Virginia; 35,561 in West Virginia; 1,119 in Maryland; 234.5 in Pennsylvania; 1,000 in New York; 3,051 in Ohio; and 5, 000 in Kentucky, for a grand total of 68,709.5 acres (of which he sold 4,457 acres before his death). In addition, in Washington, D.C., he was the owner of seven lots; in Virginia, he owned two lots in Alexandria, three in Fredericksburg, one in Manchester, six in Richmond, and two in Winchester; and in West Virginia, he owned two lots in Berkeley Springs for a grand total of 23 lots.[216] In his will, he provided for specific devises (i.e., bequests of real property) totaling 5,277 acres. As to the remaining real estate, Washington directed his executors to sell them along with his portfolio of stocks and bonds and his livestock, and distribute the proceeds among multiple named recipients. He valued these assets at $530,000 in eighteenth-century currency.[217] They were, however, far from being an exhaustive schedule of his holdings. The following is an attempt at listing some of the more obvious items not included in the foregoing valuation:

Washington's beloved Mount Vernon, consisting of about 8,000 acres of prime real estate with almost ten miles of frontage on the Potomac River and a magnificent mansion, was not part of his probate estate, as he devised it to his nephew Bushrod Washington, subject to a life estate in Martha. Bushrod occupied Mount Vernon upon Martha's death in 1802 and stayed there for twenty-seven years until his own death in 1829.

Left out of Washington's valuation were also his household furniture and fixtures, chinaware and silver, jewelry, paintings, sculpture, machinery and equipment, swords, medals, awards, and other mementos of a long career. As part of the probate estate, these were appraised at token amounts. The gold "Freedom Box," for example, presented to him as a private citizen by the City of New York in 1784, was appraised at a mere

$100. (By way of comparison, John Jay was a recipient of a similar award from the City of New York. His gold box changed hands in 2001 at a Christie's auction for $732,000. The President's box would undoubtedly have been valued substantially higher.[218])

For countless Americans, historians, and other admirers of George Washington, his most valuable possessions were his papers. Consisting of one hundred and forty thousand documents, these were the chronicles of an extraordinary life and the priceless legacy of the nation's first Presidency. The University of Virginia (in conjunction with the Library of Congress and Mount Vernon) has been compiling and publishing the entire collection, anticipating that it would occupy ninety volumes and be finished by 2023. Available at this writing are the Diaries (six volumes), Colonial Series (ten volumes), Revolutionary War Series (twenty-two volumes), Confederation Series (six volumes), Presidential Series (eighteen volumes), and Retirement Series (four volumes). All of these papers, together with his library, Washington bequeathed to his nephew Bushrod. As an indication of their worth today, a single notebook containing an annotated copy of the Constitution and the Bill of Rights, in which Washington had carefully marked in the margins certain passages covering the President's authority and responsibilities, was auctioned by Christie's in 2012 for about ten million dollars.[219]

Washington, a serial entrepreneur centuries before the term came into use with the advent of the internet, owned more than a dozen operating businesses at the time of his death. He had an active milling operation and a spinning and weaving business. He owned a tannery and manufactured shoes. He produced barrels and bricks. He had a thriving commercial fisheries business. He manufactured ropes, saddles, and harnesses. He had a busy distillery. He was into the production of fertilizer. He had a fruit orchard and a dairy in addition to his other farming activities. Some of these operations had a base of customers in markets as far away as Europe and the Caribbean. None was included in Washington's valuation of his own assets. Nor did the court-appointed appraisers show any recognition of these activities as going-concern businesses. They only listed the hard assets, such as picks, shovels, etc., at token figures. After Washington's death, these operations were all sadly abandoned with the exception of the distillery, which was taken over by Martha's granddaughter and her husband.[220] The farm and the mansion were then permitted to fall into disuse, decay, and ruin.

> *Fortunately for the nation, a proud and determined woman from South Carolina by the name of Ann Pamela Cunningham came along to rescue the home of George Washington from oblivion. Surmounting many obstacles, including the apathy of Congress, she secured a charter from the Commonwealth of Virginia for what was perhaps the first heritage preservation society in the country. Called Mount Vernon Ladies' Association, it purchased the estate from a reluctant John Augustine Washington, Jr., a collateral descendant of George's, for $200,000 on the instalment plan in 1858. Restored to its full early luster, our first President's home is now a thriving historical destination for more than a million visitors each year.*

It is a reasonable assumption that Washington was characteristically conservative in the $530,000 valuation of the assets he listed in the Schedule of Properties annexed to his handwritten will. Nevertheless, historians have accepted his assessment. His remaining real estate and other assets have never been valued. Andrew G. Gardner, writing for *Colonial Williamsburg*, cites the additional value as a lump-sum $250,000. These figures bring the total of Washington's estate to $780,000 at the time of his death.[221]

Statisticians use a variety of methodologies to convert old dollars into twenty-first-century currency. Such comparisons are, of course, riddled with uncertainty, as many aspects of life may not be transferable. A reasonable approach, which has the benefit of bypassing the complex issue of relative standards of living, would be to calculate the value of Washington's estate as a percentage of the Gross Domestic Product (GDP) of the United States in 1799, the year of his death, and compare it with the same ratio today. There is sound precedent for the use of this formula. It is common practice for modern economists to show the magnitude of federal debt by computing it as a percentage of GDP. If the use of liabilities as a percentage of GDP provides a graphic comparison, clearly, using assets for the same purpose would be equally meaningful.[222]

This computation would place the value of George Washington's estate at $34.4 billion in 2017 currency, all of it earned in his business and entrepreneurial activities in the private sector. *His service in the public sector contributed nothing to his wealth; on the contrary, it was a distinctly negative factor in his accumulation of assets.* For him, it was an immutable policy that public service was not an avenue for the accumulation of wealth. That was the standard set by him as the first President, fully expecting that his successors would adhere to that policy. Whether this is true of all his successors is a matter best left to the judgment of history.

PART II

Chapter Four

RANK, DEFERENCE, AND PREFERENCE

People think there's a rigid class system here, but dukes have been known to marry chorus girls. Some have even married Americans.

Prince Philip
Consort of Queen Elizabeth II

From the moment George Washington opened his eyes to the world at birth and for more than four decades, his life was dominated by the rules governing English culture and impacted by a spider web of British laws, regulations, and policies as applied to colonials. Imperial mandates emanating from Westminster and Whitehall defined and shaped every aspect of Washington's economic outlook. He was shackled by the multi-layered bureaucracy in London for every decision and project he contemplated.

The world of George Washington's youth was a far cry from the classless society of the republic later established in America. The notion that "all men are created equal" would have been utterly alien to the English culture of the time, which was based on an unforgiving and rigid class-and-caste hierarchical structure. At the apex of the English society sat an aloof and imperious king, to whom the law ascribed "absolute perfection." He was "the fountain of honor," incapable of any wrongdoing, and the source of all rights and privileges. He appointed the ministers who directed policy and administration, and he alone "could summon, prorogue, or dissolve Parliament." The royal will, expressed by an order in council or letters patent or other documents under the Great Seal of the realm, was the supervening authority in the British Empire. The king's subjects were bound to him by a strict moral and legal code. "Since the bond to the king was a personal and moral one, the disavowal had to be personal and moral as well," and the punishment for a disavowal of the Crown, namely "high treason," was unimaginably severe.[223]

In the crucial span of time before and during the American Revolution, Britain was ruled by George William Frederick, known as King George III, of the House of Hanover. Born in 1738, George III ascended the throne of England in 1760, the first of his line to speak English as his first language and to acknowledge his commitment and loyalty to England, giving rise to high optimism that the youthful king would usher in a fresh, honest, and perhaps even compassionate era in the monarchy. It soon became clear, however, that the rosy expectations were premature, and that the country now had a headstrong and difficult king, full of prejudices and lacking in humility and vision, and one who intended to rule and not merely reign. Throughout his sixty-year span as king, his unceasing efforts to dominate the government and manipulate the members of Parliament gained him much criticism. "Through his agents he bought and sold seats and votes, sold pensions and posts, subsidized journalists, and tried to shackle the press." In a bleak view of the king's character traits, a later popular work described George III's personality as being marked by "his fatal obstinacy, his control of party competition as the means of enforcing his will upon the government, his dogged opposition to progress, his uncouth appearance and odd manners."[224]

King George's rule was also punctuated by England's participation in a series of military engagements, about which a respected British historian, Sir George Otto Trevelyan, said that George III "invariably declared himself upon the wrong side of every conflict." As for the American Revolution, after Britain's defeat at the Battle of Yorktown, George III categorically insisted that "no blame on that account can be laid at my door" and then gave vent to his rage by adding that "knavery seems to be so much the striking feature of [America's] inhabitants."[225] Later, however, when his correspondence was compiled by Sir John Fortescue in six volumes, it showed the king's deep and extensive personal involvement in every aspect of the American war, his obsession with punishing his former subjects, and his outright refusal to consider reconciliation or compromise with the colonies.[226] George III is thus deservedly remembered as "The King Who Lost America." Unpopular as a monarch, he was also the target of several assassination attempts. After suffering from episodes of psychotic illness throughout his adult life, George III eventually became incurably insane and blind ten years before his death in 1820. Ironically, he has been the recipient of kinder treatment by American historians than those of his native land, Britain.

> *Although an implacable foe of Americans in life, His Majesty King George III now casts an amiable eye upon them as they visit his likeness at the British ambassador's residence on Massachusetts Avenue in Washington, D.C. His portrait by artist Allan Ramsey covers an entire wall at the top of the Grand Staircase there, far overshadowing a much smaller nearby portrait of one of America's favorite British leaders, Winston Churchill.*

The Prime Minister throughout the American Revolution was Frederick North, 2nd Earl of Guilford, known by his courtesy title Lord North. He was born in 1732, within two months of the birth of his future nemesis, George Washington. Their paths, of course, diverged after birth. Washington, the self-taught tobacco farmer, became one of the most respected figures in history while Lord North, scion of aristocrats and educated in the finest schools England had to offer, became the object of derision and gave rise to the taunt "the worst prime minister since Lord North."[227]

North attended Eton and Trinity College, Oxford, and spent a year at the University of Leipzig studying international law. He then joined the government, where the prerequisites for rising to high rank were said to be a combination of "high birth, a degree from Oxford or Cambridge, the ownership of estates, and the personal backing of the king." All of these attributes, plus a keen intellect and skill in debate, made North's meteoric rise in politics seem preordained.[228]

Within the first decade of his reign, George III had tried five different men as Prime Minister, but feeling ill-advised, he dismissed them one after the other, in the obvious belief that he was accountable to no one, including Parliament, in appointing and discharging officeholders. To stabilize the government, George III then turned to North, appointing him Prime Minister in 1770. North stayed in that position for twelve years, including the full span of the American Revolution.[229]

North was three years old when his mother died. His father remarried shortly afterwards. The new wife had a son from her own first marriage, who was a year older than North and who succeeded his grandfather as the 2nd Earl of Dartmouth. North and Dartmouth grew up together as brothers and were close throughout their lives. It was Lord Dartmouth who was the Secretary of State for the Colonies in North's government at the start of the American Revolution.

As children, North, Dartmouth, and George III played together. North bore a remarkable resemblance to George III, notable from their early childhood. As one writer put it, both men had many facial and physical characteristics in common – "the homely face, thick lips, light complexion and hair, bushy eyebrows." Particularly striking were the "protruding large grey eyes" they shared which, in the end, lost their sight before their deaths. Dalliances by members of royalty not being uncommon (both George I and George II kept mistresses), contemporaries believed that North was in fact the son of Frederick, Prince of Wales, and therefore a half-brother to George III.[230]

Rather than being put off by his own features, North once openly described himself and his wife as "the ugliest couple in England!" His sense of humor totally deserted him, however, when it came to dealing with the American "rebels," whom he was determined to bring to heel. This was a passion he and the king shared with equal fervor. (Perhaps

North would be aghast to learn that, in one of the ironic twists of history, Wroxton Abbey, the grand seat of his family in Oxfordshire, is now a school for Americans.[231])

The Prime Minister's vehicle for supervision over colonial affairs was the Board of Trade. Originally established in 1696 by King William II, it operated in the eighteenth century under the auspices of the Lords Commissioners for Trade and Plantations. Their carpeted and imposing offices in Whitehall had wide hallways and high columns as befitted the officials of the Crown and the Empire. For the rare colonial visitor, they projected an aura of intimidating power and aristocratic haughtiness. While several other arms of the British government were involved in colonial affairs, the Board of Trade generally served as the clearinghouse for all such matters, always subject to review and approval by the Privy Council and the king himself.

English aristocracy was a hereditary system steeped in class distinctions, with a strict protocol of "rank, deference, and preference." However, all aristocrats were not created equal. At the end of the eighteenth century, the highest levels of aristocracy consisted of dukes, followed by marquesses, earls, viscounts, and barons, all of whom numbered 287. The landed aristocrats with large estates built vast palaces for themselves and cultivated the habit of looking down upon the rest of society with inherited condescension. In a country of nine million population at the time, this small group received a whopping twenty-nine percent of national income. It dominated the government and had control of Parliamentary elections and legislation. Then there were 313 spiritual and temporal lords entitled to sit in the House of Lords. Peerage was hereditary and descended in the male line to the eldest sons, although the younger sons of dukes and marquesses could call themselves "lords" without any of the privileges of nobility. The next group in the hierarchy was the gentry, the "lesser nobility," composed of 540 baronets, 350 knights, and some 6,000 squires. The rest of society came under the heading of commoners. The aristocracy comprised a tiny fraction of the total population, but those who were fortunate enough to have been born members of its ranks enjoyed great privileges. "Not one-tenth part of the people of Great Britain had voice in the election of Parliament," an English historian acknowledged about the eighteenth century. "'Democracy' was controlled by England's wealthy landowning aristocrats," effectively disenfranchising the rest of society.[232]

Poverty was rampant for those in the lower classes, many of whom lived in Dickensian squalor. For them the opportunity to rise from humble origins to a higher level, economically and socially, was non-existent. For commoners, life was a slumgullion of misery and eternal degradation, while members of the aristocracy were isolated from the appalling living conditions of the masses in the bowels of the major cities of England. In this split-level society – the extraordinary wealth of a few and the frightful poverty of the masses – the gulf separating the aristocracy from the lower classes was absolute and unquestioned. There would be no exceptions. Lord North himself had a younger sister by the name of Lucy. In 1749, as a fifteen-year-old, Lucy fell in love with and married a boy of seventeen, a commoner with no title, no estate, and no money. It was an impetuous and rash act, an action for which teenagers have been known throughout the ages, often with little consequence. In Lucy's case, however, the punishment for marrying a tradesman was drastic, brutal, and permanent. She was disowned, expelled from the family, and treated as though she had never existed. Her father went so far in obliterating all traces of Lucy's existence as to erect a grave marker in the family cemetery showing her as having died at birth. On occasions after her marriage when Lucy happened to run into family members and greeted them, there was never any response or acknowledgement. Lucy's husband died in 1785. To survive, she was reduced to selling even the most cherished memento of her early life, a ring given to her in childhood by the Duke of Marlborough. She spent the last years of her life in the penury of her widowhood, with no hope of help from her family. She had committed the ultimate crime, attempting to corrupt the superior blood of her family with that of a lowly tradesman. She had learned a painful lesson, that in the land of aristocrats, being a commoner was no picnic. The egalitarian spirit of her youth utterly broken, Lucy died alone and penniless; she was buried in the graveyard of the local Parish Church.[233]

Britain's rigid hierarchical structure had its own characteristics. Individuals were judged by their titles and their forebears, not on their personal merit. Working to earn a living was considered demeaning for an aristocrat, who disdained commercial pursuits and lived off inherited wealth. They tended to be "clubby," attended the same schools, intermarried, and congregated together. This rarified atmosphere was saturated with an extreme level of corruption, which was highlighted by Benjamin Franklin when he said he could have bought all of Parliament, in fact the whole government of Britain, and gained America's independence for a fraction of what it cost to wage the American Revolutionary War.[234]

Kinship and nepotism were the bonds that held English aristocracy together, and patronage was the foundation of society. When members of this group were in need of funds, the likeliest source was to secure patronage positions from the Crown. They sought "pensions and appointments to which no work was attached." To a modern observer, the striking aspect of this system was the widespread practice of using one's official position for personal gain. Ironically, these activities did not have legal sanction, which Adam Smith explained by saying there were two concurrent systems of morality in the country at the time, a strict one for the masses and a loose one for the aristocracy. John Wesley was even more outspoken. In 1757, he described English morality as comprising political corruption, cheating in business, and chicanery in the courts.[235]

Britain's parliamentary government included a system of checks and balances designed to control the king's authority through the House of Commons. However, the process could be subverted by the king through patronage, the granting or withholding of government contracts, posts, or pensions, and sometimes direct payments from various funds and lists under the control of the Crown. Parliament allowed George III £800,000 and more for this civil list annually, to pay the sovereign's expenses. He used the civil list to reward his supporters with secret pensions and bribes, thus it was axiomatic in the English politics of the time that the Crown had extraordinary resources for purposes of patronage.In 1761, the House of Commons contained 204 members (out of 558) paid directly by the Crown, and in 1770 over 190 members of the House held appointive positions in the administration. In addition, George III could always count on support from those ambitious young MPs who aspired to higher office, as well as from the independent members, to tip the scales in his favor when he needed the votes. "Funds voted for secret service were in many cases remitted to Parliament in bribes." Seats in Parliament were available for purchase from various boroughs, some of which openly advertised that their votes were for sale. Like seats on the New York Stock Exchange a couple of centuries later, the seats in Parliament kept being bid up – from £3,000 to £4,000, and some had even gone for the large sum of £5,000.[236]

The King's system of patronage and bribes had its risks. While the rebellion of the American colonies was in full swing, the King's hand-picked Prime Minister, Lord North, tried several times to resign, giving as one of the reasons the poor state of his personal finances while in government service. Having already tried five others in that post without satisfaction, George III could not afford to lose North in the midst of a rebellion. So he wrote to North in 1777 offering to settle his debts for him. "You will now state to me whether 12, or £15,000 will not set your affairs in order if it will, nay if £20,000 is necessary I am resolved you shall have no other person concerned in freeing them but myself…and I want no other return but your being convinced that I love you…" North replied that his debts came to £18,000, and the King began providing the funds in installments. Later, when the American forces triumphed in Yorktown, North resigned in the face of a vote of "No Confidence" in Parliament. He still owed substantial amounts of money, including new debts incurred by him since 1777. The King once again took on North's debts, but this time he made no secret of what he thought of "his once dear Minister." When there was a delay in making a payment, one of North's creditors complained. The King replied that the delay "was not owing to any inaccuracy in me but the most barefaced fraud on the part of Lord North." It was a sad end to a relationship with a man the King had declared he loved only four years earlier.[237]

When the King appointed a governor for one of the Crown's colonies in America, it was most often a sinecure for a member of the aristocracy. The issues of merit, experience, or suitability for such a post were not important considerations in the selection. Then, once ensconced securely on the royal payroll, many an appointee stayed in London, never set foot in the colony he was to govern, and was rarely called upon to render any advice or assistance in the conduct of its affairs. Of the royal governors appointed to the colony of Virginia during the life of George Washington up until the Declaration of Independence (1732-1776), fully half did not care to subject themselves to the long and hazardous ocean voyage to America and all the "trouble with uncouth colonists and savage Indians." Another quarter of the appointees, although already in North America on military assignments, still did not bother to visit Virginia when posted as governors there, nor did they pay any attention to its oversight.[238]

An absentee governor selected a stand-in for himself, an individual who would take up residence in the colony and perform the actual duties of administering the province. Designated as the lieutenant governor, the post was considered a financial plum for non-aristocrats who would bid for it. The one selected obligated himself to rebate half or more of his compensation back to the named governor in London. This kickback arrangement worked out well for both parties: The real governor did no work and sold the job to an underling who in turn took advantage of his position as the Crown's representative in a colony to engage in various personal money-making schemes.

The reader will remember Robert Dinwiddie, the Lieutenant Governor of the colony of Virginia who commissioned young George Washington as an officer in the Virginia Militia. In his previous career, Dinwiddie had worked as the Surveyor General of the customs for the southern district of America. While in that position in 1749, he heard that Sir William Gooch, the then Lieutenant Governor of Virginia, had announced his decision to retire that year. Dinwiddie saw this as an exciting opportunity and immediately cast about to try to secure Gooch's position for himself. To succeed, he needed the approval of Willem Anne van Keppel, 2nd Earl of Albemarle, the royal governor of Virginia appointed twelve years earlier by King George II. The Earl was a combat veteran, bore the rank of lieutenant general in the British army, and had recently been appointed to the additional post of ambassador to Paris. Aware that the Earl was already a man of substantial inherited wealth, Dinwiddie anticipated no difficulties in the discussions that would follow. In fact, he was looking forward to the negotiations.

Dinwiddie's first step was to arrange for the sale of his own position as the official surveyor, which he did for an undisclosed sum. He then made his approach to Albemarle, fully prepared to offer a portion of his future compensation from the office to the named royal governor.

Dinwiddie was eager to begin his new career as the imperial representative in Virginia, by far the most populous of all the American colonies. What he had not taken fully into account, however, was the caliber of man with whom he would be dealing. Albemarle was quite aware that the post of lieutenant governor of a colony as large as Virginia was considered highly attractive, both politically and socially, and saw no reason to sell it cheaply. The Earl, soon to be appointed a member of the exalted Privy Council, also did not view the meeting with Dinwiddie as a negotiation, but as the interview of a subaltern for a job. Thrown completely off guard by the stern demeanor of Albemarle but having already left his prior position, Dinwiddie saw no alternative but to agree to His Lordship's uncompromising demand. He would be paying Albemarle £3,300 per annum for the position – an extraordinary payoff, considering that Dinwiddie's annual salary in that coveted role would be only £2,000. (As a gauge of compensation in eighteenth- century England, it is noteworthy that a wage of one pound per week for a member of the working class was considered a good income.[239])

Having gotten himself into this fix, Dinwiddie was hopeful that there would be opportunities in the post, through the collection of fees he could devise and other emoluments, at least to break even. Under the circumstances, coming out ahead could be too much to hope for.

Dinwiddie's appointment to the position was made official on July 4, 1751, precisely a quarter of a century before the American Declaration of Independence. True to his word, he managed to make the required payments as long as the Earl of Albemarle was alive. After the Earl's death, his successor, appointed in 1756, was General John Campbell, 4th Earl of Loudoun, who commanded the British army during the French and Indian War and who also had no interest in administering the affairs of a colony. Unfortunately for Dinwiddie, having already set the benchmark for the financial arrangement of the office with Albemarle, he had no opportunity to improve on it with the new Governor. He continued paying £3,300 annually, this time to Albemarle's successor.[240]

Considering the onerous commitment Dinwiddie had made in order to secure the position of lieutenant governor for himself, it is not surprising that he developed a reputation in Virginia for corruption. His constituents soon learned that Dinwiddie had "a way of turning a penny the right way, into his own pocket."[241] Shortly after he took office, Dinwiddie announced a new tax of one Spanish pistole (amounting to 16s. 8d.) as a fee for issuing patents on lands that were surveyed after April 22, 1752. This action created a furor in the colony, pitting the colonial legislature against the new Lieutenant Governor in a bitter and protracted confrontation. A flurry of petitions to London from the Virginia House of Burgesses ensued while Dinwiddie used his own political connections there to intercede for him with the Board of Trade. When the smoke cleared, the Board of Trade had sided with the Lieutenant Governor, but the Burgesses refused to go away quietly, and the controversy dragged on. Still determined to fight the unjust tax, the legislature decided to send the Attorney General of the colony, Peyton Randolph, to London to make the case that the tax was an illegal taking of property under English law. Unfortunately for the Virginians, British policy required that anyone leaving a colony had to secure permission from the governor or his stand-in. In this case, that was none other than Dinwiddie himself. Having no inclination to act against self-interest, Dinwiddie naturally refused permission. Encouraged by members of the legislature, Randolph sailed to England anyway. Claiming that the tax was designed to prevent fraud, the Lieutenant Governor continued to collect the levy he had imposed, from which he benefited personally. Eventually, a modified form of the impost was approved by the King, and Randolph was stripped of his office for leaving his home colony without having the required pass.[242] (After the Revolution, Randolph became President of the Continental Congress.)

Members of the aristocracy and other Crown appointees had many and varied opportunities for personal gain. As most commercial endeavors in the colonies required royal approval, the colonial organizers of a project had to have "the right connections" to sponsor their petition to the King. If the organizers had no direct access to members of the aristocracy in England, they tried to find indirect routes to them through lower-level

Crown appointees or influential London merchants. When Lawrence Washington, George's older half-brother, joined several other colonists to form the Ohio Company, he recognized that their only chance of success was to entice well-connected Englishmen to join their group. One of those "right connections" was Lieutenant Governor Robert Dinwiddie. They approached several others, including Colonel Henry Bouquet, the British military commander in the west, but without success. In the end, the group recruited certain London merchants for their purpose (including a well-known and highly influential broker by the name of John Hanbury) who became full partners with a share of 25,000 acres each. Having been judicious in their choice of sponsors, Lawrence and the other organizers of Ohio Company succeeded in their petition for a substantial grant of land from the Crown.[243]

Not unexpectedly, the co-mingling of official and personal positions at times had serious unintended consequences. In Dinwiddie's case, there was widespread belief that he was responsible for inflaming the passions in England against France and engulfing the world in a brutal conflict known as the Seven Years' War (the American part of which was called the French and Indian War). He did so, the colonists believed, in the interest of protecting the land in the Ohio valley belonging to the Ohio Company, of which the Lieutenant Governor was himself a major partner. For Britain, the war had a devastating impact on its treasury. For the American colonies, that engagement was no less ruinous, as the Crown ordered that they would have to bear the cost of the American theater of operation. The result of that order was to drain the reserves of gold, silver, and pounds sterling from the colonies.[244]

Dinwiddie's successor as lieutenant governor was Francis Fauquier, who was a far more popular administrator for the colony. He also turned out to be a better negotiator on his own behalf than his predecessor. The named Governor was General Sir Jeffrey Amherst, who had no interest in taking up residence in Williamsburg to administer the affairs of "colonials," whom he held in contempt. The financial arrangement he worked out with Fauquier was for only £1,500 per year, plus half the fees made by the office. Fauquier was also more politically astute in the way he took advantage of opportunities that arose during his term of office:

When presented with the chance to participate in a project called Loyal Company, for example, the Lieutenant Governor did not permit his own name to be used. It was his son who actually became the named partner.[245]

It is shocking to a modern reader to find these accounts of flagrant violations of ethics and conflicts-of-interest rules. What is equally striking is that these actions were unlawful even in eighteenth-century England. There was in fact strict prohibition against the sale of a public office, and *Blackstone's Commentaries* (a compendium of the laws of England at the time) provided a clear rationale for it:

> "No public office shall be sold, under pain of disability to dispose of or hold it. For the law presumes that he, who buys an office, will by bribery, extortion, or other unlawful means, make his purchase good, to the detriment of the public."[246]

Obviously, the statute was observed solely in the breach, not only in the case of the royal governors but in other royal appointments to the American colonies as well.[247] What is remarkable, therefore, is that history books are *not* filled with accounts of prosecutions of the violators of the law. The only comment one can make is that in societies where corruption is so deep-seated, one can almost always trace its roots to the top of the chain of command.

Even before the birth of George Washington, as already recounted, absentee royal governors were the rule, not the exception, for the colony of Virginia. It was as though the North American continent – a veritable cornucopia of undiscovered treasures in its vast uncharted terrain and populated by the sons and daughters of England who were already major contributors to the economy of the mother country – did not even rate a proper representative from the home government. It was only when the colonists' discontent over their mistreatment on multiple fronts by Britain had reached decibels audible even in London that the practice was subjected to review there. It was finally and belatedly recognized that it had been a mistake for three-quarters of a century to permit successive chief executives of a major British dominion to remain in England and dispatch subordinates to discharge their duties for them. That was why the last two royal governors of Virginia before the Declaration of Independence, Baron de Botetourt and the Earl of Dunmore, were ordered to take up their duties in Virginia personally. By then, however, the unhappiness of the Americans was well on its way toward becoming a full-fledged revolt.[248]

Norborne Berkeley, Baron de Botetourt, was the first Governor-in-Chief to travel to Virginia, live in the colony, and attempt to discharge all the duties of the office personally. The story of this royal appointment would serve as a mirror to the inner workings of the political process in England of that era. A Member of Parliament from Gloucestershire since 1741, Botetourt was also an investor in certain business projects. One of his interests was an equity stake in Warmley Brass and Copper Company, which had a manufacturing operation near Bristol, the second largest city in England, located on the west coast near the sea routes to North America. In good economic times, Warmley embarked on a major expansion project, and Botetourt borrowed heavily to increase his investment in it. As it turned out, the expansion was a complete failure, putting the company and its investors at risk of bankruptcy. Devising a clever plan to avert disaster, Botetourt petitioned the Crown to convert Warmley to a joint-stock company. There would then be, in today's parlance, an Initial Public Offering, enabling the investors to clear off their obligations with the proceeds of the sale of stock.

Unfortunately for the Baron, a vocal opposition to the petition soon developed. Opponents accused Botetourt and partners of fraud by attempting to shield their personal assets from bankruptcy, and to shift their losses to outside shareholders. With all the clamor, Botetourt's petition stood no chance of being granted. Without a public stock offering, debt service and loan maturities Botetourt could not discharge threatened financial ruin for him. Warmley soon went bankrupt, and its assets were sold at auction. The same fate (and perhaps even imprisonment) loomed for Botetourt personally. This was the point at which the Crown intervened to extricate a member of the nobility from a most unpleasant set of circumstances. To hasten Botetourt's departure from England and the angry Warmley creditors, the king ordered a ship of the line to be especially fitted and prepared to speed the new governor across the ocean.

Thus, the timely and benevolent appointment of the Baron as the royal governor of far-away Virginia was a true lifesaver for Botetourt.[249]

After serving only two years in the post, Lord Botetourt died of convulsions and fever in Williamsburg in October 1770. After his death, William Nelson, Thomas Nelson's brother, became the acting Governor of Virginia, while the Board of Trade looked for a permanent replacement. Once appointed, however, Nelson did not wish to give up the opportunity to raise fees and be rewarded with partnerships and interests in the projects of others. "As acting governor, Nelson collected a salary of £2,000 per year" with substantial additional fees and emoluments. He tried hard but unsuccessfully to extend his term as acting governor, openly admitting that he wanted "a longer run in a pretty good pasture."

To replace Nelson, the Board of Trade appointed John Murray, 4th Earl of Dunmore, in September, 1771. At the time, Dunmore was Governor of New York, and did not wish to leave that colony, complaining that his wife refused to accompany him to Virginia. However, his protests to the influential Earl of Hillsborough, president of the Board of Trade, fell on deaf ears; the appointment to the post in Virginia was non-negotiable. Finally, Dunmore grudgingly made the move to Williamsburg, arriving there two months late and in a state of indignation. He vented his anger by demanding, in addition to his salary and fees, 100,000 acres of frontier land free from the obligation of paying quit-rents to the Crown. Striking out again, Dunmore's request was disapproved in London. Nevertheless, in the tradition of other royal appointees, Dunmore's perception of the governorship was as an opportunity for self-enrichment. Many of his decisions as governor were based on his expectation of personal profit. He had no interest, for example, in restricting westward migration because he wished to receive his cut of the quit-rents that would be charged on the sale of any new tracts in that region.[250]

Another decision by Dunmore as governor involved the proposed establishment of a new colony in North America to be called Vandalia, between the Allegheny Mountains and the Ohio River. A group led by Thomas Walpole, a Member of Parliament and nephew of Sir Robert Walpole, a former Prime Minister, sought a huge grant of land from the Crown for this purpose. Lord Dunmore immediately went into action, and this time successfully used his political connections to keep Vandalia from becoming a reality, which would have removed the land from his jurisdiction and the opportunity to collect fees for himself. Vandalia never materialized.[251] Similarly, he opposed the efforts of another group known as Transylvania Company to settle the West through the purchase of land from the Indian tribes of the region. Dunmore declared their activities illegal and barred them from operating in Virginia. On the other hand, he personally became the major stockholder in another land development enterprise called the Wabash Land Company and urged the approval of its land acquisitions by the Secretary of State for the Colonies in London while concealing his personal interest in the project.[252]

In Virginia, the post of the secretary was a royal appointment under the Great Seal of Great Britain and a powerful position. Its occupant was custodian of the seal of the colony, kept its records on all births, marriages, deaths, charters from the king, and powers of attorney. He ran the land office of the colony, and issued and recorded all deeds and other real estate documents. Also issued from his office were all naturalization papers, proceedings of the courts, marriage licenses, writs for choosing members of the legislature, and fines and forfeitures. Another of the many powers of the secretary related to the British prohibition against traveling outside a colony without express permission. The secretary was most often the one to issue these passes on behalf of the governor.

The secretary also had the power to make many of the official appointments of the colony, from each of which he pocketed a portion of the annual compensation for himself. In Virginia, the power of the secretary was so great that he reportedly controlled half of the members of the House of Burgesses, who would cast their votes as he directed. It is hardly surprising, therefore, that the post of secretary was highly sought after.[253]

The holder of this position in Virginia in the 1740s was one John Carter, a member of a prominent family in that colony. He had purchased the post for a payment of 1,500 guineas per year. When he died in 1741, there was spirited bidding to fill the vacancy. Charles Carter, the decedent's brother, felt he had first dibs on the post. Even before John was buried, Charles offered £2,000 to buy the appointment, almost a quarter more than his brother had paid. Other bidders vied for the position, including one who attempted to use the clout of a London merchant to ensure the success of his proposal. All were rejected; they were told that the winning bid far exceeded their offers.

The reality, however, was different. The royal governor of Virginia, the Earl of Albemarle, had his own candidate for the position, a man by the name of William Adair. Like others in similar positions, Adair had no intention of moving to the colonies. Nevertheless, considering the power and influence of his sponsor, Adair's selection as the new Secretary of Virginia was a foregone conclusion. (Albemarle had already proven himself quite adept at outmaneuvering those who considered it their prerogative to make such selections.) Adair intended to appoint a deputy who would take up residence in Virginia, collect substantial fees as Deputy Secretary of the colony, and rebate a significant portion to Adair in London.[254]

The spirited bidding now resumed, this time for the post of deputy secretary of Virginia. The person who secured that position, beating out all others? None other than George Washington's future partner in the Dismal Swamp project, young Thomas Nelson. It was Nelson's father who had been able to out-bid all rivals to secure the deputy position for his son.

An interesting postscript to this vignette is that the last Royal governor of Virginia, Lord Dunmore, made a special effort to remove William Adair as the colony's Secretary. Dunmore wanted to appoint his own man to the job, and then share in the salary, fees, and other perks of that office. He did not succeed. This time it was a different influential lord who had his own designs for the post. The Earl of Hillsborough, who later became Secretary of State for the Colonies, wanted the revenue stream from the job of absentee secretary of the colony to go to his own nineteen-year-old son. Dunmore's efforts to co-opt the position for an appointee of his own proved totally fruitless.[255]

Chapter Five

"ALL FOR ME, NOTHING FOR YOU" ECONOMIC POLICY

Can anyone tell me why trade, commerce, arts, sciences, and manufactures should not be as free for an American as for a European?

James Otis
Colonial lawyer

British Policies and Mercantilism: George Washington was born in the era dubbed by economic historians the Age of Mercantilism. In its various incarnations, mercantilism dominated British policies for nearly two hundred years, until shortly after the American Revolution. The essence of this philosophy was that the accumulation of treasure was the crucial ingredient in the pursuit of power. Therefore, the more bullion in a country, the greater its power. Mercantilism thus provided its own peculiar formula for the measurement of a nation's economic health. No need to be concerned about Gross Domestic Product, disposable personal income, the rate of savings and investment, productivity, unemployment, wages, etc. Instead, all one had to do was simply count the amount of gold and silver in the country's treasury. Making the assumption that there was only a finite quantity of precious metals in the world, mercantilists perceived international commerce as a zero-sum game. To the followers of this philosophy, therefore, the world was a closed loop. One country could only gain at the expense of another. Like a seesaw, if one side went up, the other had to go down.[256] Mercantilists never understood that the all-important factor in an economy is the human potential, and that the true national treasure is human productivity.

From these deceptively simple precepts, Britain fashioned a panoply of policies governing its commercial relations with the outside world, particularly its colonies: It was imperative to prevent at all costs any specie from leaving the country and to ensure a constant *incoming* stream of net additional bullion. Tariffs were to be kept high on imports except for agricultural commodities and raw materials. Sea power had to be built up as a means of controlling the colonies and other foreign markets, and shipping in and out of the country had to be channeled into Britain's own merchant fleet. Adherence to these concepts took precedence over all other considerations, and the government had to be prepared to deal with any resistance to their enforcement from colonials.[257]

These principles were then incorporated into a broad system of economic rules called the Navigation Acts. One law required that all trade to and from the colonies be shipped in English flag-carriers. Another restricted the export of tobacco, indigo, sugar, and other staples from the colonies only to England. Goods from other countries had to pass through England before being transshipped to America. Another law imposed tariffs on exports of staple products from the colonies. Yet another permitted the colonists to manufacture cloth but not to export their products, even to other colonies.[258] This was perhaps the most absurd aspect of the Navigation Acts, in that it prohibited a colonist from importing goods from another colony; he had to buy them from England.[259]

Despite the starkly one-sided nature of mercantilism and the increasingly coercive nature of the laws passed by Parliament in pursuance of its goals, there were few signs of serious colonial disquiet for four decades under George II and Robert Walpole, who became Britain's first Prime

Minister in 1721. Walpole favored expansion of trade with Britain's overseas domains and put in place a policy of "wise and salutary neglect" in the enforcement of the Navigation Acts. His government took note of some colonists engaging at times in "illegal" commercial transactions with countries other than England but often took no action, recognizing that the more money the Americans made from trade, the more they would be able to spend buying English goods. His policies not only caused a substantial expansion of commerce between England and its North American provinces, but they also ensured a relatively stable environment in which the colonists could operate.[260]

The calculated benevolence of the government toward the commercial activities of the colonials, however, ended with the death of George II and the expiration of the ministries of Robert Walpole and his successors. Soon the inhabitants of Britain's possessions in America would feel the winds of change as a harbinger of a significant constriction of their economic freedoms.

King George II, who spoke English with a distinct German accent, was on the throne of England for thirty-three years. Near the end of his reign, he made it known that he had had enough of English politics. "I'm sick to death of all this foolish stuff" was how he proclaimed his distaste for the way the game of politics was played in his country.[261] On October 25, 1760, he rose at six a.m., had a cup of hot chocolate for breakfast, and retired to his private quarters to attend to his toiletries. Blind in one eye and hard of hearing, George II at seventy-seven had already lived longer than any of his predecessors. Attendants found him slumped in his private bathroom, dead of a ruptured aortic aneurism. He was buried in Westminster Abbey. His son, whom George II despised, had predeceased him. The successor to George II, therefore, became his grandson, George III, twenty-two years old at the time. As a child, he had been dull and apathetic; he could not read until he was eleven. As an adult, he exhibited strange mannerisms and ways of speech that invited parody and ridicule, such as ending every sentence with "what, what," or "hey, hey." Then, starting in 1788, he began suffering from periods of manic-depressive psychosis, and on one occasion, when his eldest son, the Prince of Wales, displeased him, George III flew into a violent rage, shoved his son against a wall, began choking him, and was restrained only with difficulty.[262] News of the king's affliction spread rapidly; Thomas Jefferson, writing from Europe in 1789, referred to the madness of George III as leaving him "in a state of imbecility and melancholy."[263]

For the American colonists, struggling to tame a mostly primitive continent while trying to create a viable economy for themselves, a harsh new era was about to unfold, one which would test to the limit their allegiance to the Crown of England. The era of "salutary neglect" would end as the new king exhibited his determination to bring the colonists fully under control."[264]

The year before the death of George II, George Washington had resigned his commission in the Virginia militia, taken a bride, and moved to Mount Vernon, eager to begin the life of an ambitious, entrepreneurial civilian. Determined to revitalize the moribund farm at Mount Vernon he had inherited from his brother and preoccupied with the reorganization and staffing of its operation, he would not hear for months the news of the old king's death. In the meantime, he continued working his farm and trying to nurture his new relationship with the trading house in London with which his bride and her first husband had worked before. He looked to England as the land of his forefathers and the source of all good for the colonists, unaware that the course of his life would soon be irretrievably changed by the far-flung operations of a few English multinational corporations.

* * *

Influence of the Chartered Trading Companies: The Seven Years' War ended in a decisive victory for Britain and its allies in 1763, gaining much prized territory for the British Empire, including Louisiana, Canada, several Caribbean islands, and certain properties in India from France; and East and West Florida from Spain. Great Britain was now established as the dominant world power, with the Union Jack flying conspicuously on every known continent. Public euphoria in England was palpable. Amid the celebratory climate, little notice was taken of another and less favorable consequence of the conflict recently ended: Wars are devastatingly expensive to wage, and this particularly prolonged one was even more so. It had depleted the British treasury and saddled it with a mountain of debt – £130 million, a colossal sum indeed at the time. The annual interest alone on that debt came to £4.5 million.[265]

For George Grenville, the British Prime Minister who also carried the portfolio of the Chancellor of the Exchequer, the fiscal shortfall posed a major challenge.

The South Sea Company: The government had actually faced a similar situation earlier in the century when it found itself burdened with a crushing load of public debt it was unable to fund. Sir Charles Spencer, 3rd Earl of Sunderland, who was the First Lord of the Treasury, and John Aislabie, the Chancellor of the Exchequer, solved the problem by means of a technique bordering on waving a magic wand! The story, now immortalized as "the Saga of the South Sea Bubble,"[266] involved the use of an entity created by act of Parliament called the South Sea Company, to which the government granted monopoly trading rights to much of South America. The plan was to persuade the public holders of British government bonds to exchange them for shares in the new company, thus wiping out all or a substantial portion of the national debt.[267]

The first step in the process was to create a public perception that the South Sea Company had a solid business, that its prospects were exciting, and that its stock was destined for great heights. The reality, however, was that the company's operations were speculative and it had virtually no prospect of ever hitting a bonanza in the region to which its monopoly applied. Spain and Portugal, the dominant colonial powers in South America at the time, left little opportunity for other nations to gain a foothold there. Perhaps a clever PR person thought to deflect attention from this reality by naming the company "South Sea" to conjure up images of lush tropical islands in the South Pacific.

Naturally, the scheme could not be carried out without securing official approvals at several levels, which required "considerable bribery and treating, both at court and in parliament, to obtain the necessary political backing." The next step was to hype the company's "trade monopoly" as leading to a substantial revenue stream in a short period of time. The company, therefore, engaged in an elaborate campaign to publicize its promising future and then started bidding on its own stock. As its share price started to rise, the company began providing easy financing to anyone who wished to purchase the stock. In less than six months, the price of each share had skyrocketed from £128 to £1,050. In this frenzied atmosphere, public holders of government annuities were given the opportunity of exchanging them for South Sea shares – which the unwary bondholders did in droves. Before the spectacular and inevitable collapse of the market in South Sea stock in 1720, the British Treasury had in one masterful stroke wiped out three-fifths of the huge debt on its books, succeeding also in ridding itself of the obligation to pay interest on that portion of its bonds.[268]

The collapse of the South Sea bubble coincided with the implosion in France of the contemporaneous Mississippi scheme. The fury of their public victims was palpable, and something had to be done to pacify them, which resulted in some of the purported "villains" being sent to the Tower of London.[269]

It would have been natural, more than four decades later, once the large deficits in the Treasury became known after the Seven Years' War, to remember wistfully the old South Sea formula for converting debt into the shares of a profitless company through sheer political and financial razzle-dazzle. Alas, the earlier times had been a simpler and more optimistic age. In the intervening decades, the capital markets had become more sophisticated. So, for the shortfall now facing the Treasury, financial legerdemain alone would not suffice.

European investors took note of the enormous national debt facing the British government in 1763 and panicked. The crisis originated in Amsterdam and quickly spread to London. Credit tightened, and interest rates spiked. The English trading houses, with which the colonists did substantial business, were caught in the ensuing liquidity squeeze. In turn, they curtailed credit to their American customers and pressed them to clear their debit balances. Like many colonial farmers whose debts had been mounting after several bad tobacco harvests, Thomas Jefferson found himself in financial difficulties and suffered greatly in the crisis.[270]

With the South Sea scheme being no longer a workable approach, the British government had to find a different formula to solve its financial plight. This time, it decided that it had an even better arrow in its quiver: it would pass on the burden of its fiscal problems to its American colonies. So Britain began imposing on its dominions in the New World a series of new revenue-raising measures including higher tariffs and additional taxes. The public relations techniques employed earlier in the century to sell the unwary English populace on accepting equity in the South Sea Company in return for their government bonds were now employed for a new purpose, namely, to sell the colonists on the notion that the new taxes being levied on them were justified to pay for their protection from Indians and other dangers!

What George III and his minister had not counted on, however, was the skepticism and intransigence of the Crown's American subjects.

The East India Company: An even worse credit crisis than the one in 1763 occurred in 1772 in England. In the preceding two years, easy credit and the beginnings of the Industrial Revolution had ushered in boom economic times in Britain, but now the down cycle was at hand. This time around, the panic may have in fact been triggered by market activity in the stock of the United Company of Merchants of England Trading to the East Indies, commonly referred to as the East India Company, which had benefited greatly from the British victory over France in the Seven Years' War.[271]

The case of this chartered trading company provides another instance of the English political process. In the seventeenth century, a member of the English aristocracy, the Earl of Cumberland, obtained a royal charter for a joint-stock company to trade in the East Indies. The company was governed by a board of twenty-four directors elected by a Court of Proprietors, and the early grant of the charter provided that every holder of £500 stock had a single vote, regardless of the number of shares owned by him. Benefiting from royal patronage, the company soon expanded its operations, secured from the British government a monopoly to operate in India, and began trading in spices, silk, tea, and opium. In 1757, under the military genius of a young man by the name of Robert Clive, the company's troops gained control of the province of Bengal, a vast territory larger than France and Spain combined, with a population of twenty million people.[272] In one military stroke, the Honourable East India Company (as it was then known in India) enhanced its fortunes to hitherto unimaginable levels by reportedly expropriating half of all the precious metals and jewels in Greater Bengal, simultaneously expanding the reach and power of the British Empire in that part of the world. By 1769, the company could count on annual revenues of £4 million, of which half would be remitted to Britain. As a reward, Clive demanded £160,000 for himself, £500,000 for his troops, £24,000 for each member of the company's governing board, and £1,000,000 of reparations.[273]

The dazzling prospects of unlimited growth and profitability caused the company's stock price to soar to dizzying heights, while its shareholders grew to 2,000 – an unusually large group in possession of high-priced £500 stock, many of whom had gone into debt to make the investment. In the meantime, the company's board of directors began adding to the feeding frenzy in the stock market by approving the payment of large dividends to shareholders, and substantial annual payments to the British government. Predictably, the good days did not last forever. The change in the fortunes of East India came after the large outlays depleted its reserves against contingencies at a critical point in its business. In a classic case of hubris causing a successful company to lose sight of its internal controls, East India began experiencing a crippling series of setbacks at every level of its operations. Shortly before the American Revolution, a famine in Bengal killed fully one-third of the local population, and the company was partly blamed for the appalling extent of the disaster. Simultaneously, its officers and agents were accused of committing atrocities in India and defrauding the Indians while stories of high living and extravagant expenditures by even its low-level expat employees began circulating in London. When the inevitable crash in East India shares came, the investors learned the added risk of buying stock on margin. The resulting liquidity crunch was as painful as it was inexorable. In the ensuing two years, prominent merchants closed their doors and stopped all payments, and there were runs on banks as a rash of bankruptcies occurred in England.Financial difficulties soon spread to the colonies.Included among the hapless stockholders of the East India Company were many of the London, Manchester, and Liverpool merchants who serviced the American colonists. Encouraged by the trading houses, colonial farmers had become accustomed to buying on credit. The same brokerage houses now withdrew their credit facilities from the Americans, pressing their clients to clear their account balances, which by the time of the Panic of 1772 had grown to a staggering £3 million. Virginia alone accounted for nearly half of that sum.[274]

In the meantime, the East India Company, unable to meet its obligations, sought a government bailout. Between 1770 and 1773, while the smoldering resentments in the American colonies were causing what had been whispered talk of a break with the mother country to become loud demands for independence, Parliament hardly took note of American affairs, giving its attention to "the Indian question," referring to East India Company. To avert the bankruptcy of so prominent an entity and its equally prominent shareholders in Parliament, the government, itself already strapped, nevertheless stepped in to advance the company £1.4 million. Shortly thereafter, the hero who had started it all, Robert Clive, committed suicide. Then, to ensure East India's continuing survival, Lord North attempted to provide it a guaranteed revenue stream by having Parliament pass the Tea Act of 1773, levying a tax on tea in the American colonies. The law met with great resistance from Americans, and the arrival of the cargo of tea at the Boston Harbor later that year became the trigger for the Boston Tea Party and the American Revolution. When news of the actions of the colonists reached London, George III made it clear that he expected the government to use force "to bring back the Americans to their duty." Lord North complied, and the rest, of course, is history.[275]

As for the East India Company, the government took complete control of its affairs in 1784, brought all its territories in India under British government dominion, and appointed a Court of Directors and Proprietors which would be overseen by a governmental control board selected by the Crown. Thus nationalized, the company became an arm of the British government.[276]

The Royal African Company: The slave trade with the American colonies was the monopoly of a joint-stock company chartered in 1672 by Parliament and called the Royal African Company of England. It was dissolved and succeeded by the Company of Merchants Trading to Africa. King George III was personally a shareholder and received regular dividends of £322 10*s* per year for his holdings. As the company grew and prospered, the Crown made certain that nothing stood in the way of the company's nefarious activities and the achievement of its trade and financial goals. Naturally, the king's involvement also ensured strong connections for the company in Westminster and Whitehall. Lord Dartmouth and Lord Hillsborough, successive presidents of the Board of Trade, went so far in supporting the activities of the company as to intervene in the foreign affairs of England for the private benefit of that entity. As late as 1771, the royal governor of Virginia was forbidden by the Crown "to assent to any law by which the importation of slaves should be in any respect prohibited or obstructed." He was further specifically directed to provide whatever assistance was needed by the company in pursuing its trade with the colony. Operating under the royal protection, by 1776 the English traders had kidnapped three million Africans, tearing them from their homes and loved ones and condemning them to the most barbaric form of bondage in America.[277]

While George Washington was a member of the Virginia legislature, the Burgesses used every technique they could devise to stop the slave trade in that colony, including the imposition of various taxes and levies to discourage its development. George III always intervened, ordering the repeal of all legislation, tariffs, and taxes inimical to the slave trade. Finally, despite the fact that some of their own members were slave owners, the Burgesses still found the practice abhorrent and reprehensible, and voted overwhelmingly in 1772 for a resolution to end it. Frustrated at every turn in their previous attempts in this matter, the legislators decided to resort to a bold and risky petition to the Crown.

Calling the practice "a trade of great inhumanity," the House of Burgesses submitted its resolution as part of a petition to the Crown to abolish the odious practice of trafficking in human beings. The Assembly of South Carolina likewise passed a law imposing a heavy duty upon the importation of slaves as a means of discouraging the practice. In both cases, George III, utterly indifferent to the cost in human suffering, contemptuously dismissed the Virginia petition and ordered the South Carolina law rescinded on the ground that "the slave trade was one of the most lucrative branches of English commerce."[278]

The chartered trading companies, such as the South Sea Company, the East India Company, and the Royal African Company, combined "the ruthless tactics of despots with the legal structure of a profit-seeking shareholder-driven joint-stock corporation." Adam Smith condemned the creation of the trading monopolies by official fiat as being abhorrent to the operation of free markets and harmful to Britain's own economic development. He could have included the development of the American colonies in that judgment as well.[279]

Influence of English Brokers: "A nation of shopkeepers" is a characterization of the English attributed to Napoleon. As in the case of most generalizations, this too needs refinement. To make it at least partly accurate, the definition of "shopkeepers" would have to be broadened to include all businessmen, financiers, manufacturers, brokers, factors, and merchants operating the English trading houses. It is a fact of history that in the eighteenth century, members of this group enjoyed unparalleled political clout at the highest levels of the British government in matters of trade, and that they exercised virtually total sway over the commercial affairs of Americans.

The policy of maintaining control over the activities of the colonists was carried out under the aegis of the Privy Council and Parliament by a panoply of different departments. For a colonist trying to understand the multiple arms of the home government exercising jurisdiction over his life, the sprawling bureaucracy across the ocean was a bewildering operational reality. The English traders and brokers with access to the levers of power had no difficulty navigating the elaborate and complex official structure, but the little guy in the American provinces hardly had a chance. This was so, even though the Board of Trade was designed to serve as the narrow funnel for the coordination and enforcement of all the mandates directed at the overseas dominions.[280] In conjunction with other Whitehall offices, the Board dealt with all complaints against the colonists, reviewed all laws passed by the provincial legislatures, and made recommendations for the appointment of colony officials. It was, however, not an independent agency; on the contrary, it was part of the political system, and its eight members changed with shifts within the government. Its president, a member of the English aristocracy, was steeped in partisan maneuvers and machinations, and was particularly sensitive to the needs and demands of special interest groups, of which none had greater access to him or influence at the Board than the English brokers and traders. They had the freedom to attend the official meetings of the Board and wielded substantial power over its decisions affecting their interest. It was common knowledge that British policy hewed closely to the desires of the traders.[281]

In any discussion of colonial affairs in government circles, there were always two goals at the top of the agenda: More revenue from the colonies for the home government and profitable business for the English merchants. The uniform instructions from London to all the royal governors of the American provinces explicitly required them to be vigilant in preventing any competition to develop in the colonies for the home companies. The governors were further instructed to enforce the policy that all payments for British imports into the colonies had to be made in gold, silver, or pounds sterling, and not in any colonial currency. It was also British policy not to permit any tariffs to be imposed by a colony on imports from England.[282]

The government archives of official records and journals kept in the eighteenth century are rife with instances of arbitrary action instigated at the behest of the English trading houses. When a colony levied a small tariff on imports to finance the construction of a much-needed lighthouse at Cape Henry, the English exporters complained to the Board of Trade, which immediately ordered the tax repealed. When English brokers found themselves with a surplus of tobacco inventory, they caused the Board of Trade to order a halt in the production of tobacco in America until further notice, thus shifting their losses onto the colonial tobacco growers, creating a crippling disruption in their operations and planting cycles. When the colonists began trading with the nearby islands of the West Indies, the British merchants took immediate action to keep exclusive control of this highly profitable business for themselves. On their behalf, Parliament imposed prohibitively high tariffs on these colonial trades. To add insult to injury, it ordered the deployment of ships of the Royal Navy to patrol the Atlantic coast and the West Indies and to seize any colonial merchant vessel in the region engaging in such activity. In these and similar cases, the pleas of American traders and farmers to London for relief, even though endorsed by the Crown representative in a particular colony, fell on deaf ears.[283]

George Washington and other planters who suffered under these arrangements were unaware of the extent of the influence and power of the English brokers over British government actions. Even the royal representative in the colony, Lieutenant Governor Sir William Gooch, was irate at the actions of the traders. "The British merchants," he wrote, "not only subjected [the farmers] to many hardships but also defrauded the revenues."[284]

Once George III was crowned, it was not long before "a powerful wave of deliberate protective legislation aimed at the colonies was enacted by Parliament," all designed to create a monopoly of colonial trade for the British houses, and to preserve and increase the cache of gold and silver in England. Foreign goods destined for America had to be shipped first to England where they would be unloaded, inspected, and subjected to import duties before being reloaded on English vessels for transshipment to the colonies. The diversion and the accompanying taxes and expenses increased shipping time and raised the prices of goods, effectively making such transactions prohibitive for Americans.[285]

Trade within the colonies was also the subject of regulation. Products destined from one colony to another did not travel unimpeded; they were subject to taxes and tariffs. Legally, a Virginia family, for example, could not, without the payment of tariffs, buy clothing from neighboring Pennsylvania. Thus, colonists would send away to England for their clothing needs, at great inconvenience and high cost. Inevitably, wrong sizes, wrong products, or other instances of negligence in observing customer instructions occurred in the shipments from England. Taxes, tariffs, duties, and similar charges applied to some products and not to others, at varying rates, and the applicable lists and rates were confusingly modified periodically to accommodate changed British needs.[286]

The colonies could export their produce and import their finished goods only in British flag-carriers with largely English crews and masters. This gave monopoly pricing power to those shipping lines. The master of a vessel carrying colonial products on board had to give a bond varying in amount from £1,000 to £2,000 to ensure that the cargo would be taken only to Britain. The penalty for violating the Navigation Acts was forfeiture of cargo and vessel, and possible imprisonment. Americans, therefore, often faced a dilemma. They could abide by the law and pay the high costs, charges, and duties, or they could turn to smuggling and bribery in the conduct of their affairs. Thus, some colonists found themselves resorting to risky behavior, at times with serious consequences.[287]

Initially, the burden of these policies fell mostly on colonial farmers. Later, British manufacturers, fearing competition from America, caused the Board of Trade to intercede in Parliament on their behalf to regulate colonial manufacturing in addition to trade. The new rules put many fledgling colonial industries out of business, such as the manufacturers of wool, yarn, and woolen cloth. England had a growing textile industry, and Parliament intended that the American colonies would remain a significant market for Britain's cloth goods.[288]

Hat-making came next. Colonial hatters produced quality hats, particularly those made with beaver pelts, which were popular in England and Continental Europe, as well as in the colonies. The Company of Feltmakers in England caused the Board of Trade to have Parliament restrict colonial production of these items. The regulations also decreed that colonial hat-makers had to undergo a seven-year apprenticeship, and the number of apprentices was strictly limited.[289]

The case of the manufacture of iron is particularly illustrative. Colonial iron production existed only on a small scale mainly in New England and the middle colonies, but as the industry grew and began to expand into finished goods, iron interests in England became alarmed and lobbied Parliament to keep the colonists from going into the business on the grounds that "they would be able to manufacture iron on cheaper terms than we can; and the meanest mechanic in Birmingham, or Sheffield, must foresee what would be the consequence if the Americans should assume to themselves this article of trade." Parliament responded by forbidding the erection in the colonies of rolling or slitting mills, plating forges, or steel furnaces.[290]

The aim of the British government was to encourage the colonists in the production of such raw materials as were needed in England. While no manufacturing was permitted, the raising of hemp and flax and the shipping of naval stores such as tar, masts, and cordage were encouraged to fill domestic requirements in Britain.[291]

Americans thus found their choices in making a livelihood limited by a multiplicity of Parliamentary acts. Southern planters (like George Washington) chafed under regulations that dictated how and where they could market their crops. Unable to sell their produce to the highest bidders in an open market or to buy their supplies and equipment from the best sources, the colonists felt they had virtually no negotiating power with British firms.[292] Nor were Northerners spared, as they found their manufacturing activities severely curtailed by the same series of Parliamentary measures affecting all Americans. Henry Knox, Washington's future Secretary of War, was one whose family suffered the loss of his father's flourishing shipbuilding business as a result of the vagaries of life under the British constraints. Another victim of British controls was Nathanael Greene, an ironmaster who later became Washington's top general in the Revolutionary War.

James Otis, the bumptious provincial lawyer whom John Adams credited with being the first to plant the seed of independence in a Boston courtroom in 1761, repeatedly posed basic questions about imperial policy.

> "Is there anything in the laws of nature and nations, anything in the nature of our allegiance," he wanted to know, "that forbids a colonist to push the manufacture of iron much beyond the making of a horse-shoe or a hob nail?"[293]

The effect of these policies was that the English and Scottish trading houses were growing rich by buying the staple exports of the American colonies and then reselling them on the European markets at the same time that the American farmers found themselves staggering under their debt loads caused by the low prices the English merchants paid them for their products.[294]

The most important colonies of Great Britain in the eighteenth century were India and America. Once Britain lost its American colonies, India "became the richest jewel in the Imperial Crown."[295] There, the aim of the Crown was to exploit that country's natural resources, a practice which continued well into the twentieth century. (India secured its independence in 1947.) British treatment of its American colonies was somewhat more complex, even though the basic goal was the same, namely, to ensure that England received the maximum benefit from its New World settlements. The American colonists, however, had a different perception of their situation. They saw themselves as free-born Englishmen, and when they petitioned the Crown to redress their grievances, they felt they were merely asserting their rights. After repeatedly complaining about the unfair treatment of the colonists by the Board of Trade at the behest of the British merchants and traders, the Virginia House of Burgesses finally had had enough. In a bluntly-worded message more than a decade before the Declaration of Independence, the legislature expressed its frustrations. The American colonists were not "a people subjugated by the arms of a conqueror," it warned, "but of sons sent out to explore and settle a new world...."[296]

William Pitt, 1st Earl of Chatham, a former Prime Minister whom English historians have anointed as "Pitt the Elder," asserted in a rousing declaration in the House of Commons: "Americans are the sons, not the bastards, of England... Taxation is no part of the governing or legislative power... I rejoice that America has resisted."[297] For this, Pitt was accused of spreading sedition by the then Prime Minister, George Grenville. Pitt and other like-minded leaders notwithstanding, *"it was beyond British upper-class comprehension how colonials could claim the same rights as Englishmen."*[298]

As the resentment of Americans against British policies was becoming acute, John Adams summarized the lament of all the colonists when he said, "We are obliged to sell our commodities to her [Great Britain] far cheaper than we could get for them at foreign markets. This difference is really a tax on us for the good of the empire. We are obliged to take from Great Britain commodities that we could purchase cheaper elsewhere. This difference is [also] a tax upon us for the good of the empire." John Adams wanted to know why Americans were given no credit for these contributions to the British economy, but instead burdened continually with a whole new set of taxes and restrictions. George Washington was even more emphatic when he summed up the attitude of the colonists toward such stealth taxes by calling them an "unconstitutional method of taxation" of the colonists and "a direful attack upon their liberties."[299]

In any event, the Revolution brought these onerous practices to a halt for Americans.

The latter half of the eighteenth century was a time of many new developments in Great Britain. Conquests abroad were providing a source of riches, early glimmers of the Industrial Revolution were a boon to the manufacturing sector, the growth of banking and finance was a means of enhancing England's standing and participation in the capital markets of Europe, and a busy trading environment was a significant contributor to the development of a bustling economy. There was a steady increase in the country's cache of precious metals, and the policymakers felt vindicated that their programs were working as intended.

In British America, on the other hand, life was following a predictable but not so productive pattern. Colonial farmers, ninety percent of the population,[300] exported their produce to Britain through British brokers. By reason of the distances involved and the delays in mail and shipments, each farmer was locked into a relationship with an English or Scottish trading house and planted his crops and placed orders for finished goods, all in reliance upon prices quoted by his British correspondent. Months later, however, after the crops had been planted, harvested, packed, and shipped by transatlantic freight to the trader, or the finished goods shipped from England, the farmer would receive a statement of his account from England, often finding out for the first time that there had been price changes. Americans had come to believe that the English merchants manipulated the prices of these colonial transactions. Washington and others complained that they had zero bargaining power with the English importers, and that the price changes went against the colonists entirely too often.

The monopoly power of the trading houses in dealing with their colonial customers – a monopoly created by Parliament and enforced by the government – put the colonists at the mercy of their British brokers. In the absence of a competitive market, the British merchants had little incentive to improve the quality of their export products or to price them attractively for the buyers. Americans felt trapped in a relentless spiral of deficits and red ink which was growing larger every year, with no light at the end of the tunnel. It was an arrangement designed to enrich one party to the trade while pushing the other party toward the poorhouse. Washington suffered in this system as much as anyone, and his correspondence with Cary & Company bears testimony to his frustration with the system.

Even those at the highest levels of the British government scoffed at the notion that if the American colonies were permitted to grow and prosper, they would be ever better trading partners for the English houses, or that the optimum trading environment was one where all the parties benefited and had an incentive to continue the relationship. With a myopia that is hard to understand today, British policies were designed to ensure that any profit from trade between Britain and its American colonies would flow in only one direction – toward Great Britain. Lord Botetourt, the royal Governor of Virginia, minced no words when he said the British merchants bore direct responsibility for the colonies boycotting British goods. Others in Britain called the power of the merchants and manufacturers "a truly pernicious influence" in the British government, "especially in extorting monopolistic privileges from Parliament."[301]

Currency: By mid-century, Britain was actively expanding its own banking sector and creating new banking partnerships. These privileges, however, were *not* extended to the American colonies. Quite the contrary. Parliament responded to strong lobbying on behalf of British merchants by passing the Currency Act of 1764, which effectively prohibited the American provinces from creating any system of uniform currency or coinage as legal tender. It also effectively ended the practice of using a rate of exchange of colonial money for pounds sterling, rendering any existing local currency worthless. It also highlighted the negative trade balance of the colonies with the mother country, which continuously drained hard currency and precious metals from America. This steady and inexorable contraction in the money supply created a serious bottleneck in the economic and infrastructure development of the colonies, with the added handicap that Americans were increasingly unable to pay their debts to the English brokers. Not surprisingly, the new law created a furor in the colonies and great commercial disruption. Benjamin Franklin candidly told the House of Commons that the Currency Act was a leading factor in driving a wedge between the colonists and the home government.[302]

Soon the scarcity of hard currency and coins reached near-panic proportions in America. With purchases from England by Americans continuing to exceed their exports to the mother country by a wide margin, debts were accumulating far beyond the ability of the debtors to service. Ironically, the colonists were financing their debit balances on the books of their English trading correspondents by borrowing from the same firms. By 1770, the accumulated colonial debt had reached £3 million, a huge sum for the times and up fifty percent from a decade earlier. With no ability to attract investments from other sources or to raise funds through the issuance of bonds or other forms of debt, the colonists found their development severely hampered. Americans believed that the policies of the home government were both short-sighted and counterproductive, as less money in circulation in America meant less purchasing power in the colonies, which was one of the contributing factors to two successive panics in Britain and parts of Europe before the American Revolution, with painful results on both sides of the Atlantic.[303]

The currency issue was far from being the only instance in which the British government found itself at cross purposes with its own policies, but it was a major one. In Whitehall, there was full awareness that "a scarcity of coin" in the colonies would slow the volume of trade with the British trading houses, and even have the potential of leading to a depression in the colonies. Nevertheless, the government's obsessive preoccupation with the dictates of mercantilism left no provision for the colonies to create their own coinage and currency.[304]

Of all the restrictions placed on the daily lives of Americans by the home government, the prohibition on the creation of a national currency was perhaps the tightest straitjacket of all. David Hume shone the spotlight on the issue when he said that money is the only "investment which men have agreed upon to facilitate the exchange of one commodity for another."[305] Deprived of its use, the colonists were forced to resort to barter – a cumbersome and clumsy process – or to pay for their local purchases in chickens, turkey, hogs, oxen, tobacco, whiskey, cannonballs, Spanish milled dollars, doubloons, Johannes, etc. The result was such a hodgepodge of money-substitutes as to border on commercial chaos. The desperate need for some sort of medium of exchange caused Americans to circulate in the colonies coins from many countries, including Portuguese,

French, Dutch, Flemish, Mexican, and even Peruvian coins. The British government again quickly stepped in, calling foreign coins "illegal currencies" and outlawing their use in the colonies.

In an official communiqué to London in 1765, Lieutenant Governor Francis Fauquier of Virginia summed up the intolerable situation in America when he wrote, "Circulating currency is growing very scarce so that people are really distressed for money of any kind to satisfy their creditors, and this evil in the colonies is daily increasing."[306]

Having received no relief whatsoever from their petitions to the Crown, by the early 1770s the colonists had about reached the limit of their frustration on economic matters affecting their lives. What with the British ban on manufacturing, on trade with any country other than Great Britain, and on the creation of a uniform currency, among many other restrictions, the colonists felt the jaws of an economic vise tightening mercilessly on them from every direction.

Protection and Obedience: George Grenville, First Lord of the Admiralty and later Prime Minister (1763-1765), was described by biographers as "intolerably conceited" and "rigid, dogmatic, and haughty." There was little patience in his soul for the smoldering resentments of "colonials." When they sought relief from the increasing restrictions on their commercial freedoms and the new and additional taxes, Grenville snapped, "Protection and obedience are reciprocal. Great Britain protects America; America is bound to yield obedience."[307]

Great sound bite! What had prompted this catchy sloganeering by Grenville was that the Seven Years' War had depleted the British treasury at the same time that the government was spending large sums on an expansion of the Royal Navy, and the land tax, excise tax, and other domestic revenue measures barely covered half of the government's debt service. Britain's financial resources were thus under severe strain, causing the minister to try to squeeze more and more revenue out of the colonies. These events were taking their toll on colonial loyalty to the mother country, and Grenville's stern admonition was designed to provide a rationale for Britain's actions and serve as a warning to the colonists as well. Despairing of ever receiving a fair hearing in London, Americans lamented that the mother country was displaying a "captious and unbending spirit" toward them.[308] The problem with Grenville's slogan was that the "obedience" part was explicit, the "protection" part less clear.

Britain did in fact maintain certain garrisons in the American colonies, but until the outbreak of hostilities with France during the French and Indian War, their cost was trifling. As Benjamin Franklin observed, "The colonies cost England nothing in forts, citadels, garrisons, or armies to keep them in subjugation. They were governed at the expense of a little pen, ink, and paper." Before fighting began in that particular conflict, there were only about five hundred English soldiers in all of America, and the colonies kept their own militias at their own expense. Once the war with the French troops broke out on American soil, Britain sent six thousand troops to America, and the colonists were ordered to reimburse the mother country for the cost of that engagement – an order which came close to bankrupting the colonies. Between 1755 and 1762 the contribution of Virginia alone was £440,000 sterling to the French and Indian War, with the result that all the supply of gold and silver in the colony was taken for the payment of troops in service. New York contributed £535,000, Pennsylvania £540,000, and Massachusetts £800,000. The total for the North American provinces was £2.5 million sterling, a huge sum for the strapped colonies.[309]

After the Seven Years' War, then Prime Minister John Stuart, 3rd Earl of Bute, called for the permanent deployment of fourteen infantry regiments in the colonies, about 10,000 men, and the Secretary of War informed Parliament that after the first year, all costs of the army stationed in America would be borne by the colonies. The policy recommendation for this action was originated in the Board of Trade and included an explicit statement that "the main purpose of stationing a large body of troops in America was *to secure the dependence of the colonies on Great Britain*." [Emphasis added.] As one historian described it, the British army in North America "was almost entirely stationed in the new colonies and the Indian reservations, as much to control the inhabitants there as to defend them." Thus, many in the colonies actually believed that the maintenance of garrisons on American soil by the British, which was presented as being for the protection of the colonists, was in fact for protection *from* them. When a member of the Grenville government explained that these Americans are being "protected by our arms," Colonel Isaac Barré, a plainspoken, battle-scarred veteran of the French and Indian War turned Member of Parliament who knew the colonies well, took the floor and in a passionate speech expressed shock and amazement at the distortion of the truth. "They [the Americans] protected by your arms?" he thundered. "They have nobly taken up arms in *your* defense…" Others who kept a close eye on developments in North America from Britain expressed early skepticism about the willingness of the American colonies to continue to support the imperial ambitions of waging wars to gain additional colonies, openly asserting that it was "an improbable assumption that colonial assemblies would always be ready to vote funds to subsidize an army over which they had no control."[310]

There was widespread belief among the colonists that the presence of British forces was for the protection of imperial interests such as the fur trade and the retention of Indians as customers of British merchants, and that any military engagements taking place on American soil among the major powers of the day – Britain, France, and Spain – were strictly in furtherance of their quests for territory or advantage in commercial trade.

For Americans, what posed grave danger to their population were the continuing raids on western settlements by various Indian tribes, in which whole families were wiped out, houses and barns painstakingly built with scarce parts by manual labor burned down, and livestock taken. George Washington carried with him heartrending memories of settlers who lived in constant fear of such raids and who had begged him for help. "I see their situation," Washington wrote, "know their danger, and participate in their sufferings, without having it in my power to give them further relief than uncertain promises." In 1763, British forces under General Jeffrey Amherst did in fact make an attempt at protecting the colonies from Indians in a conflict known as Pontiac's War, but the result was so prolonged and bloody, with major casualties suffered by Amherst's forces, that it caused the government in London to make a 180-degree turn in its Indian policy: It issued a sweeping order to the colonists to say out of the Indians' way! That historic decision was documented in the Royal Proclamation of 1763, which prohibited all settlement beyond the Appalachian mountain range from Canada all the way to Alabama and

Mississippi. From that point forward, protecting the American colonists from Indian raids was not high on Britain's agenda. For the government in London, "Indian danger was considered primarily a matter of *colonial* interest," and the provinces were expected to assume the burden of their own internal defense, for which they should not have "the slightest expectation of any reimbursement" from the mother country.[311]

Attempts at courting the Indian tribes by the British government did not stop with the Proclamation of 1763. After winning the French and Indian War, Britain took over Canada from France, acquiring for the English trading houses a monopoly of the highly profitable fur trade with Indian trappers. Simultaneously, Britain became the dominant supplier of manufactured items to Indian tribes in North America. Thus, the mother country's perspective on the Indian issue differed greatly from that of the Americans. Far from providing protection to the colonists from attacks by Indian tribes, British policy was to court the same tribes and spend large sums on presents for the Indians every year with the object of securing their friendship, an arrangement which continued for more than a decade after the American Revolution.[312]

There was one area in which British protection was important for the colonists, and that was against piracy on the high seas. Britain's agreements with the North African corsairs provided for free passage for ships of the British Empire, including colonial merchant vessels used in trade with Great Britain. However, even this was not an unmixed blessing: To secure this protection was far from routine. George Grenville had issued a whole set of new regulations designed to tighten the collection of customs duties in the colonies, and the process of securing sailing clearance now required the submission of an application to London through the royal governor of a colony, accompanied by an affidavit, a bond, and several other documents. In addition to the frustrating amount of red tape involved, the realities of transatlantic communication inevitably resulted in costly delays in the sailing schedules of the ships. Francis Fauquier, the Lieutenant Governor of Virginia, wrote to the Admiralty on June 22, 1764, on this very point, stating that the merchants in Virginia were "in great distress" by reason of the delays in receiving the passes and "are daily applying to me for them." Faced with such obstacles and frustrations, in time the colonists came to believe that the new shipping regulations were designed neither to facilitate their transportation needs nor their trade.[313]

Under Grenville, British control of the colonies reached levels hitherto unknown in America. The Royal Navy was used to enforce purely administrative regulations, and British soldiers patrolling the towns and the increased numbers of British officials were a constant reminder of the power of Britain over the colonies.[314]

Controlling Those Rowdy Colonials: While commoners in eighteenth-century England did not rate high on the social and economic scale, "colonials" were also deemed low on the hierarchy of class and caste, and government policy placed ever greater restrictions on their actions. Thus, little escaped the reach of imperial control in London when it came to colonial matters. This process was understandable for larger questions of colonial policy such as the westward movement of population in America, Indian relations, and other high-level and complex issues, but the need for official intervention from across the Atlantic was much less clear for a whole host of routine matters. As if the multitude of orders prohibiting and restricting the commercial activities of the colonists was not sufficient safeguard to ensure British control over colonial affairs, an endless list of everyday minutiae also required review and approval by the bureaucracy in Whitehall. Even the royal governors had little authority to act on their own in the colonies; their instructions from London got down into the weeds, covering such matters as dealing with drunkenness and other vices, the posting of marriages, the naturalization of immigrants, etc. Another item particularly covered was the treatment of Catholics in the colonies: They were to be kept from any official colonial position, even elective ones, by any means possible, and all colonial appointees had to swear an oath to uphold this policy.[315]

Mercantilism had geographic consequences as well. As is clear from the foregoing narrative, the colonists were greatly dependent on British imports from across the Atlantic Ocean. It was the policy of the Privy Council and the Board of Trade to keep the colonists "as near as possible to the Ocean" to continue their dependence on trade with England. While most European settlement patterns involved the strategic location of some major cities in close proximity to flowing bodies of water, the colonial pattern favored settlement locations easily accessible to Britain's seafaring vessels. Thus, "of the twenty largest cities in the colonies, only one (Lancaster, Pennsylvania) was not a port."[316]

PART III

Chapter Six

THE NASCENT FIELD OF ECONOMICS

Rulers fall into three categories: those smart enough to figure things out for themselves, those smart enough to understand the explanations of others, and those too stupid to do either.

Richard Brookhiser
Historian

"*George Washington knew nothing about economics!*"

Of all the myths that have sprung up about our first President over the years, few have received more mindless repetition than that one, and none deserves closer scrutiny.

It is true, of course, that a PhD in macroeconomics George Washington did not have, nor an MBA in finance, but then neither did anyone else in the eighteenth century. To visualize life as it existed at the formation of the republic, we have to put ourselves in a 1780s mindset and turn our intellectual clocks back more than two centuries. Obviously, viewing the events and people of bygone years through the prism of today's standards would lead to a mischaracterization of the earlier era. To paraphrase the admonition of historians, one cannot view eighteenth-century conditions with a twenty-first-century sneer!

Back then, America was a nation of farmers. With a population of two and a half million, the country was sparsely populated, and much of its infrastructure at the most basic level. A network of four-lane highways crisscrossing the country, often clogged with traffic, was centuries in the future. What existed were horses and wagons traveling on dirt roads and dusty, muddy, and rocky trails connecting the major population centers, and primeval overgrowth and forests in other areas. And as the only means of contact with others not in one's presence was by the written word, communication was a painfully slow process.[317]

At the time, Americans were dependent on news and other information from Europe, but transatlantic mail had long built-in delays. A letter to Thomas Jefferson in Paris from James Madison in Philadelphia on May 15, 1787, to vent his frustration about the tardiness of delegates to the Constitutional Convention, did not reach France until two months later, when the Convention was already more than halfway through its proceedings.[318] Newspapers from London often took months to reach the colonies. Even the wildest imagination could not have foreseen the advent of instantaneous global communication. As for serious books, most had to be imported from England and other European countries, a practice affordable by few. Understandably, therefore, books tended to be treated with the gravity and care accorded special treasures.

Formal schooling was not widespread, particularly in the rural communities. Families in a position to do so sent their children to England for a "proper education," in the obvious belief that the same quality of schooling was not available on this side of the Atlantic. There were only eight colleges in existence in all the colonies (vs. 5,300 in the country in 2015. The College of William and Mary was the only one located in the South.[319]

University degrees were rare in the general population, being mostly the province of philosophers, academics, and lawyers. No university in America conferred PhDs in economics at the time, nor taught a curriculum leading to an MBA. (The first graduate program in business in the United States was set up by Harvard one hundred and thirty-three years after the Declaration of Independence, in 1908.) In one particular field, however, there was no shortage in the country from the earliest days. America, it seems, has always been blessed with an abundance of legal talent! Many of the individuals who took an active part at the birth of the United States were lawyers, but there was no economist among them. At the signing of the Declaration of Independence in 1776, there was a plethora of lawyers (25 to be exact, out of 56), plus merchants, farmers, physicians, and even a minister, but not one economist. At the Constitutional Convention of 1787, there were even more lawyers (32, this time, out of 55), in addition to merchants, politicians, farmers, teachers, and physicians, but again no economists. A distinguished historian listed seven men who were the key leaders at the founding of the United States, of whom only two — Benjamin Franklin and George Washington — were non-lawyers. The law was not so much a skilled profession as the route to becoming a member of the coveted ranks of the gentry and a possible political career. Alexander Hamilton, Thomas Jefferson, John Adams, and James Madison were all lawyers, as were John Jay, Patrick Henry, Gouverneur Morris, James Monroe, Edward Rutledge, Edmund Randolph, Charles Pinckney, John Quincy Adams, and many others.[320]

In the eighteenth century, a finance-based economy was not even a gleam in the eyes of the most optimistic American. Nor could anyone have imagined that one day the spires of the financial district of New York would soar into the sky. As for the study of economics, during most of Washington's life the field did not even exist as a separate and distinct science, and the term "macroeconomics" would not be coined for another two centuries. A telling statistic on this point would be how many of the early U.S. Secretaries of the Treasury were economists. During the first hundred years following Washington's inauguration, there were thirty-nine Treasury Secretaries. Here is the composition of the list among different professions:

Lawyers	35
Other	4
Economists	0

To find an economist at the head of the Treasury Department, one would have to go forward one hundred and eighty years after Washington was elected President. (Joseph W. Barr, who served as Secretary of the Treasury by a recess appointment under President Lyndon Johnson in 1968, was the first holder of that office to hold a degree in the field. He had an MA in Economics from Harvard.[321])

As is evident, economics was not exactly a known profession in the country at the time, let alone a flourishing one. There were, of course, many businessmen like George Washington, all of whom were engaged in their own commercial pursuits and in creating jobs. In reality, they were the very people whose activities became the stuff of economics, and whose behavior was studied by later economists in order to formulate their theories. However, for most of the eighteenth century, economic thought was at a basic level. To judge how basic, consider a respected biographer's observation that "[t]he 'science' of economics was new, still in its first blush." His surprising frame of reference? Early twentieth century.[322]

Early Economic Thought: Long before the emergence of macro and micro economics, monetary economics, Keynesian economics, behavioral economics, neoclassical economics, econometrics, and scores of other new, sometimes radical, and increasingly sophisticated approaches to the field, there were essentially two dominant economic philosophies in Washington's time, those of the physiocrats in France and of the mercantilists in Britain and a few other European countries.

The physiocrats celebrated farmers and farming. François Quesnay, a royal physician in France in the eighteenth century and a founder of *physiocratie*, believed that land was the source of all wealth in a country, and that commerce and industry were only productive as ancillary activities for agriculture.[323] His followers believed that cities were to be shunned as artificial creations, that man should live in nature, and that there should be little government control. As a school of political economics in the eighteenth century, this philosophy enjoyed great popularity in France. In America, Thomas Jefferson was probably its strongest proponent.

There is no evidence that George Washington had any particular awareness of that school of thought. What is known, of course, is that he had a deep interest in land as an asset class. "Our welfare and prosperity depend upon the cultivation of our lands," he wrote, "and turning the produce of them to the best advantage."[324] The records of his private activities clearly indicate, however, that he believed more was required to fulfill the needs of society than land and agriculture. In his own operations at Mount Vernon, he had to develop a myriad of manufacturing and other functions to complement his agricultural base. It is a reasonable assumption, therefore, that he would not have been a follower of Quesnay in his exclusive emphasis on agronomy, had Washington even known about him.

With the philosophy of the mercantilists, on the other hand, Washington was intimately familiar. He had endured their dictates from birth and for more than forty years before the Declaration of Independence. Americans, however, were not the only ones critical of that school of thought. The new approaches of the brilliant English and Scottish political philosophers named John Locke, Dudley North, David Hume, and Adam Smith must have been like a breath of fresh air to America's Founding Fathers, many of whom were familiar with the works of these iconic thinkers. At the Constitutional Convention, as in the countless public and private debates preceding it, the philosophies of these writers were the subject of continuous discourse. Despite the high cost of purchasing books from England, many of the Founders, including George Washington, Thomas Jefferson, Benjamin Franklin, Robert Morris, James Madison, and others, had copies of the works of one or more of these early thinkers.[325]

John Locke was born in Somerset, England, in 1632, a hundred years before the birth of George Washington. He studied medicine and became a physician. Then there came a time when he had to perform emergency surgery to save a man's life. The operation was successful, and the patient, the Earl of Shaftesbury, prevailed on Locke to join his staff. The two developed a long relationship, with Locke becoming an indispensable political advisor to the Earl. After the death of his patron in 1680, Locke increasingly devoted his time to writing. His *Essay Concerning Human Understanding*, on which he had been at work for almost twenty years, was published in 1690 and was an immediate success. Locke's great contribution to the advancement of human thought was based on a three-pronged principle of political philosophy: He questioned the divine right of kings, he believed in the natural law of the equality of men, and he was a strong believer in the institution of private property. He died in 1704.[326]

Dudley North (1641-1691) was the son of the 4th Baron North. As a child, he was abducted by gypsies but later recovered by his family. In his youth he traveled extensively, trading in Smyrna and Constantinople (now Izmir and Istanbul) before returning to England a wealthy man. He was then knighted, elected to Parliament, and appointed to oversee the Treasury for the Crown. His earlier travels led him to become a strong believer in free trade and free markets, and a passionate advocate of the belief that any interference in the market mechanism of pricing would harm an economy. He argued against the basic tenets of mercantilism, pointing out that gold and silver were not the source of wealth for a country; rather it was human enterprise that created national prosperity.[327]

David Hume was born in 1711 to a wealthy Scottish family, and started attending the University of Edinburgh when he was twelve years old – coincidentally, in the same year his future friend and fellow philosopher Adam Smith was born. Hume's writings focused on an analysis of the nature of man and challenged many of the established philosophies of the day. He believed that the role of government was to provide a credible system of laws and to protect the private property of its citizens; that onerous public debts and an overstretched system of taxation retarded economic growth; and that theology could lead to dangerous delusions. Considering the aristocratic structure of the society at the time and the prevalence of strong religious beliefs, it is not surprising that Hume's philosophy was branded as heresy. Nevertheless, his two-volume *Essays, Moral and Political* was well-received. Later, he wrote his most popular work, the six-volume *History of England.*[328]

Hume was well-known through his books to the delegates to the Constitutional Convention of 1787 in Philadelphia. His strong anti-mercantilist views, his belief that individuals were the drivers of economic development, and his emphasis on the sanctity of private property made him a favorite of Americans struggling to create a sound governmental structure for the new nation. Highly sympathetic to the grievances of the

North American colonists, Hume did not conceal his disdain of British policymakers when he asked publicly, "How could we expect a form of government to maintain its authority at a distance of three thousand miles when it could not make itself respected or even treated with common decency at home?" The British government blamed him for putting "constitutionalist" ideas into the minds of the colonials, causing them to demand their rights as full British citizens.[329]

Stimulated and energized by Hume's egalitarian philosophy, Americans declared their independence the year he died of an internal disorder at sixty-five. Adam Smith wrote a most affectionate eulogy about him. "The extreme gentleness of his nature," he wrote, "never weakened either the firmness of his mind or the steadiness of his resolutions."[330]

The person credited with ushering in modern economics as a separate science in the English-speaking world was *Adam Smith*, a brilliant Professor of Philosophy at the University of Glasgow in Scotland. Smith was born in June 1723 in Kirkcaldy, Fife, on Scotland's east coast about ten miles from Edinburgh. His father died before Adam's birth; he was raised by his mother, who never re-married and devoted her life to the son she adored.

Adam received a classical education before attending Glasgow University at fourteen. He spent three years there, and then six years at Balliol College, Oxford, where he learned about David Hume's work on political philosophy. At Oxford, however, Hume's writing was seen as poisoning young minds and banned. When Adam Smith was found reading it, he was given a strong reprimand by the school authorities, and his book confiscated. Nevertheless, Smith found Hume's philosophy transformative and used it as a basis for his own economic treatise. Later, when Smith had the opportunity of meeting Hume, the two quickly became the closest of friends.

Smith deviated from the traditional philosophical topics of his day to concentrate instead on human motivation in commercial matters, and on how individuals and societies accumulated wealth. His ground-breaking economic text, published in March 1776, was titled *An Inquiry into the Nature and Causes of the Wealth of Nations*. Because it was an erudite work by a philosopher, it initially had a small print run, as the publisher expected it to attract little public attention. Instead, it became a success and underwent five revisions, the last edition coming out in 1789 with the substantial print run of 1,500, making it a best seller for the times. Few books have had as much impact on the era in which they were published and beyond.

Smith's thesis was that Britain had adopted a flawed economic system, and that neither precious metals, as the mercantilists advocated, nor land, as the physiocrats believed, was the proper pathway to a nation's commercial wellbeing. Rather, the wealth of a society depended on the people's ability to produce goods and services in an environment of free markets and free trade. He advocated a reasonable level of taxation and prudence in government spending. As his stature grew, his advice was sought by leaders of the government on a wide range of issues including taxation policy, the burgeoning national debt, the financial crisis engendered by the East India Company, and the worsening Anglo-American relations. He was also elected a Fellow of the prestigious Royal Society.

The year 1776 was an eventful year for Smith. He saw the publication of his book, heard Americans declaring their independence from Great Britain, and grieved the death of his good friend and fellow Scotsman David Hume in Edinburgh. *The Wealth of Nations* had great impact on the leaders of the American Revolution – a fitting tribute to Adam Smith, who had always been critical of Britain's treatment of its American colonies. Shortly afterwards, Smith was appointed a Commissioner of Customs, moved to Edinburgh with his mother, and ceased writing.[331]

Another European whose thinking on economic and financial matters attracted attention in America was a Swiss national by the name of Jacques Necker (1732-1804), who actually served for seven years as the Finance Minister of France. His three-volume treatise, *Traité de l'administration des finances de la France,* was published in 1784. Robert Morris and Alexander Hamilton were both intimately familiar with Necker's text. While serving as the Superintendent of Finance in the early 1780s, Morris was in regular correspondence with Necker and arranged to have his book translated into English. (Other European philosophers writing on economic subjects, Turgot in France and Beccaria in Italy, were virtual unknowns in America.)

How much of the economic work of the early philosophers was familiar to George Washington has been the subject of debate among researchers. An avid reader, he kept in his library at Mount Vernon a copy of Smith's *Wealth of Nations* in three volumes in the original tree calf binding, with Washington's bookplate and autograph atop the table of contents in each volume (now in the George Washington Collection at the Princeton University Library). He also kept a copy of Locke's *An Essay Concerning Human Understanding* in two volumes, originally published in 1689. Washington's copy, bearing his autograph, was the 1775 edition. The last known owner of this book was John F. Hurst, a Methodist bishop and one-time president of American University in Washington, D.C., who sold his copy in May 1904 to an unknown buyer for $650. The imprimatur of these authors – the unmistakable influence of Adam Smith and to a lesser extent of John Locke and David Hume – is evident in Washington's writings. Aside from his reading material, Washington had close association in the Confederation government with Robert Morris, the Superintendent of Finance, and his deputy, Gouverneur Morris (no relation). Later, during the Constitutional Convention, with Washington and Robert Morris both preoccupied with the fiscal exigency and other matters of national scope, they conferred on an astonishing fifty-two occasions outside the actual meetings, according to his diary. Washington thus kept current on the economy and the few economic source materials available in America at the time.[332]

Other episodes in Washington's life also point to a person deeply preoccupied with issues of economic import:

The year is 1751. *George Washington has recently spent three months in Barbados with his half-brother Lawrence, whom he loves dearly. It has been an unbearably painful period in young George's life, watching helplessly while his brother's health deteriorates day by day. He is now on the way back home from the only trip he ever takes outside America.*

During the long voyage back to Virginia, George has much to say about the economy of Barbados, making frequent entries in his diary. He remarks on the absence of the vital middle class in the population, evidenced by the large gap between the rich and the poor. "There are few who may be called middling people," he observes. "They are either very rich or very poor." Given the island's natural resources, George is baffled by the inability of the inhabitants to create a prosperous economy for themselves. Drawing on his own knowledge of agriculture, he writes about the growth of fruit, particularly pineapple, on the island, and the cost and quantity of the production of sugar and rum. He is puzzled by the high rates of interest that prevail there. With his ever-present entrepreneurial eye, he also notes that the British West Indies would be a promising market for the products of the colony of Virginia.[333]

> Nineteen-year-old George's commentary in his diary about the economy of Barbados shows the strikingly analytical and inquisitive bent of his intellect.

It is 1781. *Washington has been engaged in a prolonged war against the most powerful military and economic power on the planet, Great Britain. On another front at home he has been engaged in a different sort of skirmish. For almost six years, he has been pleading with the Continental Congress to provide money with which to pay his troops and to purchase food, clothing, shoes, blankets, and equipment. Congress is dependent on the states to provide the requisite funding, but its members are mired in squabbles among themselves. The government has also exhausted its credit with the American public, as well as with its foreign lenders. The treasury is empty, and the currency and notes issued by Congress have depreciated to worthlessness. "If there is not a very great and sudden change of measures it will be next to impossible to keep the Army together," Washington warns.*[334]

Frustrated at every turn, Washington turns repeatedly for money and supplies to his friend Robert Morris, the financier and member of Congress. Over and over, Morris digs deep into his own pocket, puts the arm on his friends and professional contacts, and comes up with money, provisions, supplies, equipment and even boats for the revolutionary cause, including crucial help in the decisive battle at Yorktown.

The desperate economic posture of the nation continues even after the ground war is won. The Continental Congress appoints Morris as the economic czar of the country and directs him to prepare a plan of action for dealing with the mounting foreign and domestic debts of the government and devise a program for the restoration of fiscal soundness and public credit. Morris complies. In a series of detailed reports, he describes the steps necessary to restore solvency and public confidence. As they have done during the war, Morris and Washington hold frequent conversations about the causes of the economic and fiscal problems of the country. When he has prepared his report, Morris provides Washington with a draft. They review and discuss Morris's program before its submission to Congress, sometimes with the participation of Robert Livingston, Secretary of the Department of Foreign Affairs, on questions arising about the pending loans from foreign governments. Washington is in accord with Morris's diagnosis of the situation, as well as his prescribed remedies for pulling the nation out of its fiscal plight.[335]

Morris advises Congress that it is of paramount importance that all public debts, whether foreign or domestic, be consolidated and funded at their face value, that the obligations between the Union and the states be clarified and settled, and that the methodology of funding and servicing the collective liabilities be approved. It is imperative, he adds, that Congress charter a national bank to revive and enhance both public and private credit. The bank would also serve as the payment agent for the government, receive deposits and make loans, and share its ownership between the United States government and public investors. As the dilemma of how to get the states to act as a union is on everyone's mind, Morris believes that the bank would be a strong factor in achieving that goal and would "unite the several states more closely together in one general money connection."[336]

To raise immediate revenue, Morris recommends several measures, including the imposition of a 5% duty on imports and the setting-up of machinery for the collection of taxes in each state. Morris also considers it vital that Congress authorize the establishment of a single national currency and the organization of a mint. Morris is only able to secure congressional authorization for a few of these steps. He sets up a network of receivers for the collection of taxes, organizes the Bank of North America and sees to its proper staffing and operation, begins preliminary efforts to establish the dollar as the national currency and to organize the mint. To tide over the Confederation government in its state of exigency, Morris issues notes secured by his personal credit and delivers them to the army paymaster for distribution to the unpaid soldiers.[337] *The overall effectiveness of Morris's program, however, depends upon securing a stable source of revenue for the country. Despite the emergency nature of the government's financial situation, Congress is unable to pass any tax measures. Its very first step is thwarted by the intransigence of the governor and legislature of a single state, the country's smallest, Rhode Island. Other initiatives by Morris get bogged down in congressional indecision. Morris is horrified by the apathy of the members of the Continental Congress about their legitimate obligations to foreign lenders, as well as to the many patriotic Americans who gave up their life savings during the Revolutionary War to buy government bonds.*

Without a source of revenue to bear the expenses of running the government and to fund existing and future foreign and domestic debts, it is impossible to restore public credit. Laboring under the illusion that additional loans will be forthcoming from Europe to stave off total collapse, Congress refuses to face reality. Morris is blunt in his warning: "To expect that foreigners will trust a government which has no credit with its own citizens would be madness."[338] *Having substantially exhausted his personal resources in tiding over the insolvent government, Morris finally resigns in frustration after four years. The country's economic slide continues inexorably.*

> For Morris, the experience was an object lesson on the perils of the political process. Even more important, he became deeply concerned about the inadequacy of the Confederation structure for the government. For the future President of the United States, the event constituted an economic baptism by fire. Ten years later, after the Confederation government was replaced by the federal structure, Alexander Hamilton, as the Secretary of the Treasury in President Washington's Cabinet, followed the broad outlines of Robert Morris's plan to rejuvenate the government's financial posture.

Fast-forward to 1787. *Delegates from all thirteen states have arrived in Philadelphia to begin a monumental initiative, devising a new governmental framework for the nation. With many of the best minds of the era among the delegates, it is hoped this will be the first step toward solving the ills of the country. The location of the meeting, the Pennsylvania State House,339 is rich in historic significance, reminiscent of George Washington's appointment as Commander of the Continental Army in 1775, the signing of the Declaration* *of Independence in 1776, the design of the American flag in 1777, and the adoption of the Articles of Confederation in 1781.*

The delegates, however, are not focused on past events. Rather, there is an expectation of great national achievement here. The atmosphere is charged, the energy palpable. The chorus of voices ebbs and flows in lively discussion and discourse in the halls, and the names of the great Scottish, English, and other European thinkers and philosophers are invoked freely. Some of the delegates are resistant to the notion of a strong central government, perceiving it as replacing the old British tyranny with a new home-grown variety. Others believe that only an energetic federal structure can pull the Union together and ensure its survival. The extent of the representation of each state in the proposed national legislature is also a contentious topic. The elder statesman at the Convention, the venerable Benjamin Franklin, acknowledges the reality that the members of the assembly all have "their prejudices, their passions, their errors of opinion, their local interests, and their selfish views." He would have them park their egos at the door.[340] *The lawyers in the group – a majority of the delegates – are in their element, voluble and persuasive, relishing the advocacy of one position and the disputation of another. Some members keep their eyes on the strategic consequences of their resolutions, others choose to parse the wording of every sentence.*

There being great urgency to the task, it is imperative that the delegates remain focused on drafting a Constitution acceptable to all within a reasonable timeframe. If recent experience with the impotent and ineffective Continental Congress is any guide, it requires a monumental exercise in leadership to keep the delegates, representing so many divergent views, working together harmoniously in this new setting. It is obvious that the selection of the presiding officer for this group is a crucial choice.

All eyes turn to George Washington. It is known that he was extremely reluctant to leave Mount Vernon to attend the Convention but relented when the point was urged by his closest advisors that without his presence the Convention stood little chance of accomplishing anything meaningful. He has put his standing as a national icon on the line by agreeing to come, but his presence has given "the Convention and the proposed Constitution a prestige that they otherwise could not have had." He is the delegate unanimously voted to be the presiding officer, the chairman of the Convention.[341]

It is a wise choice. Washington's calm confidence is heartening to the entire group. Over the span of nearly four months, he allots each delegate all the time he needs to argue his cause, and the discussions unfold until all the issues are crystallized. When, inevitably, disagreements arise and passions flare, Washington skillfully defuses the tensions and refocuses on the topic of the moment. He often employs his famous "gift of silence"[342] *during the long speeches of the delegates, obviously aware that a chairman who actively participates on one side or another of a debate, or who telegraphs his own position in other ways, becomes an advocate, losing effectiveness as the leader and coordinator of the group. As Washington knows, there is a myriad of tools available to a chairman to nudge and subtly influence the direction of proceedings without compromising his own role. He acknowledges that he is "restrained from offering his sentiments on questions pending in the house."*[343] *He is thus singularly successful as the understated consensus builder and presiding officer of the Convention.*[344]

Throughout, Washington is deeply engrossed in the substance of the discussions. He is in daily attendance. He also spends countless hours with many of the delegates outside the formal meetings. In particular, he spends many sessions with Robert Morris,[345] *with whom he shares a financial focus of vital importance in shaping the economic agenda of the nation. To the task at hand he and Morris bring entrepreneurial backgrounds, and financial as well as operational experience. Even though there are several delegates who have achieved success in business careers, Washington, Morris, and Hamilton bring their own unique economic perspective to the proceedings.*

The final draft of the Constitution mirrors the broad outlines of George Washington's deeply-held convictions about the republican form of government, with which the economic needs of the nation are inextricably interwoven. The landmark document envisages the supremacy of the federal laws and treaties in the Supremacy Clause. To provide for a cohesive union, the Privileges and Immunities Clause gives every American the "right of access to resources and a right of trade without the limitations of state boundaries," and the Full Faith and Credit Clause provides that the public acts and records of each state shall be given full faith and credit in all other states.[346] *The Commerce Clause provides for the regulation of commerce with foreign nations and among the several states. Other sections provide for the protection of private property, including protection against the taking of property without just compensation, and sanctify contractual obligations. There are also provisions for a national currency, a postal system, the protection of intellectual property, and the empowerment of Congress to pass laws relating to bankruptcy.*

Benjamin Franklin, addressing George Washington, announces thoughtfully but proudly the sentiment shared by many at the Convention: "I consent, Sir, to this Constitution because I expect no better, and because I am not sure that it is not the best." The document is also one in which Washington believes wholeheartedly, and for which he becomes a powerful advocate. "I am fully persuaded," he writes to Henry Knox, "that it is the best that can be obtained at the present moment, under such diversity of ideas as prevail."[347]

> The Constitution was then forwarded by Congress to the states for ratification, a process that turned out to be far from smooth. Many in the country opposed the provisions of the new charter for fear they would be abused, thus trampling upon the rights and interests of ordinary citizens. Others fretted about how the untried system provided by the new Constitution could work in practice. George Washington worked tirelessly, using all his persuasive powers, as well as his unrivaled popularity and prestige, to ensure the ratification of the new national charter. Without his overt support the nation would not have ratified it. "Be assured," James Monroe reminded Thomas Jefferson, "his [George Washington's] influence carried this government." In the end, only Rhode Island and North Carolina refused to ratify the Constitution, but all others had joined the Union.[348]
>
> The country was jubilant. "We have become a nation," everyone said, "the freest and most enlightened" in the world.[349]

It is 1789. *Washington has been inaugurated as the first President of the United States. The unhappy state of the country's affairs and particularly the fiscal problems inherited from the Confederation government are very much on his mind. He leaves to Vice President John Adams, Senator William Maclay, Congressman James Madison, and others the resolution of basic protocol issues, such as whether the President should be addressed as "His Excellency," hold periodic levees for visitors, etc.350 Washington himself casts about to gain as much insight as possible into the substantive affairs of the government. Congress* *has not yet gotten around to authorizing him to recruit his own department heads, so he turns to carryover Confederation administrators to request reports on the military situation, foreign affairs, and the fiscal state of the country. In response, he is bombarded by detailed material from them, arriving piecemeal over several months. The Treasury's memoranda on the state of the country's finances are the most voluminous. They provide extensive details on all the outstanding obligations of the government.*[351]

To assimilate the complex fiscal issues involved, Washington pores over the data and takes meticulous notes, identifying each category of indebtedness, maturity dates, accumulated interest, and total arrearages. He then personally prepares a digest of the tangled and complex federal debt structure, and continues until the intricacies of the financial condition of the nation form into a recognizable pattern for him.[352] *Already familiar with the broad issues at stake, he has isolated and quantified each of the elements into a mosaic of the prevailing American financial posture. What would be a fair solution for the emotionally-charged issue of the debts of the states to the federal government, as well as the debts of the federal government to the states? Should there be a set-off for those states that responded fully or partially to requests for funding from the Continental Congress? What would be a practical way of dealing with the existing government notes and bonds when purchased at substantial discounts? How can the government deal with the arrearages of foreign debt-holders? What would be the source of funds used in the repayment of all these obligations, and if new borrowing would be involved, what would be the rate, the maturity? How to arrange for a dependable stream of revenue for the federal government without causing a whole new set of resentments in the population?*

It is vintage George Washington "Problem-Solving 101": Reduce the complex fiscal state of the United States to the simplest elements, then ask questions that go to the heart of the problem.

Among the papers of George Washington is a document that purports to provide preliminary solutions to the vexing fiscal issues facing the country. It is in Washington's hand, written contemporaneously with his research into the finances of the government after becoming President but before he had assembled his Cabinet. A respected historian dates it as of October 1789.[353]

The document is in outline form and visualizes multiple sources of ongoing revenues for the national government, consisting of import duties of 5%, an excise tax of 5% to be shared with the states, and revenues from fees "on civil process" and from postal services. It proposes to fund the liabilities of the federal government to the states through a bond issue bearing interest at 6%. It calculates that an impost of 5% on imports would yield about $1.5 to $2 million per year.

It further provides that (a) if the government were to refinance its existing foreign debts by floating a new loan in Europe in the amount of $12 million at 5% interest, the proceeds would pay off the existing foreign obligations as well as take care of government expenditures for one to two years; (b) after servicing the new debt from the proceeds of import duties, the balance could be used to pay interest on the obligations of the federal government to the states; (c) part of any surplus would be allocated "toward the creation of a sinking fund to retire the debts of the Union," and (even anticipating government "open market" operations) refers to the purchase of "debts at their market price;" and (d) any remaining balance would be designated for military expenditures and contingencies.

Chapter Seven

A PRESCRIPTION FOR GOVERNANCE

The origin and onset of the American Republic contain lessons of which posterity ought not to be deprived.

James Madison

Washington was inaugurated in March 1789. Months before the event, it was a foregone conclusion in the nation that the Presidency was Washington's for the taking. Washington, however, genuinely struggled with the prospect of once again giving up the life he cherished at Mount Vernon to take another turn at public service. He had been busy rebuilding his home and business operations there as both had suffered serious deterioration in his absence during the war years. After the war, he fervently desired to continue that work. He had made no secret of his wish "to quit the walks of public life."[354]

Nevertheless, the message from newspaper editorials and the barrage of mail arriving daily at Mount Vernon was that no one else could be trusted to unite America, and that without him the success of the new government might be at risk. For those who desired to influence Washington, this was an effective approach, designed to appeal to his highly developed sense of duty and honor. At some level, he too must have known that if the Presidency were offered, he could not refuse to serve. Therefore, even before he was officially offered the position, he was considering plans on how to address the multitude of challenges that faced the nation.

Washington's lifelong habit of early and thorough preparation now led him to try to be ahead of the curve. He began reviewing in his mind the condition of the country and the available options for solving its problems. There were several people with whom he could consult, but all were scattered in different cities. Alexander Hamilton, his aide during the War, was now practicing law in New York. Thomas Jefferson, with whom Washington had worked on the Declaration of Independence, was still in Paris. James Madison, then a sitting Member of Congress, was at Montpelier in Virginia and the closest to Mount Vernon geographically. So he was one prospect to whom Washington could turn for advice on the interpretation of the applicable provisions of the new Constitution. His longtime military aide, David Humphreys, was now living and working at Mount Vernon as Washington's secretary. He would be available to perform research and to prepare notes for him. But in the end the task of formulating a plan for leadership was his and his alone at that point. Fortunately, with a front-row seat at every critical stage in the development of the country, he had spent years thinking about the crucial issues. It was now time to hone his ideas into a national agenda.

Washington had begun preparing the nation for the urgent tasks that lay ahead almost immediately after the victory at Yorktown. With the country facing civil unrest and economic stagnation in the aftermath of the Revolution, Washington could not help but feel deep uneasiness about the prevailing state of affairs. He had not won the American independence at such a great cost in American lives only to see the nation slide into chaos. He recognized that the military success of the Revolution was no guarantee of the political success of its aftermath – an assessment confirmed by the later history of scores of other revolutions. Therefore, once the Treaty of Paris was signed in 1783, Washington began a non-stop letter-writing campaign to his large network of correspondents, including the governors of all thirteen states and other leading citizens of the new republic. He was calling for urgent action on the country's problems and recommending solutions. In the six years before 1789, he wrote more than a thousand such letters. Despite the seriousness of the crisis, the letters also reveal Washington's optimism about the immense natural advantages enjoyed by the country and the new opportunities that would be created in a nation founded upon the principles of freedom and equality applied to all its citizens. "There are few," he admitted, "who rejoice more fervently in the expectation that the beams of prosperity will break in" upon America.[355]

But first the country needed to be put on a sound economic footing. The finances of the government were in need of total overhaul, and public credit required priority of attention and resources. The government had to make a serious effort to meet all its obligations, both domestic and foreign. "I had indulged the expectation," he wrote to Thomas Jefferson in Paris, "that the new government would enable those entrusted with its administration to do justice to the public creditors and retrieve the national character." Over and over he stressed the need for action on the arrearages and defaults on the debts of the national and state governments, and on the unpaid wages of the soldiers who had fought valiantly in the Revolutionary War. "If I can form a plan for my own conduct," he wrote to the Marquis de Lafayette, "my endeavors shall be unremittingly exerted ... to extricate my country from the embarrassments in which it is entangled through want of credit." Honor as well as practical necessity demanded, Washington wrote, that all government obligations be "paid to the uttermost farthing."[356]

Washington had been painfully aware during the war years that the public treasury was in desperate need of funding, and he recognized that this was still the case. Therefore, ensuring a stable revenue stream for the government was a matter of urgency. This could be assured through the establishment of tariffs and "taxation continued and regularly collected."[357]

He also knew firsthand that financial development was a vital key to economic growth. As he could personally attest, the nation was in urgent need of the infrastructure for private credit to fund commercial activity and capital projects – resources that had been in dire shortage during the colonial period.

In Washington's youth, Britain's blanket prohibition against the creation of a uniform currency in North America had led to chaos in the daily lives of the colonists. If the new U.S. government evinced any hope of promoting commercial prosperity for its citizens, it had to attach the highest priority to the establishment of a national currency. Without it, commercial activity, particularly trade among the states, would be difficult to develop. "If there cannot be money found to answer the common purposes of education, not to mention the necessary commercial circulation, it is evident that there is something amiss in the ruling political power..."[358]

Equally important for the economic revival of the country was its safety from foreign encroachment. "The restriction of our trade, and the additional duties which are imposed upon many of our staple commodities" continued to take a drastic toll of the domestic economy. National security considerations, therefore, required immediate attention, as they would also be of aid in removing obstacles to free trade for Americans in their international commerce. "I cannot avoid reflecting with pleasure on the probable influence that commerce may have on human manners and society in general," Washington wrote. "I indulge a fond, perhaps an enthusiastic idea...that the period is not very remote when the benefits of a liberal and free commerce will pretty generally succeed to the devastation and horrors of war."[359]

The judiciary was also on Washington's mind. It was vital that Americans have an impartial judiciary "for the speedy administration of Justice," with judges whose competence and integrity were above suspicion. Safeguarding the rights of citizens and equal justice for all had to be the dominant principles of the American judicial system. Without a sound judiciary which would command public confidence and respect, economic development would be seriously hampered. "We have a new national character to establish," he had written earlier, "and it is of the utmost importance to stamp favorable impressions upon it; let justice be then one of its characteristics, and gratitude another."[360]

With ownership of farms and homes being of fundamental importance in the land, protection of private property and the establishment of a sound system for the chain of title on real estate were paramount. As Washington knew from personal experience, the colonial period had left a legacy of a confusing and complex process for determining the state of title to real property. The same piece of land might be owned by multiple parties – by one who received it from the Crown, another whose claim was based on prescriptive use, and yet another who bought it for trinkets from an Indian tribe. Washington clearly recognized the economic importance of reforming the land system and setting sensible precedents regarding property transactions.[361]

While the ratification of the Constitution had caused the nation to proclaim jubilantly that "now we are all Americans," Washington had firsthand experience with the wide gulf separating the states from one another. Encouraged by the policies of Great Britain to go their separate ways, the colonies had become insular. During the years when each colony issued its own currency, it routinely rejected payment in the currency of any other colony. So Washington knew that the union of the thirteen states achieved on paper was far from a reality, each state viewing itself as a separate sovereignty. Every American had to understand, Washington asserted, that without a strong Union binding the nation together, the republic would be in danger of dissolution. It was imperative, therefore, that there must be an indissoluble union of all the states under a single federal government, and that the states must be prepared to set aside their regional jealousies. All citizens had to learn that they were now members of one Union, that they were Americans and not Virginians, New Yorkers, Pennsylvanians, or Georgians. Washington thus espoused a theme close to his heart – a countrywide domestic market. At his most enthusiastic, he rejoiced that "[i]n Pennsylvania they have attended particularly to the fabrication of cotton cloths, hats, and all articles in leather. In Massachusetts they are establishing factories of duck, cordage, glass and several other extensive and useful branches. The number of shoes made in one town and nails in another is incredible. In that state and Connecticut are also factories of superfine and other broad cloths." He was exultant that "we shall soon be able to furnish ourselves at least with every necessary and useful fabric upon better terms than they can be imported." Commerce, he noted, "is the best, if not the only cement," that can bind all the people together in the country.[362]

Promotion of education was also vital for political as well as economic reasons, as an educated workforce was a crucial element in economic growth. As he had done repeatedly before, he urged the creation of a national university (for which he later bequeathed £5,000 in his will,) and federal assistance to institutions of higher learning. "Knowledge," he would write later, "is in every country the surest basis of public happiness."[363] Authors would also deserve encouragement by the establishment of copyright legislation. Equally important to growth and innovation would be the encouragement of inventors by establishing a proper system of patent protection. He would also establish a uniform system of weights and measures, as well as national coinage.

* * *

Proposed Inaugural Address: As Washington prepared to take the leadership of the new republic, he set out to commit to paper his program for solving the problems facing the United States. With a few pages of scribbled notes prepared under his direction by David Humphreys, his private secretary, he set out to capture in writing many of his long-held convictions about the needs of the country. He managed to distill the essence of his strategies, judgments, analyses, and plans into a single document that constituted the George Washington prescription for the governance of the United States. Even though filled with personal and deeply-moving sentiments, he nevertheless crafted, on the one hand, a plan for dealing with the immediate problems facing the nation and, on the other, a veritable blueprint for its long-term development, all in one extraordinarily clear and precise presentation, with loud echoes of David Hume, John Locke, and Adam Smith running through its pages.

Without the marvelous convenience of word processing equipment, Washington produced a seventy-three-page manuscript in longhand, in his own distinctive style. What came from his quill pen was the future President's vision for the United States – his response to the nation's clarion call for leadership, and it was vintage George Washington: concise and pragmatic. It would be the defining agenda of his Presidency, America's first economic development program – probably the first in the world.[364] He intended that the document he carefully drafted would serve as his inaugural address to Congress, along the lines of speeches made by British monarchs at the opening of Parliament each year. These customarily contained extensive policy recommendations, as distinct from the speech made upon a king's accession to the throne, which did not. Washington's proposed speech was thus a fusion of tradition and innovation, designed to set a new course for the nation, call widespread attention to the policies he would support in his administration, and underscore the importance of preserving the fragile experiment in self-government begun in 1776. In assessing the contribution of the first Presidency to the development of the American society, this is a work of such disproportionate importance that it merits full coverage here.[365]

With a dramatic endorsement of the republican form of government and a direct stab at Britain's system of royalty and aristocracy, Washington set the tone for his inaugural speech with these electrifying words:

> "I rejoice in a belief that intellectual light will spring up in the dark corners of the earth; that freedom of inquiry will produce liberality of conduct; that mankind will reverse the absurd position that the many were made for the few."

Then Washington launched into a catalog of the concrete issues facing the nation.

On National Debt: A primary concern of this document was the national debt. Washington took his audience through a tour of recent history, reviewing the events that had brought all Americans together to the moment of inauguration. Referring to the unhappy era of serving under a tyrannical king and the Revolution which followed, Washington harkened back to John Locke and the observation that "mankind are believed to be naturally averse to the coercion of government." He reminded his audience that little thought had been given before the war to the enormous cost involved in "resisting to blood," and in fighting an enemy whose resources were "inexhaustible," whose "fleets covered the Ocean," and whose battle-hardened troops "had harvested laurels in every corner of the globe." America, on the other hand, was not even organized as a nation, and had made no preparations for prolonged armed conflict. The most important need for waging a war, "money, the nerve of war, was wanting." Purely as a matter of necessity, the treasury had "to be created from nothing."

Washington's love of his country and his pride in his countrymen, then came through in jubilant tones:

> "If we had a secret resource of a nature unknown to our enemy, it was in the unconquerable resolution of our citizens, the conscious rectitude of our cause, and a confident trust that we should not be forsaken by heaven. The people willingly offered themselves to battle."

As for the means of fighting a war – arming, clothing, and feeding the troops, and procuring for them the implements of hostility – they "were only to be found in anticipation of our future wealth." All the government could do was to borrow for the most pressing emergencies, and to keep "our brave troops in the field unpaid for their services." Congress went heavily into debt in Europe, and Americans had to step forward and lend their life savings to support the war effort, so the long campaign left the country with a load of debt and ever-weakening paper currency. With the "ravage of farms, the conflagration of towns" resulting from the war, the decline in the country's affairs was predictable, leaving it in default on all its debts. In a masterful understatement of the war's awesome achievement, Washington added that peace on terms "that could gratify our reasonable desires… was at length obtained."

It was clear that putting the finances of the government on a sound footing and restoring confidence in its creditworthiness were matters of the highest priority. Making a direct appeal to Congress, Washington said, "I have a confident reliance that your wisdom and patriotism will be exerted to raise the supplies for discharging the interest on the national debt and for supporting the government during the current year, *in a manner as little burdensome to the people as possible.*" (Emphasis added.) This could be accomplished, Washington proposed, by levying "a general, moderate impost upon imports; together with a higher tax upon certain enumerated articles." Washington was certain that the American public would be willing to contribute a modest portion of their income to support their government, and that they would take pride in knowing they were paying the lowest taxes among nations.

On the subject of public debt, Washington also counseled his successors, as well as Congress, to avoid "throwing upon posterity the burden which we ourselves ought to bear."[366]

On the New U.S. Constitution: Referring to the Confederation period, Washington then asked the indulgence of his audience to "speak on so unpleasant a subject as the rotten part of our old constitution." The Confederation was a government "formed on the defective models of some foreign confederacies, in the midst of war, before we had much experience." He referred to "the impotence of Congress under the former confederation…. [as] without some speedy remedy a dissolution of the Union must have ensued…." Congress "possessed no power of carrying into execution a simple ordinance, however strongly dictated by prudence, policy or justice. The individual states, knowing there existed no power of coercion, treated with neglect whenever it suited their convenience or caprice the most salutary measures of the most indispensable requisitions of Congress."

The country's affairs being in a deplorable state, a convention was called to devise a new system of government to replace the confederacy. The delegates were all aware of the "feebleness" of the prior model, he noted – they had "purchased wisdom by experience." As for the product of that convention, the U.S. Constitution, Washington made his position perfectly clear: "I have been induced to conclude that this government must be less obnoxious to well-founded objections than most which have existed in the world."

Relying on the election process to weed out those who would arrogate to themselves greater power than the Constitution provides, he said: "Nor can the members of Congress exempt themselves from the consequences of any unjust and tyrannical acts which they may impose upon others." During the Constitutional Convention, he had "attentively heard and read every oral and printed information on both sides of a question." He was thus convinced that the Constitution is really in its formation a government of the people, and in its operation a government of laws. Then, referring to the tripartite structure of the legislative, executive, and judicial branches of the government, he stated that no other government "ever contained so many checks and such efficacious restraints to prevent it from degenerating into any species of oppression."

On the National Union: The bedrock issue still to be hammered home to every American, as Washington saw it, was that the country was now one nation, not thirteen separate, independent countries. "The culture of separateness of the former colonies, originally fostered by the mother country, was almost the undoing of our struggle for independence. It should now be abundantly clear to all that regional differences have to be subordinated to the welfare of the entire nation." Otherwise, the United States of America, for which so much American blood was shed, "would not survive even for a day if regional jealousies pulled the Union asunder." As he had already stressed in his earlier messages, Congress would have to set aside the regional interests and prejudices of its members, promote trade among the states, and enact legislation of benefit to all Americans.

To this end, Washington put the improvement of road transportation and communication at the top of his agenda, as it would also bring the people and communities closer together. "While the individual states shall be occupied in facilitating the means of transportation, by opening canals and improving roads, you will not forget that the purposes of business and society may be vastly promoted by giving cheapness, dispatch and security to communications." To enhance the exchange of information throughout the Union, he contemplated that the federal government would arrange for the conveyance of newspapers and periodical publications in public vehicles free of charge through the Post Office.

On Defense: A matter of great urgency was to make the country safe for Americans, as relative security and freedom of action were vital for economic development. For Washington, therefore, the ominous presence of hostile forces surrounding the nation made such security issues paramount. Even though the government could ill afford to arm itself at this time, he believed that "to be prepared for war is one of the most effectual means of preserving peace." He advocated that we should "train our youths to such industrious and hardy professions as that they may grow into an unconquerable force." Washington also recommended that every encouragement should be given to the creation and expansion of the merchant marine. This would be a source of sailors for the navy in the event of war. He believed that Americans had a natural genius for naval affairs, and that in time "we shall possess such a nursery of seamen and such skill in maritime operations as to enable us to create a navy almost in a moment." Washington also advocated creating a grand provision of warlike stores, arsenals and dockyards.[367]

And then, despite the weakened state of the country's military and fiscal preparedness in the aftermath of the Revolution, Washington deemed it prudent to issue a warning to the European powers.

> "As to any invasion that might be meditated by foreigners against us on the land, I will only say that, if the mighty nation with which we lately contended could not bring us under the yoke, no nation on the face of the earth can ever effect it, while we shall remain united and faithful to ourselves."

On International Trade: Washington viewed security considerations as vital for the economic development of America. As the disruption of the country's trade by foreign forces was taking a drastic toll of the domestic economy, Washington believed that it was imperative for the government to initiate negotiations with foreign powers to settle existing differences and to establish trade relations. He fully intended to cultivate friendly and harmonious relations with all foreign powers. "We may more at our leisure meditate on such treaties of amity and commerce as shall be judged expedient." As he saw it, the appointment of consular representatives abroad would also enhance these goals, the persons to be selected on the basis of merit and from different parts of the United States.

The recent British embargo of American shipping was also on Washington's mind. Nevertheless, he took pride that "the enterprising spirit of our citizens has steered our vessels to almost every region of the known world," where they were received with tokens of uncommon regard. "An energetic government will give to our flag still greater respect, while a sense of reciprocal benefits will serve to connect us with the rest of mankind in stricter ties of amity."

Washington would also attach priority to the development of domestic commerce over foreign trade: "Internal commerce is more in our power," he wrote. "An intercourse of this kind is well calculated to multiply sailors, exterminate prejudices, diffuse blessings, and increase the friendship of the inhabitants of one state for those of another." He would improve and expand the postal system and road building as he deemed the dissemination of information vital to interstate trade. Likewise, he would foster the expansion of communication in the country through the growth of newspapers and other periodicals.[368]

On the Judiciary: Washington gave Congress a clear signal about the importance he attached to the establishment of a sound judiciary. "The complete organization of the Judicial Department was left by the Constitution to the ulterior arrangement of Congress. You will be pleased therefore to let a supreme regard for equal justice and the inherent rights of the citizens be visible in all your proceedings on that important subject."

On Corruption: Washington could not miss the opportunity to put everyone on notice that patronage and nepotism had no place in his administration, and that all appointments would be based solely on merit. "In all our appointments of persons to fill domestic and foreign offices," he wrote, "let us be careful to select only such as are distinguished for morals and abilities. Some attention should likewise be paid, whenever the circumstances will conveniently admit, to the distribution of offices among persons belonging to the different parts of the Union." Then, with a disapproving eye toward the system of corruption prevalent in Great Britain, he asserted, "We should seek to find the men who are best qualified to fill offices: but never give our consent to the creation of offices to accommodate men."

On Manufacturing: Washington made specific recommendations for the advancement of America's manufacturing capability, which had been long suppressed in the colonial period by British mandate. He would increase the production of many manufactured products, as well as agricultural commodities, to levels far above what existed at the time. By way of example, he proposed that "if the quantity of wool, flax, cotton and hemp should be increased to ten-fold its present amount (as it easily could be), I apprehend the whole might in a short time be manufactured, especially by the introduction of machines for multiplying the effects of labor, in diminishing the number of hands employed upon it." Washington, however, was uncertain how quickly the country could industrialize. "Even the mechanics who come from Europe," he lamented, "as soon as they can procure a little land of their own, commonly turn cultivators."

On Other Initiatives: Washington then listed a whole series of initiatives for his administration. He exhorted Congress to be particularly mindful of the general welfare. "I trust you will not fail to use your best endeavors to improve the education and manners of a people; to accelerate the progress of arts and sciences; to patronize works of genius; to confer rewards for inventions of utility; and to cherish institutions favorable to humanity. Such are among the best of all human employments." He also recommended the passage of legislation for the establishment of just weights and measures, and for the regulation of currency and commerce. Nor would he miss the opportunity of addressing the cherished dream of his earliest days – the expansion of western territories. "The western states will probably long retain their primeval simplicity of manners and incorruptible love of liberty."

On What the Future Holds: As he had in his letters, Washington could hardly contain his optimism and jubilation about America's future and the foundation that could be laid for a durable prosperity for the nation. "Can it be imagined that so many peculiar advantages, of soil and of climate, for agriculture and for navigation were lavished in vain? Should not our souls exult in the prospect! Though I shall not survive to perceive with these bodily senses but a small portion of the blessed effects which our Revolution will occasion in the rest of the world; yet I enjoy the progress of human society and human happiness in anticipation."

Washington then took pains to caution against aggressive territorial expansion in the manner of many European governments. Americans, he counseled, "should guard against ambition ... We should not, in imitation of some nations which have been celebrated for a false kind of patriotism, wish to aggrandize our own republic at the expense of the freedom and happiness of the rest of mankind."

On Personal Considerations: Washington's proposed inaugural address also included some items of a personal nature. He talked about the stresses of service as the Commander of the Continental Army. It was not in his nature, he said, "to be insensible to the sufferings, or to refuse a share in the toils and dangers" to which his troops were exposed. He felt he did not need to recount the details of "the complicated cares, the cruel reverses or the unusual perplexities inseparable from his office." He then went on to say that after the war ended, nothing was more agreeable to him than the status of a private citizen, and that "my leaving home to take upon myself the execution of this office was the greatest personal sacrifice I have ever, in the course of my existence, been called upon to make."

Becoming introspective, he again expressed his deepest desires. "I have now arrived at that sober age when...the love of retirement naturally increases," while "the objects of human pursuit ...lose much [of their] captivating luster." He was not smitten with "the frivolities of ceremony or the baubles of ambition." With longing that clearly comes through his prose, he admitted that when the war ended and he returned his military trust to Congress, he felt it was time "to compensate for the inquietude of turbulent scenes by the tranquility of domestic repose" through a reversion to his agricultural roots – always a source of delight to his mind. Showing his disdain for a system of hereditary rule, he remarked that he had no heirs, "no child for whom I could wish to make a provision, no family to build in greatness upon my country's ruins."

And finally, Washington gave himself the privilege of being a little preachy. "In public as in private life, let the eternal line that separates right from wrong be the fence....I most earnestly supplicate that Almighty God, to whose holy keeping I commend my dearest country, will never offer so fair an inheritance to become a prey to avarice."

The whole of Washington's proposed inaugural address contained a far more comprehensive program than the foregoing summary would suggest. Unfortunately, however, the address cannot be reproduced here in its entirety as major portions of the manuscript have been irretrievably lost through a series of unfortunate circumstances: the lax oversight of the Presidential papers by their custodian, the thoughtless actions of an early researcher and compiler of Washington's writings, and an offhand remark by an aging James Madison nearly forty years after Washington's death.

Madison's Impact on Washington's Economic Blueprint: Once he had completed writing his speech, Washington felt the need to confirm that the program he had outlined would pass muster from a constitutional perspective. The presidency was a blank slate, and he was acutely aware of the precedent-setting aspect of his actions and decisions. Always thorough in his preparations for a public function, he also had to make certain that his proposed inaugural presentation did not exceed the limits placed on executive power in the new Constitution. He once complained of an "unfitness of ability to judge legal questions arising out of the Constitution." Then too, perhaps his feelings about the lack of a formal education, with which he had been haunted all his life, had reared up anew, sending him on a quest for validation.[369]

Washington had first met James Madison briefly in 1781.[370] A few years later, at the Constitutional Convention of 1787, he observed Madison's contribution to the debates on the structure of the new government and was equally aware later of Madison's diligent efforts in support of the Constitution during the ratification process in Virginia. These prior interactions led Washington to turn to the Congressman to advise him on constitutional law.

In late January 1789, Washington sent his manuscript to James Madison through the Fredericksburg postmaster,[371] asking him to review the draft and pass on its appropriateness for the occasion under the Constitution, anticipating that Madison might suggest a few revisions. Washington judged, however, that the young Congressman might be reluctant to criticize his senior's work product, and that a small stratagem might serve to encourage him to give his honest opinion about the draft. Washington's transmittal letter, therefore, made a veiled reference to his assistant and secretary David Humphreys as "a person under this roof" with whom, if Madison should desire, he could discuss the speech.

Some writers have interpreted this reference as an indication that Humphreys was actually the author of Washington's proposed inaugural address. There is scant evidence to support that assumption. Humphreys was not exactly a person to whom anyone would look to produce a comprehensive legislative agenda for the United States Congress. He wrote romantic plays and indifferent poetry. He aspired to write a biography of Washington but managed to produce only a jumble of notes.His real claim to fame, of course, was that George Washington was his patron and employer. Succeeding U.S. Presidents have used multiple speechwriters for their presentations, but this was not the case here. The reality was that Humphreys' contribution to Washington's seventy-three-page draft consisted of only a few sheets of notes on the writings of Hume, Locke, Smith, and others, nine pages in all, which have in fact survived and are now on deposit at the Rosenbach Museum and Library in Philadelphia.[372]

As for Washington's attempt to secure corroboration of his approach to Congress at his inauguration, matters did not proceed as he had visualized. The unexpected turn of events that befell Washington's manuscript can only be understood in light of the evolving political philosophies of the nation at the time, and particularly those of Madison and Jefferson.

By the last decade of the eighteenth century, the leaders of the American Revolution had become aware of the political forces unleashed by the democratic process and had begun to refine their concept of the system that would best serve the nation. Though fervent believers in a free society, they were already beginning to diverge from one another over the question of what exactly a republican government entailed. While still evolving, the competing perspectives were slowly taking shape. One of those philosophies would come to be identified with Thomas Jefferson and James Madison. Both were brilliant lawyers and scholars, with high energy levels. Neither was a good speaker; Jefferson's voice was soft, almost effeminate, Madison's weak but harsh. Both came from wealthy families, part of the landholding aristocracy of Virginia. Jefferson, tall, stooped, and loose-jointed, with hair that rose in loose waves on his head, was older and senior, and better known in the land. Madison was small in stature, awkward in demeanor, and introspective and bookish in personality, all of which concealed a calculating mind and a strong drive. Both men had a casual attitude toward money and accumulated substantial obligations in their lifetimes. Both preferred to work by indirection, even misdirection, rather than direct confrontation. The two had first met at the time of the Declaration of Independence, but, as will become clear, they had not started out by sharing the same space on the political spectrum.[373]

Having been personally involved in the Continental Congress as one of its members, Madison was intimately familiar with the fundamental flaw of a government model based on a loose confederacy among the states. He had seen the impotence of the earlier Congress and the national chaos caused by the absence of an effective central government. During the Revolutionary War, Congress's repeated attempts at raising revenue for the war effort through a modest tariff on imports had failed by the requisite unanimous vote when Rhode Island refused to go along. Two Congressmen, Madison and Hamilton, had been delegated to try to persuade Rhode Island to change its position. They failed in their mission, much to their joint-frustration. Later, when the Revolutionary War was won and the nation entered into a Treaty of Peace with Great Britain, Congress failed for weeks to achieve the requisite quorum to ratify the vital document that would confirm the nationhood and independence of the United States.

With such experiences fresh in his mind, Madison was a proponent at the Constitutional Convention of the kind of national government that would restore public confidence and set the country on a course of prosperity. After the Convention had completed its work, Madison was equally passionate and diligent in working to ensure the ratification of the Constitution by the states. He had even collaborated with Alexander Hamilton and John Jay in writing the Federalist Papers, describing the benefits of the proposed Constitution and urging its ratification.

> "In framing a government which is to be administered by men over men," wrote Madison, "the great difficulty lies in this: You must first enable the government to control the governed; and in the next place oblige it to control itself."[374]

Madison believed that the tripartite structure of government provided in the Constitution was the best system for exercising control over the activities of the executive departments. In his home state of Virginia, he demonstrated his continuing commitment to the Constitution by taking on its most vocal opponent, no less an icon than the popular former governor, Patrick Henry. Madison's success in this debate ensured that Virginia would cast its crucial vote in favor of ratification.[375] "A powerful national government," Madison had asserted in the *Federalist Papers*, "would strengthen rather than weaken the liberties to which Americans were strongly attached."[376]

Once the process was completed and the Constitution had gone into effect, Madison was elected to the new Congress, where his dedication to hard work and mastery of the legislative process, as well as his close relationship with George Washington, quickly won him a position of great influence. It did not take long for Madison, as a leading member of the federal legislature, to refine his political and economic convictions. It was here that observers have noted the remarkable shift in position some have called Madison's about-face; he publicly declared it in a speech on the floor of the House on September 4, 1789. That is the day in which he became the spokesman for a new opposition faction which was in time dubbed the Jeffersonian Republicans. Madison came to believe, actively and passionately, that in the tripartite system of government envisaged by the Framers, it was Congress that represented the will of the people and the President's role was limited to carrying out the mandates issued by Congress. And so, on his own and through interactions with Thomas Jefferson, Madison developed serious reservations about Presidential authority, subjecting him to criticism for taking inconsistent positions. Madison's views on politics and the government were becoming increasingly aligned with the Jeffersonian concept of republicanism.[377]

Thomas Jefferson had been the American minister in France from 1784 to 1789, residing in Paris, almost all of it during the Confederation period. He was thus spared many of the frustrations endured by sitting members of the Continental Congress during that difficult era, unlike Madison and Hamilton. Jefferson's initial comments from Paris appeared to favor the Constitution, expressing admiration for the skill of its Framers (whom he revered as "demigods") for successfully weaving the conflicting regional and political positions of the delegates into an acceptable document. During the ratification process, however, he took a new look at the structure of the federal system envisaged in the Constitution and was aghast. To him, reposing authority in the central government, rather than in the state governments, would constitute a betrayal of the principles of the Revolution and could lead to tyranny. It is not surprising, therefore, that Patrick Henry, George Mason, and other opponents of the Constitution counted Thomas Jefferson as one of their allies. Circumspect in his correspondence with Madison, Jefferson was nevertheless active behind the scenes against the new landmark document and the federal structure envisioned by it. "I have sworn upon the altar of God," he would later write, "eternal hostility against every form of tyranny over the mind of man." As an eminent historian described it, "Jefferson had so much confidence in the natural harmony of society that he sometimes came close to denying any role for government at all." Jefferson himself was even more direct. "I am convinced," he wrote to another Virginia planter, "that those societies (as the Indians) which live without government enjoy in their general mass an infinitely greater degree of happiness than those who live under European governments."[378]

Jefferson's strong opinions were not limited to the structure of government; they also covered many issues relating to the governance of specific segments of society. With no skill in finance and no particular patience with financial matters, Jefferson had always harbored an abhorrence of the "creditor class" – i.e., the business and banking world in general – whose practitioners he viewed as leeches upon society. He had a particularly unfavorable impression of British brokers and merchants on whose books he had run up large bills. When eventually they tried to collect, Jefferson became bitter, believing they were unfairly pushing him to the brink of bankruptcy. The trauma of these experiences and the specter of disgrace and lifelong odium that could have ensued haunted him throughout his days.[379]

Jefferson also looked with equal disfavor upon European-style manufacturing facilities employing large labor forces, which he perceived as corrupting "the morals in the mass of cultivators." So, for him, the industrial and financial development of the country was not only far from a priority, it was to be shunned at all costs. Taking a leaf from the physiocrats, he idealized the farmer as exemplar of republican virtues and expressed the desire to keep America as an agrarian society and, therefore, virtuous. "Those who labor in the earth," he wrote, "are the chosen people of god." He went farther, however, than the French philosophers he admired. Along with his antipathy toward business and finance, he also felt distrustful of cities and what they represented: "I view great cities as pestilential to the morals, the health and the liberties of man." What he wanted for America was a peaceful and perhaps unchanging bucolic haven.[380]

The other political theory soon became identified with Alexander Hamilton. While the followers of Jefferson focused on the evils of British colonial rule and the tyranny of an inherited royalty, the followers of Hamilton concerned themselves with the more recent experience of the discredited Articles of Confederation in which the thirteen states constituted essentially a "friendship league" with a central government that had no power of execution. This group believed that the crucial need for the country at the time was to put power into the hands of "energetic government."

As the views of Jefferson and Madison on the role of government would became more refined and focused, they would become increasingly estranged from Hamilton on both domestic and foreign policy. They would differ with him over such matters of crucial national import as the assumption of state debts by the federal government, the establishment of the Bank of the United States, the resolution of the Whiskey Rebellion, the ratification of Jay's Treaty, and the like.

President Washington, on the other hand, saw good elements in both ideologies. He came from a farming background so he identified with Jefferson's cultivators. He also understood the growth-oriented financial and economic ideology of Hamilton. He did not sympathize with Jefferson's disdain for the business and financial sector, nor with the aristocracy and corruption ingredients which were significant elements in Hamilton's philosophy of government. As the ensuing chapters will make clear, Washington's model differed in significant respects from those of both Hamilton and Jefferson.

This was the state of affairs when Washington sought out Madison's opinion on his draft of the inaugural address. Washington knew that Madison had the requisite mastery of the relevant portions of the Constitution, but it is unclear if he had any sense how Madison might be disposed to interpret them. There is no record that Washington was aware at the time of Madison's political beliefs, particularly those that related to Presidential power and congressional prerogatives.

Madison received Washington's voluminous package at Montpelier in late January. A quick scan of its contents alerted him to what Washington proposed to do when inaugurated. The notion of the future President presenting a detailed program to serve as the country's legislative agenda was utterly unexpected. During the Constitutional Convention, Connecticut's delegate Roger Sherman had made a strong argument that the Presidency was really "nothing more than an institution for carrying the will of the legislature into effect." At the time, a majority of the delegates, including Madison, disagreed with Sherman and actually visualized a significant role for the President in the legislative process. It is clear that by 1789, however, Madison had come full circle. He now believed that the President's sole function in domestic policy was to execute the laws passed by Congress. Sherman would have been delighted to hear that Madison was now a convert.[381]

In Madison's eye, Washington was attempting to inject the Presidency into the legislative process, and his proposed speech represented an attempt at usurping congressional authority. It was nothing less than an overstepping of the boundaries of the tripartite government by the executive branch. It was not only unthinkable, but highly disquieting. If allowed to stand, it would set a dangerous precedent.

It was now clear to Madison that Washington intended to preside over an energetic executive branch, and that he would use the power of the Presidency to shape the republic into an integrated political and economic union – an empire – which would have fundamental strategic consequences for the political process. Jefferson and others had already warned that creating a vast union was an absurd and highly impractical idea.[382]

Madison's negative opinion of the manuscript should, of course, be viewed in the context of his politics. It was not in character for him, however, to be direct, to explain his misgivings, and to invite a dialogue with Washington on the issue of Presidential authority. It would not do for him to put the spotlight on the gulf in political philosophy that now separated the future President from the person known to be his Constitutional advisor. Introspective and even somewhat reclusive, Madison had already developed a reputation for being a backroom operator, skilled at misdirection to achieve his goals. Thus, when he responded to Washington's request for advice about his proposed address, Madison carefully avoided dealing with its contents. Rather, he stressed that the speech would not be well received by members of Congress as it would remind them of the operating mode of the English king George III, whose tyranny was still fresh on everyone's mind. Madison needed to say no more. He had scored his point masterfully without revealing his true reservations about the speech. Madison then prepared a brief set of general remarks – eight pages in all – as a substitute for what Washington himself had compiled. Madison's draft comprised mostly the main elements of his personal legislative agenda; it would surely help to have Washington endorse them in his inaugural speech. It was Madison's version, with few changes, that historians believe Washington delivered as his inaugural address.[383]

And that is how the nation was deprived of the first President's full agenda for the strategic direction of the country and its economic renaissance.

Madison's perspective on Washington's proposed inaugural address placed him squarely on the wrong side of history. The Presidential election process in the United States, by and large, has produced strong personalities who perceived it as part of their job description to recommend specific legislative programs to Congress. Succeeding Presidents have not only done so, but have used whatever influence or pressure was available to them to secure the adoption of their agenda by Congress. There is in fact broad support in the Constitution for Presidential involvement in the legislative process. It provides that the President shall "from time to time give to the Congress information on the state of the Union, and *recommend to their consideration such measures as he shall judge necessary and expedient.*" (Emphasis added.) The Constitution also granted the President, over James Madison's strong objection, the power to veto bills passed by Congress, subject to being overridden by a two-thirds vote of both houses. It also provides for a significant Presidential role in setting policy during the implementation phase of legislation enacted by Congress.[384]

Madison himself had been an active participant in the deliberations that led to the inclusion of these provisions in the Constitution. And yet, as a leader in the Congress of the new republic, he did not view the legislative process as a cooperative one between Congress and the President. Rather, he saw it as a contest of power between the two branches of government, as though it were a seesaw, with each side vying to gain ascendancy.Thus it was that thirty-eight years later, when asked, Madison would still dismiss and belittle Washington's original draft of his inaugural speech.[385]

Jared Sparks' Impact on Washington's Speech: Most historians acknowledge that Washington's seventy-three-page proposed inaugural address is perhaps "the most valuable political document of Washington's entire career."[386] What became of that manuscript would bring tears to the eyes of those who would treasure the first President's legacy as crucial in the preservation of early American history. This priceless document ended up in the hands of a thoughtless researcher who was oblivious of its value and set out to destroy it. As a respected Washington biographer characterized it, the text of the first President's inaugural address became "the victim of the most horrendous historical vandalism" ever perpetrated.[387] Here is the story in a nutshell:

George Washington bequeathed his substantial library, as well as all his papers (except his private correspondence with Martha). to his favorite nephew, Bushrod Washington, the heir to Mount Vernon and a future Supreme Court justice. In the early nineteenth century, a man by the name of Jared Sparks was compiling Washington's papers in book form and asked Bushrod for information about his famous uncle.[388] Bushrod responded by turning over to Sparks all of the papers of the first President. In the course of his research, Sparks was surprised to come across Washington's undelivered inaugural manuscript, about which there had previously never been any public information. Uncertain about the provenance of the document, on May 22, 1827, Sparks sought advice from James Madison, still alive at seventy-six and living at Montpelier. Sparks inquired about this previously unknown and puzzling manuscript in President Washington's distinctive handwriting, and asked Madison if its existence should be suppressed. In reply, Madison chose to say nothing about his perception of the conflict between congressional prerogatives and Presidential authority. Instead, he dismissed the document by calling it "strange," implied that its disclosure would be embarrassing to the legacy of President Washington, and expressed his firm concurrence that the document should be suppressed.[389]

Sparks had to have been elated. On the one hand, he would do a favor for the object of his biography by destroying the ill-fated manuscript; on the other hand, he had discovered a clever marketing and promotional ploy when his book was published. He would cut up the proposed inaugural speech into pieces and give away the fragments to buyers of his book as mementos of the handwriting of the great hero. And that is how this historic document ended up in pieces scattered all over the United States and Europe. Over the years, through a monumental effort by scholars, some of the fragments were located and laboriously pieced together to reconstruct about 5,600 words, probably only one-third of the original writing. The remaining fragments, if indeed they have survived the wear of the centuries, are waiting to be found in basements and attics across several continents.[390]

Most historians share in the pessimism that "it seems certain that only a small percentage of the entire document will ever be recovered." Nevertheless, his vision of a prosperous American economy, based on an innovative and hitherto unknown economic model formulated months before he put his Cabinet together, is discernible from the remnants of his proposed inaugural address, his other writings, his legislative initiatives, and his Presidential actions and pronouncements. And when one sets Washington's goals as thus outlined against the web of policies and other initiatives he put in place during his two terms in office, it is clear that he in large measure succeeded in achieving what he had set out to do in his economic development program for the country.[391]

Ironically, therefore, in the end Madison's actions did not affect the outcome. Washington's proposed inaugural address had been only a prequel to the President's concrete actions. His plans to unveil his full program during his inauguration may have been adroitly sidetracked, but he was in no way deterred in his resolve to create a lasting infrastructure for the strategic economic development of the United States.[392]

Chapter Eight

THE ENTREPRENEURIAL MODEL: A GAME-CHANGER

Economists try to prove that something that works in practice works in theory.

Baumol, Litan and Schramm
Professors

Britain's policies toward its colonies in the eighteenth century had a surprising and hidden aspect: They had a strong dose of central planning about them.

The concept of a "planned economy" as a prescription for government control of market forces would not rise to the level of a recognized economic theory until the second half of the nineteenth century. Nevertheless, in eighteenth-century Britain, a high level of government control was equated with prosperity for the country, as mercantilists "would chain the economic system to national power."[393] Let us therefore revisit those policies, already broadly covered in earlier chapters, in this new light.

Britain dictated which industries could be developed in the colonies and which could not. While farming was a permitted activity, manufacturing was severely restricted. The colonists found their access to sources of supply, as well as markets for their produce, closely circumscribed, not only internationally but even domestically among the colonies. For all practical purposes, they were forbidden to trade with any country other than Great Britain, constrained in their choice of shipping lines for international exports and imports, and prohibited from establishing a common currency. Travel by Americans was restricted. Britain required a colonist to secure a pass before leaving his or her own colony for any reason whatsoever, regardless of the destination. The intrusive nature of these and other policies reached beyond purely commercial matters and into a colony's legislature, where every attempt at legislative action was scrutinized in London and subjected to veto if found incompatible with aims of the home government.[394] Taken altogether, the full array of British laws and policies had to have been a central planner's dream come true, but for the Americans snared in the labyrinthine bureaucracy across the ocean, it was a real-life nightmare.

Adam Smith, who kept a close eye on the developments in the New World, called Britain's approach to the governance of its colonies "invidious and malignant."[395] Americans felt Smith was giving voice to their own deepest frustrations when he wrote:

> "To prohibit a great people from making all that they can of every part of their own produce, or from employing their stock and industry in the way that they judge most advantageous to themselves, is a manifest violation of the most sacred rights of mankind."[396]

In essence, the impact of British rule under George III was akin to placing an economic straitjacket on the colonists. Therefore, when Americans rose up against the Crown of England, the revolt was not only against the commercial policies already described, it was also a decisive rejection of a planned economy being imposed on them from London. Thus, more than two centuries before the fall of the Soviet Union late in the twentieth century, Americans had already rejected that system as part of their own revolution.

For a person with Washington's energy and drive, the frustration of living under the arbitrary and often contradictory orders coming out of London would not have been easy to endure. The experience of living under these restraints was the crucible in which he learned firsthand what it meant to be deprived of a reasonable level of freedom in the pursuit of one's trade or profession. He took away from that period a keen sense of the factors that hamper economic growth and stifle the entrepreneurial spirit in a society. It was what had driven him to take part in defying the Crown of England.

In the eighteenth century, Britain was possessed of neither broad-based affluence nor equal justice for all. This was particularly so in interactions with its overseas dominions. The objectives of most of its policies toward America were indeed puzzling, as they were short-sighted and self-defeating. Perhaps nations, like individuals, have to undergo their own maturation process. Fortunately for Britain's colonies in North America, even when its policies were counter-intuitive, it still contributed to progress, albeit by showing a future leader of the colonies how to achieve better results by doing the opposite!

It was fortunate for the nation that Washington's in-depth experiences in the private and public sectors turned out to have been superb preparation for solving the country's economic malaise when he became its first President. It was as though he had been groomed from birth for the job now thrust upon him. It made him uniquely qualified to pass on an enduring economic legacy to succeeding generations of Americans. As a respected historian remarked, "[T]he fact is that Washington was the only man who measured up to the job."[397]

* * *

Modern American Presidents are often expected, by the necessities of present-day elective politics, to produce economic miracles in four-year bursts. Such expectations inexorably lead Presidents to resort to short-term political solutions for long-term economic challenges, running the risk of setting off dislocations in the system in later years. The dictates of modern politics notwithstanding, the reality is that a strategic economic model, like good wine, has a fermentation period often counted in years, producing results sometimes long after the administration that initiated it has left office.

Economics is organized common sense. It is the "study of mankind in the ordinary business of life," as Alfred Marshall, the great nineteenth-century economist, asserted.[398] As for economic theory, it is basically a verbal description of human experience, for the human mind always finds a way to interpret experience within a recognizable context.[399] Economists often speak of the law of cause and effect and point out, for example, that Adam Smith, in developing his theories about the creation of wealth, drew on his knowledge of commercial and financial progress in Scotland and England. And that Keynesian economics evolved from its author's particular experience of living during the waning years of the British Empire. In modern times, however, the field has become highly mathematical and esoteric in its analyses, placing it beyond recognition by those outside the profession. As one practitioner acknowledged, "If you ask an economist where's a good place to invest, which industries are going to grow, where the specialization is going to occur, the track record is pretty miserable. Economists don't collect the on-the-ground information businessmen do."[400] And another admitted, "When new acquaintances learn what I do for a living, they routinely ask, 'So how should I invest my money?' I wish I knew."[401] Others acknowledge that "any correlation between [economic] theory and business results is likely to be coincidence."[402] Clearly, while the freedom to create and innovate is the paramount ingredient in a free economy, job creation is a product of commercial activity. Naturally, a degree in economics would always be a plus, but formal education in that field is not the exclusive qualification for determining what commercial activities contribute to full employment, lead to prosperity, and raise a society's standard of living.

That economics is an empirical discipline is indeed a fitting comment for Washington's approach to the field, for despite his familiarity with the work of the political philosophers of that era, his ideas about the American economy were primarily shaped by his common-sense view of the life of a colonial. Even without the theoretical insights of the later economists, he had a clear perception that imperial policies had restricted normal commercial activity in America and stifled the innate drive of the colonists to foster growth and prosperity within their own communities.[403] It was what had propelled him to take part in defying the Crown of England. Over the years, he had naturally pondered the desirable long-term financial and commercial goals for the nation: What should be the economic trajectory of America? Should he follow the model put in place by Britain during the colonial period, which already had deep roots in society? Should he continue the practice of keeping tight central control over the commercial activities of Americans as Britain had done? Or should he strike out in an entirely different direction? And if so, what should be his guide for this nation's economic design into the future? If the people were freed from the bureaucratic red tape and arbitrary strictures that had been imposed on them during colonialism, would they then re-channel their energies into creating whole new enterprises? Would they even expand commerce across the other colonies and create a natural American market?

The backdrop of living and working in colonial America had thus served for Washington as the beacon lighting the way toward the economic revival of the country. "I think I can see a path," he wrote, "as clear and as direct as a ray of light" to lead the nation to economic prosperity. Washington's eerily prescient economic insights, developed during four decades of living and working under colonialism, was that the shackles had to be removed from Americans so they could enter into any business, trade in any market, and feel secure in the ownership of any asset. He visualized a society where success was not dependent on one's title, and where working hard and earning a living were not considered demeaning to a person. His vision, therefore, was not to continue British policies but to reverse them; not to emulate British culture but to foster equality; not to sow the seeds of patronage and corruption but to establish a policy of meritocracy and fairness; not to have a rigid class structure but to encourage and facilitate upward mobility for all; not to restrict home ownership to landed aristocracy but to enable home and farm ownership for all the people; not to place obstacles in the path of the creators of new enterprises but to encourage new business formation.

Washington's Promethean economic blueprint for the country was thus the antithesis of the top-down design inherent in Britain's policies for the governance of its American dominions. In his formula, the focus was on the *individual* as the lynchpin of the system, and his or her creativity, restlessness, and tolerance for risk as the high-octane fuel for dynamic growth. It would be an approach tailor-made for the ones who would start small, work hard, inevitably suffer losses and heartbreaks, but who would be unstoppable in their drive to see their projects come to fruition. Extraordinary resiliency of character, Washington knew, was as vital in business as it was in warfare. With unquenchable optimism, therefore, he saw America as an incubator for the entrepreneurial spirit long before the term was coined. *In essence, what he later did as President was to reshape the economy of the United States into the kind of environment in which he himself would have thrived as a businessman.* Washington's economic model was thus clearly patterned after his own image!

A century later a renowned scientist, Michael Faraday, described his formula for success as "having a model to teach me what to avoid."[404] Obviously, Washington had independently arrived at precisely the same formula, as for him the colonial period was an extraordinary tutorial on how *not* to run an economy. No modern candidate for a PhD in macroeconomics had such lessons drilled into his or her psyche more effectively. As a corollary, Washington also quite naturally developed an appreciation for those elements that would lead to a flourishing economic environment, such as fostering initiative, creativity, and risk-taking. In effect, he learned about the ingredients needed for a nurturing entrepreneurial society from taking note of what the British had *not* done in America.

The entrepreneurial spirit, of course, has always been with us. It is a phenomenon deeply rooted in the human psyche. What the first President set out to accomplish was to ensure that this spirit had the means to flourish in America. His program called for him to put in place the requisite infrastructure and governmental mindset to transform the society into a nationwide entrepreneurial environment. Every individual in the new republic would then have the opportunity of pursuing his or her economic aspirations. Washington's aim as President, he wrote, was "to establish a general system of policy, which if pursued, will insure permanent felicity" for the nation.[405]

To accomplish his vision, he spearheaded the executive, legislative, and societal initiatives described in the remaining chapters of this book, of which the following are a few highlights:

I

In eighteenth-century England, the society was rigidly stratified. Aristocrats, a tiny fraction of the population, were granted many exclusive privileges. They disdained commercial pursuits as demeaning and relied on patronage from the Crown and appointments to official positions to which were attached almost limitless opportunities for self-enrichment. The U.S. Declaration of Independence, on the other hand, had included a monumental pronouncement that all men were created equal. If only the reality matched that grand declaration! The American society, however, was patterned after the English model of that era, and even some of the Founders were not immune to exhibiting the same haughtiness toward commoners prevalent in the home country.

Washington regarded the British culture of aristocracy, nepotism, patronage, and corruption as inherently incompatible with his economic vision for the United States. He was determined to level the playing field for all Americans. Unequal treatment arising from one's lineage, family connection, and the like had to be eradicated from society, appointments had to be made solely on merit, and shame at working for a living had to give way to pride. Then, and only then, would the opportunity for wealth creation, home ownership, and access to education be broad-based, open to all, and sustainable for the long term.

II

In a flourishing economic system, the protections accorded private property and contract rights had to be regarded as sacrosanct. The U.S. Constitution provided for these safeguards, but to preserve and enforce those rights required a judicial system consisting of qualified and respected justices operating in an environment free from the taint of political or other pressures.

During the colonial period, the judiciary was an unremarkable element in society. Courts were an integral part of the political machinery of government, and judgeships were often the rewards for the political or social standing of candidates, with little or no regard for legal training or ability in such appointments.

Washington was convinced that a competent, honest, and easily-accessible federal judiciary was an essential ingredient in his vision. It was the rock upon which the entrepreneurial structure he visualized would be erected. If judges were incompetent, biased, corrupt, or showed favoritism, or if they were vulnerable to external pressures, then Washington's economic model would not long remain sustainable.[406]

III

Starting a business in England in that era was fraught with serious risk. Failure – often the fate of start-ups, then and now – would land the unfortunate entrepreneur in the dreaded debtor's prison, an outcome too horrific to contemplate. Corporate charters would insulate one from liability but they were rarely granted by the Crown, and then only to exalted members of the English nobility.

In the colonies, dealing with the red tape and bureaucratic obstacles across the ocean presented a formidable challenge to anyone aspiring to run his own company. For Washington, therefore, creating a favorable environment for starting businesses was of paramount importance for the country.

IV

In British America, a farmer or businessman in need of a loan had to seek it from the same British broker through whom he exported his own products and imported the finished goods the colonists were not permitted to manufacture domestically. The borrower would have to adhere to whatever terms and rates the British factor dictated. Then, too, credit availability was on a demand basis and strictly at the whim of the lender, who could – and did – withdraw his credit facility whenever his own circumstances so dictated, often with little advance notice to the borrower.

Washington had learned much from the experience of operating under this one-sided system. He had particularly learned the imperative of dodging the credit squeezes periodically emanating from across the ocean and knew other planters who had barely escaped the infamy of default. The scarcity of credit and other financing methods, however, had not ended with the Revolution; rather, it had dogged Americans beyond the colonial period and well into the Confederation era.

During the colonial period, Washington and others were aware of the existence of capital markets and banking organizations in several cities in Britain and elsewhere in Europe which greatly facilitated commercial transactions and industrial projects. Even though the colonies were prohibited from erecting a similar financial structure on their side of the Atlantic, Washington was eager to have the chance to do so. For him, therefore, the creation of a financial infrastructure was an essential element in the economic program he visualized for the country.[407]

V

Britain's regulation of its North American provinces restricted trade to exports and imports as a two-way street between Britain and the colonies, with minor exceptions in the case of a few other British dominions. If Americans found other sources of supply or other markets for their commodities, British rules made such transactions prohibitively expensive and therefore impractical. Trade among the American colonies themselves was subject to similar burdens. The colonists had no alternative but to hew closely to the bilateral arrangement with the mother country.

Washington viewed these policies as major stumbling blocks to the development of the domestic American economy. Unfettered by inveterate mercantilist preconceptions and buoyed by the influence of British philosophers such as Adam Smith, Washington and many other Founders had emerged from their experiences in British America as strong believers in free trade. He therefore set for himself the challenging task of negotiating trade agreements with the existing and potential trading partners of the United States, and otherwise creating commercial relations with most of the developed nations of the world. On the domestic side, Washington visualized a vast American market, which would not only create a vital and thriving commercial hub for internal and external trade, but would additionally cement the Union of the states, linking them together in an enduring system of cooperative and collaborative commercial enterprise. These he viewed as vital elements in fostering a flourishing American economic environment.[408]

VI

Americans learned the hard way, even after the conclusion of the ground war in the American Revolution, what it meant to be powerless to protect themselves from the encroachments of foreign powers on U.S. soil, the imposition of blockades on American ports by hostile naval forces, and the capture of vessels of the American merchant marine by marauders and pirates, and the enslavement of their crews.

Washington, of course, was keenly aware of the cost to an economy of being on a war footing, and of how armed conflict could drain a country of its fiscal underpinnings. He was equally cognizant that a nation's vulnerability to aggressive moves by foreign powers would not provide the optimum conditions for a flourishing economy. Under the exigent circumstances of the United States at the time, Washington knew he had to tread carefully through the minefields of overt foreign designs on the new republic. He would use diplomacy whenever and wherever possible to save the nation from another military confrontation so soon after the devastation of the Revolutionary War and pave the way for growth and prosperity to take root in the American economy.[409]

Washington was unflagging in his efforts to see his economic vision become reality, but the path to achieving that goal was hardly free from dissent. There was widespread opposition to his initiatives throughout the nation, skepticism in Congress, and contentious discord within his own circle of advisors and in the administration itself. Despite the many obstacles, Washington succeeded in implementing substantial and broad portions of his program. Thus it was that this extraordinary man, with no PhD in macroeconomics, no MBA in finance, and no JD in law, provided the United States with the single most effective economic infrastructure the world had ever known.

What Washington put in place in his two administrations was an entrepreneurial architecture rooted in the hard realities and experiences of his own professional life, and tailor-made for the struggling new nation. Focused on building the essential ingredients of America's long-term economic structure and utterly oblivious to any thought about who received the kudos, Washington did not even name the system he so carefully created. The French had already been talking about "entrepreneurs" before John Stuart Mill, an English political philosopher, first introduced the term into the consciousness of the English-speaking world in the nineteenth century.[410] Even as a description of Washington's own private activities, that term did not immediately come to the minds of the early historians.

It is not surprising, therefore, that in the scores of biographies about the life of George Washington, one searches in vain for any reference to his monumental contribution to the design of the economic system under which America has thrived for more than two centuries. Incredibly, no one has connected the dots back to our first President.

It is true, of course, that the economic trajectory of a country is often perceived only in retrospect through the working of its components, and is therefore an implicit, rather than an explicit, plan. It is mostly the authoritarian regimes, with their managed economies, that make public announcements of their multi-year economic goals. The foundation of Washington's economic vision, on the other hand, was self-reliance and individual initiative, the very antithesis of central planning. Besides, it would not have been at all in character for him to label his program "the Grand Design" and trumpet its launching with modern-style press conferences and great fanfare.

* * *

When attempting to explain how people's behavior affects their commercial environment, economists follow the methodology of other social scientists in that they use empirical research to develop mathematical models and formulate theories which are useful to understanding the myriad of ways in which mankind makes its way in the business world. Journalists who write their observations of events and human activities also make contributions to developments in this area of knowledge. Nevertheless, formulation of theory has been primarily the province of academic economists. The best-known award in the field, the Prize in Economic Sciences in Memory of Alfred Nobel, awarded since 1969, has been largely directed toward the academic and theoretical practitioners in the field.[411]

Washington's model eventually found its way into the perspective of the theoreticians. In economics, cause and effect have their own cycle and maturation process; there is naturally a lag between the observation-and-analysis phase of the research and the actual formulation of theory.[412] What is astonishing is how long it took economists to recognize the design President Washington had put in place for the U.S. economy. As one economist readily admitted, "As a rule, economists don't know much about history."[413] In reality, it took the theoreticians more than a century before they recognized this new system, baptized it the "entrepreneurial economy," and wrote about its attributes. By then, the world had already entered The American Century, and the phenomenon of the country's dynamic national economy could hardly have escaped notice.

Focusing on the extraordinary growth of commercial activity in the United States, economists observed that Americans were starting businesses, developing new products and services, improving society's living conditions, and creating jobs, all at hitherto unparalleled rates. Joseph Schumpeter (1883-1950), an Austrian economist who taught at Harvard through the Great Depression, is generally credited with being the first to devise theories about the entrepreneurial society in 1911. He argued that innovation, as the crucial ingredient in economic growth, resulted from the work of entrepreneurs, whom he called "wild spirits," in a society. Other Austrian economists who had escaped the rise of Hitler in Europe brought added attention onto the entrepreneurial model as creating acceptable economic conditions for the greatest proportion of the people. One in particular, Friedrich Hayek (1899-1992), a professor at the University of Chicago and one of the most intriguing thinkers of the twentieth century, provided an elaborate description of the entrepreneurial view of the market process in his *Road to Serfdom*. Published in England in 1944, the first print of the book sold out within days. The Readers Digest, then at the height of its popularity as a magazine, featured a condensed version of the book in 1945, causing Hayek to become a celebrity on both sides of the Atlantic. For his work in the field, Hayek received the Nobel Prize in 1974, the Order of the Companions of Honour in England in 1984, and the U.S. Presidential Medal of Freedom in 1991.[414]

Hayek was an unabashed believer in the freedom of the individual as essential to a progressive economic policy. He also believed that government control of the economy led to suppression of the freedom of thought and speech, and that economic freedom was a vital ingredient of political liberty in exactly the same way that command economies are crucial to totalitarian governments. He subscribed to a line from Walter Lippmann he deemed an apt description of his own economic philosophy: "The generation to which we belong is now learning from experience what happens when men retreat from freedom to a coercive organization of their affairs."[415]

By mid-twentieth century, others were increasingly engaging in discourse about what had made the United States an economic powerhouse. Ludwig von Mises, Milton Friedman, Edmund Phelps, and other notable economists fleshed out the theory of the entrepreneurial economy, describing it as a system which encourages innovation and creativity in a society more effectively than any other design. By the time the new millennium had arrived, the quantum of literature about the entrepreneurial society had proliferated beyond all expectations. It is now axiomatic that this model provides the optimum long-term opportunity for raising a country's standard of living, which accounts for the rapidity with which much of the rest of the world is borne along.

Members of the Austrian School deserve great credit for writing and theorizing about the entrepreneurial society, and for their astute analysis of its benefits. Equally important, they deserve credit for their courage in the face of widespread disdain from within their own profession. For their criticism of central planning and their championing of free markets, these economists were widely labeled as cranks and skeptics. As late as 1989, only a few months before the collapse of the Soviet Union, the most popular economic textbook in American universities, authored by a Nobel Prize-winning economist, praised Soviet-style "command economies" as models of productivity.

Some go so far as to give credit for the design of the entrepreneurial system to the economists of the Austrian School. This is, of course, ironic; they did not *create* the entrepreneurial economy; they only *discovered* and recognized its existence. The alternative would be akin to crediting William Herschel, the astronomer who discovered Uranus, with creating the planet!

Biographers have often recorded that George Washington was steadfast in his convictions about the principles of the republican form of government. For him, however, those principles comprised both political and economic freedoms in a seamless whole for the society to be fully productive.

What will be most remembered about the Washington Presidency was how he orchestrated a multi-pronged assault on all the problems faced by Americans during the turbulent last decade of the eighteenth century. There were, of course, many challenges, but what was happening on the economic front was inspirational, though hardly linear in its progression. Once Washington's program was in place and an appropriate lag allowed for his policies to take root, the nation underwent an astonishing metamorphosis and a prolonged burst of entrepreneurial energy. The President's formula being so devised as to enable every individual to give rein to his or her creative energies, the upshot was to foment an exhilarating, busy, bustling, noisy, ever-changing environment in which people could feel free to innovate and take risk, revel in the opportunity of doing so, and reap the personal satisfaction and rewards of such efforts. It resembled a dam breaking, releasing countless pressures kept in check by two centuries of British rule and the chaotic Confederation period. The resulting massive changes were unprecedented, transforming the American society, as the President had intended.

There is virtual unanimity among historians that these changes actually occurred on the economic front; some even assert flat out that "perhaps no country in the Western world has ever undergone such massive changes in such a short period of time."[416] What is often missing from the historiography, however, is the original impetus for these impressive changes. Many have simply attributed them to the American Revolution, putting the socio-economic cause-and-effect in the context of "the Revolution happened, ergo these changes." There can, of course, be no doubt that the Revolution changed the political environment by lifting the strictures of colonialism from the nation, but the economic system remained broken. The Revolution provided political transition without any underpinnings of a new economic order. Thus, what followed the Revolution was hardly impressive economic performance. Quite the contrary. The country's Gross Domestic Product had taken a precipitous dive in the interval between the Revolution and the first Presidency.[417] Then Washington's economic design burst upon a nation hungry, even impatient, for the implementation of its tenets. They quickly became the norm for the country, so much so that their origin has been lost in history. The crucial elements of change were actually two:

The first was the ratification of the new U.S. Constitution, which created a vital change in the political structure of the government and provided broad protections for certain aspects of economic activity. History, however, provides multiple instances of such landmark documents being defiled by power-hungry leaders. Washington himself was forthright about such dangers when he wrote,

> "No compact among men (however provident in its construction and sacred in its ratification) can be pronounced everlasting and inviolable. If I may so express myself, no wall of words [and] no mound of parchment can be so formed as to stand against the sweeping torrent of boundless ambition on one side, aided by the sapping current of corrupted morals on the other."[418]

James Madison was equally emphatic. The Constitution, he wrote, "is of no more consequence than the paper on which it is written, unless it is stamped with the approbation of those to whom it is addressed... the people themselves."[419] Washington and Madison both knew whereof they spoke. Emblematic of the truth of their words was the widespread practice in Britain – with total impunity – of the buying and selling of official positions, which was in fact strictly prohibited by a statute notable for being completely ignored at all levels of the government. Washington's foremost priority, therefore, was to foster a firm tradition of deep and abiding respect for that basic American charter, as otherwise the Magna Cartas of the world could be all too easily ignored. Aware that any crisis could serve as an excuse to expand federal power, Madison had also warned against "the old trick of turning every contingency into a resource for accumulating force in the government." Washington, therefore, set out to inculcate upon the minds of the populace the foundational precepts of a free republic, and to promote a massive cultural belief in the imperative of compliance with the provisions of the new U.S. Constitution by ensuring that the Supreme Court of the United States would be staffed with justices who would be respectful of that landmark document and would ensure its survival through their opinions and decisions.

The second element was the painstaking step-by-step process of putting in place the ingredients of an entrepreneurial society designed and implemented by President Washington. The accumulated literature about the entrepreneurial society makes it abundantly clear that this kind of economy requires a set of dynamic infrastructural elements to bring it into being, and that it simply does not occur spontaneously like the rising of the sun.[420]

Historians are in accord that American society was thus transformed and that "people and their energies were let loose in an unprecedented outburst,"[421] as evidenced by the creation of new commercial enterprises, the general prosperity in cities and towns, the active trade of the United States, and the booming demand for U.S. government bonds in London, Amsterdam, and other European financial centers. The system worked so well, with built-in delays for such a program to mature and bear fruit, that nominal GDP for the United States during the last decade of the eighteenth century grew by an average of 9.78% per year, and that by the 1820s the economy of the United States had already caught up with that of Great Britain in output per capita.[422]

The Many Faces of George Washington

Farmer

Struggling to extricate himself from dependence on his London tobacco broker, Washington became a serial entrepreneur, creating a thriving and self-sustaining farming and manufacturing village at Mount Vernon.

Soldier

Washington's rise to commander of the Virginia militia was meteoric, but he found the condescending attitude of British officers hard to take. Loss for Britain, decisive gain for American independence.

President

Washington put in place the economic model later economists called an entrepreneurial system. Actually, what he did was to undo and reverse the British economic structure for its American colonies.

The Courtship of George Washington

George Washington called on Martha Dandridge Custis at her home on the Pamunkey River in 1758. She had other suitors, but Washington's commanding personality soon won her hand.

Martha Washington

Comely and warm-hearted, Martha was a devoted wife throughout George's demanding life. While their private correspondence was never made available, one can easily surmise that theirs was a storybook marriage.

Mount Vernon

The house George Washington inherited from his brother Lawrence

George had fond memories of his early life at Epsewasson, the family's small cottage on the Potomac River. Lawrence, the older half-brother George idolized, inherited the house from their father and renamed it Mount Vernon.

The residence at Mount Vernon with George Washington's improvements

Washington spent a lifetime renovating and expanding Mount Vernon, including building a piazza of his own design for entertainment on the shores of the Potomac River. Mount Vernon now draws more than a million visitors every year.

Lawrence Washington

Lawrence, George Washington's beloved half-brother and role model, took over George's upbringing after their father's death. A farmer and businessman, Lawrence's affairs were at the takeoff point when he succumbed to tuberculosis and died at 34.

Lord Fairfax

Thomas, 6th Lord Fairfax, was the first English aristocrat in Washington's life. Impressed with his sixteen-year-old neighbor, His Lordship often invited George on his favorite pastime, foxhunting. He also helped George in his surveying practice.

Daniel Parke

Daniel Parke, the grandfather of Martha's first husband, was a handsome rogue in whose presence no married woman was safe. Although he had a wife and two daughters in Virginia, he also fathered illegitimate children on two continents. After his violent death, his heirs waged a no-holds-barred fight over his estate. Dubbed by historians as the Dunbar suit, it dragged on for more than two generations, went up on appeal to the Privy Council, and drew in no less a personage than the Lord Chief Justice of England. Eventually, it even embroiled Washington in its backwash.

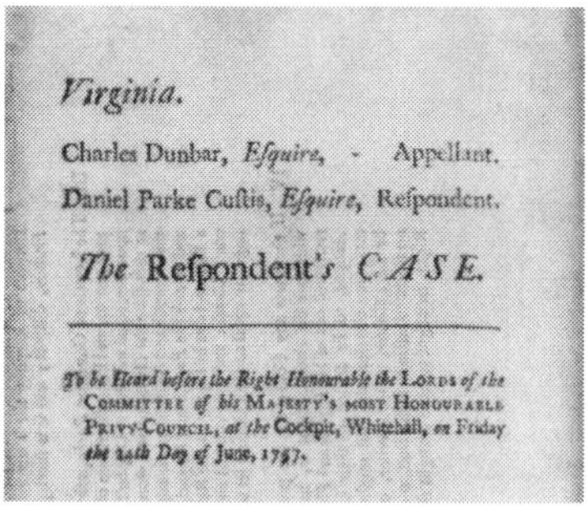

Virginia.

Charles Dunbar, *Esquire*, - Appellant.

Daniel Parke Custis, *Esquire*, Respondent.

The Respondent's *CASE.*

To be Heard before the Right Honourable the LORDS *of the* COMMITTEE *of his* MAJESTY'S MOST HONOURABLE PRIVY-COUNCIL, *at the* Cockpit, Whitehall, *on* Friday *the* 24th *Day of* June, 1757.

Appeal to the Privy Council in London

Washington's Library

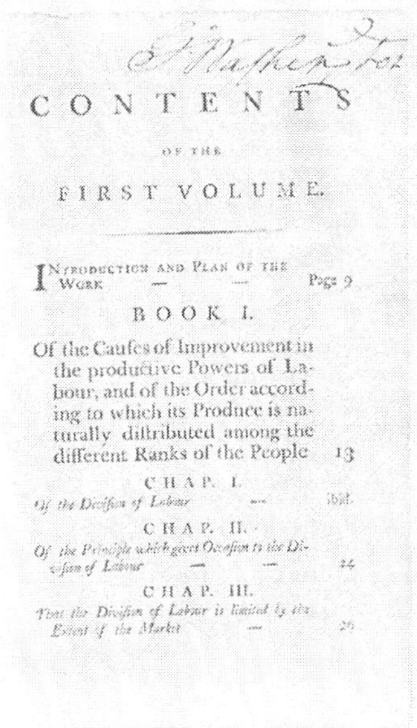

CONTENTS

OF THE

FIRST VOLUME.

INTRODUCTION AND PLAN OF THE WORK — — Page 9

BOOK I.

Of the Caufes of Improvement in the productive Powers of Labour, and of the Order according to which its Produce is naturally diftributed among the different Ranks of the People 13

CHAP. I.

Of the Divifion of Labour — ibid.

CHAP. II.

Of the Principle which gives Occafion to the Divifion of Labour — — 24

CHAP. III.

That the Divifion of Labour is limited by the Extent of the Market — 26

George Washington's signature and bookplate on Vol. I of Adam Smith's *Wealth of Nations*

Economics was hardly a known field in Washington's time. In the English-speaking world, Adam Smith was the best-known practitioner of this new branch of knowledge. His *Wealth of Nations* became a bestseller in its time. Washington had a three-volume set of the 1789 edition, now in the Washington Collection at Princeton University.

Date	Mr. John Parke Custis Dr	Curr. Mony £	s	d	Sterling £	s	d
1759 Oct.	Balle of your Acct Currt then settled & approvd of by the Genl Court [and] 485 lb. Tobo.	£ 617.	7.	¾			
	To the said 485 lb. Tobacco @ 20/ prCt	4.	7.				
	To James Gildart Esqr. for ⅔ of £151.0.4¾ for Negroes Cloathing				£ 100.	13.	7
	To 4 pair Cotton Sheets and Beds for Overseers and Workmen	17.					
1760	To Sundrys for his own use Vizt 8¾ yds Irish Linnen £3.14.3 ¾ Cambrick 12/6 1¼ yds Linnen 3/1½ Toys 3/9 Books and Marbles 3/11 Callico for a double Gown 10 1 Yard fustian 2/. A pair of Silver Buckles 15s. A Suit of Cloaths for his Man £3.15.1½. 7¼ yards illegible (as 12/6 and a pair of Shoes for ditto 4/.	11.	6.	2			
	To Joseph Valentine for Sundrys allowed him at Settlement Vizt. for his own Wages £70 paid the Mill Right 10£ 15/. the Taylor £2.4.10. The Weaver £1.13.4 the Glazier 9/9 for building a Boat 25s. Mending Seines 20s. taking up [illegible] 39/6. 15 Bushels of Oats to Sow 21/3. Toys 4/. an Augur 1/3. Tobo Knives 7/6. Milk pans 26/7½ horse Collars 3/6	92.	11.	6½			
	To Mrs Washington's [share] of the Rents on the other side	43.	2.	8			
	To Sundrys for his own use Vizt. Shipd. by Robert Cary Esqr. & Co. £23.19.7 School Books 5/. a pair of Shoes for his Man 4/6		9.	6	£ 23.	18.	7
	To two Seines for Fishing at your Plantations				28.	5.	4
	To Joseph Valentine for Sundrys allowed him at Settlement Vizt. Paid Roger Tandy's Wages £40. Benja. Piggots £8 Lewis Smith £5 for James Mer dies share of Corn £5.16.10½ for David Goddens ditto £7.4. for Wm B ates ditto £6 Doctr Amsons Acct £1.1.8 Doctr Jas Carters £18.13.10. Doctr Wm Carter 13s. Mr [Andrew] Franks £1.2.6. The Smiths £3.9.3¾. The Taylors 19/1. The Midwife 10/ for bringing things over the Bay 20s. for 2 pr Wool Cards 5s. for 2 horse Collars 2/6 for fixing the Seines 3/9. for a Barrel of Tar 12/6. for the Poll and Land Tax to the Sheriff of York £9.6.8½	113.	..	7¾			
	To Law Charges for one half of £5 and 2/3 of £187.9. paid Mr Mercer pr Acct.	127.	9.	4			
April	To Balle now due to John Parke Custis besides 1/3 of 51 hhds Tobo Contra				1456.	19.	[illegible]
		1026.	18.	8¾	£ 1609.	17.	11 [illegible]
	Miss Martha Parke Custis Dr						
1760	To Sundrys for her own use Vizt. Shipped by the Capt. [illegible] £30.6 paid the mantuamaker 23/ illegible Cambrick 5/ Toys 3/ illegible 3 prs of Stocking 4/6 Callico for a Gown illegible yds illegible bag holland 10/ 4 yds Irish Linnen 36/ illegible making a pair of Silk Do 3/9 illegible	£ 7.	4.	11	£ 30.	6.	
1761.	To Ditto vizt knitting a pr of Silk Stockings 4/. School Books 7/6		11.	8			
	To Law Charges for one half of £5 and one [sixth] of £187.9 paid Mr Mercer by Acct.	33.	14.	10			
April	To Balle now due exclusive of the third of 51 hhds Tobo e Contra wch Colo. Washington agrees to Assign Bonds and £1650 Bank Stock for	7880.	17.	8 [illegible]	£ 2228.	5.	8
		£ 7922.	9.	1 [illegible]	£ 2258.	11.	8

We the Subscribers have pursuant to the Order of the Honble. the General Court examined...
Children John Parke Custis and Martha Parke Custis to whom the said George Washington is Guardian...
the Ballances as due April last according to the several Accounts hereunto annexed. Given under...

Guardian Accounts

Washington managed the assets of his stepchildren, Jacky and Patsy, as well as Martha's separate dower estate, under a court order. He kept meticulous records for their benefit.

Transcript of a page from the account book Washington kept for his stepchildren, John Parke Custis and Martha Parke Custis, the original being damaged and rendered illegible with the passage of years.

Thomas Jefferson

Jefferson's unfamiliarity with the currency markets cost him dearly in a personal transaction, saddling him with a mountain of debt to his English bankers for the rest of his life.

Alexander Hamilton

As Secretary of the Treasury, Hamilton successfully revamped the credit markets of the United States. Brilliant, articulate, and opinionated, Hamilton did not pull any punches in his rivalry with Jefferson.

James Madison

Madison's small stature and sickly frame concealed a steel-trap mind. Washington relied on him for advice on the new Constitution. Madison became the most astute legislative tactician of his time.

John Jay

Urbane, polished, eloquent, and a formidable negotiator, John Jay was the most able U.S. representative on the international scene. When a student at Columbia, he was almost expelled for refusing to rat on his classmates. Among his many honors was that he was the first Chief Justice of the U.S. Supreme Court.

Robert Morris

As a thirteen-year-old orphan arriving in Philadelphia from Liverpool, Robert Morris found an unpaid apprenticeship in a small trading company. At fifteen, he devised a scheme to corner the market in flour and made a huge profit for his employer. Later, he became the financier of the American Revolution. He was the one who recommended Alexander Hamilton as Treasury Secretary to President Washington.

Phillis Wheatley

Phillis Wheatley, the first published poet of African-American descent, wrote a poem in support of General Washington in 1776. He was encouraging in his praise of her and invited her to visit him in Cambridge.

President Washington's First Cabinet

Washington created the Cabinet style of administration, patterned after the council of officers under his command during the Revolutionary War. His handpicked department heads were: left to right, Secretary of War Henry Knox, Secretary of State Thomas Jefferson, Attorney General Edmund Randolph (facing away), Secretary of the Treasury Alexander Hamilton, and the President himself.

Bank of the United States

The mere mention of a banking institution reminded Americans of the unfairness of the British system of aristocracy. Hamilton had to fight hard to get a congressional charter for his Bank of the United States. Once founded, its shares skyrocketed in value.

The White House

President Washington overseeing the building of the White House

Congress passed a resolution to build the nation's capital on a no-man's-land on the Potomac River and assigned the task of implementing it to George Washington. With no federal funds and an impossible timetable, Washington had to rely on his dealmaking skills to get the project off the ground.

The Queen of Spain

Elegant and vivacious, Queen Maria Luisa had an affair with her handsome royal guard, Manuel de Godoy. She then importuned her husband, King Carlos IV, to elevate her paramour to be the prime minister of Spain. In the tug-of-war between the U.S. and Spain for control of territory, it was Godoy whom President Washington outmaneuvered to secure a most favorable treaty for the United States.

PART IV

Chapter Nine

ARISTOCRACY OR PARADIGM SHIFT: A NUANCED TAPESTRY FOR A NEW REPUBLIC

No great improvements in the lot of mankind are possible until a great change takes place in the fundamental constitution of their modes of thought.

John Stuart Mill

For centuries before the American Revolution, European monarchs were the absolute rulers of their subjects. In foreign relations, they engaged in war as though it were a game, showing virtually no concern for the safety of civilians and the destruction of their homes and properties, no compassion for the wounded and dying soldiers, and certainly no mercy for the captured enemy combatants. Peace was a precious transitory interlude amid continuing warfare with continental neighbors. Bent on self-aggrandizement and using the public treasuries as personal piggy banks, the royal heads of state built monuments to themselves on the backs of their subjects. For these rulers, the enhancement of the lives of their common citizens was not an agenda item.[423]

When Americans chose George Washington as their President in 1789, onto the world stage stepped a new kind of leader, one who would leave no doubt in anyone's mind that the launching of the United States heralded an entirely different approach to the governance of a nation. For him the lofty pronouncements in the Declaration of Independence were not mere philosophical concepts, and he would not countenance the tainting of the new republican experiment with vestiges of the Old Order from Europe. "Duty" and "responsibility" were rock-solid core values for him, and he would pull into his orbit other like-minded individuals and mold them into a team of energetic public servants dedicated to the common good.[424] Along the same lines, he was also a fervent believer that politicians were never free to make promises they did not intend to keep or to make statements they knew to be untrue. "I do not recollect," he declared, "that in the course of my life I ever forfeited my word or broke a promise made to anyone." To him it was a heartfelt axiom that "to promise what one does not perform is at all times wrong."[425]

Much needed to be done to create the country envisaged by the new Constitution. A major missing ingredient was ease of travel. With abysmal roads, rare to non-existent accommodations, coaches breaking down, horses going lame, bridges washing out, and serious other hazards, travel was arduous and at times dangerous. Even short distances required great physical endurance to travel. It is not surprising, therefore, that most people of that period rarely ventured outside the confines of their own towns or hamlets. The poor transportation also hampered another ingredient vital to the welfare of the country, namely postal service. There were few post offices, and mail delivery was unreliable and haphazard. Washington was determined to expand the highway system, and to substantially enhance the country's postal reach.

By the time the United States emerged from its Revolution, the country extended from the Atlantic in the east to the Great Lakes in the north, the Mississippi River in the west, and nearly to the Gulf of Mexico in the south – a vast territory, as large as France, Italy, Spain, Britain, and Ireland combined. European monarchs, already uneasy about the American experiment in the republican form of government, were convinced that a population spread over such a huge area would never become one nation, would never be governable from one center, and would eventually become a collection of minor squabbling fiefdoms.[426]

As for the Americans themselves, now that they were no longer bound together by their allegiance to the English Crown, they preferred to see themselves as New Yorkers, North Carolinians, Virginians, Georgians, etc. The sense of separateness, first instilled in them by British colonial policy, was by then too deeply ingrained in the culture to be swept aside by the single act of winning the Revolution. Alexander Hamilton was so concerned about the disunity and distrust among the states that he came up with a plan to protect his home state of New York from potential incursion by other states. Knowing that the Continental Army would be disbanded as soon as a peace treaty was signed with Great Britain, he proposed to George Clinton, the Governor of New York, in February 1783 that the state should offer free land to the soldiers to keep them from leaving New York. If a conflict were to break out with another state, New York would thus have a trained fighting force within its own population.

> "It is the first wish of my heart," Hamilton wrote, "that the Union may last, but feeble as the links are, what prudent man would rely upon it? Should a disunion take place, any person who will cast his eye upon the map will see how essential it is to our state to provide for its own security."[427]

The Europeans, of course, were not satisfied with merely making cynical pronouncements about the United States but worked actively to bring about the country's fragmentation. When he became President, George Washington was determined that the self-serving predictions of European leaders of America's inevitable failure would never come to pass, and that their agitations against the Union would never succeed. The mission he set for himself was, therefore, abundantly clear: The regional jealousies and distrust would have to be subsumed into a sense of national pride. He would do all in his power to bring the country together, strengthen the sense of Union, encourage commerce and intercourse among the states, and create a vast domestic trading market and a cohesive national economy.

George Washington had a Promethean blueprint for creating a dynamic economy in the country by nurturing the innate American spirit of enterprise, essentially transforming the society into a nationwide entrepreneurial environment. To accomplish this vision as President, he spearheaded the specific executive and legislative measures described in the remaining chapters of this book. There was, however, an additional ingredient in his strategy, one that was discernible empirically from a close study of his writings and actions, and understandable only in the context of the moral burdens of colonialism. This new element was designed to ensure that the President's strategic program would provide economic security for *all* Americans, and not merely for those in the upper classes of society.

Patterning themselves after the British society of the time, Americans had naturally adopted the English attitudes on such fundamental issues as equality, risk-taking in commercial matters, entry into business, and the like. At the dawn of the republic, the customs and morals transplanted from England were as interwoven into the daily lives and deepest beliefs of the former colonists as their physical environment. These mores constituted the sum total of the American culture at the time. They were also the primary motivations in the people's economic decisions.

Focusing on these core values, Washington wove a nuanced tapestry of disparate initiatives designed to wean the society away from the legacy of aristocracy and corruption at the individual level, and insularity and distrust at the state level. He had a vision of encouraging cultural norms based on diametrically different elements from those inherited under colonialism. The process would produce nothing less than a tectonic shift in American culture. The many and varied building blocks of this undertaking included the tolerance of diversity of views, seeing to it that freedom of the press is solidly in place in everyone's mind, the development of national communication and transportation systems, availability of educational opportunities, encouragement of literary efforts and inventiveness, the nurturing of a vast domestic economic bloc, the creation of public and private credit markets, and removal of bureaucratic red tape from business formation. Washington viewed these principles as timeless, and while policies would change to adapt to new circumstances, the underlying elements were meant to endure through the ages.

Such a sustained and cohesive program for the governance of the nation being wholly unfamiliar at the time, George III, the quintessential role model for the Old Order, paid his Revolutionary War nemesis the ultimate compliment when he said Washington was "the greatest character of the age."[428]

A powerful tool in the economic development of a society is its culture, which can have a decisive impact on saving, investment, and other elements of commercial life. Long underappreciated by academics, this conclusion is now better understood by sociologists and an increasing segment of modern economists, who acknowledge that the rise of a free enterprise society is essentially a cultural phenomenon. David Landes, the noted author of *The Wealth and Poverty of Nations,* asserts flat out that culture makes all the difference, a hypothesis shared by F. Fukuyama, Thomas Sowell, and other distinguished social scientists and economists.[429]

In a free society, however, one cannot simply legislate a new and improved culture into existence, nor launch major societal changes without ensuring that they would be acceptable to those most affected by them. It is also a given that any fundamental adjustment in the mores of people would meet strong resistance, as cultural norms are seamlessly enmeshed into the deepest beliefs of every society, and that resistance to change is often a built-in human trait.[430]

Replacing an anemic, risk-averse culture with a robust and dynamic entrepreneurial one requires a long incubation period.[431] Such transformations are usually measured in years, if not in generations. To bring about such attitudinal changes would require a time frame that exceeded any one President's tenure. All Washington could do, therefore, was to plant the seeds. History shows that he did so to great effect.

The focus of this chapter will thus be on several socio-economic trends discernible in the Washington era.

* * *

Inequality and Corruption: In eighteenth-century England, the stratification of people into the aristocracy, gentry, and peasantry was hardwired into the English psyche. The nobility's perch at the apex of society was believed to be pre-ordained by Providence. Dividing the population into classes was thus viewed as fundamental to the organization of the nation. Peerage denoted special privilege, and its members were the ones most often appointed to important political offices by the Crown. Money and power followed aristocracy, and British lords built vast palaces for themselves. Peers had annual incomes as high as £50,000, lesser noblemen £4,000 to £20,000, and the titled gentry £3,000 to £4,000. By way of comparison, farmers and tradesmen earned £40 to £300 per year.[432]

Those in the lower classes existed to serve the lords and were treated with haughtiness and scorn by the aristocracy. "Mankind are …properly to be considered under two great divisions," one writer proclaimed only half facetiously, "those that use their own hands, and those who employ the hands of others." A distinguished historian went so far as to say that to the English aristocrats, the mass of commoners was "little more than 'cattle'."[433]

But those were English views. Americans would have been fully familiar with this harsh hierarchical system but would never subscribe to such haughty and discriminatory practices.

Or would they?

> Alexander Hamilton called them "the unthinking populace." Thomas Jefferson called them "hackneyed rascals." John Adams called them "vulgar, rustic." Others called them "ignorant," "selfish," "illiberal," "idiots."

Whom were Messrs. Hamilton, Jefferson, Adams, and others talking about? These great Founders of the American republic, who believed that "all men are created equal," must have been talking about some fairly disreputable members of society. Were they? Actually, no. They were talking about ordinary people – the plain, average, hardworking common American folk, from whom these "gentlemen" were eager to distance themselves both socially and culturally.[434]

Let us not judge our Founding Fathers too harshly, however. After all, they grew up in British America, and the long colonial period had led Americans to admire and emulate the English system of royalty and aristocracy as the ultimate human model, and to embrace British manners and attitudes. "The whole community," Benjamin Franklin explained, "is regulated by the example of the king."[435] Clearly, the American Revolution had hardly dismantled all the indicia of that aristocratic model as it was deep-rooted and required a furious onslaught to dislodge.

During the period of British rule, Washington had been aware that designating an individual as a "colonial" automatically relegated him or her to lower-class status. He had personally experienced this affront in his own life. The sting of such treatment would not be easily forgotten by a proud man. For him, therefore, equality was a heartfelt conviction. He believed that the class-and-caste system was wholly antithetical to republican ideals and destructive of the vibrant spirit of innovation in people. In England, there had existed neither political nor economic equality. To Washington, equality was thus a basic pillar of the economic structure.

Washington believed that it was vital to expunge from public consciousness the aristocratic disdain for the lower classes. There should be honor, not shame, in working for a living and engaging in a vocation or trade. Nor should there be a ruling class, or titles or privileges conferred by the government, or honorifics for Washington himself or anyone else. It was foolishness for the President to be called "His Most Benign Highness" as John Adams proposed, or "His Highness the President of the United States of America and Protector of the Rights of Same" as was proposed by a committee of the U.S. Senate. Madison remembered Washington's annoyance at the efforts "to bedizen him with a superb but spurious title."[436]

Washington's personal rejection of English aristocratic culture was indeed remarkable. As a farmer, businessman, member of the legislature, and part of the plantation society of Virginia, he had worked several decades in British America under a system that subsisted on patronage and corruption, kickbacks and rebates, and a complete lack of enforcement of conflict-of-interest rules for public officials. Even in such an environment, by all accounts he had been quite successful. And yet, at the first opportunity, he had unhesitatingly turned his back on practices that he believed sapped the energies of honest and hardworking citizens and entrepreneurs, and redirected those energies into unhealthy channels and possible antisocial involvements. If permitted to grow, corruption would adversely impact entrepreneurial activity and taint every aspect of life down to its economic, political, and judicial underpinnings. Washington firmly believed that the legacy of English culture required an overhaul to fit the republican mold.[437]

As President, Washington was determined to prevent corruption, or even the appearance of it, from taking root in the American society and government. He took great pains to make his official appointments purely on merit and would not permit personal or political considerations to affect his judgment in making his selections. Washington was particularly unmoved by pressure to make appointments based on family relations, friendships, or personal *quid pro quo*. When his own nephew, Bushrod Washington, petitioned his uncle for a federal appointment, Washington resorted to the metaphor of a giant with all-seeing eyes out of Greek mythology to explain his refusal. "My political conduct," he wrote, "must be exceedingly circumspect and proof against just criticism, for the eyes of Argus are upon me, and no slip will pass unnoticed."[438] Perhaps nothing highlighted Washington's abhorrence of the class-and-caste system and his dedication to merit and equality than his appointment of an illegitimate orphan as his first Secretary of the Treasury. "His integrity was most pure," Jefferson would later observe of Washington, "his justice the most inflexible I have ever known, no motive of interest or consanguinity, of friendship or hatred, being able to bias his decision."[439]

Washington believed that an educated workforce was crucial to equality of opportunity in an active economy in the same way that an informed voter was fundamental to political democracy, and that general education in the population had a leveling tendency. Unlike the monarchs of old, Washington believed in the worth of an educated nation and its contribution not only to a free political order but to the economic advancement of society. In his pronouncements, therefore, he repeatedly placed emphasis on the availability of educational facilities throughout the nation for all who desired it. Equality of economic opportunity and equal access to educational institutions were thus the keystones of Washington's model. He repeatedly urged the establishment of a national university and made personal contributions to certain schools.[440]

Washington also had an intense aversion to the widespread English practice of using one's official position for personal enrichment. Anyone in a position of authority was simply assumed to engage in multiple money-making schemes at the expense of the general public. It was a corrupt – and corrupting – cultural trait. An Englishman by the name of Henry St. John, Viscount Bolingbroke, had written extensively about the bribery and corruption prevalent in the British society. He was dismissed out of hand in England, but his brand of journalism resonated with Americans, including George Washington and Thomas Jefferson.[441] Washington saw these influences as self-reinforcing, corrosive elements in the political and economic fabric of a society. James Madison expressed his own deep frustration with such practices when he lamented, "[H]ow easily are base and selfish measures masked by pretexts of public good and apparent efficiency."[442] Washington's proposed inaugural address was designed to put everyone on notice that corruption in any form would not be tolerated in his administration. He personified what he preached. He never denigrated or commercialized the office of the Presidency while he occupied it or even afterwards. When companies he had helped organize offered him gifts of stock as tokens of appreciation, he simply refused to accept compensation if there was any participation by the public sector. The canal projects described earlier clearly demonstrated his conviction that mixing public service and personal enrichment was anathema to honest government.

Paradoxically, many of the objectionable activities prevalent in the English society were illegal even in that era. The widespread practice of selling one's official position to the highest bidder, for instance, was specifically prohibited by statute.[443] It was obvious that laws in and of themselves would be insufficient to establish a new cultural trait. Washington would, therefore, contend for the hearts and minds of Americans through his actions as President, banking that the attitudes he and his Cabinet projected would be powerful influences in shaping the new culture of the American society. It was also fortunate for the implementation of his program that his own extraordinary popularity would ensure that the public would emulate his example and his pronouncements – an operating mode that in later centuries would be dubbed "the Presidential bully pulpit."

During his Presidency, Washington also exhibited an unshakable conviction that transparency was essential in government affairs, and the free flow of information was vital to expose corruption in American society. He also warned against the development of an arrogant aristocracy among government officials. He presciently mentioned the troublesome practice by Congress of exempting its own members from the laws they imposed upon the nation, thus creating an imperious and privileged subculture in American society. Washington warned that such a system could only serve to erode the people's confidence in their government.[444]

* * *

Debtors' Prison: The entrepreneurial society visualized by George Washington for the United States faced a formidable obstacle to its development in the eighteenth century: Nothing stifled the spirit of risk-taking in business more than the harsh punishments routinely meted out to anyone who could not pay for a purchase, defaulted on a loan, or was otherwise unable to discharge an obligation.

The poor in twenty-first-century America do not know how well-off they are, relative to the destitute in eras past. Today, a complex network of public and private support systems provide a modicum of relief for those living below the poverty line, making life at least bearable. But pity the poor at the dawn of America's founding. If they could not pay for the goods and services they purchased or repay a loan, the consequences were harsh indeed.

Among the many laws that the American colonies inherited from England were ones mandating imprisonment for defaulting debtors. In the eighteenth century, the inability to pay one's debts was a sign of moral turpitude, and this view shaped the legal system, which meted out severe punishment for the non-payment of one's debts. And yet, debt was ubiquitous in the colonies. Britain's economic policies governing its North American dominions, coupled with the nearly constant state of political and military upheaval which existed at the time, all conspired to put the finances of colonial farmers and businessmen in the red on a continuing basis. Americans in large numbers suffered economic setbacks so acute that, by the latter part of the eighteenth century, one out of three householders was at risk of defaulting on his or her debts.[445]

Some of the contemporary descriptions of debtors' prisons in America in the eighteenth century were "human slaughterhouses," "dismal cages," and "loathsome dungeons." These were no exaggeration; even violent and hardened criminals often fared better behind bars than those who could not meet their financial liabilities.

Debtors in jail had to provide their own food, fuel, and clothing. Since they were in jail for being without funds, they had to beg or steal scraps of food from other prisoners, rely on the generosity of family and friends or the beneficence of a local relief society, or do without. As a result, pleas of starvation were reported by debtors for every cell in the country. Severe overcrowding, unsanitary conditions, and disease were also rampant. Abuse of prisoners by the guards, physical punishment and even mutilation were common. An appalling example of such facilities was the Newgate debtors' prison in Connecticut. It consisted of an underground cavern to which the only entrance was a ladder down a shaft leading to wooden pens in which scores of inmates were jammed together, their feet shackled and their necks chained to beams in the roof. "The darkness was intense; the caves reeked with filth; vermin abounded…"[446]

During the yellow fever epidemics which swept the Mid-Atlantic States with distressing frequency in the eighteenth century, free citizens would flee from their homes and communities. The City of Philadelphia moved its hardened and violent criminals to a jail outside the city at the height of the epidemic to reduce contagion, but it left behind the inmates of its debtors' prison surrounded by disease and death in the most inhumane conditions imaginable – an intentional act designed to reduce overcrowding in the jail.

"As the law now operates," wrote William Keteltas, publisher of a newspaper entitled *Forlorn Hope*, "it is a greater crime to run into debt, however fair the prospect of paying, than to rob a man on the highway, commit a rape, or burn a house." As these deplorable conditions brought to light the humanitarian tragedy of imprisonment for debt, the need for change became all the more evident.[447]

The great irony here is that during the Confederation era, Congress itself incurred substantial debts at every level of its activities. It owed money to foreign governments and investors, to its own soldiers who had put their lives on the line for their country, to the hapless widows and orphans who, trusting their leaders, had put their life savings into promissory notes and bonds issued by the government, and to the individual states. *And Congress was in default on all of these loans.*

So, while ordinary citizens were daily being thrown into prisons with sub-human conditions for the crime of non-payment of even small debts, their government was shamelessly engaging in precisely the same practice on a massive scale with impunity.

Compulsory servitude to one's creditor was another possible fate confronting an insolvent debtor in the eighteenth century.[448] In this, immigration was a major factor, as America then was being deluged with new immigrants of whom only a fraction could pay their passage from Europe to America. Impoverished and working-class Europeans, eager for the promise of a better life in the New World, had to be prepared for servitude upon landing on American shores.

Indentured servitude could last as long as seven years. Most indigent immigrants would sign a contract before boarding a ship, then endure the long and gut-wrenching Atlantic crossing before arriving on American soil where they would be sold to the highest bidder. Many came willingly, but some were convicts sent to America by Great Britain. Underage immigrants were usually forced to serve until the age of twenty-one. Often these children were not even willing immigrants but rather kidnap victims sold into service in the colonies.[449]

Occasionally, a person already on American soil had the opportunity of choosing the indenture route, in lieu of debtors' prison, in satisfaction of a debt. Or he or she could do so to fulfill a special need. In a particularly striking case, an indigent man desperate for medical help bound himself for four years to one who promised to ease his suffering. Similarly, an orphan might be indentured by the court to a master who would teach *him* a trade or *her* sewing skills. Poor parents might even indenture their children to ease their own financial burden or to ensure that their offspring received a certain kind of job training. Thus, indentured apprenticeship, another form of servitude, was common in the eighteenth century. Benjamin Franklin, being the youngest son in a family of seventeen children, was indentured to his older brother for the unusually long term of nine years for the labor-intensive job of apprenticeship to a printer. He was twelve at the time. Being a servant to his brother did not spare Benjamin from the usual beatings apprentices received at the hands of their masters. And so, at the first opportunity, he fled Boston with only the shirt on his back, eventually arriving in Philadelphia at the age of seventeen broke, dirty, hungry, exhausted, and bedraggled.[450]

Fortunately, Franklin's case turned out spectacularly well both for him and for the country. Several other leaders in early America, including Robert Morris (later U.S. Senator) and Henry Knox (later Secretary of War), had also served apprenticeships in their youth and fared well afterwards, but most indentured servants did not do so well. When they were subjected to severe abuse, they had little recourse to the law. And when they fled from their masters, upon recapture they found their term of indenture extended sevenfold the number of missed days of work. Women were particularly vulnerable as, in addition to the usual abuses such as insufficient food, clothing, or rest, female servants could suffer sexual assaults from their masters. If a woman became pregnant, most states would compel her to compensate her master for lost efficiency during the late stages of her pregnancy, the cost of medical attendance at delivery, and time spent caring for the infant.[451]

George Washington never believed in the existence of a "moral economy of debt" and was compassionate about the crushing burden of financial obligation carried by many colonial families to the English trading houses. "That many families are reduced almost, if not quite, to penury and want," he wrote to George Mason, "from the low ebb of their fortunes, and estates daily selling for the discharge of debts, the public papers furnish but too many melancholy proofs of." After the Revolution, Washington argued forcefully that the payment of long-delayed army wages to his impoverished troops be made a priority of the Continental Congress. "To disband men… before their accounts are liquidated and the balances ascertained would be to set open the doors of the jails, and then to close them upon seven years' faithful and painful services."[452]

In his own affairs, Washington was loath to withhold a helping hand from a friend in need of temporary funds, a debtor truly unable to meet his obligations, an immigrant striving to bring his family to America, or an acquaintance seeking to finance a college education for his son. Thomas Posey, who had served with Washington in the Forbes campaign, repeatedly borrowed money from him to consolidate debts to others and avoid imprisonment. Washington was equally reluctant to press hard for the collection of his loans. He would not resort to lawsuits and jail for a debtor, sometimes despite strong provocation. At times, he would even agree to sign a Letter of License, granting a debtor a respite of several years to discharge his obligation. Although he never tired of urging friends and others that debt must be repaid promptly when due, he believed that imprisonment for debt was an unproductive and overly harsh system of punishment. So he donated funds to the Society for the Relief of Distressed Debtors, an organization that attempted to relieve the harsh conditions in debtors' prisons.[453]

During this period, bankruptcy, insolvency, and servitude were all matters of state law and thus differed in their impact on the parties depending on the jurisdiction. The profusion of inconsistent laws was a source of economic confusion, as creditors who did business in more than one state faced varying systems, sometimes with diametrically different results in similar transactions.[454]

Recognizing that a credit-based economy required some standardization of bankruptcy laws to function smoothly, the Framers of the U.S. Constitution in 1787 empowered Congress to pass national bankruptcy laws. That measure evoked little opposition, the only dissenting vote being cast by the delegates from Connecticut who feared that a federal bankruptcy statute, like an old English law, would permit the execution of debtors. Most Framers, however, agreed with James Madison that "… the power of establishing uniform laws of bankruptcy is so intimately connected with the regulation of commerce, and will prevent so many frauds where the parties or their property may lie or be removed into different states, that the expediency of it seems not likely to be drawn into question."[455] And so the Constitution granted Congress the authority to "establish uniform laws on the subject of bankruptcy."

In Washington's first term as President, an attempt at reform was made through the introduction of a bankruptcy bill in the House of Representatives in December 1792, but the increasing conflict between the commerce-minded Hamiltonians and agrarian-minded Jeffersonians in Congress in large measure prevented it from becoming law. Thomas Jefferson was strongly opposed to the bill, fearing that it would "render all the landholders of this state liable to be declared bankrupts."[456] Others, however, supported the bill on the grounds that to encourage the re-entry of unfortunate businessmen into the marketplace, some provision was needed for the discharge of one's debts. James A. Bayard, the chief sponsor of the bankruptcy bill, said, "No commercial people can be well governed without [a bankruptcy law]. Debts of great magnitude must be contracted; and the most honest and prudent man may, by accidents and misfortunes incident to commerce, be deprived of the means of making good his engagements." William Maclay, the Senator from Pennsylvania, once said of debtors' prison, "Liberty is the soul of life. Life without it is misery. . . . Once shut up, the prisoner's property is sure game." And with that, the Senator launched a passionate attack on the practice of putting debtors in prison.[457]

In time, an almost imperceptible awareness began to emerge that economic, not moral, causes were at the root of most failures, that even foreign events and wars created hazards that could precipitate business failures in America, and that debt was most often an "economic risk," not "moral delict." "A world governed by a moral economy of debt," one writer explained, "did not require much in the way of statutory regulation."[458]

Many prominent Americans, including several Founding Fathers, were among the victims of the debtors' prison system. The most famous was Robert Morris. His service in the government during the early 1780s was crucial to the victory in the war against Great Britain, but it cost him dearly in his personal financial affairs. After the war, to make up for lost time, he rapidly accumulated large land holdings. Unfortunately for him, the economic cycle turned against him at the same moment that a spike in interest rates resulted in a sharp slowdown in real estate development. Unable to meet his loan payments, he was taken to a dreaded debtors' prison in Philadelphia, broken and penniless in his old age.[459]

Washington brought the public spotlight on the barbaric practice of debtor incarceration when he made a dramatic visit to Robert Morris in prison in 1798. He was accompanied on the visit by Martha's grandson, eighteen-year-old George Washington Parke Custis, whose description of the visit shows how profoundly Washington was affected by the experience: "The old man [Morris] wrung the hand of the chief

[President Washington] in silence, while his tearful eye gave the welcome to such a home. . . The financier of the Revolution, whose talent, whose credit sustained the cause of his country in that country's utmost need! Whatever may have been his misfortunes, say his faults, did not his generous services 'plead like angels, trumpet-tongued, against the deep damnation,' of such a home for his age?"[460]

Later, on September 21, 1799, shortly before his death, Washington took the time to write to Mrs. Morris: "We hope it is unnecessary to repeat in this place how happy we should be to see you and Miss Morris under our roof for so long a stay as you shall find convenient before you return to Philadelphia, for be assured we ever have and still do retain the most affectionate regard for you, Mr. Morris, and the family."[461] The letter was signed by George and Martha Washington.

Morris was not the only prominent citizen to suffer debtors' prison. James Wilson, a justice on the U.S. Supreme Court, was imprisoned in several states successively for bad debt and died of malaria and a stroke. William Duer, a member of Congress, a New York judge, a signer of the Articles of Confederation, and Secretary to the Board of Treasury of the United States, was another prisoner of debt. His financial failure and subsequent imprisonment triggered a veritable panic in New York, and in a cascading effect caused many of his creditors to end up in debtors' jail in turn.[462]

Of all the disincentives built into the colonial system for entrepreneurial activity, none was more dangerous than failure – failure to complete a project, failure to succeed, and failure to pay one's debts. For those who thus failed, the environment was an unforgiving one, and the future bleak indeed. Such draconian consequences to failure were serious deterrents to entrepreneurial risk-taking. Washington showed his disapproval of this system in various ways, giving rise to a movement to reform the system and the appointment by the House of Representatives of a commission to draft a new bankruptcy bill. Congress managed to pass a bankruptcy statute shortly after Washington left office. Even then, it survived for only three years before it was repealed during the Presidency of Thomas Jefferson.[463]

Washington's conviction that a system of providing credit was crucial to the functioning and flourishing of commerce was shared by many, and as more people became comfortable with the concept, credit became elevated to the level of business necessity. The President's businesslike attitude toward debt and credit, whether public or private, found expression even in his Farewell Address to the nation: "As a very important source of strength and security, cherish public credit," he wrote. "One method of preserving it is to use it as sparingly as possible."[464]

The seeds of reform planted during Washington's tenure in the late eighteenth century did in fact bear fruit in the nineteenth. Unfortunately, it also took a bloody Civil War, which resulted in the passage of the Thirteenth Amendment to the U.S. Constitution in 1865, which abolished involuntary servitude, along with slavery. A permanent system of national bankruptcy relief finally occurred in 1898 – a full century after Americans found Washington's visit to a Philadelphia prison an inescapably shameful reminder of that blot on the national character. In the end, it was public revulsion against the unjust severity of criminal punishment for a purely economic misfortune that helped abolish the hated debtors' prison system.[465]

* * *

Entry into Business: Americans naturally followed the example of England in business matters as much as they did in their social interactions. In the English society of the time, the ingredients for the achievement of financial success were as available to members of the aristocracy as they were *in*accessible to commoners. In a republic, on the other hand, equality of all citizens meant that everyone had to have access to wealth. If the route to the accumulation of assets was open only to a select group of people, as had been the case in Britain, then the republican system would also be operating on the same inherently unfair basis.

During the colonial period, entry into business was fraught with a formidable array of obstacles. British policy restricted the colonists from entering into a variety of commercial activities, particularly those that would put them in competition with English businesses. The dire shortage of capital was another major deterrent, as credit and financing were only available from British sources, if at all. Even permitted activities often required prior approval from London. A petition to the Crown to start a project inevitably involved lining up support for it from influential members of the English aristocracy – a complicated and challenging transatlantic process that required extraordinary skill, resources, and patience – as well as support from one or more political leaders in the particular colony involved. This level of corruption was endemic to the business life of the time.

The colonists were not only restricted in their choice of businesses on which they could embark, but also the form in which they would operate. To create a corporation in Britain required an order from the Crown and an Act of Parliament. "In England," declared the Royal Solicitor in his definitive text on eighteenth-century English laws, "the king's consent is absolutely necessary to the creation of any corporation."[466] The king used this prerogative to grant special monopoly powers to favored members of the aristocracy, carving out for them exclusive spheres of activity in such fields as the slave trade, the opium trade, or trade with a particular region of the world, sometimes with his own personal involvement as a shareholder.

Even if a petitioner succeeded in securing a Royal charter, he would still have to reckon with the fact that the Crown was designated by law as "the visitor" of every corporate entity, empowered to participate in its affairs and delve into its operations at any time. "The founder of all corporations in the strictest and original sense is the king alone...," Blackstone asserted. "The king is constituted by law *the visitor* of all civil corporations." [Emphasis in original text.] [467] The Crown thus cast a long and forbidding shadow in the boardroom of every corporation, providing unending opportunities for him to grant patronage and otherwise encroach upon the legitimate functions of a commercial organization. In practice, the grant of a corporate charter – a parchment with frilly chirography to which was affixed the imposing Great Seal of Great Britain – was a rare occurrence. Like the medieval priests who were the sole repositories of occult knowledge, and resisted sharing it, the Crown was at his most parsimonious when it came to opening up his trove of corporate charters to more than an occasional recipient. It was no wonder that the general public viewed these entities with suspicion and distaste, and that respected philosophers such as David Hume and Adam Smith were openly critical of them.

The business community in England could see great value in employing the corporate form for their commercial activities, but its exclusivity, high cost, inordinate delays, and long odds against obtaining the requisite royal approval discouraged its use. If only there were a way of infusing the features of a corporation into a different kind of entity, then a petitioner would be spared the labor of struggling through the bottleneck at the Crown level. Inevitably, this led to the invention of a clever new device called the *unincorporated* joint-stock company, which could be used in the process of creating a public market for the stock of manufacturers, trading companies, and others. As designed, its major advantage was that it obviated the need for a royal charter or Parliamentary approval.[468]

Alas, but the excited proponents of this new commercial tool had been too optimistic. The Crown was not about to remain passive in the face of an obvious attempt at curtailing its control over the business affairs of the country. All too soon, Parliament passed a law forbidding joint-stock companies from operating without a royal charter, putting an end to their proliferation.[469] The new law also had an added advantage from the government's standpoint: It would forestall the development of any competition in the capital markets for the South Sea Company, which at the time was blatantly hyping the price of its own stock with government backing.

In the American colonies, the story was much the same as in Britain itself. Although royal grants made possible the chartering of a few schools, towns, and churches, starting a business in corporate form required a petitioner to work his way through the many layers of British bureaucracy. As we have seen, this was a difficult and time-consuming process for the English nobility; for a mere colonial on the other side of the ocean, it was an immense challenge. It is no wonder, therefore, that by the end of the seventeenth century, the only chartered joint-stock company in North America was the Hudson's Bay Company. During the eighteenth century, the Ohio Company, the enterprise led by George Washington's half-brother Lawrence, also operated under a royal charter.[470]

This state of affairs changed little after the colonies declared their independence. Only a smattering of new charters were issued in the United States before Washington took office in 1789. Most businesses such as flour mills, fisheries, foundries, glass works, whiskey manufacturers, hat and button makers, trading companies, and the like were either sole proprietorships or small partnerships. If a group of colonists desired to start a business, its members sometimes resorted to operating through "articles of association," a contractual entity with most of the indicia of a partnership. George Washington did so when he organized the Dismal Swamp Land Company, as did Alexander Hamilton for a client when he was in law practice.[471] Almost all commercial organizations thus operated in colonial times without the benefits that inhere in the corporate form of organization. It was a real damper on new business formation.

President Washington was familiar with British business practices, some aspects of which clearly did not fit the economic model he had in mind for Americans. To him, a vital ingredient for the creation of an active and bustling economy in the United States was through the removal of bureaucratic obstacles and various forms of payoff in commercial endeavors.

In Washington's first term, Alexander Hamilton as the Treasury Secretary asked Congress to issue a charter for a new corporation named the Bank of the United States. Hamilton may well have expected smooth sailing in Congress for this petition as only ten years earlier, Robert Morris, then the Superintendent of Finance in the Confederation government, had similarly petitioned Congress for a corporate charter for a bank, and it had been routinely granted.

What Hamilton found instead was heated and broad-based opposition to the establishment of a banking corporation by the U.S. Congress. The mere mention of corporate charters was reminiscent of their aristocratic origins in England. A segment of the American populace, remembering why they had rebelled against British royalty, could find no room for corporations in the new republic. These anti-charter advocates emerged in full force in the debates in Congress and in the press.

As congressional debates unfolded, the bitter conflict and public outcry surrounding the organization of the Bank of the United States left an indelible mark on the national landscape. Ironically, as will become clear shortly, the antagonism to the issuance of federal corporate charters became the single most important factor in the skyrocketing expansion of the corporate form of business in America.

Meanwhile, there was a noticeable uptick in the tempo of commercial activity, and much was happening in the country on all other fronts. President Washington, wasting little time on clever rhetoric, political posturing, or finger-pointing, was devoting serious attention to solving the urgent international and domestic problems he had inherited from the Confederation government. He had put together a Cabinet of respected department heads and was closely monitoring their activities. Foreign encroachments still posed grave danger to Americans, and he was using restraint and diplomacy to navigate the minefield of international entanglements, with help from Thomas Jefferson and others. On the domestic front, he was proceeding with high priority to put in place the elements of the entrepreneurial society he visualized for the United States. He was focused on launching the new United States Supreme Court at the apex of the federal judiciary and providing for it the most credible and enduring foundation possible, with help from John Jay and others. Washington's efforts in this area were as much to create a respectable court system as to aid the country's entrepreneurial development. Likewise, the fiscal difficulties of the government were being tackled at multiple levels, with help from Alexander Hamilton and others. The vestigial colonial restrictions on permitted commercial activities were already becoming a distant memory, and with rising public confidence that the nation's affairs were in capable hands, there was the beginning of a stimulating business climate and a pervasive sense of optimism about the economy.

Inspired and emboldened by the new and favorable environment, those desirous of creating new businesses in the country – and thus incurring substantial personal risk – began a quest for an efficient and stable form of commercial organization which would also protect them from the dreaded debtor's prison in the event of failure. Their search brought them to the old and tarnished English corporate charter: Could it be revived and retrofitted for use in the boisterous new entrepreneurial atmosphere in America? Could it be so configured as to be suitable for speedy business formation?

The corporate form, moribund and unpopular in Britain and France, upon examination proved to offer several attractive features. For one, it eased what Hamilton called "the fear of want of success in untried enterprises." In essence, it bestowed upon its owner the incalculable benefit of *keeping him out of jail!* In the event the venture failed (as often happens, particularly to startups), the corporate form insulated the owner from any liability beyond his original investment. It thus served as a bulwark between him and the savage conditions of the debtors' prison. This feature of the corporation, which we simply take for granted today, was indeed a lifesaver in those early days. It had other advantages as well. It allowed for a large and efficient scale of operation; it was a boon for financing capital-intensive projects; it provided for perpetual existence, ensuring continuity of management; and it could lead to the development of stock and bond markets as it had in Europe.

Despite these attributes, the corporate form did not appear to have a promising future in the United States. Its opponents continued to view it as a tool of the aristocracy and a source of special privilege for the favored few, as had been the case in Europe. Unmindful of the dramat ic societal and commercial differences between the United States and European countries, the American charter opponents perceived corporations as toxic to society – just another form of corruption. Even the capacity of a corporation to permit an expanded scale of business operation was viewed negatively by its opponents, who feared it would lead to the growth of large factories and the exploitation of workers. They also saw the creation of securities markets as "stock jobbing," and therefore evil. Perhaps the feature that most inflamed the anti-charter passions was the perpetual life of corporations. Americans had never been fond of the British laws of descent, which were designed to give members of the aristocracy the power to keep wealth in multigenerational hands by providing for the exclusive right of inheritance of the eldest son (primogeniture) or limiting inheritance to a specific line of heirs (entail). The American opponents of corporations viewed the perpetual existence of these entities as similarly contributing to the concentration of wealth in a small group of shareholders.[472]

The Anglo-French rivalry that appeared to be a perpetual feature of the eighteenth- century European geopolitical landscape had its respective advocates in the Washington administration, with contrasting opinions on corporate charters. Thomas Jefferson, a confirmed Francophile, viewed corporations as emblematic of the corruption inherited from the British system, and their possible proliferation as most unfortunate for the United States.[473] On the other hand, Alexander Hamilton, an admirer of British culture, believed that corporations were useful commercial devices.

With various and scattered business groups evaluating the corporate form, a consensus inevitably emerged that this type of organization could be well adapted to the American commercial environment, and that it should be resuscitated from the limbo to which it had been relegated in Britain. To counter the strong opposition of the anti-charter group, however, the proponents needed equally strong political support. With no organized backing, their prospects were not too bright.

It so happened that the state governments, inspired by an energetic executive branch at the federal level, were actively seeking opportunities on which *they* could capitalize. The outcry against federal corporate charters in the debate over the organization of the Bank of the United States seemed to create a void tailor-made for the states to fill. If the issuance of such licenses by the federal government was anathema to many Americans, then the public should welcome the alternative of the *states* taking on that responsibility. True to their role as "laboratories of democracy" in the federal system (as later described by Supreme Court Justice Louis Brandeis), the states did not take long to recognize the special opportunity presented to them. They could bring in banks, insurance companies, manufacturing plants, and other new businesses into their own backyards. These entities would create jobs, enable public financing of many infrastructure projects such as roads, canals, turnpikes, etc., and otherwise enhance the local and regional economic development efforts. To achieve these worthy goals, the state governments would obviously need to encourage the process through the passage of favorable legislation. A state could even subscribe to the stock of such entities or grant other reasonable privileges to entice them to locate there. It was an exciting scenario, and several of the states were prepared to step into the breach with unabashed zeal.

The charter proponents thus found the strong political support they sought in a most unexpected quarter: the state governments. It was a natural and potent alliance, and in time various state legislatures began setting up the requisite machinery for the granting of these licenses. They passed enabling legislation and established fairly streamlined processes for its administration. These developments led to a revival of the corporate form and the expansion of its reach in commercial matters. The ease with which any qualified person wishing to start a business in America could secure a state license resulted in the untrammeled proliferation of corporations. They thus became a normal part of the business landscape in the country, as manufacturers began turning out woolen cloths, foundries produced iron forges, others made hats and buttons, nails, and even ships. Printing and publishing became staple operations in most of the major cities. Then came turnpikes, canals, gun manufacturing, chocolate making, even a company to clear and deepen river channels, and a farming corporation. Among these businesses, the ones that attracted the most capital to a state were banks, insurance companies, canals, bridges, and turnpike operations.[474] (Later, the railroads became the corporations with the largest market capitalization.)

Not all states followed the same pattern, however. New York, home today to hundreds of thousands of corporations, was surprisingly reluctant to accommodate them in the eighteenth century. By statute, it required a two-thirds vote of both houses of the legislature to grant or renew a petition for a corporate charter! Other states, mindful that the excitement generated by a new issue of stock could sometimes drive the price to unsustainable heights (as had happened in 1791 in the IPO of the Bank of the United States, also that of the Schuylkill and Susquehanna Navigation Company), placed limits on the number of shares any one buyer could acquire in the initial offering of a corporation. In the same vein, some placed limits on voting rights to keep any one individual or group from gaining control of a company.[475] In time, however, one vote per share became the norm.

As corporations held annual meetings for the election of directors, the public became aware that the power and authority of the directors were carefully circumscribed both by statute, and by the articles of incorporation and bylaws. It also became clear that the corporate charter in America was the antithesis of its use in Europe, and that corporations were democratic institutions of uncommon economic benefit for the common man or woman. In this way, the proliferation of corporations and their general availability stripped them of their aristocratic and privileged aura, and contributed greatly to the flourishing of the entrepreneurial economy.

What Americans had done, in effect, was to transform a European device for exclusive aristocratic profit into an unparalleled opportunity for wealth creation for the masses and an instrument of increased productivity and accelerated commercial development. Just as the *un*availability of corporate charters had served to discourage innovation and risk-taking in business, so did their *availability* serve as a great incentive to embark on the entrepreneurial path for many who would otherwise have been reluctant to risk starting an enterprise. With the formation of a rudimentary public market for stocks and bonds, even small investors could participate in business opportunities previously out of reach for them. Little wonder then that the corporate charter became a popular tool for the economic growth of the entire nation. Thus, despite formidable initial opposition, corporations flourished, and starting businesses suddenly became preposterously easy in America. By the end of the decade of the 1790s, the volume of business formations in corporate form in America soared to nearly three hundred. Interestingly, James Madison, the leading anti-charter activist in Congress, had no qualms about establishing corporations at the federal level when he later became President. Having obviously undergone a change of heart on the issue, he signed the charter for the Second Bank of the United States in 1816.[476]

One can imagine the reaction of the English and French at finding their much-maligned business device dusted off, revived, and made into a new and exciting tool of commercial development. Amazed at the economic renaissance happening in America, they could only look upon the innovative use of the corporate device for business purposes regardless of class and caste, and wonder at the cleverness of the brash and venturesome Americans![477]

* * *

Freedom of the Press: Long before Washington became President, his life was a phantasmagoria of encounters and interactions with individuals all across the land and from all walks of life. He was a passionate advocate of better communication though better roads, better mail service, better and cheaper delivery of newspapers and magazines, and better domestic and international trade. He recognized instinctively that the more cross-cultural exchanges among people, the greater the opportunity for innovation, experimentation, and cross-pollination of ideas. Some crowns of Europe were reputed to believe that it was not good for the common people to be too well informed. Washington was a fervent believer in the opposite view. He was, in fact, an impassioned advocate of a strong and vibrant press corps. He believed that the democratic process required the public to receive full information about the debates on pending bills in Congress. His views, however, did not have the full support of Congress as some members feared the establishment of "a court press and court gazette," which could be used to manipulate popular opinion and to consolidate political power. Despite such opposition, Washington remained a strong advocate for better communication in the country through newspapers and other publications, and his Presidency saw robust growth for the American press. Newspapers in fact became the cheapest and most widely available sources of information in the country.[478]

The press was also Washington's potent tool in his campaign against corrupt practices by government officials and politicians. He had an unshakable conviction that freedom of the press was the hallmark of the democratic process and vital for achieving transparency in government. As the first President of the United States, he was determined to establish an enduring precedent for that freedom as a vital and irreplaceable element of American culture. He never deviated from that resolve, even when faced with great pressure to rein in journalists who were seen as abusing their privilege.

If Washington appreciated the press, the feeling was fully reciprocated for years. Through the decade of the 1780s, his press coverage was universally warm and laudatory. He was mindful, however, of the fleeting nature of such sentiments, and concerned that there might come a time when the public and the press would turn on him. True to his prediction, by the time he was into his second term, a noticeable chill had permeated that relationship. Words like "apostate" and "imposter" began to find their way into press accounts describing Washington. Then, as his Presidency neared its end, the tone became even more strident. He was accused of betraying his own troops, of being a hypocrite and a traitor to republican ideals.[479]

The greatest underlying cause of these increasingly vituperative attacks was the emergence of partisan politics and party-affiliated newspapers, stemming from the conflict between the Federalists led by Hamilton and the Anti-Federalists led by Jefferson.

By 1791, Jefferson was prepared to take his rivalry with Hamilton to another level. While still a part of the administration, he hired an acquaintance of James Madison named Philip Freneau as a clerk in the State Department with the sole function of creating and editing an opposition newspaper. At thirty-nine, Freneau had already had a series of short-term careers as a divinity student, a school teacher, a poet, a privateer in the West Indies, a sergeant in the New Jersey militia, a prisoner of the British, and brief stints with five successive newspapers. In October 1791 he left New York for Philadelphia to work for the Secretary of State. The newspaper he founded while serving in that post was called the *National Gazette*. It became, under Freneau's editorial guidance, a harsh critic of all supporters of the Constitution – Alexander Hamilton, the administration, and even the President himself.[480]

The first issue of the *National Gazette* appeared on October 31, 1791, and soon the attacks against the administration began in earnest. In progressively bolder articles, Freneau questioned Vice President John Adams's moral fitness to hold public office and accused Alexander Hamilton and others of "plundering" the resources of the country, of colluding with foreign speculators, and of promoting a system of "perpetual taxation." Freneau ridiculed the plan to design the coins of the United States bearing Washington's image, and took the President himself to task for losing his republican perspective and currying the "favours of monarchial mystery" and "the buzz of the aristocratic few."[481]

Other newspapers began to defend the administration. One such newspaper was the *Gazette of the United States*, edited by John Fenno, a former teacher and aide to Revolutionary War general Artemas Ward.

Alexander Hamilton, not known for backing down from a fight, was quick to pick up the gauntlet laid down by the *National Gazette* and began responding forcefully with articles of his own, written under a pseudonym in the *Gazette of the United States*. It thus became a battle of the two *Gazettes*, of Freneau vs. Fenno. In reality, of course, it was Jefferson vs. Hamilton. Convinced that the President favored his Treasury Secretary over his Secretary of State, Jefferson permitted his resentments to lead him, through Freneau and his newspaper, to extend his hostility to Washington himself.

As the journalistic tones grew increasingly partisan and shrill, Washington felt saddened that "the seeds of discontent, distrust, and irritations which are so plentifully sown" would tear the nation asunder and damage the standing and prestige of the United States in the international arena. And when the Neutrality Proclamation, Whiskey Rebellion, Jay's Treaty and other serious and thorny issues took center stage in the public mind and raised national tensions, the pressure on the President from hostile newspapers spiked in intensity, railing against his every decision and even his personal integrity.[482]

Washington was aware that politics was played most deviously by some, but he deplored such tortuous plots and machinations. He would hope that open dialogue between opposing views would lead to cleaner politics and greater harmony at the highest levels of government. His response to the increasingly bitter thrusts and parries of the two Gazettes, therefore, was to attempt to effect a truce between Hamilton and Jefferson, the two men at the center of the literary storm. He regretted the lost opportunities for productive thinking and wished that the feuding parties would find more useful vehicles for their energies. "How unfortunate," he wrote to Jefferson in August of 1792, "that, while we are encompassed on all sides with avowed enemies and insidious friends, internal dissensions should be harrowing and tearing our vitals."[483]

Although he considered the pages of the *National Gazette* to be a series of "outrages on common decency," Washington counseled "charity in deciding on the opinions and actions of others." It was his earnest wish, he wrote, "that instead of wounding suspicions, and irritable charges, there may be liberal allowances, mutual forbearances, and temporizing yieldings on all sides."[484]

Alas, Washington's efforts were in vain, and the tattered relationship between Hamilton and Jefferson was beyond repair.

Then, in 1792 Hamilton publicly exposed the covert arrangement between Jefferson and Freneau, and with it, Jefferson's sponsorship of the attacks upon Washington. "In common life it is thought ungrateful," Hamilton wrote, "for a man to bite the hand that puts bread into his mouth; but if the man is hired to do it, the case is altered."[485] Once this became known, Jefferson pulled the plug on *The National Gazette*, resigned as the Secretary of State, and departed from the administration in 1793. Freneau had lost his patron, his government sinecure, and funding for his newspaper, which ceased publication and went out of business. The journalistic cudgel was then passed on to Benjamin Franklin Bache, editor of the *Aurora.*

Bache was the grandson of Benjamin Franklin, but Bache's acerbic style bore little resemblance to the subtle and passionate wit of his high-minded grandfather, the lovable best-selling author and publisher. Franklin, who died in 1790, would have been aghast had he lived to see the strident tone of his grandson's approach to journalism. By October, the *Aurora* had declared open season on Washington, claiming the President had "dark schemes of ambition," was politically degenerate, and had an "insipid uniformity of mind." Once begun, the attacks quickly increased in volume and pitch. "If ever a nation was deceived by a man," he wrote, "the American nation has been deceived by Washington." The *Aurora* accused him of being "the source of all the misfortunes of our country." An equal-opportunity slanderer, Bache also took aim at John Adams, whom Bache called "a ruffian deserving of the curses of mankind."[486]

The *Aurora* reserved some of its most incendiary language for the moment of Washington's retirement. As the former President prepared to make his final departure from the capital in Philadelphia, Bache's paper declared, "If ever there was a period of rejoicing, this is the moment." At the same time, the *Aurora* revived old charges of "corruption" and "political inequity," and accused Washington of complicity in both.[487] Despite Washington's decision not to respond to such attacks, the *Aurora* could not escape the wrath of other citizens. A short time after the accusations appeared, a group of people ransacked the headquarters of the *Aurora* and destroyed much of the printing equipment. Although Bache's sense of dramatic timing and scurrilous intent were extraordinary, the *Aurora* reflected the increasingly partisan tone of the press at the time.

In spite of the vituperative nature of these attacks, Washington rarely flinched in public at his treatment by the press. He believed that if "the general tenor" of his executive conduct "would not stand the test of investigation, a newspaper vindication would be of little avail." Even in private, he feigned calm indifference to the assaults on his reputation and honor. "However much they might continue their outrages on common decency," Washington wrote Henry Lee, "I have a consolation within . . . that neither ambitious nor interested motives have influenced my conduct. The arrows of malevolence, therefore, however barbed and well pointed, never can reach the most vulnerable part of me." His protestation to the contrary notwithstanding, he could not entirely shield himself from the wounds to his pride and worried that Bache's unfair attacks would eventually corrode his reputation, "for drops of water will impress (in time) the hardest marble."[488]

When newspapers adored Washington and promoted his policies, he staunchly supported the freedom of the press. When they castigated him, fabricated inflammatory stories about him, and relentlessly engaged in personal attacks on his character, Washington remained steadfast in his protection of that freedom, certain that the value of a free press far outweighed its abuses. Despite his fears that the unremitting partisan sniping could lead to political discord and civil discontent, he never attempted to rein in or muzzle any member of the press, nor resort to such dubious devices as government-funded news organizations.[489]

A different attitude prevailed in the years immediately after Washington left office. During the Presidency of John Adams, Congress passed and the President signed into law the Alien and Sedition Acts, a series of statutes designed to prevent aliens and American citizens from undermining the stability of the federal government.

The Sedition Act made it a high misdemeanor to "unlawfully combine or conspire together, with intent to oppose any measure or measures of the government of the United States." The act criminalized the publication of "false, scandalous, and malicious writing" about the government or its officers, and made it a crime to "resist, oppose, or defeat any ...

law or act; or to aid, encourage or abet any hostile designs of any foreign nation against the United States, their people or government."[490] Proving "the truth of the matter contained in the [libelous] publication," was, however, a complete defense.

While the statute was in effect, its enforcement resulted in the arrest and conviction of ten editors, including several who were staunch friends and supporters of Thomas Jefferson. Those included William Duane, editor of the *Aurora,* and Matthew Lyon, a Representative from Vermont and a journalist. Another, Thomas Cooper, a Pennsylvania politician, was indicted and convicted for a statement impugning President Adams's honor and political competence. He was fined $400 and sentenced to six months' imprisonment. President Adams offered to pardon him, but Cooper insisted that he would not accept a Presidential pardon unless it were accompanied by a public apology from Adams. The President refused, and Cooper served out his prison term. Congress nevertheless refunded Cooper's fine.[491]

Benjamin Franklin Bache, whose work was the primary inducement for the enactment of the Sedition Act, was arrested for libel but died before he could be brought to trial. Of course, actual convictions under the Act did not reflect the full effect of the legislation; the threat of prosecution doubtless exerted a chilling effect on some journalists who were never arrested or indicted. The Sedition Act expired on March 3, 1801, the last full day of the Adams Presidency.[492]

In the United States, freedom of the press is now firmly entrenched in the American culture. It is guaranteed by the First Amendment to the U.S. Constitution and has been consistently protected by the U.S. Supreme Court from incremental erosion. President Washington's restraint in the face of strong provocation legitimized the First Amendment's guarantee of that freedom, and his forbearance set the foundation for that guarantee to become more than mere words on paper.

Unfortunately, much of the rest of the world has not shared in the same historical development. Sadly, even in the twenty-first century, episodes of intimidation and imprisonment of journalists are everyday occurrences in various countries. In the five years ending in 2014, for example, 352 journalists were killed, 988 imprisoned, 4,187 arrested, and 9,332 beaten or physically threatened. In many countries, those in power use the media in much the same way as they use the judiciary – as tools for the enforcement of the government's will. In a worldwide index assessing the state of media freedom, fully two-thirds of the countries fall below the minimum acceptable level. The reality is that media freedom is one of the first to be sacrificed by authoritarian leaders, and a society pays a heavy price for the derogation or loss of this fundamental liberty.[493]

* * *

Copyrights and Patents: Imagine a society without intellectual property laws. An author would have no protection against piracy, nor an inventor against infringement. A writer might work for years on a book, and if it proved popular upon publication, there would be nothing to keep others from simply reprinting it without paying the author any royalties and without facing any legal consequences.[494] Likewise, if there were no patent system in place, there would be less incentive to invent, and the few innovators who still functioned would be tempted to keep their inventions secret. That was pretty much the state of affairs in the United States until George Washington assumed the Presidency.

These concerns about the lack of copyright and patent protection resonated deeply with George Washington. He recognized that the economy of the United States suffered without the crucial incentive to innovate that recognition of intellectual property provided. He knew that the entrepreneurial economy he envisioned for the United States could only flourish if innovation were an active ingredient in the economic and marketing mix.

James Madison, similarly concerned, lamented that there was a "want of concert" about intellectual property.[495] In September 1787, the Constitutional Convention, chaired by George Washington, laid the groundwork for uniform national copyright and patent protection by granting Congress the power to "promote the progress of science and useful arts."

The absence of debate during the Constitutional Convention, however, did not signify unanimity of opinion on intellectual property protection afterwards. It became the subject of debate within some of the states during the ratification process of the Constitution, the most notable dissent coming from Thomas Jefferson. Not a delegate at the Convention, he let his opinion be known from Paris. "The benefit even of limited monopolies," Jefferson wrote James Madison on July 31, 1788, "is too doubtful to be opposed to that of their general suppression."[496]

Washington was of a different view. He had always taken a personal interest in technology. Historian Timothy Ferris describes an occasion when George Washington and Thomas Paine spent a night on a creek in New Jersey "lighting cartridge paper at the water's surface to determine whose theory was correct about the source of swamp gas." On his land, Washington often experimented with new methods of composting and treading out wheat, and successfully innovated in other aspects of agriculture. Aside from his own inventions, he showed a keen interest in such developments by others. He was, for example, an early purchaser of the rights to a revolutionary type of grist mill. Even in the twilight of his life, when he heard about a new threshing machine in 1797, he immediately got in touch with the inventor, Thomas Coleman Martin, to find out how his machine worked. "I am," he wrote to Martin, "perfectly willing to allow the patent fee if it exists." By such means, he had as thorough a grasp of contemporary technology applicable to his private sector involvements as anyone in America.[497]

Washington's grasp of the importance of new technology – and patent rights as an inducement to innovation – was prescient. So when Congress adjourned its first session without taking up an intellectual property bill as a priority agenda, the President decided to nudge the legislators into action. In his first State of the Union Address on January 8, 1790, he drove the point home that the country had an imperative need to encourage the creation of new discoveries through the patent system. "I cannot forbear," he wrote to the legislators, "intimating to you the expediency of giving effectual encouragement as well to the introduction of new and useful inventions from abroad, as to the exertions of skill and genius in producing them at home." The result was an immediate scramble in Congress to act on the President's admonition. In its response, the Senate affirmed on January 11 that "literature and science are essential to the preservation of a free Constitution," and the House followed suit on January 12, saying "We concur with you in the sentiment…that science and literature will contribute to the security of a free government; in the progress of our deliberations, we shall not lose sight of objects so worthy of our regard."[498]

Congress then proceeded at an astonishing pace to fulfil Washington's recommendation. On January 25 the House appointed a committee which within three days produced a bill to "Promote the Progress of the Useful Arts." It was introduced to the House on February 16, 1790, and with some amendments was passed and went into effect with the President's signature on April 10, 1790. From a standing start, Congress had produced a major piece of legislation in only three months.[499]

Washington's grasp of the importance of new technology and, by extension, patent rights as an inducement to innovation was prescient. The legislative wheels were quickly set in motion and the requisite statute enacted.[500] Later, in February of 1793, Congress passed a revised patent act, eliminating the requirement that Cabinet members evaluate patent applications. The new statute streamlined the application process, and placed the responsibility for patent evaluation on private citizens and on the court system.[501]

The existence of the early federal patent system has been called the secret of the great success of the United States – one of the provisions that "most influenced the destinies of the American people." Twenty-first-century economists now recognize that "inventive activity is primarily responsible for the improvements in technology that contribute to sustained increases in per capita income." The biggest factor contributing to the proliferation of inventions in America was the entrepreneurial environment fostered by Washington during his two terms in office. It provided the most favorable condition for innovation and the sustained economic growth that followed in the nineteenth century. In this connection, recent scholarly research on inventive activity points to an interesting historical conclusion, namely, that once a system of patent protection is available in a country, the crucial factors for the stimulation of inventions are the existence of an active commercial market on the one hand, and the expansion of waterways on the other.[502]

Ironically, despite all the brouhaha surrounding the advisability of establishing a patent system, there were in fact three renowned inventors who never applied for patent protection. Their names should not come as a surprise. They were Benjamin Franklin, Thomas Jefferson, and George Washington, each of whom had multiple inventions to his name.[503]

Chapter Ten

A CLEVER LEGISLATIVE MANEUVER

The principle of spending money to be paid by posterity under the name of funding is but swindling futurity on a large scale.
Thomas Jefferson

On September 8, 1789, Congress voted to build the permanent capital of the United States on the banks of the Susquehanna River in Pennsylvania. This action was supposed to put an end to the heated national debate about the location of the capital that had been going on for more than a decade, but it did not even come close. In fact, the intense competition among cities to be selected continued unabated despite the vote. Various groups from around the country, convinced of the merits of their region, would not let a mere congressional resolution stand in their way. They continued to beat the drums for the unique advantages of *their* city, whether of harbors, navigable rivers, thriving commercial hubs, networks of roads, educational institutions, or a long history.

Every state participated in this contest. In all, thirty cities were in contention including Annapolis, Baltimore, Boston, Charleston, Havre de Grace, Lancaster, New York, Philadelphia, Princeton, Trenton, Wright's Ferry, and others. They all lobbied hard for the prize, eager to benefit from the real estate and construction boom that would surely follow Congress and the President to their new home. They also anticipated that the city chosen for the honor would see skyrocketing land values, a thriving business environment, super-charged development of roads, bridges, and residential and commercial properties, and a spike in local population. The annual economic value of the capital to a region, once estimated at $100,000, was continually being upgraded until Thomas Jefferson put the figure at $1 million, an astronomical sum at the time.[504] With monuments designed by the nation's best sculptors thrown into the mix, as well as great expanses of parkland and lawns in the capital city, there was indeed much to capture the imagination of the eighteenth-century public, politicians, and municipal authorities.

The advocates for the various locations played a no-holds-barred game, and their representatives in Congress pulled out all stops in their political maneuvers and plots. The press joined in the fray by plastering their newspapers with florid editorials praising the virtues of their favorite cities above all others. In Congress new alliances were being formed daily, only to fall apart before the day was out, causing the site selection to result in the proposal and subsequent rejection of sixteen different sites. One newspaper suggested only half facetiously that Pierre L'Enfant design a mobile capital on wheels![505]

By the spring of 1790, the long list of contenders had been substantially whittled down. To all appearances, this was now a two-way race between New York and Philadelphia or another site in Pennsylvania. As between these rivals, however, there was no clear winner on the merits. New Yorkers argued that their city, already host to the executive and legislative branches of the federal government, could be seamlessly transformed into the permanent capital of the United States, making it the ideal site for the purpose. Besides, they pointed out, New York was a major port, a cosmopolitan center, and a bustling hub of finance, trade, and agriculture, while unceasing new construction activity was giving it a fresh and elegant look that attracted visitors from near and far.[506] As for Pennsylvania, two different sites were drawing support from that state's delegation in Congress. One was a location on the banks of the Susquehanna River, which had been the focus of the resolution of September 8. The other was German Town, a Philadelphia suburb. With a population of over 42,000, Philadelphia was the largest city in the country. Founded in 1682, it had deep roots in the nation's early struggle for liberty, having hosted the Founders for the signing of the Declaration of Independence and later the Framers for the Constitutional Convention. The Liberty Bell, which had served as a potent symbol of America's commitment to freedom, was housed there. Philadelphia was also a flourishing hub of business activity, a major port, and a center for transatlantic trade. It was, therefore, a strong contender in the race.

There were drawbacks to both sites. New Yorkers were proud of their flourishing city, but what the city lacked was an energetic advocate for their cause. Alexander Hamilton, who would have been expected to lead the charge, was preoccupied with the effort to get his fiscal program through Congress and was working behind the scenes in a futile effort to buy votes for his legislative package in return for throwing his weight behind the choice of a Pennsylvania site. Besides, James Madison was openly expressing his opposition to New York, calling it a city of grasping financial speculators whose lust for money would inevitably corrupt national politics and imperil America's destiny as an agrarian and republican paradise. Like Madison, Jefferson aspired to build the federal district as far as possible from the taint of urban industrialism.[507]

To say Philadelphia was not a favorite site for Southerners would be a gross understatement. "I would as soon pitch my tent beneath a tree in which was a hornet's nest," declared South Carolina Congressman Aedanus Burke, "as I would vote for placing the government in a settlement of Quakers." Support for Philadelphia was not unanimous even among its own congressional delegation. Senator William Maclay, a dour and cynical man who looked at the world through a haze of suspicion and dread, was dead set against the choice of Philadelphia. Being from Harrisburg, he preferred a site on the Susquehanna River. Besides, with the issue of slavery evoking strong passions in the nation, the Southern delegation in Congress was committed to opposing any attempt at locating the capital north of the Mason-Dixon Line, and hinted at secession and breakup of the Union if their wishes were disregarded.

With competing sites jockeying for support, bargaining and behind-the-scenes negotiations were in full swing in Congress. Determined to push his funding program through Congress, Hamilton began lobbying key Pennsylvania lawmakers intent on making a compact for their favorite sites. He first approached Senator Maclay with the proposition that, in return for Maclay securing votes from the Pennsylvania delegation in favor of Assumption (of states' debts by the federal government), Hamilton would throw his support behind the choice of the Susquehanna site as the capital. Maclay's reaction was explosive. He was aghast by what he viewed as a blatant attempt at subverting the democratic process through buying votes, and was shocked that Hamilton would stoop to such underhanded shenanigans. Maclay turned Hamilton's proposition down flat.

Undeterred, Hamilton sent two emissaries on June 11, 1790, to propose a clandestine meeting with Robert Morris, Pennsylvania's other Senator. Morris, intrigued, responded that he would be taking a walk the following morning along the Battery, an open-air embankment nestled on the tip of Lower Manhattan. Should Hamilton happen by chance to be there at the same time, the two could work out any pending matters between them.[508]

At sunrise the next morning, Morris arrived at the Battery wearing a top hat and carrying a walking stick, looking very much like a successful urbanite taking a morning constitutional. A dapper and well-groomed Hamilton arrived shortly afterwards. As the two men strolled along the embankment, Hamilton laid down the terms of the deal he proposed. If Morris could deliver one vote for the Treasury's funding plan in the Senate and five in the House, Hamilton would arrange for the New York delegation to support a permanent capital on the Delaware River or at German Town. Openly skeptical that Hamilton could deliver on his part of the proposal, Morris responded that he would be satisfied if Hamilton could garner support for the choice of Philadelphia as the *interim* capital. Hamilton confidently agreed, and the two men parted ways.[509]

Morris was quickly able to secure the concurrence of the Pennsylvania delegation to the deal he had made with Hamilton, except for the recalcitrant Maclay's vote, but managed to persuade George Read, the

Senator from Delaware, to go along with the plan.[510] Much to Hamilton's dismay, however, he soon learned after a few days of vigorous lobbying in Congress that he would be unable to round up the votes to fulfill his part of the bargain. He so informed Morris, and their deal was off, throwing the choice of the capital up in the air again amid much confusion and frustration by the lawmakers.[511]

"Negotiations, cabals, meetings, plots and counterplots have prevailed for months past without yet ripening to any decision," complained Representative William L. Smith of South Carolina.[512] The situation became murkier still when Baltimore began a last-minute push to be selected as the capital, resulting in a mad scramble to reconstitute old alliances and coalitions along new lines. The admission of Rhode Island into the Union and the subsequent arrival of its congressional delegation on the scene further muddled the diverse array of factions in Congress looking for potential partners.[513]

* * *

While the legislators were struggling with the capital city dilemma, a search of a different sort was causing yet another political firestorm: The solution to the public debt.

War is expensive, and the American Revolution was no exception. From the time the legendary shots were fired at Lexington and Concord until the signing of a peace treaty eight years later, the rebellious young nation wrestled with the shockingly high cost of maintaining an army engaged in fighting the most formidable military force in the world. To make matters worse, the Continental Congress had neither the authority nor the structural capability to tax the income of its citizens, impose tariffs on imports, or place excise taxes on manufactured products. All too often during the war, Washington had to pass the arm on his friend Robert Morris to get emergency funds. Legend has it that on one occasion, Morris, in desperation, visited a Quaker who was known to have buried a chest of currency in his backyard. "Morris literally dug the cash and sent Washington two parcels of hard money."

No obstacle, however, stood in the way of Congress resorting to a method used countless times by succeeding governments, namely, turning on the printing presses. Throughout the long conflict, Congress not only issued paper money but also relied on – and almost exhausted – every other option available to it to raise the necessary funds. It applied for loans from foreign countries, borrowed from its own citizens, and even, when all else failed, requisitioned supplies from the states in hopes that grain, horses, and foodstuffs might magically appear where demands for cash had yielded little. In the end, independence from Great Britain would wind up costing America $165 million. Roughly a third of this amount was borrowed from domestic and foreign creditors (excluding states' obligations), so that after passing through the crucible of war and forging a new government, Americans confronted a debt burden of about $52 million. How exactly could this sum ever be repaid? That was the challenge that motivated many of Washington's initiatives upon taking office as the nation's first chief executive.[514]

The printing of paper money to finance the Revolution started as early as 1775. Called "Continentals," these dollars were equated by Congress with Spanish milled dollars. The first print run in June of that year was for $2 million, quickly followed by another million a month later. By year's end, the total was $6 million. The presses were halted for good in 1780 after printing over $241 million.[515] The Continental dollar depreciated steadily beginning in 1776, with a sharp decline occurring immediately after the British capture of New York. The situation only worsened as the war dragged on. In many places, farmers and merchants selling their goods at market stopped accepting the Continental as payment, preferring to sell at very low prices for hard currency rather than for high prices in worthless paper dollars. Foreign suppliers were equally reluctant to accept the Continental in payment for goods. The existence of hyperinflation in the country was by then unmistakable. Currency depreciation was at such an alarming rate that Washington lamented to John Jay in April 1779 that "a wagon load of money will scarcely purchase a wagon load of provisions." The full emission of $241 million put in circulation lost nearly all of its value, removing a massive amount of wealth from the assets of Americans.[516]

The Continental Congress also turned to European governments for help in financing the war, either in the form of loans or immediate cash assistance. France was quick to respond. Unwilling to incur the wrath of Britain by openly providing financial aid to its rebellious colonies, however, France secretly arranged for private French citizens to enter into contracts to purchase tobacco from America for future delivery, with the payment of two million livres ($400,000) to be made in advance. Once France signed a treaty of alliance with United States in 1778, the secrecy was no longer necessary. From that point on and extending into 1783, primarily through the unceasing and prodigious efforts of Benjamin Franklin, France spared no effort to help the new nation. It then made a series of subsidies and loans to the U. S., openly provided military assistance, and engaged in joint operations against British forces. France's King Louis XVI showed such deep commitment to the American cause that when the Dutch proved unwilling to trust the creditworthiness of the U.S. government, he stepped forward and borrowed the money from the Dutch personally, turning the proceeds over to the United States.[517]

After France persuaded the Spanish king to enter into the war on the side of the United States, Congress sought to borrow $5 million from that government as well, but the effort was not well received in Madrid. After a great deal of foot-dragging, Spain eventually came up with a mere $174,000 in loans.[518]

The Dutch reluctance to extend credit to the U. S. evaporated once the British forces were defeated at Yorktown. John Adams, the U.S. representative in Amsterdam, suddenly found better reception for his loan applications than he ever had before. Between 1782 and 1784, a private syndicate composed of Dutch investors lent the American government a total of seven million guilders ($2.8 million).[519]

Congress also borrowed from its own citizens. In every state, a Continental loan office managed by a state commissioner sold certificates in denominations from $300 -to $1,000, bearing 4% interest. Rather than operating as circulating currency, these "loan office certificates" had the characteristics of government bonds and were intended to serve as investment-grade instruments with a specified annual yield. Most of these certificates were bought by northern buyers, with holders in only three states (Pennsylvania, Connecticut, and Massachusetts) accounting for two-thirds of all purchases. Initially, the maturity of the certificates was set at three years, but with no means of redeeming them, Congress raised the interest rate to 6%.[520]

After the war, the cash-strapped Continental Congress paid off the arrearages in salaries and wages of the troops and debts to wartime suppliers with loan office certificates and other unsecured paper. Comparable to government bonds, these instruments soon found their way into the trading markets. The failure of Congress to pay interest in specie on these instruments caused them to depreciate rapidly in value. The only purchasers, therefore, were the speculators who hoped that someday Congress would redeem the paper at par. Eventually, with the Continentals becoming nearly worthless, the government began using these certificates as a fallback medium of exchange.[521]

At war's end, the country was in fiscal chaos. Facing a catastrophic collapse of its credit, the Continental Congress appointed Robert Morris, a respected financier, as the Superintendent of Finance. He set out to get the books of the government in order, to determine exactly how much it owed and to whom. Morris then prepared detailed reports, outlining for the Continental Congress the steps necessary to restore solvency and public confidence.[522]

Morris also took time to talk over these issues with George Washington, who was still Commander of the Continental Army after Yorktown. During the war, the two had held frequent discussions about the economic and fiscal problems of the country. So, when he was made Superintendent of Finance, Morris provided the general with drafts of his reports to Congress to satisfy himself that he and Washington saw eye-to-eye on the government's financial problems and the prescribed remedies.[523]

Morris wrote Congress that it was vital that all domestic and foreign debts be discharged or funded at their full face value. It was imperative that Congress charter a national bank to revive and enhance both public and private credit.[524] To raise immediate revenue, Morris recommended several measures, including the imposition of a 5% duty on imports and the setting-up of machinery for the collection of taxes in each state. Morris also considered it important that Congress authorize the establishment of a single national currency and the organization of a mint.

Morris was only able to secure congressional authorization for a few of these steps. The effectiveness of this program depended upon securing a stable source of revenue for the country. Despite the emergency nature of the problems, however, Congress was unable to pass any tax measures. Morris's prodigious efforts were stymied by a strife-ridden Continental Congress.[525]

By the time 1789 rolled around, the large debt burden incurred in wartime was still a formidable challenge for the new government. President Washington saw it as his mission to restore fiscal order and inaugurate a new era of responsibility, integrity, and enterprise.[526] He therefore offered the post of Secretary of the Treasury to Robert Morris. Being unwilling to serve himself, Morris recommended for the post the bright young man he had mentored when Superintendent of Finance, none other than Alexander Hamilton.

Washington appointed Hamilton as Secretary of the Treasury on September 11, 1789.

Despite Congress's new taxing authority, government coffers were empty. Incredibly, Hamilton's first act in office was to borrow money – to meet payroll![527] The Treasury's estimate of the foreign debts of the government, primarily to France and Holland, totaled about $12 million. Revolutionary War debts of the states, to be assumed by the government, amounted to about $25 million, a slight overestimate. Domestic debts of the national government were about $27 million, with accumulated interest of $13 million bringing the total to $40 million. The sum of all these figures came to about $77 million, to be discharged or funded at full face value by the federal government. In 1790, this figure represented about almost forty percent of the young nation's Gross National Product.[528]

The Treasury's "Report on Public Credit" laid out in detail the administration's plan for restoring the financial credibility of the federal government. It proposed to Congress the adoption of a long-term funding system that would ensure the payment of interest on all existing debt, thus restoring the credit of the United States. It provided for a three-pronged approach to establishing a fiscal framework for the new nation: Foreign debts were to be repaid promptly in accordance with the terms of the original loan agreements, and the timetable and amounts specified.[529]

Domestic debts were not to be paid off and discharged but to be restructured and their overall cost to the government reduced.[530] The federal government would assume all outstanding debts of states arising from the Revolutionary War by exchanging federal securities for state debt certificates, replacing thirteen different types of certificates with a single security payable in specie and transferable across state lines.[531]

Consistent with Washington's operating style, Hamilton submitted a draft of his report to the President for review. Washington gave his approval on Saturday, January 2, 1790. Hamilton then finalized the report and submitted it to Congress two weeks later, on the 14th.[532]

A political storm of great magnitude was stirred up by the report's recommendation that the government's liabilities would be discharged at their full face value. The concerns centered on the fairness of paying the current certificate holders at par in specie. These instruments had been trading in the market at substantial discounts since issuance, and in many cases their holders had changed repeatedly over the years. Opponents of the Treasury report focused on the discounts at which many soldiers had sold their certificates and objected vehemently that the Treasury's proposal would give a windfall to the financial purchasers. "Speculators," "stock jobbers," "leeches upon society" were some of the more benign terms applied to the current owners of those notes, and Congress had no interest in giving this undesirable segment of society the huge payday the Treasury proposed. Many members saw this as stripping the poor to increase the wealth and influence of the rich.[533]

Taken together with the distrust of financiers prevalent throughout American culture at the time, the surge in rhetoric against "moneymen" posed a significant obstacle to the approval of the Treasury report. James Madison argued that the proposed plan threatened the republic by creating a class of moneyed individuals whose wealth derived not from productive industry but from the act of defrauding the poor, and he proposed an alternative system, called "discrimination," under which the present creditors would be paid the average price at which the securities had traded two years earlier, with the difference between that and the current price paid to the original holders.[534]

Using parliamentary tactics later uncharitably labeled "stupid" by John Adams, Madison and other opponents of the bill stalled its passage for several months. The delay had the ironic result of giving added opportunity for investors in New York, Philadelphia, and elsewhere to continue their buying spree, driving up the prices of securities and creating more windfall for the purchasers.[535] Hamilton warned that Madison's plan would entail abrogating the contractual commitment of the government to the creditors at the time the transaction originally transpired.[536] *As will become clear, Madison was being far more clever than John Adams or anyone else realized at the time.* He had an agenda for his delaying tactic that no one yet suspected.

The President was fully cognizant of the passions surrounding these issues. At the end of the war, he had taken the time to caution his troops against the ill-advised practice of "disposing of their notes and securities of pay at a very great discount." The investors who purchased the notes, he told his troops, "must hereafter obtain the full payment of their nominal value." He had also expressed regret that "necessity will compel [some soldiers] to part with their certificates for whatever they will fetch...; this will place them in the hands of unfeeling avaricious speculators."[537] At the public policy level, however, Washington was equally aware that the establishment of credit, whether for the government or in the private sector, entailed the certainty of repayment, and he felt obliged to support the use of executive power to strengthen public credit.[538]

Little support for Madison's plan materialized in Congress. In the end, the House of Representatives rejected Madison's discrimination plan by a vote of 36-13, with nine of the votes in favor coming from his home state of Virginia.[539]

The collapse of Madison's plan still left open the question of whether Congress would approve the Treasury's proposal of all state debts being assumed by the federal government. Congress was aghast at this part of Assumption. Several states had made Herculean efforts to pay off or curtail the debts incurred during the war, while others had simply let their obligations slide. Many members felt that treating all states alike would be highly unfair, rewarding those profligate states that had made no effort to repay their debts at the expense of the prudent ones that had. Debt repayment being closely linked with the taxing power of a governing authority, there was fear that Assumption would swell the size and power of the federal government at the expense of the states, endangering the ideals of fairness and equality for which the Revolution had been fought.[540]

So, after weeks of acrimonious debate, on April 12, 1790, the House voting as a committee of the whole defeated the proposed assumption of state debts by the central government by a vote by a vote of 31 to 29.

* * *

Despite the pre-eminence of New York and Pennsylvania as the strongest contenders for the choice of the capital city, there was yet another entry in the race – a site on the banks of the Potomac River, even though it was generally considered to be of only marginal interest and to have little to recommend it.[541] The Potomac, stretching hundreds of miles through countless acres of productive farmland, seemed the perfect choice to those who prized the nation's agrarian roots. The river also offered a natural connection to the interior, serving, in Jefferson's words, as "the only point of union which can cement us to our western friends when they shall be formed into separate states."[542] To the further credit of the site, Virginia's republican credentials could not have been improved upon, having given birth to many a Revolutionary hero. However, while New York and Philadelphia were thriving cities, the region along the Potomac consisted mostly of green fields, farms, and swampland. It had already been proposed once in the House and once in the Senate, and decisively defeated both times. The widely held opinion was that "the Patomacke scheme is so absurd that very few expect Congress will ever go there."[543]

It was, of course, true that the proposed Potomac site was neither a population hub nor a center for transatlantic commerce. What it had going for it above all else, however, was a determined champion in the person of James Madison. Like many a Virginian, Madison felt proprietary about that flowing body of water and was passionate in his belief that the banks of that river were the ideal location for the capital of the United States. While Morris, Maclay, Hamilton, and various members of the northern and southern delegations were delivering long orations about their favorite cities and otherwise plotting and maneuvering, forming and shifting alliances, devising ever-changing schemes – and getting absolutely nowhere – Madison was a quiet presence on the scene. His vigilance never faltered – poisoning the well for other proposed locations and swooping in when he saw an opening. In his school days at Princeton, sickly and diminutive "Little Jemmy" had been easy to overlook and underestimate. To appear to be unassuming was a role that James Madison had continued to cultivate as an adult, having found that working quietly and by indirection was of substantial advantage in the give-and-take of the legislative power structure.

Earlier, Robert Morris had moved to delete "Susquehanna" from the resolution of September 8, 1789, and to substitute Philadelphia suburb "German Town" in its place. When the votes were counted, the energetic and ebullient Morris had made surprising headway. The vote was nine for, eight against. Morris, however, had not counted on the obstinacy of his fellow Pennsylvanian. When Maclay stood up to vote, to the horror of the supporters of Philadelphia he cast his vote against the resolution. The vote was now tied, nine to nine. As the President of the Senate, Vice President John Adams was called on to break the tie. He deliberated, made a speech about the pros and cons of the competing Pennsylvania sites, and finally came to the point. He would cast his vote in favor of the location at German Town, about six miles northwest of the Philadelphia city center.

The Residence Bill, designed to establish the capital of the new United States, was then sent to the House. Assessing the mood of his fellow representatives, Madison realized that the bill was headed for approval in the lower chamber as well. This would put an end to the search for the capital city. Philadelphia will have won the coveted prize, and the cherished hopes and dreams of all Virginians about the Potomac site will have come to naught. If he did not act – and quickly – the ball game would be over, and the priceless opportunity of locating the capital on the banks of the Potomac would be lost forever. At this stage in the proceedings, however, he knew there were few options available. With his well-developed sense of the legislative process, he recognized that direct action would be perceived as confrontational and quite likely backfire on him.

This was the moment when Madison's brilliance as a legislative tactician and backroom operator would manifest itself. In his most unassuming manner, he raised the issue of whether federal or state law would govern in the new capital and then proposed an innocuous-sounding amendment to the Residence Bill to the effect that Pennsylvania law would remain in effect unless Congress voted otherwise. As Madison had accurately judged, the issue of what law would govern in the new capital was perceived as a mere technicality by the members, a detail that was of little interest to them at this point. Quite typical of a lawyer, many would think, to see all issues through the narrow prism of the law. With little debate or fanfare, Madison's amendment was adopted.

What had just taken place was actually a matter of no small moment. No one in the House appeared to have been particularly concerned that, after the passage of Madison's amendment, the whole bill would have to be sent back to the Senate for a new vote. With the legislative term ending the next day, the Senators were eager to get on the long, dusty roads to their homes and families; they would be postponing consideration of the matter until the next session. Congress thus adjourned without having settled on the location of the capital city, giving the proponents of the Potomac site crucial additional time to ferret out the perfect opportunity to push their cause.[544]

It was a vintage performance by Madison – quick, devious, and devastatingly effective.

Despite Madison's parliamentary maneuvers, the Potomac's prospects were still not promising. Virginia and Maryland state officials, however, were undaunted and launched a full-scale campaign on behalf of the site. They informed Congress of their willingness to cede sovereignty and land, as required by the Constitution, in exchange for the honor of becoming home to the national capital. The proponents of the Potomac region stressed its strategic location as being squarely between the North and the South, making the area an attractive compromise. Its many opponents, however, considered the idea of building the capital in the wilderness impractical and costly in the extreme.

Madison had actually tried to enlist the support of George Washington for the Potomac site earlier without success. He had raised the question in a letter to Washington back in August 1788, but the query did not elicit the hoped-for response. Washington divulged little of his own personal preference.[545] Despite his silence on the subject, however, his earlier efforts on behalf of the navigation of the Potomac River had not escaped public attention.[546] Nevertheless, as President, Washington stayed above all the political jockeying by competing constituencies and declined to enter the debate on the location of the capital. He was particularly careful about this decision because of the proximity of the Potomac River site to Mount Vernon, as it bore on his integrity in office.

Madison, trying to capitalize on the President's popularity, did not fail to note that the geographic midpoint of the north-south axis of the United States was not just the Potomac, but Mount Vernon itself. He also tried to garner support from the Northern representatives and took the floor in the House to chide those who called the Potomac a Southern body of water. He went to great pains to give everyone a geography lesson, contending that the Potomac was in fact a Western river. Another Virginian, Thomas Jefferson, had famously asserted that the Potomac, requiring only one seventeen-mile portage, was an ideal route to the West.

* * *

And so, while the selection of a site for the capital of the United States was on everyone's mind, so was the Plan of Assumption. At this point in the spring of 1790, however, the chances of a tidy resolution to either problem seemed slim indeed. With passions running high on both issues, the stage was inevitably set for legislative horse-trading – a skill in which Madison excelled. His intervention in the matter proved decisive for both the funding bill and the choice of a site for the capital of the United States.

To Hamilton, the acrimonious tone of the congressional debates over his Assumption plan was highly disquieting. He perceived the likely failure of his fiscal package as an ominous herald of doom for the new republic. He confided his forebodings to Thomas Jefferson when they ran into each other in front of the President's house, and Jefferson invited him to dinner the next day, June 20, 1791, at his residence on Maiden Lane to discuss the matter. The following night, in addition to being a good host and providing a fine meal (a habit Jefferson had cultivated during his sojourn in Paris), another contribution by Jefferson was to invite James Madison to the affair. In his long and frantic search to garner support in Congress for his funding bill, Hamilton had overlooked Madison as a possible and effective ally. So, at the dinner, he quickly took advantage of Madison's presence to describe in detail the importance to the nation of his fiscal program, as he had done the previous day to Jefferson.

That Jefferson had brought his two guests together that night was hardly fortuitous. One of them, he knew, was desperate to pass his fiscal package through Congress, the other shared with Jefferson a deep eagerness to see the permanent capital placed on the banks of the Potomac River. It was a legislative match made in heaven. Madison shrewdly recognized that this was the opportunity he had been waiting for to ensure the selection of George Town as the site of the new capital. With support from as prominent a figure in the administration as the Secretary of the Treasury, members of Congress would assume they were carrying out the President's wishes when they voted for the Potomac site. In turn, Hamilton was already aware that the Pennsylvania delegation would be prepared to vote for Philadelphia as the temporary capital of the United States.

With dinner and drinks smoothing the discussion, a plan of action began to take shape. Madison agreed to mute his opposition to Hamilton's fiscal plan and try to find the necessary votes within the Virginia and Maryland delegations to pass the required legislation authorizing the funding of all existing federal, state, and foreign debts. In exchange, Hamilton would work with Robert Morris to arrange temporary residence of the capital in Philadelphia, with the permanent home planned for an unspecified location on the banks of the Potomac. (Ironically, this was the same deal Madison had proposed to Robert Morris nearly two years before, on August 28, 1789.[547]) The meeting thus ended with both sides having accomplished their most fervent goals. Whether Jefferson, a devotee of fine French wine, toasted the success of the discussions at the night's end his writings do not reveal.[548]

That dinner is a contentious incident in the annals of American politics, and some historians have openly expressed skepticism of Jefferson's version of the event. If the evening actually transpired as Jefferson reported, it was an early instance of backroom politics in America – a practice not exactly favored by the voters. Jefferson was proud of his part in arranging for the nation's capital to be placed on the banks of the Potomac. "This way," he wrote James Monroe, "there will be something to displease and something to soothe every part of the Union but New York, which must be contented with what she has had." He did not, however, wish to be remembered as the man who had engineered the approval of a plan he believed was designed to give a financial windfall to the hated "moneymen." In his version of the events, therefore, he shrewdly inserted a *mea culpa:* He had only agreed to the Plan of Assumption "with a revulsion of stomach almost convulsion." He rued the day he had succumbed to Hamilton's plaintive arguments and arranged the dinner at his behest. "Of all the errors of my political life," he lamented, "this has occasioned me the deepest regret."

With Jefferson, Hamilton, and Madison acting in concert, and in confidence that the plan would meet with the approval of the one whose concurrence was indispensable (i.e., the President), the process moved forward swiftly. Last-ditch efforts by Baltimore and New York to throw sand into the legislative machinery did not change the outcome. The Senate approved the Residence Bill by a vote of 14 to 12 on July 1, 1790, and the House passed it 32-29 eight days later. Surprisingly, there was speculation both in Congress and in the press as to what the President would do, some even anticipating a veto. Washington put a stop to all speculation by signing the Residence Bill into law on July 16. To enact such an important piece of legislation, the entire process had consumed the astonishingly brief period of only twenty-six days after the celebrated dinner at the Jefferson residence.

Barely taking a breather from its labors on the selection of the temporary and permanent capitals, the Senate on July 15, 1790 took up the bill for the funding of all debts assumed by the government. William Maclay, the curmudgeonly Senator from Pennsylvania who looked down on his colleagues from his height of six feet three inches, kept a detailed journal of the events of that day. As the Senate opened, John Adams, the Vice President and thus president president of the Senate, "took up the funding bill without any call for it." Maclay was shocked by the proposal of "taking two so dissimilar objects together" and made his objection known. Adams listened impatiently while Maclay spoke and then, ignoring the protest, called for the vote. Unaware of any secret agreement or backroom arrangements, Maclay sat dumbfounded as he witnessed the proceedings that day in the Senate chamber in New York. The resolution relating to Funding and Assumption was passed on August 4, 1790, putting into action most of the administration's recommendations set forth in the report of the Secretary of the Treasury six months earlier.[549]

Debate on the bill had been rigorous and intense, pitting the supporters of the funding plan against those who argued that public debt inevitably brought excessive taxation, corruption, and a dangerous centralization of power. For the moment, the argument had been resolved in favor of the Treasury's proposals. Madison and his allies settled for the promise of a light tax burden and the commitment that the government's interest obligations would be met promptly and regularly. The national debt would still exist, but through the creation of a sinking fund and by earmarking some taxes specifically for interest payments, it was argued that such government liabilities would not reach staggering proportions.[550]

The President, whose outsize popularity and influence were crucial elements in almost all political developments in the country, had always been in favor of the assumption of state debts. He had been deeply troubled by the opposition to the Plan of Assumption in the south, particularly in Virginia, where the public seemed "irritable, sour, and discontented." He was equally chagrined by Madison's statements against the Plan, although Washington was certain that Madison had been actuated by the purest motives and most heartfelt convictions.[551] The resentment of the people of Virginia toward the new government was unfortunate, for "the cause in which the expense of the War was incurred was a Common Cause." Some states had borne a greater burden in funding the war than others, but all had pledged themselves to stand by each other at the start of the conflict. Assumption was without doubt a just policy, Washington noted, and the debt should be borne collectively by all the states through the fair and just administration of the federal government.[552]

In its final form, the Funding Act of 1790 identified which taxes would be used to repay the principal and interest of specific debts, created a sinking fund from the proceeds of the sales of western lands, and authorized the President to negotiate for $12 million in new foreign loans to settle the old. Effective October 1, all those holding Revolutionary War Certificates (in any of their myriad forms) would be eligible to trade in their old claims for a new issue of government bonds. The exchange would be entirely voluntary; a holder did not have to trade in the certificates to retain his or her rights as a creditor. The law also outlined a procedure for the assumption of state debts.[553] As for foreign debts, the government authorized its agents in Europe to negotiate a loan from a Dutch syndicate to refinance earlier Dutch loans and to discharge wartime debts to France and Spain. Americans were becoming optimistic that the European capital markets would begin to view U.S. debt as worthy of credit, and perhaps even lean toward channeling some capital into the new republic.[554]

In achieving passage of the Funding Act, the administration had created a new, vibrant, and thriving trading environment for domestic debt. Once it took hold, the capital markets flourished throughout the 1790s. Boston, Philadelphia, and Baltimore all had some form of securities markets, but it was New York that emerged as the central hub of trading activity. In a sign of confidence in U.S. securities, foreign buyers, particularly the Dutch and the French, began accumulating substantial holdings of such debt instruments, and American merchants hurried across the Atlantic to sell securities to syndicates in London, Paris, and Amsterdam. These activities had a ripple effect on other areas of the U.S. economy; some investors even purchased government debt to use as collateral on loans for other business endeavors.[555]

As expected, the rising value of U.S. securities attracted increasing attention in the capital markets of Europe. By 1794, the United States had the highest credit rating there, with some of its bonds trading at significant premiums. A year later, $20 million (out of a total of $70 million) in American debt was owned by foreigners, which rose to $50 million after the turn of the century and shortly before the purchase of Louisiana. Charles-Maurice de Talleyrand-Périgord, the noted French foreign minister, spoke for many Europeans when he said that American bonds were "safe and free from reverses. They have been funded in such a sound manner and the prosperity of this country is growing so rapidly that there can be no doubt of their solvency." When at one point in 1797 U.S. bond prices rose over their British counterparts in the London market, the event was perceived as indisputable validation of the underlying economic causes of the American Revolution. The reality, however, was that American securities abroad were to some extent benefiting from the low interest rates prevailing in Britain. Investors in France and the Low Countries had been heavy purchasers of British securities, driving their prices to great heights, and their yields (which naturally moved in the opposite direction from price) commensurately to very low levels. These same investors, in search of safe and better-yielding instruments, now flocked to American bonds. Regardless of the cause, the flood of foreign capital reaching American shores in the 1790s fueled explosive economic growth, giving rise to new enterprises and expansion in agriculture, manufacturing, and communications in the country.[556]

Washington expressed satisfaction at the result. As he would mention in his Second and Third Annual Addresses to Congress, the Funding Plan had been an important step in the nation's path toward fiscal stability. Ever upbeat, Noah Webster reflected the public mood when he wrote, "The establishment of funds to maintain public credit has an amazing effect upon the face of business and the country.... Commerce revives and the country is full of provision. Manufacturers are increasing to a great degree, and in the large towns vast improvements are making in pavements and buildings. Indeed, you may easily conceive what an immense difference it would make in a young country."[557]

Ironically, Thomas Jefferson, an implacable enemy of bankers and financiers during Washington's Presidency,

> *became a major beneficiary of the flourishing capital markets and the enhanced public credit of the United States. As President, attempting to finance the purchase of Louisiana from Napoleon Bonaparte, he and Albert Gallatin, his Swiss-born Treasury Secretary, were able to pull off the largest deal of the era through Baring Brothers of London and Hopes and Company of Amsterdam. The loan of 80 million French Francs ($16 million) was staggering in sheer size, causing a Baring partner to admit that "We all tremble at the magnitude of the American account."*[558]

* * *

Once the selection of the Potomac site was finalized and the Residence Act was passed by Congress, the losers in the capital lottery unleashed a tidal wave of fury and scorn upon those they believed had manipulated the process. The members of the New York congressional delegation were highly distraught by the loss, and predictions abounded that in the absence of the federal government, grass would soon grow and wolves would appear on Wall Street. After the Senate voted on the bills and adjourned, Maclay continued to sit pensively as the members filed out of the chamber, dismayed at the triumph of back-room dealing and secrecy over open discussion and deliberation. He recognized "that the whole business was prearranged." He had only one comment. "The President of the United States," he concluded, "has (in my opinion) had a great influence in this business…, his name goes to wipe away blame and silence all murmuring."[559]

Nothing in Washington's correspondence or diaries indicates that he played the Machiavellian role Maclay described. The President had remained largely silent on the issue of the capital throughout that fevered summer, beyond noting occasionally to correspondents that the issue preoccupied Congress with great intensity. To the Marquis de la Luzerne, Washington wrote on August 10 that he hoped the passage of the Residence Bill had "stilled" the debate "in as satisfactory a manner as could have been expected."[560]

Chapter Eleven

THE CENTER OF THE UNION

Washington intended this to be a Federal city. When a man comes and walks these city streets, he begins to feel that this is my city; I own a part of this Capital.

William Howard Taft

"An Act for Establishing the Temporary and Permanent Seat of the Government of the United States" provided that Philadelphia would be the interim capital for ten years and authorized the President to choose a site on the Potomac River to serve as the permanent seat of the federal government. Having finally resolved the wrangling over the location of the capital, Congress washed its hands of any further involvement in the project until 1800, when the federal offices would be moved from Philadelphia to the new city. Congress then turned its attention to other matters, its members satisfied that they had done their part and content to leave it up to the President to build the capital city. If they were aware of the immensity of the task they had assigned to Washington, the record provides no evidence of it.[561]

The Residence Act required the President to locate the capital city along the Potomac River 65 miles northwest of George Town as the crow flies, or 150 miles along the course of the river.[562] Much of it was familiar ground to Washington, but he still intended to inspect the territory from the new perspective of locating the capital city there. He would have to familiarize himself personally with the contour and lay of the land, the demographics of the region, accessibility of highways and nearby ports, availability of other infrastructure and the needed labor force, and countless other factors crucial in urban planning. He would also have to take account of the defensive posture of the location in the event of war. And so, in mid-October,1790, the President departed from Mount Vernon on a reconnaissance tour of the entire sector. It would be an extensive area to traverse on horseback.

If Washington had expected the trip to go as it had when he traveled as a private surveyor or real estate developer, he was in for a surprise. At every stop along the way, residents came out in throngs to sing the praises of their community and point up its positive attributes as a potential home for the capital. Each town boasted about its superior climate, the quality of its soil, and the excellence of nearby roads, filling Washington's ears with a nonstop refrain of promotional appeal.

In the company of members of the local community, Washington inspected the grounds in the vicinity of George Town and the land between Rock Creek and the Eastern Branch (now the Anacostia River). He then rode upriver toward the confluence of the Potomac and the Conococheague Creek (an Algonquin name pronounced co-no-co-cheeg), for which some in Congress had expressed a preference, in the belief that placing the capital there would permit all three states of Pennsylvania, Maryland, and Virginia to share in the benefits.[563]

Washington's tour of the federal territory fanned the flames of speculation, creating anticipation among the region's landowners. There was a rumor that Washington had ordered three separate surveys of various areas along the Potomac River that fall. There was general expectation that the President would announce his decision during his December address to Congress, but he was not quite ready to proclaim the site of the capital then and made no mention of it. Washington may have found the arguments in favor of one site or another compelling, but he would still follow his preference of not disclosing his plans prematurely.[564] Perhaps he was also carefully setting the stage in his attempt to secure a viable arrangement from the landowners.

Washington was, of course, fully aware of what would happen once he announced the precise location of the federal buildings: There would naturally be a scramble by developers, investors, and even ordinary members of the community to grab all the available tracts in the vicinity of the designated site at pre-development prices in the expectation that there would be a substantial increase in value as the city center began to take shape.

There was much to be done, and the next four months were a blur of activity. Acutely aware of the ten-year deadline imposed by Congress on the work, Washington wasted no time in getting organized. To put together the team to manage the day-to-day operation of the project, he needed to recruit three commissioners, a chief surveyor, and an architect and city planner. He also intended to appoint a high-level person to take overall charge of the capital initiative.

Washington sought the services of a seasoned architect who could unite aesthetic concerns with the more practical dimensions of urban planning to produce a design for an elegant, modern capital city. To fill this role, he turned to Pierre Charles L'Enfant. Born in Paris in 1754, Pierre had been raised in artistic circles. His father's paintings adorned the walls of the palace of Versailles, where he had served as an official painter to the royal court. Pierre himself underwent training at the Royal Academy of Painting and Sculpture in Paris before enlisting in the army and receiving an appointment to the engineering corps. In 1776, the young soldier joined an elite cadre of engineering, artillery, and cavalry officers, including the Marquis de Lafayette, who would cross the Atlantic to offer their services in aid of the American Revolution. During the war, L'Enfant demonstrated great courage under fire and was seriously wounded in battle. He also performed military engineering tasks such as the design and construction of fortifications. When not engaged in combat, he illustrated drill manuals, designed medals and insignia, drew portraits of military officers, and sketched scenes of camp life, including several during the campaign at Valley Forge.[565]

After the war, L'Enfant spent several years in New York practicing architecture and landscape design, and in the process established an impressive reputation for his work. The Common Council of New York City raised $65,000 and hired L'Enfant to redesign and rebuild the old city hall into an ornate Federal Hall for the inauguration of the first President of the United States, an engagement which L'Enfant completed in record time. Washington was so impressed with the new design of the structure that he asked L'Enfant to give Martha a personal tour of the building.[566] Washington was also familiar with other buildings and houses in New York where L'Enfant had served as the architect.

Tall, lanky, and ambitious, L'Enfant shared Washington's aspirations for the future capital city. His notion that the district should be designed on a scale that would allow for its evolution as the capital of a global power coincided with Washington's own ambitions for the capital.[567]

The President was aware of Thomas Jefferson's deep and abiding interest in architecture. Washington shared the same interests with his Secretary of State, whose views he sought on how to implement the Residence Act. Jefferson advised that it was "the wish, and perhaps expectation" of Congress that Washington would take an expansive approach to the federal territory designated for the capital. Acting on the advice of his Secretary of State dated September 14, 1790, Washington recommended the following January that Congress amend the Residence Act to shift the boundaries of the permissible area four miles further to the south, which would serve to square off the tract of land originally designated by Congress. This would add about thirty-odd square miles to the federal territory on the Virginia side and include the City of Alexandria (and, incidentally, about 1,200 acres of land owned by Washington himself and 950 acres owned by George Washington Parke Custis, now the site of Arlington National Cemetery). Congress did so on March 3, 1791.[568]

When it came time to appoint a high-level person to take overall charge of the capital project, the President felt well advised to put Jefferson in that position, which he readily accepted. Washington then authorized him to hire L'Enfant as the chief architect for the project.

Being engaged as the chief engineer/architect of the capital of the United States was the fulfillment of L'Enfant's lifetime ambition. He could hardly wait to start this exciting project and rushed south from New York City, arriving in George Town on the evening of March 9, 1791. He began working at his customary feverish pace the very next morning.[569] Despite a heavy downpour that drenched every inch of his skin and clothing within minutes, he set out on horseback, armed only with a sketchpad and pencil, to traverse the landscape and familiarize himself with its contours. In the weeks that followed, L'Enfant became a familiar sight on the grounds of the federal territory. With an innovative and imaginative approach to architectural design, he began scoping out the most suitable sites for various structures and worked almost non-stop on a set of plans, visualizing the sodden landscape as a magnificent and cosmopolitan city, a shrine to republican virtue, and the envy of all civilized people.[570]

At the same time, L'Enfant studied the plans for other grand cities he considered comparable to the new capital, such as Rome and Paris. He requested Jefferson to provide him with any drawings he had of the well-known buildings on the Continent. In April, Jefferson sent him the plans of Frankfort-on-the-Mayne, Karlsruhe, Amsterdam, Strasburg, Paris, Orleans, Bordeaux, Lyons, Montpelier, Marseilles, Turin, and Milan, all of which Jefferson had collected during his travels across Europe.[571]

On January 24, 1791, the President informed Congress that he had designated the boundaries of the new federal district between George Town and the Anacostia River. Other than a small community in George Town itself, the land chosen by him was largely devoid of urban structures and only sparsely inhabited. Dotted with the occasional small farm and corn or tobacco plantation, the future district consisted mostly of woods and grasslands, interspersed with tidal marshes, hillside bluffs, and scenic stands of ancient trees. Along the Anacostia and Potomac Rivers, the ground was low and flat, with sycamores, willows, and birch trees carving graceful arcs to the sky. Farther north, the land rose in a series of hills and rocky outcroppings from which sprang numerous small waterways that, once joined as creeks, flowed together toward the rivers and the bay below. For generations, inhabitants of the area had fished the waters of the Potomac for herring, shad, and sturgeon, while turkeys, quail, deer, and other wildlife abounded on the shore.[572]

In building the city that would one day be known as Washington, D.C., the President faced a challenge that would intimidate even the most seasoned urban planner. He had to turn a farming community and wooded wilderness into a maze of streets, buildings, and public spaces pulsing with humanity and signs of progress. The cityscape and the culture it supported would have to suffice not merely as a local market town or regional commercial hub but as a grand and imposing metropolis "worthy of the nation" that had birthed it. This would require planning, design, and construction on the largest and most imaginative scale possible in that era.[573]

When passing the Residence Act, Congress had made no appropriation for the capital project. Clearly, the losers in the name-the-capital sweepstakes had not given up completely. They had made certain that Congress allocated no funds for the acquisition of the land, the initial surveys, preparation of site plans, engineering and architectural services, and countless other development costs, nor even for the construction of the buildings into which the government offices would move. If that were not enough, they had also made sure the President was given the incredibly tight timeframe of ten years in which to build an entire city from scratch. That the project was destined to fail was clearly the expectation. The enabling legislation could thus all too easily unravel at the first sign of difficulty during the development phase of the capital city.[574]

The President would have to identify, within a hundred square miles of land, the precise location on which the capital city would be built, acquire thousands of acres, select the design of the entire city, arrange for the development of miles of roads and all city amenities, erect the required federal buildings including the President's house and the meeting place of Congress – *and accomplish all this within the impossible deadline of ten years and without a nickel of federal funds!*

A lesser man would have considered the project an insurmountable challenge and thrown up his hands in frustration. Washington, however, was driven by a messianic optimism about the future of America and was convinced that to keep the fledgling republic from being torn asunder under the weight of its regional jealousies and conflicts, there was a crucial need for a symbol in which the entire nation could take pride, namely, a capital worthy of the expanded future role on the global stage Washington visualized for it. It was worth any price to keep the Union together, and he would not be deterred by lack of federal funds from making the dream of a grand national capital a reality.[575] As it had been during the war, this too was a do-or-die effort in which he and the nation dared not falter.

By March 1791, Washington was prepared to have a meeting with the landowners in the area of the future capital city and personally assess the feasibility of working out a reasonable arrangement with them. So, before embarking on his tour of the southern United States, Washington stopped off in George Town. Despite a difficult trip getting there, he immediately went to Suter's Tavern, a popular gathering place for businessmen and others on High Street (now Wisconsin Avenue).

His first appointment was with the three district commissioners to discuss their plans for the management of the capital city project, and then he met with surveyor Andrew Ellicott to review the results of his preliminary survey of the proposed district.[576] The meeting with Pierre Charles L'Enfant, next on his agenda, was the one he had been keenly anticipating. An excited L'Enfant, voluble, passionate, and gesticulating throughout a breathless presentation, used rough pencil sketches to pour out his ambitious vision of the American capital. He recommended that the district incorporate all the land in between the Eastern Branch, Potomac River, Rock Creek, and the hilly terrain to the north. To the south, he described a picturesque wooded hillock a short distance from the river which stood "like a pedestal waiting for a superstructure," and which he called Jenkins Hill (on the mistaken assumption that a nearby farmer named Jenkins owned the land). He would put upon this hill the two houses of Congress (now Capitol Hill), which would be grand structures and give "a majestic aspect" to the city. Jenkins Hill would serve as the epicenter of the public buildings, and the other government offices would be placed at pleasing angles around the surface of the hill and radiate outward along eighty-foot avenues fixed in a striking diagonal formation. From the crest of Jenkins Hill, the city would be visible for miles, and the whole spectacular arrangement, L'Enfant prophesied, would draw visitors from around the world.

L'Enfant surpassed himself when it came to describing the residence of the President: it would be "a magnificent edifice" conveniently connected to "Congress House" by a boulevard a mile long and wider than any road that then existed in North America (now Pennsylvania Avenue). Nearby would lie the commercial hub of the capital. The federal city, he assured Washington, "would soon grow of itself and spread as the branches of a tree toward where they meet with most nourishment."[577]

Over and over, L'Enfant reverted to his favorite theme: the district must be planned and designed with sufficient grandeur to accommodate the day the population of the capital would swell to a million people. One day, L'Enfant predicted, the city limits would expand well beyond the four thousand acres encompassed within his sketches to cover the full allotted one hundred square miles of land. This was heady stuff, outstripping even Washington's ambitions for the federal city.[578]

The next item on Washington's agenda was the meeting with the proprietors of local real estate, in which he had to achieve a challenging set of twin goals. He had to acquire thousands of acres of land at or near the banks of the Potomac River without the cash to pay for it *and* find a way to raise the staggering sum of a million dollars for the development and construction of the city.

At the outset, he had to be mindful that the individuals with whom he was meeting appeared to be qualified real estate investors and not *un*sophisticated farmers. Nor was Washington so naive as to believe that high ideals and lofty patriotic overtures could sway the proprietors into making decisions not in their commercial interest. Public project or no, a sophisticated landowner could not be expected to part willingly with his land without receiving in return meaningful and specific commitments and guarantees – undertakings that Congress had not authorized the President to make. Which of the landowners present at the meeting could be persuaded to convey his property to the government on favorable terms and which would be likely to hang tough was also unknown at the moment. Nevertheless, it is safe to assume that Washington had planned the minuet with the George Town landowners with his customary attention to detail and was fully cognizant of the obstacles to success.

What Washington had going for him, of course, was that he was skilled in negotiating and making deals in land transactions from his civilian life. Perhaps he even relished the chance to practice once again a trade he knew well. He would first size up his audience and then carefully tailor his approach to them.

Nevertheless, could even the high-octane energy and dealmaking mastery of a George Washington pull off such a vast, complicated, and costly project? How would he go about acquiring so much land without the money to pay for it? Were the required technical knowledge and skilled management even available in the country for an undertaking of this magnitude? And, most important, was it even humanly possible to build an entire city on scrubby stands of alder and tobacco fields within the unimaginably tight timeframe mandated by statute? Some in the nation may have thought Washington was superhuman, but was he also a magician?

Present at Suter's Tavern for the meeting, either individually or through representatives, were twenty major landowners from George Town and seven from Carrollsburgh, the elbow of land wedged between the Potomac River and the Eastern Branch. He was aware that, despite his best efforts, the rumor mill had been working overtime in the local marketplace and a speculative fever had gripped the landscape. He had also received reports that a bitter dispute had already arisen between the group based in George Town and the other in Carrollsburgh, both vying to have their land designated as the center of the planned government office buildings. Washington recognized that this internecine quarrel provided him with the perfect starting point to set the tone of the meeting. Quickly taking command, he began by stressing forcefully the need for cooperation between the two groups, telling them that they should forge "a common cause" toward the achievement of a larger goal. If they joined forces and came forward with the right offers of land, this would "secure" the federal district, vindicate Congress's choice of the Potomac as the site for the nation's capital, and ease concerns that the internal conflict of the landowners would delay the start of construction.

Feeling somewhat chastised, the proprietors were now anxious to hear what was in store for them. Having used the stick, Washington was now ready with the carrot. He began by giving his audience a glimpse of the future city that would be built on the banks of the beautiful river flowing near where they stood: The broad 160-foot wide boulevards radiating out from the magnificent structures housing Congress; the elegant mansion for the President that would rival the best that Europe had to offer; the other imposing government edifices; the bustling commercial establishments to serve their needs; the city's many circles, squares, and parks; and the pleasing monuments, obelisks, and fountains; all built on a scale far more substantial and opulent than anything that existed in North America.

For landowners who had visualized the capital as a small hamlet of a few government offices, Washington's description surpassed their highest expectations for the use to which their land would be put. It was a compelling, even mesmerizing vision of the capital city, its grandeur almost breathtaking, for which the President freely gave much of the credit to his talented and highly imaginative French architect.

By this point in the meeting, Washington had managed to strengthen the resolve of the proprietors to do whatever was necessary to ensure that they would participate in the enchanting panorama he had laid before them. This was their once-in-a-lifetime opportunity, and they would not care to miss out on it.

Having carefully established the framework for the discussion, Washington was now ready to present his proposal.

In his civilian activities, when approaching a business transaction Washington had always shunned bargaining, haggling, nitpicking, stalling, and the customary process of starting negotiations with a hidden agenda. Now, as President, he felt an even greater need to be direct. He began by telling his audience that no separate tract from George Town or Carrollsburgh would be "adequate to the end of insuring the object." The new city would comprise not only both communities but much of the land in between. Then, once Andrew Ellicott had completed his surveys, the land would be divided into lots, of which the George Town and Carrollsburgh proprietors would retain half. For any additional land taken for public use, such as squares, walks, and the like, the government would pay the proprietors £25 ($66.67) per acre. For the ground taken for roads, streets, and alleyways, the proprietors would receive nothing. The timber and wood on the land would belong to the owners. The proprietors would pay the government £12 10s ($33.34) per acre for any building and improvements belonging to a landowner and permitted to remain in the city. Conversely, if any such building was required to be demolished, the government would pay the owner its reasonable value. Washington then adjourned the meeting to give the landowners time to ponder his proposal overnight.

Having carefully thought over the approach laid out for them by Washington, and convinced that they would recoup far more than the value of the scrubland they would be giving up by the skyrocketing prices of their remaining acreage as the development of the capital took shape, the landowners on March 30, 1791, agreed with the proposal before them.[579]

Washington had sought advice from both Jefferson and Madison on the legal aspects of the prospective discussions and already had in hand the necessary documentation to memorialize the transactions. The press later reported that the proprietors had "cheerfully entered into the necessary business of making the proper conveyances."[580]

Today, town-sector developers are accustomed to dedicating the roadways and parks of a project to the community at no cost to the municipality, thus making the dedication of land part and parcel of an overall development plan. When Washington was negotiating with the landowners, however, what existed were only a few preliminary sketches by L'Enfant. No full development plan as yet existed, nor was the requisite financing in place for it. The proprietors were agreeing to part with thousands of acres for no payment, even before the site plan was in place and approved, and long before the first shovelful of earth had been removed. What the government intended to do – and Washington made no secret of it at the meeting – was to turn right around and sell these same lots to raise money for construction. He had obtained ten thousand lots and all the land needed for roads and avenues at no cost, and hundreds of additional acres for plazas, fountains, etc., at rock bottom prices.[581]

Washington then wrote Jefferson to inform him of the outcome of the negotiations with the landowners in the federal district. "All the land from Rock Creek along the river to the Eastern Branch... the whole containing from three to five thousand acres," Washington explained, had been ceded to the government by the area landowners. "When the whole shall be surveyed and laid off as a city (which Major L'Enfant is now directed to do), the present proprietors shall retain every other lot." He also told Jefferson about L'Enfant's plans for the capital being comparable in size to London or Paris, or to use a scale more familiar to Washington's contemporaries, "as large as the occupied portions of New York City, Boston, and Philadelphia combined."[582] Jefferson chose not to mention his serious reservations about this grand plan at that point.

L'Enfant, of course, was delighted that his vision had won the approval of the President.

What had been accomplished was a true feat of dealmaking, one that has served as a template for successive generations of municipal officials in the United States.[583] Washington permitted himself a rare moment of satisfaction at the outcome. "The business," he wrote in his diary, was thus "happily finished."[584] He made it look easy.

Accompanied by L'Enfant, the President later visited the federal site on horseback. Washington approved of Jenkins Hill as the site for the Capitol, but he asked that the "Presidential Palace" be moved a short distance to the west, placing it on higher elevation to provide an unobstructed view of the city. As for the layout of the city streets, the President endorsed L'Enfant's innovative use of diagonals in place of a strictly traditional grid but asked that their total number be reduced. Mindful of the land auctions that would be held to raise revenue for the city's development, Washington wished to decrease the number of awkwardly-shaped fragments of land that would generate less revenue when sold to the public.[585]

Washington had done his part, and all the pieces were in place for the project to move forward at an accelerated schedule. The execution of this vital national undertaking was now in the hands of the commissioners, the chief surveyor, the chief architect, and Thomas Jefferson as the administration's point man to provide oversight. Washington himself had a government to run. He had to attend to the never-ending stream of crises facing the fragile new republic – Indian massacre of settlers, rebellion against the excise tax on whiskey, the threat of war with Britain over its capture of American merchant ships and other transgressions against U.S. sovereignty, disputes with revolutionary France, the feud between his two most important Cabinet Secretaries, Hamilton and Jefferson, which was threatening to undermine the effectiveness of his administration, on and on ad infinitum.

Jefferson took supervision over L'Enfant's work, directing him to report on his progress "about twice a week, by letter, say every Wednesday and Saturday evening."[586] L'Enfant obliged by sending a letter two days after his arrival. It quickly became evident that L'Enfant's concept of the city was at odds with that of Jefferson.[587] L'Enfant had visions of Versailles, broad boulevards, and beautiful sculptures. On the other hand, Jefferson's vision of the perfect life for Americans was living in small hamlets and ploughing their small farms. As for the capital, his vision was of a collection of buildings erected within a twenty-block grid in which to house the federal government. The President was unaware of the divergence between Jefferson and L'Enfant on the design and scope of the capital. Washington wanted a capital worthy of his own vision for the United States and shared L'Enfant's aspirations as well as his esthetic sense. Jefferson, in contrast, detested cities as monuments to urban decay and depravity. Obviously, it would not be long before Jefferson's expectations would clash with those of L'Enfant. Face-to-face encounters and open dialogue, however, were not Jefferson's preferred style. He would hold back until the right opportunity arose to neutralize the chief architect. [588]

So, as time wore on, a whole series of misunderstandings, misadventures, and mistakes plagued the progress of the work Washington had so carefully orchestrated. Only the President's determination kept the project alive and functioning. He had no choice but to keep a close eye on the district as it grew in fits and starts. Even though Jefferson maneuvered to have L'Enfant fired, what survived was still George Washington's grand vision for the capital city as developed by his imaginative and talented French architect. Under Washington's steady hand, the development of the President's House and the Capitol buildings gradually inched forward. By late summer 1797, the residence was very nearly complete, needing only a roof atop its graceful crown. Likewise, the north wing of the Capitol was ready for roofing.

Throughout spring and summer of 1791, while plans proceeded for the new capital on every front, most people assumed the city would be named in honor of either George Washington or Christopher Columbus. Indeed, these two names were the ones bandied about most frequently in newspapers, pamphlets, and broadsides.

Touring the district in April 1791, William L. Smith, Congressman from South Carolina, found himself so captivated by L'Enfant's rhapsodic description of the future capital that he pronounced it "grand and romantic," and then proposed the name "Washingtonopolis" for it. The *Gazette,* a popular Philadelphia journal, proposed the name "Columbus." Others came up with "Columbian Federal City," making an adjective out of Columbus's name. Several newspapers published a jaunty little ditty referring to the capital as "Washingtonople." The matter was finally settled on September 8, 1791, when Secretary of State Thomas Jefferson, Congressman James Madison, and the three commissioners officially designated the capital as the City of Washington and the federal territory as the District of Columbia.[589]

Traveling through the area in September 1796, Henrietta Liston, wife of the Scottish diplomat Robert Liston, commented that everything about the prospective capital impressed her, especially its Potomac location, which struck her as "noble and beautiful, strongly resembling Constantinople." Her husband counted as many as one hundred buildings under construction, including a fair number of public edifices.[590]

The capital city remained a work-in-progress when Present Washington's term ended. On the day of his official retirement from the Presidency, Washington must have felt gratified when, en route to Mount Vernon, he was greeted with a sixteen-gun salute as he rode past the site of the almost-finished President's House and the dozens of buildings under construction in the capital.[591] Once installed in retirement, Washington continued to oversee the project from Mount Vernon. His successor in office, John Adams, was happy to let Washington take the lead on all matters relating to the capital, being himself largely uninterested in the project. Fall of 1797 found the aging former President making daily trips back and forth into the district in a silver phaeton, providing him ample opportunity to take note of any problems he encountered or observed along the way. Washington's involvement in the district continued to be far-reaching and influential. He never ceased to press the commissioners, albeit quite gently, to speed up construction of the Capitol. He chose locations for various government departments, offered opinions on public squares and other open spaces, and promoted the establishment of a national university and a national botanical garden.[592]

The capital continued to be a major preoccupation for George Washington as long as he was alive. The year after his death, the government moved its offices from Philadelphia to the city named after him, as scheduled. Like so many other ambitious and worthy projects he had started in his private and public involvements, Washington sadly did not live to see the fruition of his mighty labors in this public endeavor. Without him, the United States would have never embarked upon the creation of the magnificent city that became the grand symbol of the American Union, a capital befitting the powerful and prosperous nation the first President saw in its future. Nor would the capital have been built without federal funding and on the impossibly tight timetable set for it by Congress had it not been for his awesome determination in the face of overwhelming obstacles and challenges.

Chapter Twelve

JUDICIAL DIGNITY AND LUSTER

There are more instances of the abridgement of the freedom of the people by gradual and silent encroachments of those in power than by violent and sudden usurpations.

James Madison

In an authoritarian government, the head of state can, even on a whim, override or invalidate the actions of the legislature. In the United States, no one could exercise that kind of power – to strike down acts of Congress or challenge the authority of the head of state. Right?

Not so. This is the story of who does in fact wield that kind of awesome power in this country.

Even in the twenty-first century, it is a rare country that does not routinely receive accusations of corruption and bias in its judiciary. Most often, the courts and judges are part of the enforcement arm of the government, much like the police. They are there to carry out the will and whim of the head of state and provide him or her with a thin veneer of judicial gloss for actions against dissenters, political rivals, and other "enemies of the state." Russian and Chinese governments do not have a monopoly on such practices; similar stories of serious due-process violations abound from most other countries as well.[593] These reports are daily reminders of the dark and sinister side of the court system in many corners of the world.

Judicial corruption, whether it arises from political intimidation and pressure, bribery and graft, or any other form of undue influence, becomes a pervasive and toxic overlay on all aspects of society. It saps the morale of a nation, undermines public trust in its government, interferes with the administration of justice and the punishment of crime, and jeopardizes the sanctity of contract and property rights. It inevitably leads to mediocrity in the quality of judges and other government officials, and to dismayingly inefficient court processes for potential litigants. Not surprisingly, systemic corruption also erodes foreign and domestic confidence in the local investment climate, leading to long-term adverse economic consequences. Once established, the scourge of corruption becomes endemic in a country's culture, virtually impossible to uproot.[594]

In the United States, the federal judiciary is wholly independent of the head of state. It is also independent of the legislative branch of the government. The U.S. Supreme Court, sitting at the apex of the federal judiciary, serves as the final arbiter in the land on matters of the law. It is the country's last resort against tyranny, arbitrary government action, and unfair laws and regulations. It can declare as arbitrary the actions of the executive branch and strike down laws enacted by the legislative branches of the federal and state governments as unconstitutional and therefore invalid. The Supreme Court is not only *not* subservient to the U.S. President and other branches of the government, it can in fact override their acts and declare them unenforceable.

The U.S. Supreme Court receives universal respect for its independence, the quality of its opinions, and the depth of professional commitment and skill of its justices. It wields its awesome powers judiciously and with great restraint and dignity. Americans and non-Americans alike can count on the Court's impartiality, fairness, and competence. It is the envy of countless people in countries whose judiciaries lack independence and have no power to defy authoritarian political or military leaders.

How did this come about? Is America's good fortune in this respect the product of accident and pure chance?

This chapter covers the roots of our solid federal judicial structure. It is the story of how our first President, not a lawyer himself, took great pains to launch the United States Supreme Court on a solid foundation based on two essential ingredients that have endured through the centuries:

First of all, he intended to establish a firm tradition of appointing only "the fittest characters" to serve on the highest court in the land. His selections would be based solely on merit – not wealth, nor friendship, personal favoritism, or even a family connection with himself.[595] His own nephew had to wait for another administration to find a high-level federal appointment as Washington felt there were other and better-qualified candidates.[596] So, being Washington's relative was actually a distinct handicap. (President Adams did in fact appoint Bushrod Washington, the nephew, to the Supreme Court.)

Second, the President had an overarching principle which he enunciated when he sent to his initial appointees a ringing endorsement of their vital role in the American republic:

> I have always been persuaded that the stability and success of the national government, and consequently the happiness of the people of the United States, would depend to a considerable degree on the interpretation and execution of its laws. In my opinion, therefore, it is important that the judiciary system should not only *be* ***independent in its operations***, but as perfect as possible in its formation.[597] [Emphasis added.]

This message from the first U.S. President to the members of the first U.S. Supreme Court on the eve of embarking on their circuit-riding duties contained a pronouncement of epic proportions. He was unequivocal that the federal court system would be "independent" in its operation – independent of the executive branch, independent of Congress, and wholly independent in its judgments and rulings. It would be impervious to politics, undue influences, and public or private pressures of any sort.

It would thus be the hallmark of this country's federal judiciary that it would be wholly free from corruption.

Washington's message to the justices was, of course, consistent with all of his actions and policies, but in the context of the governmental environment in an eighteenth-century world, this was as much a fundamental change in the running of a government as creating a republic was to a world dominated by hereditary kings and aristocrats. Even in the twenty-first century, most countries have yet to achieve a judiciary not subservient to the policies and wishes of the executive branch. (In a corruption index created by Transparency International for 180 countries, each of which was ranked on a scale of zero to 100, with 0 being the most corrupt and 100 the least, two-thirds of the countries surveyed scored below 50 in 2017.[598])

More than two centuries later, economists, in identifying the elements of a successful national economic environment, have come to recognize that those two factors identified by our first President are indeed crucial for an entrepreneurial society.[599] Had Washington not articulated his requirements, and had he not laboriously ensured that they became ingrained in the judicial structure he bequeathed to the nation, the cancer of corruption and incompetence would have reduced the American government to the level one sees in so many countries to this day. Were it otherwise, and were the President's appointments less than eminently qualified jurists operating independently, "the Court," as one distinguished scholar wrote, "might have become a reliquary for political hacks."[600]

Monday, February 1, 1790, was heralded as an important day in the life of the new American republic.[601] The highest tribunal of the United States would open for business in the Royal Exchange building at the foot of Broad Street in New York City, and members of the press and the public would have the opportunity of attending the new Court's opening ceremony and acknowledging their support of the institution.

The Judiciary Act, recently passed by Congress, provided for the establishment of the Supreme Court, and it became law upon the President's signature. Then, in a clear demonstration of the urgency he attached to the creation of a sound judicial system in the new republic, Washington submitted the names of six highly qualified persons to serve as the first justices on the very day the Act took effect. At a salary of $4,000 per year for the Chief Justice, and $3,500 for each Associate Justice (compared with $6 per day for Members of Congress when in session), the compensation scale was not unattractive for the times, and once the advice-and-consent process of the Senate had been completed, the Court was ready for business.[602]

The opening day of the Court was thus the culmination of the expectations and passions that were raised in debates on the need for a strong federal judiciary. Despite the blustery cold, a sizable gallery, including many lawyers and reporters from around the country, gathered to witness the historic event. The Chief Justice and two of the Associate Justices, clad in their somber black and red robes, were clearly prepared to proceed, as were those in the visitors' gallery, including the press.[603]

Soon, however, the hopeful spectators began to drift away in disappointment. To act, the Supreme Court required a quorum of four justices, and the fourth, much less the fifth or the sixth, had yet to appear. So the Chief Justice had to adjourn the new Court that day without transacting any business.[604]

The Court today is ensconced in a majestic building with massive bronze doors at the top of a marble entrance on First Street, N.E., in Washington, D.C., across from the U. S. Capitol grounds, it would be difficult to imagine that the highest judicial symbol of the nation had a somewhat inauspicious beginning.[605] However, the delay in achieving quorum on the opening day was merely the labor pang of birth. In time, the solid foundation laid by the careful selection and appointment of superior justices would bear fruit and lead the Court to the position of unparalleled respect it has come to occupy.

The Court did in fact muster the required quorum soon after its opening day to plunge immediately into a heavy docket of the justices' circuit-riding responsibilities. Then, as the Court's jurisdiction was mostly appellate, it had to wait for cases to percolate from the lower federal courts. It was a year and a half before the justices, sitting as members of the Supreme Court, handed down their first decision.[606] However, in their alternate roles as judges in the circuit courts, they passed on many issues of national importance, which later served as the bases for major Supreme Court decisions.

Each of the justices nominated by President Washington contributed greatly to American politics and jurisprudence, and as their caseloads grew, so did their importance.[607] By their decisions in the Circuit Courts, the early justices not only provided precedents of constitutional interpretation, but also succeeded in their primary objective of bolstering and consolidating the new federal government.[608]

The first Supreme Court performed the vital function of establishing the rule of law in the new nation and laid the foundation for the judicial structure of the country. No federal courts having existed previously, there were no federal judicial precedents on which to rely, nor any cemented understanding of the scope and limits of the powers of the executive, the legislature, or the states. The early Court had to address almost every issue that came before it from scratch.

Today, the Court's prestige and significance derives in no small measure from its ability to invalidate the decisions of Congress and the President – i.e., the power of judicial review.[609] The vital principles of our republican form of government – namely, judicial review and the supremacy of federal laws – were in fact first tested in Circuit Court cases by the same Supreme Court justices appointed by President Washington. Later, these principles were incorporated into the well-known foundational cases of constitutional law which arose under Chief Justice John Marshall in the second decade of the Court's existence,[610] such as *Marbury v. Madison*, which asserted the Supreme Court's power to strike down unconstitutional federal laws, and *McCulloch v. Maryland*, establishing the Supreme Court's power to invalidate the unconstitutional actions of states.

In this country, we take great pride in the Court's power of judicial review. It sets the United States apart, boldly and uniquely, from the multitude of governments that consider the judiciary an arm of the executive branch and effectively subservient to it. Back in the eighteenth century, however, there were detractors to the whole concept. Thomas Jefferson rejected it outright. He saw the role of the Supreme Court as strictly limited to the application of statutes to individual cases. Perhaps he was again showing the influence of the French judicial culture on his views, but he would allow no special powers in judges to interpret the Constitution.[611]

Operating in an environment of national economic weakness and international geopolitical instability, the first Supreme Court had to be particularly mindful of the impact of its decisions on the fragile condition of the country. The President stressed at every opportunity that it was vital for the nation to act as a united whole, to set aside the regional jealousies and conflicts, and that the Union could only be strengthened if the rule of law were applied and obeyed across all boundaries.[612] This entailed basic respect for the decisions, character, and judgment of the justices on the nation's highest court. It also meant that the federal judiciary had to be prepared, in appropriate cases, to subordinate state laws to federal necessities, as the Supremacy Clause of the Constitution provided. For the fledging national economy to survive, for example, property rights had to be uniformly recognized and protected, and this required the active intervention of the federal judiciary. State courts could generally be trusted to protect the property rights of their own citizens; however, where the rights in question belonged to foreign nationals (particularly if they were British Loyalists), state courts could not be trusted to strike down state laws that interfered with those rights.[613] Without consistent enforcement in the United States of the property and contract rights of foreign nationals, trade with America would be seen as risky by Europeans and others. Thus, the vital foreign commerce of the country would be jeopardized.

While the President's power to appoint Supreme Court justices is today taken for granted, this was far from a foregone conclusion to the drafters of the Constitution at the Convention of 1787. The Framers were concerned about the concentration of power in the hands of one man. With the evils of English tyranny still fresh in their minds, they were mindful of the risk of abuse of power by a President. "The people," warned South Carolinian John Rutledge (whom Washington would later nominate to the Supreme Court), "will think we are leaning too much toward monarchy." James Madison recommended vesting the appointment power in the Senate alone, a body he perceived as more stable and independent than the House of Representatives, of which he himself was a member.[614] In the end, the matter was resolved by providing that the President would nominate candidates, and the Senate would confirm them.

The Constitutional Convention also engaged in vigorous debate over the advisability of establishing lower federal courts. The unanimity with which the Framers agreed on the creation of the Supreme Court dissolved at the mention of additional federal courts. Touching on the highly sensitive issue of the balance of power between the states and the federal government, the matter evoked strong passions among the Framers. Many believed that establishing inferior courts would encroach on states' rights.[615] Citizens across the nation were already nervous about the impending concentration of power in federal hands; every additional grant of authority to the central government would only increase resistance to the new Constitution. Others argued that states, accustomed to setting their own policies, may not choose to enforce important national policies at the expense of local prerogatives. As Edmund Randolph of Virginia put it, "The courts of the states cannot be trusted with the administration of the national laws. The objects of jurisdiction are such as will often place the general and local policy at variance."[616]

During the Constitutional Convention, Virginia's James Madison and Pennslvania's James Wilson were unflagging in their support of a system of inferior federal courts. In light of the strong opposition, a compromise was suggested. To mitigate the potential obstacles to the ratification of the Constitution, they proposed that the entire matter be put in the hands of Congress. The provision would allow but not require the federal legislature to establish inferior federal courts. With a sigh of relief at ducking yet another controversy, the Convention accepted the compromise provision.[617]

There were, of course, many other contentious issues raised at the Constitutional Convention, including the life tenure of justices, whom voters could not remove no matter how egregious their corruption or incompetence. All were in the end resolved, but naturally not to everyone's satisfaction.[618]

Once the requisite nine states had ratified the Constitution, the President wasted no time in seeking to fulfill its mandates. Faced with the daunting task of creating a federal judicial system from scratch, he and members of Congress were unanimous in the need to address the organization of the judiciary as promptly as possible. The Senate and the

House began work in April 1789, but it was not all clear sailing. Many of the issues which had generated heated oratory at the Constitutional Convention were now raised anew in Congress, with undiminished passion, until finally the Judiciary Act, a landmark piece of legislation for the new nation, was signed into law by President Washington on September 24, 1789.[619]

The Act set up the Supreme Court of the United States, to be composed of one Chief Justice and five Associate Justices. It was to meet at the "seat of government" (then New York City). It divided the United States into thirteen judicial districts, each with its own one-judge district court.[620]

The President spent months putting together the criteria he would use for the selection of nominees to the Supreme Court, and then began sifting through dozens of names of potential candidates. Congress might legislate about the duties of Supreme Court justices, but the President had the constitutional prerogative of choosing them.[621]

Today, a nomination to the high court is often the subject of impassioned oratory and controversy, engendering riveting political theater and media fanfare. One might surmise that in the early republic, this process must have been simple and straightforward. On the contrary, the choices were even then far from cut-and-dried. Unlike modern U.S. heads of state, our first President had no teams of investigators for his recruitment projects, nor any public relations advisors for counsel in the selection process. He had to rely solely on his own judgment.

Washington was acutely aware of the vital role the judiciary would play in shaping the economic and political fate of the new nation. The respect accorded the Court would depend on the caliber of the men he appointed to the bench, the quality of their opinions, and the soundness of their judgments. If the first Supreme Court could not command respect and trust, the judicial branch would be seen as weak and ineffectual, destabilizing the whole structure of the federal government. The "due administration of justice," the President wrote to John Rutledge, was "the strongest cement of good government," and "essential... to the stability of our political system." Vice President John Adams aptly characterized the gravity of the search process when he said, "The national character, public credit, private confidence, public liberty, private property, everything that is sacred, precious or dear, depends so much on these judges." So Washington took great care to choose the ablest of men who would bring "*dignity and luster* to our national character."[622]

With so much at stake in the actions of the early Court, it was of the utmost importance that its judges be individuals of the highest caliber. "It has been the invariable object of my anxious solicitude," Washington wrote, "to select *the fittest characters* to expound the laws and dispense justice."[623]

Washington sought candidates possessed of first-rate legal minds and strong commitment to the U. S. Constitution as the symbol of the unity of the nation. They would be men of proven judgment, whom the public already held in high regard. As Vice President Adams wrote, rather wistfully: "It would have a happy effect if all the judges of the national supreme court could be taken from the chief justices of the several states."[624]

Washington's nominees to the first Supreme Court were superb lawyers who brought wide-ranging experiences to their role as justices. Some had deep foreign affairs exposure, others extensive legislative backgrounds, still others knowledge of admiralty, etc. Some had served as delegates to the Constitutional Convention of 1787; all had worked tirelessly to secure the ratification of the Constitution in their individual states. Washington was also understandably biased in favor of those who had participated in the American Revolution. Several had actually fought in the war; others had been active politically during and following the Revolution. All the nominees also had significant other political résumés, having held state offices of one kind or another: governors, attorneys general, delegates to Congress, or some combination of those positions. Almost all were super-achievers and had experienced meteoric rises in their careers.[625]

A reputation for honesty and fair dealing was also high on the list of qualifications the President looked for in a candidate. An unfavorable reputation in the community was indeed decisive to disqualify the individual as was the case with Arthur Lee, about whom Washington wrote to Madison: "[Arthur Lee] has applied to be nominated one of the Associate Judges but I cannot bring my mind to adopt the request. The opinion entertained of him by those with whom I am most conversant is unpropitious." The President was being diplomatic. Arthur Lee had been an opponent of the Constitution during its ratification process in addition to having a bad reputation among his peers. He stood no chance with the President.[626]

Washington was also sensitive to regional diversity, to avoid the appearance of favoring any particular state. Every state felt that it deserved to have a native son on the bench, an awkward state of affairs in that there were more states than Supreme Court seats to be filled. This was an issue on which feelings ran high. So Washington tried to maintain "a remarkable geographic balance" on the Court to give it sufficient credibility to enforce the laws in each region of the nation.[627]

Newspapers were keenly interested in the judicial appointments, and each paper had its own candidate. The *Federal Gazette*, a popular Philadelphia publication, argued that Pennsylvania was "entitled" to provide the new Chief Justice, especially given that the President hailed from the South and the Vice-President from the East. A newspaper from Massachusetts recommended three candidates, all of whom were citizens of that state: Adams, Cushing and Dana. (One, at least, made it.)[628]

Naturally, Washington was also mindful (as, indeed, have been all the succeeding Presidents) of how the new Court would enhance or impede his own strategic vision for the country. As the presiding chairman at the Constitutional Convention, he had sat through the debates on the powers given to the Supreme Court and was fully aware that it was to be the final arbiter on matters of extraordinary national import. The jurisprudence established by the individuals Washington chose could dramatically help – or hinder – his long-range plans for the growth and prosperity of the nation.

The choice of the first Chief Justice would be especially daunting. It would have to be a person of national and international renown, one whose abilities and achievements would cloak the Court with instant substance and credibility. The nominee's organizational skills would bring structure to the new tribunal and create a template for its members in dealing with the many conflicting pressures to which they would find themselves subjected.

Washington finally settled on one whose long list of credits included playing a leading role in negotiating the Treaty of Paris to end the Revolutionary War and in the ratification of the Constitution; one whose personal involvement had already been crucial in dealing with major domestic and international controversies; and one who had a keen awareness of the multitude of tensions among the states, between state and federal power, and between the United States and foreign powers. That man was John Jay of New York, super-lawyer, envoy extraordinaire, and a natural leader.

Washington put John Jay at the top of his list of Supreme Court nominees. For the five Associate Justices, a larger group of potential candidates was available, each with his own special talents and strengths. He selected the five who would eventually serve, all of whom had reached the zenith of their judicial and political careers in their own states. Some originally came from impoverished homes, others from influential or well-to-do families. Some were immigrants to America and had been foreign-born. All had managed to secure a first-rate education. They were James Wilson of Pennsylvania, William Cushing of Massachusetts, John Rutledge of South Carolina, John Blair of Virginia, and James Iredell of North Carolina.[629]

On September 24, 1789, President Washington sent to the Senate his nominations for the positions of justices of the Supreme Court of the United States.[630] The Senators appear to have been awed by the quality of the nominees, exulting, as one did, that no "judiciary in the world is better filled."[631] The Senate provided its advice and consent to these nominations in only two days.

Given the multitude of factors to be taken into account in making judicial appointments, it is a testament to Washington's judgment, as well as his political skills, that his selections were generally well received. Those who feared the establishment of a powerful federal government, however, objected to the appointment of Wilson, whose support of a strong federal government was too well established for their comfort.[632] Then there was the Senate, which had expected to play a more active role in the appointment process and was disappointed by Washington's self-sufficient approach to judicial nominations. "I understand that some of the Senate are disgusted," one Senator wrote of Washington, "that he leaves or is likely to leave to the Senate the power of rejecting the person nominated and nothing more. They expected to act more in the quality of an executive council."[633]

Nevertheless, Washington's nominations satisfied most people. A former aide ran an informal survey to determine the public reactions and found that people were, for the most part, well contented with the new justices. "I heard it repeatedly said in Halifax," he wrote, "that the Supreme Court would be the first Court in the world in point of respectability."[634]

Despite the plaudits, serving on the highest tribunal of the land was hardly a cushy job. Quite the contrary. The justices had to do double duty: They were responsible not only for carrying out the business of the Supreme Court, but also for holding court twice a year in one of the three circuits.[635] This semi-annual judicial travel became known as "circuit riding." One justice had to travel 1,900 miles in his circuit, often under harsh conditions.

> "Stages ran irregularly, broke down, or were missed by the barest of time periods. Horses replaced them and at times became lame. Roads were execrable, making travel by stage or horse severe. Sporadic criminal activity affected the roving jurists, and at times personal possessions were simply lost. Accidents were common, disease was a near neighbor, and fatigue was a constant companion. The entire lifestyle was ... more than the strength of any man can bear."[636]

Writing in September 1791 to his wife, James Iredell described one of his nights on the circuit: "The accommodations were in some places very bad, particularly at a very rascally house where I had the misfortune to be obliged to put up on Saturday night, a parcel of worthless young fellows sitting up drinking, gaming, cursing and swearing all night. I think I never had a more effectual lesson against swearing, and hope to profit by it."[637]

Washington invited the justices to share their circuit-riding experiences with him, but they readily admitted they loathed the practice.[638] It was the cause of frequent turnover of justices on the first Supreme Court, but Congress refused to change it. Sending the justices around the country was designed to give the Court greater recognition and credibility, bring the government to the people, and promote public confidence in the new federal structure.[639] As far as Congress was concerned, however, its most important benefit was that it saved the cost of hiring more judges.

As Supreme Court justices, Washington's appointees rendered opinions that reflected respect for the Constitution, for the limits of judicial power, and for the rule of law.[640] Although often overlooked in favor of their successors, the earliest justices insisted upon American sovereignty and the superiority of federal law over state laws. In the face of significant temptations to blur the line between judicial, executive, and legislative functions, they stoutly maintained judicial independence. In so doing, they helped clear the way for the ensuing political, social, and economic successes of the United States.

The true test of the independence of the Court arose over a request for an advisory opinion from the Washington administration.

In February 1793, France declared war on Britain, precipitating yet another armed conflict in Europe which threatened to engulf the fledgling United States as well. Americans were subjected to strong conflicting tugs and pulls toward one or another side, and this was so even within Washington's own administration. Attempting to thread carefully through the minefield of conflicting treaty obligations, the President was determined to avoid war if at all possible. Then on April 22, 1793, he issued a Proclamation of Neutrality, declaring that the United States would "pursue a conduct friendly and impartial toward the belligerent powers."[641] He needed legal advice on the international law aspects of remaining neutral.[642] Perhaps an opinion from the Supreme Court would guide his policies and bolster the credibility of his actions in the eyes of the American public and the French and British governments.[643] The Supreme Court's authority would "ensure the respect of all parties."[644]

Thomas Jefferson, writing at the behest of the President, asked the Supreme Court "consistent with well-established English custom" for an advisory opinion about the duties and obligations of the United States under its various treaties and under international law. The President himself, however, had misgivings about asking Supreme Court justices for an advisory opinion. In his letter to Jefferson on July 18, 1793, the President cautioned that "the Judges will have to decide whether the business which it is proposed to ask their opinion upon is, in their judgment, of such a nature as that they can comply."[645]

The justices unanimously rejected the request for an advisory opinion, basing it on the Separation of Powers clause of the Constitution, "lines of separation drawn by the Constitution between the three departments of government – their being in certain respects checks on each other...."[646]

Washington had made certain that the Supreme Court would be independent in its operation, and the Court had just demonstrated it.

At the dawn of American independence, what was of fundamental concern to the people was the scope of the powers granted to the national government and the possible abuses of authority that might occur as a result. In debates about the creation of the Supreme Court, many harbored the fear that an extensive federal judiciary – colluding with a strong centralized federal authority and isolated from the public – would lead, once again, to a system of aristocracy and oppression as had occurred during the colonial period under the British monarchy.

Having been personally involved in the debates during the formation of the republic, Washington was familiar with these concerns. He knew that the transition from a confederation of more-or-less independent states to a republican form of government would be neither easy nor immediate, and that the delicate balance inherent in federalism would be constantly tested. In the international sphere, he was painfully aware of the country's lack of ability to wage another war against a major foreign power, so he relied on his appointed justices to handle these matters with such dignity, firmness, and impartiality as to impress – and defuse – potentially explosive foreign confrontations. He was not disappointed. Time and again the justices brought their extraordinary legal talents to bear on these problems to render decisions that demonstrated great sensitivity to their international impact.[647]

Even though George Washington did not live to see the full breadth and impact of the decisions handed down by his judicial appointments, history acknowledges that the justices of the new Supreme Court made vital contributions to the establishment of the rule of law and the sanctity of contracts and property rights, and that they also laid the foundation for the decisions made in the next decade by Chief Justice John Marshall establishing the power of judicial review and the supremacy of federal laws and treaties.[648]

Chapter Thirteen

THE PARADOX OF PAPER MONEY

I believe that banking institutions are more dangerous to our liberties than standing armies.

Thomas Jefferson

It was Tuesday, February 22, 1791, George Washington was turning 59, and the City of Philadelphia was going all out to impress him on his birthday.[649] The celebrations began at noon on Tuesday with a parade by the Artillery and Light Infantry Corps marching down Market Street to the President's house. Then members of both Houses of Congress and other dignitaries and foreign envoys walked in procession,[650] while hundreds crowded near the President's house trying to catch a glimpse of its celebrated occupant. Then the Liberty Bell rang out, cutting the crisp winter air with a clear tone to remind all of the cause of liberty. (The Bell would ring for the last time on the same day in 1846, when it cracked while ringing out in celebration of George Washington's birthday.)

There was a ball that evening in the new Concert Hall on Chestnut Street, with a late dinner served between ten and eleven[651] to Vice President and Mrs. Adams, many members of the U.S. Congress and of the Pennsylvania legislature, and three hundred and fifty other prominent guests.[652]

It was a beautiful function. Philadelphians had wanted to show the President how much they appreciated his presence in their city. Perhaps, if he were sufficiently impressed, the government would stay in Philadelphia.

As the evening drew to a close at midnight, the guests departed in their carriages, the click-clop of horses' hooves against the cobblestone streets breaking the silence in the pale light of hundreds of oil lamps lighting the route for the horses to follow. Washington too retired to his house. It had been a long and eventful day. He was preparing to send a ransom payment to free American sailors held captive by the Barbary pirates, an extremely distasteful but necessary step. In another unpleasant but necessary duty, he was dispatching two officers to Ohio in preparation for a counterattack on Native American tribes in that region who had been raiding the local settlements.[653] Despite many challenges, Washington was in high spirits. The nation was making great strides on multiple fronts. He expected to receive Jefferson's recommendations shortly for the appointment of several additional consular officers in foreign capitals. New states were being added to the Union, and he was sanguine about the progress of his economic program.

As was his custom, Washington rose early the next morning to get in an hour's horseback riding before starting another demanding day. But he had more than pirates and Indians on his mind that morning as he climbed the steps to his private second-floor office. On his mahogany desk for his signature was a bill designated as the "Act to Incorporate the Subscribers to the Bank of the United States." Next to it sat the draft of a veto message prepared for him by James Madison that would forever silence the emotional debates surrounding the bank bill. Whichever document Washington signed would have deep implications for the nation's fiscal posture.

* * *

The administration's plans to revitalize the American economy included on-going efforts to put the country's financial infrastructure on a sound footing. As an integral part of these initiatives and with the approval of the President, the Treasury under Hamilton issued two reports to Congress in December 1790. The first, its Report on Public Credit, was intended to lay the groundwork for the second, a proposal to organize a national-level institution called the Bank of the United States.[654] The bill sitting on the President's desk that morning was designed to create this new entity, a sort of central-bank-cum-commercial-bank – not exactly a familiar sight to Americans in the eighteenth century. There had been no experience with such institutions in colonial times, and hostility toward "moneymen" had been widespread even before the Revolution. This new administration initiative, therefore, had an uncertain outcome in the U.S. Congress.

Earlier, while still serving as an aide to George Washington, a youthful Alexander Hamilton, full of enthusiasm for the concept of creating a national bank gleaned from his readings about the history of the Bank of England, wrote about it to Robert Morris, at the time the foremost financier of the age. Later, when Morris was engaged in a serious effort to restore fiscal soundness to the Confederation government, Hamilton continued his exhortations about the Bank of England. In a classic case of taking coal to Newcastle, a young and brash Hamilton again wrote Morris about the importance of organizing a banking institution for the country. He credited the Bank of England with Britain's success on the world stage. "Great Britain is indebted for the immense efforts she has been able to make in so many illustrious and successful wars essentially to that vast fabric of credit."[655]

Now that he was the Treasury Secretary, Hamilton continued his explorations about a national bank, this time in a rousing defense of the proposed bank in his report to Congress in 1790. It was a first-rate tutorial dubbed by historians as "Banking 101" for members of Congress, and it was vintage Alexander Hamilton – clear, detailed, and wordy!

Writing to Congress, Hamilton called the bank "a political machine of the greatest importance to the state." It would serve as the clearing agent for the payment of national debts and as the principal depository of federal funds. Combined with other initiatives of the administration, it would also help promote domestic industry and diversify the economy by pumping cash and credit into a wide array of productive enterprises.[656]

The bank could also be of help in the establishment of a national currency. In 1790, the real issue for the bank bill was the issuance of paper currency with which the Bank of the United States would be tasked. The President and his Treasury Secretary both recognized the urgency of this project for the country, but it was a most sensitive subject at the time. For one thing, the Constitution contained no grant of such authority to Congress. Americans still bore the scars of the ill-fated Continental dollar, which had depreciated to zero in value, causing massive losses in the general population. For most people, there was now an obsessive embracing of specie and bullion, referred to as "coin" in common parlance, and a corresponding aversion to paper money. Hamilton had to convince the public that the paper currency issued by the Bank of the United States would be acceptable in payment of taxes and all government debts and accounts, and be redeemable in specie upon demand with no pre-conditions, as Adam Smith had advocated.[657]

The Treasury had to deal with other public concerns as well. If the bank were managed by the government, opportunities for malfeasance would multiply, especially in times of emergency when the bank would be called upon to lend large sums to finance government operations. To allay such concerns, the Treasury proposed that the bank would be a public-private partnership in that its charter would be issued by the government, but its ownership would be largely in private hands. Likewise, private citizens would be in charge of the bank's management, but their focus would be on acts of "public utility" such as expediting payments on behalf of the Treasury, serving as the depository of federal funds, aiding in the regulation of the money supply, facilitating the collection of taxes, and other similar functions. The government would also retain certain rights of ownership and be entitled to its pro-rata portion of the dividends.[658]

Paradoxically, the notion of private investors being the primary beneficiaries of the proposed bank was equally unpalatable to the public, fueling criticism that the institution would become a tool of the wealthy. This the Treasury dealt with by using the only precedent available from pre-Revolutionary America, namely, the colonial land offices, which had been institutions managed by government employees for the benefit of all colonists. It would be unwise to stray from this tradition, Hamilton knew, since many harbored fears that a privately-owned bank would become a pawn of special interests and leave the ordinary citizens out in the cold.

Hamilton proposed that investors could use government securities to pay for three-quarters of the purchase price of stock in the Bank of the United States. The securities would thus form a part of the capital stock of the bank, boosting the demand for the government's debt instruments while providing price support for them in the marketplace.[659] Rather than expanding the borrowing capacity of the federal government to limitless dimensions, the Treasury recommended that government securities should match but not exceed the bank's portfolio of loans generated from the private sector and comprise no more than eight or nine percent of the outstanding federal debt.[660] The bank would therefore accumulate capital in the form of "coin" and government securities, and issue bank notes in greater volume than the quantity of bullion it had on hand.[661] The banking and funding systems would thus work together to promote the growth of the capital markets.[662]

When the Treasury's Report on a National Bank was released to Congress in December 1790,[663] it sparked an immediate reaction among those who viewed finance as an unsavory profession. The question of whether the proposed bank would become an instrument of financial progress or simply another windfall for moneyed interests was the key point of contention in the coming debate. Nevertheless, in the U.S. Senate, the "Act to Incorporate the Subscribers to the Bank of the United States" fared well. There, the report was routinely referred to a committee whose composition included members knowledgeable about business, and the Senate passed it by voice vote in January 1791. It was then received by the House of Representatives, where a different fate awaited it.[664]

In long speeches, the anti-banking faction in the House fulminated against the proposal as being the brainchild of speculators and moneymen, believing that the bank was clearly "calculated to benefit a small part of the United States – the mercantile interest only," wrote James Jackson, a Congressman from Georgia and a staunch ally of Thomas Jefferson.[665] In addition to provoking the ire of the agrarian and anti-finance contingent in Congress, the bank bill also stirred opposition among Southerners, who feared that the twenty-year lifespan of the bank charter would give the government an excuse to remain in Philadelphia, near its financial anchor, rather than to move its operations to the new Potomac capital in Georgetown as planned.[666]

Spearheading the opposition in the House, James Madison threw down the gauntlet on February 2, 1791, and spoke forcefully against the bill.[667] As the champion of the anti-charter and anti-banking faction, Madison was a curious choice. During the Constitutional Convention of 1787, he had tried to secure for the federal government the explicit power to grant charters of incorporation – the opposite of the position he now so passionately advocated.[668]

In an astute legislative ploy, Madison diverted the debate away from the emotional argument that banks were harmful to society to a lofty intellectual plane. Taking the high road, he shrewdly contended that the proposed legislation was unconstitutional. "Is the power of establishing an incorporated bank among the powers vested by the constitution in the Legislature of the United States?" Madison asked incredulously. Pausing for effect and pulling himself up to his full height, he then answered his own question. The bank, he thundered, "was condemned by the silence of the Constitution."[669] Other like-minded Congressmen then began making similar charges on the floor of the House.[670] This argument became the primary objection to the bank bill, enabling the bill's proponents to concentrate their firepower on the legal issue raised by the opposing faction.

On the House floor, the campaign in support of the administration's proposal was led by Fisher Ames, a representative from Massachusetts, and Elias Boudinot, former president of the Continental Congress and now a representative from New Jersey. Boudinot quoted passages from Madison's own writings contradicting his contention that chartering a bank violated the U.S. Constitution. After much spirited debate, the Madison faction failed to carry the day. With the prestige of the President supporting the bill, the House voted to pass it on February 8, 1791, by a vote of 39-20,[671] which was followed by the final vote of approval by the Senate on February 12. The bill was then presented to George Washington for his signature on February 14, 1791.[672]

From his cramped offices at Sixth and Market Streets, Washington carefully followed the proceedings in the House. Having been exposed to business and finance from his earliest days, particularly as they related to real estate, farming, and international trade,[673] he harbored no doubts about the vital need for the proposed financial institution as a tool for the restoration of public credit.[674] Adam Smith, whose writings influenced much of Washington's thinking, attached great importance in his *Wealth of Nations* to the Bank of England as the source of financial support for Great Britain. The book suggested that one of the principal mechanisms by which a nation could accumulate wealth was through the establishment of a banking system. "The trade of Scotland," Smith wrote, "has more than quadrupled since the first erection of the two public banks at Edinburgh."[675]

Reflecting his instinctive understanding of the crucial role of a national bank as a financing vehicle for a government, Washington once asked Wakelin Welch, managing partner of his London trading company, whether Great Britain had not been enabled "by means of the Bank [of England] to continue the war" against the United States. Aside from demonstrating his grasp of the wartime funding operations of the British government, Washington was also trying to make a case that Cary & Company owed him reimbursement for certain losses sustained on his farm during the war. Mr. Welch was not about to oblige, nor debate such philosophical issues with his famous American client.[676]

Washington later demonstrated his confidence in eighteenth-century U.S. banking by providing in his will that the proceeds of the sale of the real estate assets in his estate were to be invested in bank stock for Martha's benefit, and the dividends paid to her.[677]

During the debate over the bill, its opponents cannily decided to raise no questions about the usefulness of the bank as an instrument of growth for the economy. They knew full well they could not match wits with Hamilton on the subject of finance, which is why they chose to attack the bill on an issue to which Washington was known to be most sensitive, namely the constitutionality of granting a congressional charter to such an entity. The President believed that the federal Constitution was the best that the mind of man could devise, and he had worked tirelessly to select the first justices of the U.S. Supreme Court to ensure their adherence to its tenets and to the rule of law. He believed that to play fast and loose with that landmark document would put the republic in peril. Constitutional mandates had to be viewed as sacrosanct as otherwise public respect for the rule of law – which he regarded as the lynchpin of a free society – would be eroded. Understandably, therefore, Washington was uneasy about the prospect of his administration being associated with an act of dubious constitutional precedent. He had never had the benefit of a formal education in the law, but he also did not bring any dogma or preconceived notions to the debate swirling about him. He would rely on his personal experiences in the private sector as well as his skill at perceiving the nuances that could alter the course of consideration. So, to judge the pros and cons of the debate, he would resort to his lifelong habit of listening to all sides of an issue, then judge its merits for himself. On this process would now hang the ultimate fate of the fiscal program of the United States.

Having worked out his approach, Washington wasted no time in seeking comment from all quarters as soon as the bill cleared both houses of Congress. His first step was to turn to James Madison, the bill's chief opponent. The President respected the Congressman's opinions on the Constitution and wanted to hear from him personally and in detail. He did so over several sessions, throughout which Madison was authoritative and unequivocal in his assertion that the bank bill was unconstitutional. As he had done on the floor of the House, Madison demonstrated his encyclopedic knowledge of the Constitution to support his position that there was no authority in any of its provisions for the organization of a bank by the government. He then added what he considered the *pièce de resistance*: The twenty-year period of the bank's stay in Philadelphia was entirely too long. "Twenty years was to this country," he said, "as a period of a century is to the history of other countries, there was no calculating for the events which might take place." Moreover, in another ten years

Philadelphia would no longer be the capital city. Madison stressed that the President should exercise his veto power for the first time and lay this matter to rest in a decisive manner.[678]

Madison was not the only Virginian to oppose the organization of a national bank. In January, Beverley Randolph, the governor of Virginia, wrote Washington about the proposed legislation, enclosing a resolution passed by the General Assembly of that state, asserting that the bank bill was "dangerous to the rights and subversive to the interest of the people."[679]

Senator William Maclay of Pennsylvania, a scrupulous note-taker, also had reservations about the bill. Writing in his journal on December 24, 1790, he revealed his early misgivings about the plan, expressing concern that a national bank could be "an aristocratic engine," and "a machine for the mischievous purposes of bad ministers."[680]

Washington habitually kept an eye on the press.[681] A writer calling himself "Z" wrote at length in the *Federal Gazette*, which had the largest readership, in opposition to the bank bill. Invoking the Constitution, "Z" contended that "the power of laying taxes and borrowing money" was not "synonymous to the granting charters of incorporation to a number of private men for the purpose of an exclusive trade through the Union for twenty years."[682]

Henry Knox, his Secretary of War, was convinced that the government was not authorized to create an institution of the proposed bank's size and influence. He too advised Washington to veto the bank bill.

Washington then turned to his Attorney General, Edmund Randolph, for a legal opinion on the subject. The two conferred over several sessions between February 8 and 11, 1791, after which Randolph followed up with a written opinion on February 12. He too was unequivocal that the bank bill was unconstitutional, and that the "necessary and proper" clause provided no basis for the extension of federal power in the manner proposed. "Let it be pronounced as an eternal question to those who build new powers on this clause," Randolph warned, "whether the latitude of construction which they arrogate, will not terminate in an unlimited power in Congress?"[683]

The President also sought the opinion of Jefferson, who was already known to harbor a deep suspicion of bankers, moneyed interests, and financial investors. "I have ever been the enemy of banks seeking to filch from the public their swindling and barren gains," Jefferson would later write to John Adams.[684] Not surprisingly, therefore, in his response to the President, Jefferson agreed with Madison that the bill strayed beyond the boundaries of congressional power as laid out in the Constitution.[685] In his letter to the President on February 15, Jefferson cited the Tenth Amendment, which states that "the powers not delegated to the United States by the Constitution, nor prohibited by it to the states, are reserved to the states respectively, or to the people." Jefferson then attached to his letter a copy of a speech on the subject by Madison.[686]

Jefferson was also apprehensive that the bank bill would further expand the scope and reach of Hamilton's power and responsibility within the administration. In this Jefferson was joined by several members of Congress. Elbridge Gerry, a respected Congressman from Massachusetts, had spoken for all like-minded opponents of the Treasury's initiatives when he expressed deep concern that the Secretary was being given "a greater influence than the President of the United States has, and more than is proper for any person to have in a republican government."[687]

For Jefferson and others who viewed Hamilton as pro-British and pro-monarchy, the fact that the proposed Bank of the United States appeared to be substantially patterned after the Bank of England deepened their suspicions about Hamilton's motives. Thus, they viewed the pending bill as constituting not only a threat to state power but a fundamental assault on the republican structure of the new nation.[688]

Time was running out on the President's decision. He had carefully reflected on the pros and cons of the arguments since the bank bill had passed, but he had not concluded his analysis and deliberation. The bill was presented to the President on February 14. If he failed to act within ten days, it would become law without his signature. The President penned a letter to Hamilton on February 16. "It... [is] my duty to examine the ground on which the objection [to the bill] is built," he wrote. He then enclosed the reports of Attorney General Randolph and Secretary of State Jefferson, and requested Hamilton's opinion on the constitutionality issue. "That I may fully possess the argument for and against the measure before I express any opinion of my own, I now require, in like manner, yours on the validity and propriety of the above recited Act," Washington wrote. "I give you an opportunity of examining and answering the objections contained in the enclosed papers. I require the return of them, when your own sentiments are handed to me (which I wish may be as soon as is convenient); and further, that no copies of them be taken."[689]

Hamilton quickly set to work. Like all government offices at the time, his quarters at the Treasury on Third Street between Chestnut and Walnut Streets were sparsely furnished. His desk, a plain pine table covered with a green cloth, was piled high with files and papers next to a China vase,[690] and including a copy of the charter of the Bank of England. The 1791 Philadelphia city directory listed two hundred and eighteen employees in the Treasury Department, versus seven, including two chargés d'affaires in Europe, for the State Department, and a mere dozen civilian employees in the War Department.

By the third week in February, the President had two documents in hand. One was a letter of apology from Hamilton. "The Secretary of the Treasury sends his respects to the President of the United States, to request indulgence for not having furnished his reasons on a certain point. He has been ever since sedulously engaged in it, but finds it will be impossible to complete before Tuesday evening or Wednesday morning early. He is anxious to give the point a thorough examination."[691] The other document was from Madison, the draft of a veto message of the bank bill, a not-so-subtle hint to the President to take the easy road and affix his signature to it.

On the night of February 22, the city of Philadelphia had drifted off to sleep while its dimly-lit streets were patrolled by thirty-two watchmen who cried the hour. Hamilton had been working feverishly on his response to the President for a week, and now his frenzy was about to culminate in "the most famous all-nighter in American banking history" as he worked by candlelight on his opinion "concerning the constitutionality of the bill for establishing a national bank." Faced with a torrent of strong, even angry opposition from within the administration and in Congress, he needed to mount a convincing defense. The President had been in complete accord on every aspect of the plan to restore financial confidence in the United States government, but if he were not fully convinced of the constitutionality of what was being proposed, he would not hesitate to veto the bank bill. The President was rock-solid in his determination to set a precedent of respect for the Constitution.[692]

Hamilton sat glued to his chair, writing his response to Washington in longhand, the pages falling from his desk to be picked up by his wife Elizabeth, who then hurried off to copy them. When it was done, Hamilton permitted himself a moment of indulgence to mention his sleep deprivation to his boss. "The Secretary of the Treasury presents his respects to the President," he wrote in his cover letter, "and sends him the opinion required which occupied him the greater part of the night."[693]

Mindful of the historical importance of the occasion, Hamilton was formal in the opening paragraph of his commentary. "The Secretary of the Treasury," he began, "having perused with attention the papers containing the opinions of the Secretary of State and Attorney General, concerning the constitutionality of the bill for establishing a national bank, proceeds, according to the order of the President, to submit the reasons which have induced him to entertain a different opinion."

In his law practice, Hamilton had found it useful to overwhelm his courtroom opponents with voluminous written material, a practice that would be popularized in another century as a "Brandeis brief" (named after a successful lawyer and later justice of the U.S. Supreme Court, Louis Brandeis). So, while Jefferson made his case against the bank bill in 2,100 words and Randolph in 3,350, Hamilton's defense was made in a mind-bending essay of 13,000 words. Nor was he content with merely expounding a different interpretation of the relevant provisions of the Constitution, as Washington had requested. Fully aware of the President's sensitivity to charges of unconstitutional action, Hamilton set for himself the mission of totally demolishing his opponents' arguments point by painstaking point. Laying out his presentation with precision and detail, he based his case on the premise that no draftsman of the Constitution could have possibly foreseen all the circumstances under which the government would be called upon to act, and that, therefore, certain powers are implied in that document.[694] If Congress were not specifically granted the power to incorporate a bank, neither had it been explicitly forbidden from doing so. "It is not denied that there are implied, as well as express powers; and that the former are as effectually delegated as the latter." He was forceful in taking the position that "every power vested in a government is in its nature sovereign and includes...a right to employ all the means requisite and fairly applicable to the attainment of the ends of such power, and which are not precluded by restrictions... specified in the constitution, or not immoral, or not contrary to the essential ends of political society."[695] Spelling it out further, Hamilton then gave the President the justification for the constitutionality of the bank bill: "The means by which national exigencies are to be provided for, national inconveniences obviated, national prosperity promoted are of such infinite variety, extent and complexity, that there must, of necessity, be great latitude of discretion in the selection and applications of those means." If one were to accept the opinions of Jefferson and Randolph, Hamilton argued, then the federal government would be powerless to act in countless instances, such as in taking up arms against the Indian tribes or against smugglers. "The practice of government," he concluded, "is against the rules of construction advocated by the Secretary of State."[696]

On the morning of February 25, 1791, the bank bill sat on George Washington's mahogany desk, on the second floor of what had once been Robert Morris's bathhouse. By this time, the President felt confident that this much-needed piece of legislation did not contravene any provision of the United States Constitution. However, mindful, perhaps, that many in the House and the Senate had voted in favor of the bank bill because it had originated in his administration, the President wished to demonstrate his convictions that there existed a real need for such a banking institution in the American society and that the bill did not contravene any provision of the U.S. Constitution. He was thus prepared to sign the bank bill without further delay. He did so on February 25, 1791, bringing to a close – for the moment, anyway – a contentious debate hinging on the relationship between legislative power and constitutional precedent.

The Bank of the United States received a charter for twenty years, along with a promise of exclusivity. Congress would grant no other bank charters during that period. The Bank would issue 25,000 shares at $400 each, of which three quarters could be payable in government securities, for a total of $10 million. Eighty percent of the bank's capital would come from private subscribers who were allowed to purchase shares in four installments, payable over eighteen months, reducing the immediate need for specie. Bond prices would thus be supported as individuals bought them to convert into bank stock.[697] Foreigners would also be permitted to own stock in the bank, but in their hands the shares would be non-voting. The charter allowed the bank to collect deposits, make loans at a maximum interest rate of six percent, and issue up to $10 million of paper currency. To restore order to the chaos existing in the currency of the country, the bank's capital would provide the backing for emissions of paper currency, subject to the limitation of two to three times such capital. As for voting rights, Hamilton rejected the approach of one vote for each shareholder, irrespective of the number of shares held, as used by the Bank of England, and chose instead one vote for each share, which in time became the prevailing American approach. Stockholders of the bank would elect its board of directors, which in turn would appoint a president, cashier, and other officers. The bank could buy bills of exchange and trade in bullion, but its dealings in real property were limited to land and buildings required for its own accommodation and assets pledged by borrowers as collateral and seized upon the occurrence of an event of default. The federal government would accept notes issued by the bank for all taxes and other payments. With ownership of twenty percent of the stock, the government would be the largest shareholder in the bank, but it would not control its day-to-day operations. "What nation was ever blessed with a constant succession of upright and wise administrators?" Hamilton asked rhetorically. "The keen, steady, and, as it were, magnetic sense, of their own interest, as proprietors, in the Directors of a Bank, pointing invariably to its true pole, the prosperity of the institution, is the only security, that can always be relied upon, for a careful and prudent administration."[398]

As for the location of the bank's headquarters, Hamilton wrote to the President that a large commercial city with a great deal of capital and business would be the fittest seat for the bank. Philadelphia was presented as a city generally favorable to the establishment of a national institution, where in fact the first such entity (the Bank of North America) had been headquartered. The bank, therefore, would be based in Philadelphia for an initial term of twenty years, after which it would be moved to the new capital.[699]

When the bank bill became law, Philadelphians were exultant, and hopeful of keeping the government in their city on a permanent basis. They had already begun the construction of a mansion on Ninth Street for the President's exclusive use (in size fully two-thirds the modern While House), although Washington was not particularly supportive of this initiative. Perched at the octagonal desk in his office in Philadelphia, the President had a view facing south and east. Even with the bank bill in front of him, he looked out wistfully in the direction of Mount Vernon – toward the garden where he restored his soul.

To allow for the widest possible participation by residents of all the states, and considering the slow pace of communication and transportation at the time, the bank's charter provided that the subscription books would remain open until July 4.[700] Accordingly, in July 1791, six months after receiving its charter, the bank made the first public offering of its stock. Like many IPOs some two centuries later, the shares promptly became hot stock; they were snapped up within two hours after the subscription books were opened. An explosion of demand then drove up the price quickly to seven times the amount set at the initial offering.[701] As Hamilton had written earlier to Robert Morris, "The men of property in America are enlightened about their own interest and would easily be brought to see the advantages of a good plan."[702] Nonetheless, aware that many buyers had borrowed heavily to finance their investment, and that there was danger that share prices might soar above their underlying value, Hamilton took steps to avoid the fate that had befallen the shareholders of the South Sea Company after the collapse of the market for that stock resulted in massive public losses in England. Hamilton wasted no time in acting to dampen the demand and increase the cost of borrowing for investors, successfully averting a crash in the bank stock.[703]

Among those who came into a windfall profit as a result of the frenzied demand for the bank stock were thirty members of Congress, prompting another round of acid commentary from Madison, Jefferson, and other critics of finance. "The Bank shares have risen as much in the market here as at Philadelphia," Madison reported to Jefferson in early July. "The subscriptions are...a mere scramble for so much public plunder, which will be engrossed by those already loaded with the spoils of individuals."[704]

Once the bank was established, the Treasury Department quickly relinquished all control over it, as pledged. Thomas Willing (1731-1821), a respected banker, former partner in Willing and Morris, and former president of the Bank of North America, was appointed president of the Bank of the United States. Even before the main branch in Philadelphia opened for business on December 12, 1791, the stockholders voted to establish branches in Boston, New York, Charleston, and Baltimore.[705] So, while its detractors looked on in disdain, the bank began its work with vigor. By the spring of 1792, it had established the branches authorized by the shareholders and began accepting deposits and transferring money for the Treasury. Ironically, Hamilton was far from being pleased by these developments; obviously he had not expected that the institution he had fathered would so quickly begin to act independently of him. "The whole affair of the branches was begun, continued, and ended," he wrote, "not only without my participation, but against my judgment... I was never consulted."[706]

The bank's ability to lend to the government in times of difficulty became increasingly useful in later years. Washington's support of this institution at a time when banking was frowned upon even in principle set a critical precedent for the new nation and its future entrepreneurs. "The establishment of public credit is an immense point gained in our national concerns," Washington wrote after the passage of the bank bill. "This I believe exceeds the expectations of the most sanguine among us, and a late instance, unparalleled in this country, has been given of the confidence reposed in our measures by the rapidity with which the subscriptions to the Bank of the United States were filled. In two hours after the books were opened by the commissioners, the whole number of shares were taken up and four thousand more applied for than were allowed by the institution. This circumstance was not only pleasing as it related to the confidence in the government, but also it exhibited proof of the resources of our citizens."[707]

The year following the passage of the bank bill, Congress also passed the Coinage Act of 1792, which established the Mint and created the office of Director of the Mint at a salary of $2,000 per year. Still using the Spanish milled dollar as the model, Jefferson, Hamilton, and others then specified the exact amount of standard silver or other metal to be used in each coin.

After its charter was granted, Jefferson wrote to Madison that all Virginia residents who cooperated with the Bank of the United States should be prosecuted for treason in the Commonwealth of Virginia, and if convicted be sentenced to death. "The power of erecting banks and corporations," Jefferson exclaimed, "was not given to the general government; it remains then with the state itself. For any person to recognize a foreign legislature [i.e., the United States Congress] in a case belonging to the state itself is an act of treason against the state. And whosoever shall do any act under color of the authority of a foreign legislature, whether by signing notes, issuing or passing them, acting as director, cashier or in any other office relating to it, shall be adjudged guilty of high treason and suffer death accordingly by the judgment of the state courts."[708]

Chapter Fourteen

THE EUROPEAN THEATER – BRITAIN

Without economic security there can be no national security – and vice versa.

George Osborne
Chancellor of the Exchequer

When George Washington assumed the Presidency in 1789, the threat to American homes and families was real and immediate, and the traumatic memories of the recent war were still fresh. Foreign and domestic enemies threatened the United States from all sides. To the west, various Native American tribes, egged on by Britain and Spain, were raiding western settlements. Spain controlled portions of the southwest, and its forces prevented American access to the Mississippi River. To the north and northwest, Britain retained control of Canada, the navigation of the Great Lakes, and the military posts ceded to the United States by the Peace Treaty of 1783. On the high seas, the country's ships were fair game to hostile forces of other nations, and Britain's superior navy and discriminatory trade policies restrained the international trade of the United States. Although France presented little direct threat to this nation initially, that country's volatile domestic situation and its antagonism toward other European powers posed the risk that it would drag the United States into a European-born conflict.

Having fought a revolution at least partly to escape the severe constraints placed on their economic development by Great Britain, Americans had high expectations that, once freed, they could engage in trade on a global basis, find new markets for their products, and buy manufactured items from the most favorable sources worldwide. All too soon the realization came that independence did not automatically translate into the fulfillment of the commercial expectations of Americans. Each of the major powers of the day (Britain, France, and Spain) created its own peculiar set of problems for the United States, threatening America's national security and inhibiting its economic progress.

President Washington was painfully aware of the country's lack of military preparedness, as well as its fragile financial circumstances, and was determined to find peaceful solutions to these great-power issues, if at all possible. While mindful of the deterrents to the nation's development – danger to the country's security from foreign powers and the impediments imposed by them on the commerce of the United States – Washington was equally cognizant of America's inability to remove these obstacles by the use of force. He made it clear that war was "unwise . . . in the extreme" and carried the guarantee that the United States' "weight would be but small; though the loss to ourselves would be certain."[709] He had to find peaceful ways of securing in the international arena the essential privileges for the creation of a prosperous American economy. He described peace as "the most powerful instrument of our rising prosperity," and was single-minded in his pursuit of commercial treaties with the major powers of the day to achieve that prosperity.[710]

Years later Washington would speak optimistically of the day when America would "possess the strength of a giant and there will be none who can make us afraid."[711] Until that glorious day arrived, he was emphatic about the urgency of buying time to put the nation's affairs in order. "Twenty years' peace," he noted, "with such an increase of population and resources as we have a right to expect, added to our remote situation from the jarring power, will in all probability enable us in a just cause to *bid defiance to any power on earth.*"[712] [Emphasis added.] Despite Washington's firm conviction that domestic prosperity required peace, however, events outside his control conspired to make this goal ever more elusive.

The President had set a daunting task for himself. To accomplish his objective of creating commercial relations with all European nations through a network of appropriate treaties – all without firing a shot – would require patient determination, fortunate timing, and extraordinary diplomatic skills. In the Revolutionary War, Washington had demonstrated that he could be a resolute field commander. In the post-war era, he showed equal talent in a different sort of war – mobilizing all the diplomatic resources available to him to play the major powers against each other and to attempt to gain every possible advantage for the United States in his quest for the long-term commercial development of the new republic. The country's economic prosperity depended on it.

Under the 1783 Treaty of Paris, Britain recognized the American colonies as independent states. At Washington's inauguration as President more than five years later, however, many of the essential terms of that treaty still remained unfulfilled. The troublesome military presence of British forces on the northern border of the United States combined with the existence of the thorny unresolved issues of trade and navigation made for an untenable state of affairs, causing a second war between Britain and the new American republic to seem, if not inevitable, at least probable.[713]

Under the Treaty of Paris, both countries promised that "creditors on either side shall meet with no lawful impediment to the recovery of the full value in sterling money, of all bona fide debts heretofore contracted."[714] The federal government did in fact "earnestly recommend" to the states to provide restitution for confiscated property. The states, however, unused to submitting to federal control over their affairs, resisted these recommendations. During and immediately after the Revolutionary War, Americans had fallen massively in debt to English merchants. Southern states, and Virginia in particular, were the most affected by the debt crunch. The "earnest recommendation" of the federal government thus rang hollow to the creditors.[715]

The first American tribunal addressing the issue was the Circuit Court in Richmond, Virginia. The ever-eloquent Patrick Henry, as counsel for the defendant debtor, not only won the case, but in the process made certain that the outcome sent a clear signal to all British creditors: They would not prevail in American state courts. Other Southern states then followed the model set by Patrick Henry's defense in Virginia.[716]

Upon taking office, President Washington immediately looked for the means to halt the escalation of tensions with Britain. As the two countries had yet to establish full diplomatic relations, neither nation wished to be the first to send an ambassador to the other.[717] If Washington wished to negotiate with Britain, he would have to take the first step. In October, he consulted with John Jay, whose credentials in the arena of international relations were unmatched in the country, and who was handling the foreign affairs portfolio pending Thomas Jefferson's acceptance of his appointment as Secretary of State. Jay concurred that sending a special envoy to His Majesty's government would be the best way to test the extent of England's interest in concluding a bilateral commercial treaty with the United States and resolving the issue of Britain's western posts. Jay suggested Edward Bancroft as a candidate for the mission. Bancroft, an American physician and businessman, was born in Massachusetts in 1744 and had served as secretary to the American Commission in Paris during the Revolutionary War.

Washington also consulted with Alexander Hamilton about the selection of an envoy. He agreed that it was a useful approach and recommended Gouverneur Morris for the job. Gouverneur (no relation to Robert Morris) had served as the deputy to the Superintendent of Finance in the Confederation government. Washington had observed Gouverneur as a delegate to the Constitutional Convention and judged him to have a sharp intellect and a great vision of the future of the young republic.[718] He was tall, handsome, and charming, with a notable sense of humor. He was also a brilliant negotiator. An early accident had left him with only one leg, which did not slow him down at all in his many activities.[719] A week after these discussions with Jay and Hamilton, Washington appointed Gouverneur Morris to the unofficial mission of envoy to London with instructions to determine whether the British "incline to a treaty of commerce with the United States on any and what terms," whether they could be persuaded to abandon the western forts, and whether they would be willing to pay compensation for the property taken during the war.[720]

If there were a drawback to his selection, it was that Morris was a great admirer of French culture and might have been viewed as a Francophile by the British. "I consider France as the natural ally of my country," Morris had written to William Carmichael, the American chargé in Madrid on February 25, 1789. "I love France."[721]

Washington's diaries provide no other clue for the choice he made, but his judgment in rejecting Edward Bancroft was another of the many indications of the President's remarkably intuitive perception of people. Bancroft was lauded at the time as an American patriot, but in reality he was a British agent spying on Benjamin Franklin and other American representatives in wartime, passing secrets to his English handlers through coded messages concealed in trees and other methods of communication with London, for which he received a pension of £200, later raised to £500, from the British Secret Service. Bancroft's treason remained secret until certain British diplomatic papers were declassified in 1891.[722]

When Morris arrived in London in February 1790, Britain stood on the threshold of war with Spain and France.[723] The prospect encouraged Britain to expand the Royal Navy. As volunteers did not appear in sufficient numbers, Britain increased its impressment of Americans for sea duty. U.S. protestations and outrage notwithstanding, the British continued for decades their odious practice of shanghaiing Americans to serve on their ships.[724]

In the meantime, Spain found itself faced with a British ultimatum. Upon reflection, the Spanish court decided it was unprepared for a contest of wills with the Royal Navy. Madrid threw in the towel and capitulated, and the war clouds between the two countries dissolved. It then became clear to Gouverneur Morris that without the pressure of an impending military conflict, Britain had no interest in good-faith discussions with the United States. Discouraged and frustrated, he ended his mission and left England in July 1791, convinced that the British were not in a serious negotiating mode.[725]

The British position vis-à-vis the United States had actually hardened after Washington's inauguration, in some measure by reason of the influence of the English brokers and merchants in the government. When it came to relations with America, the man with whom to reckon was Charles Jenkins, 1st Earl of Liverpool, known as Lord Hawkesbury. As President of the influential Committee for Trade, Hawkesbury was hostile in the extreme toward the United States. He was adamant that Britain should not abandon its garrisons in America, that the carrying trade in the Great Lakes area should be confined to British vessels only, and that access to the Mississippi River should be secured for Britain. He was dead set against permitting Americans to continue to trade with the British West Indies. He also urged the government to take the necessary measures to ensure that the new territories of Kentucky, Vermont, and others should not become part of the United States but remain independent. On April 17, 1790, Hawkesbury detailed these positions to Foreign Secretary George Grenville, and thereafter official British policy toward the United States came to mirror the blueprint formulated by Hawkesbury.[726]

By mid-1791 relations between the U.S. and Great Britain had become increasingly tense. In the summer, Britain finally agreed to send a diplomatic representative to the United States. His name was George Hammond. At the age of 28, he became the first envoy from Great Britain to the United States, arriving in Philadelphia in October 1791 to present his credentials. He reported to his superiors in London that the President had received him with "utmost politeness and respect." His meeting with Alexander Hamilton was also cordial and friendly.[727]

Unknown to the Americans, Lord Grenville had sent Hammond to the United States with a stern set of instructions: The forts would not be removed from American soil, American breaches of the peace treaty had to be rectified, the debts and properties of the British had to be repaid and restored, etc. Furthermore, Britain would not look kindly upon Americans attempting to settle in the areas occupied by the British. If questioned about British complicity in the uprisings by Indian tribes along the frontier, Hammond was to deny, deny, deny. Clearly, Hammond had sailed for the United States with full recognition of the increasing difficulties between the two governments.[728]

One of Hammond's first acts in the United States was to compile a comprehensive list of American laws and court decisions which, in the judgment of the British government, violated the 1783 treaty. When forwarding this long list to Thomas Jefferson as Secretary of State, Hammond complained that "there does not exist a single instance of a recovery of a British debt in [American] courts."[729]

Upon receipt of Hammond's unfriendly bill of particulars, Jefferson responded in kind and provided a long list of America's grievances against Britain.[730] Thus, each side blamed its non-performance on the actions and violations of the other. As for the legalistic bills of particulars presented by Hammond and Jefferson to each other, a more contentious set of correspondence could not have been imagined. It was all lucid and well written but wholly devoid of a scintilla of compromise on which peace negotiations could be advanced between the two countries. They left little room, or hope, for reconciliation.

Hamilton was aghast at Jefferson's letter to Hammond. He favored a much less dogmatic response than the one drafted by Jefferson and made his case to Washington in language one could only describe as vintage Hamilton – impassioned and well-reasoned but in its own way as uncompromising in tone as Jefferson's letter to Hammond. The hostility between the two Cabinet Secretaries, already begun over their diverging positions on other issues, now became inflamed as a result of their respective attitudes toward Great Britain and France. Pulling no punches, Jefferson called Hamilton "the servile copyist of [English Prime Minister] Pitt."[731]

If Washington believed that the United States could not be in a more explosive international situation, he had not counted on the irrational behavior of revolutionary France. He had been unanimously elected to a second term in February 1793, just as France declared war on Britain, catching the American government by surprise and putting the U.S. in an ominous position vis-à-vis the great powers.[732] The President was on a brief visit to Mount Vernon when word of France's declaration of war reached him. He was immediately galvanized to try to pull the United States from the brink of war without promoting riots and upheavals at home. "My visit to Mount Vernon (intended to be short when I set out)," he wrote to Henry Lee, "was curtailed by the declaration of war by France against Great Britain and Holland; for I foresaw in the moment information of that event came to me at that place the necessity for announcing the disposition of this country towards the belligerent powers; and the propriety of restraining, as far as a proclamation would do it, our citizens from taking part in the contest."[733]

In London, the issue of whether the U.S. would join the war on the side of France was a subject of intense speculation. Hammond's instructions were to gather as much intelligence on the matter as possible while simultaneously sparing no effort to work toward ensuring that the U.S. stayed neutral in the war. Without consulting with the President, Alexander Hamilton took it upon himself to assure Hammond that the President was determined to keep the U.S. out of European entanglements, and, even more important, that there were no secret understandings with France.[734] For Lord Grenville, deeply engrossed in the conflict with France, this was indeed valuable intelligence garnered from the American side.

As the Secretary of State, Jefferson was furious with Hamilton for his unauthorized dealings with foreign envoys, his unilateral pronouncements on U.S. foreign policy, and his distinct tilt toward Britain in disregard of America's obligations under the 1778 Treaty of Amity with France. Hamilton had the Treasury portfolio, but he permitted himself to encroach upon areas outside his ambit of primary responsibility.[735]

Washington had invented the cabinet form of administration in order to have the good minds of all his department heads available for consultation on the major issues facing the country, but outside of Cabinet meetings each department head was responsible for his own portfolio. The diverging views of Hamilton and Jefferson were transforming their personal relationship into open animosity, much to the chagrin of the President, who prized collaboration among his Cabinet members and detested unproductive bickering. Aware of the rising tensions, he still chose not to take direct and forceful action, nor to reprimand Hamilton for his unauthorized foreign policy forays. Perhaps Washington remembered that even the mildest rebuke had caused Hamilton to submit his resignation as his aide-de-camp during the war. For once, the President's legendary command-and-control skills seemed to have deserted him. He tried to bring about a reconciliation without resolving any of the substantive issues that were creating an ever-widening gulf between Jefferson and Hamilton. Sadly but predictably, Washington's attempts at brokering peace between his brilliant Cabinet Secretaries proved fruitless, with serious and lasting consequences not only for his administration but for American politics.

Washington faced a constitutional conundrum.[736] Of immediate importance was the weight to be given any pre-existing obligations to France. The 1778 Treaties of Amity and Alliance with France concluded during the Revolutionary War provided for a "perpetual" alliance between France and the United States. They obligated the United States to rise to the defense of French possessions in the New World, to permit French privateers to carry captured prizes to American ports, and to deny the same privilege to ships of any hostile power. At the time, John Adams had declared the agreements a "rock upon which we may safely build," but their impact in the present circumstances was not entirely clear.[737] The issues required careful consideration. If France were at war with England, would American obligations under the Treaty of Alliance require the U.S. to go to war on France's behalf?[738] Would the treaty require the U.S. to protect the French West Indies if attacked? Was the U.S. obligated to prevent British military ships from accompanying British merchant ships into American ports and their privateers from retrofitting in the U.S.? Should a proclamation be issued for the purpose of preventing interference by American citizens in the war between France and Britain?

With his customary caution, the President collected all the divergent views.[739] Hamilton was in favor of the United States remaining neutral in the war. Jefferson, who had consistently favored maintaining the pre-existing alliance with France, was predictably opposed; however, he did not stop there. Perhaps impelled by conversations with James Madison, the ever-vigilant protector of the prerogatives of Congress, Jefferson argued that the President lacked the constitutional authority to declare neutrality and only Congress could do so.

The President listened, and then made his decision. With an emphatic declaration that "the duty and interest of the United States require that they should with sincerity and good faith adopt and pursue a conduct friendly and impartial toward belligerent powers," Washington proclaimed America's neutrality in the war on April 22, 1793. U.S. citizens would now be prohibited from participating in the European conflict and from carrying contraband to any of the warring nations. All citizens were warned that the President had instructed officials to seek out and prosecute violations of the proclamation.[740]

The President's congressional opponents objected strenuously, fearing that the course chosen would inevitably lead to war, but they did not prevail.[741] Nevertheless, being a realist, Washington fully recognized that the Proclamation of Neutrality was far from a panacea for the United States, and that the country had to be super-vigilant in maneuvering between British and French interests on the one hand, and America's economic and political concerns on the other.

The President raised the question of America's relations with Britain and France at a Cabinet meeting and specifically opened for discussion the issue of whether America's treaty obligations toward France were still binding on the United States. Hamilton cited a treatise on international law by Emerich de Vattel in support of the position that, as France had a government different from the one with which the treaties had been concluded, they no longer constituted binding obligations on the U.S.[742] Jefferson presented an equally strong argument that the regime change in France did not affect the validity of the treaties between the two countries. Either interpretation of international law, if adopted by the administration, risked alienating one of the two warring foreign powers.[743]

Washington might declare American neutrality, but maintaining it would be a challenging undertaking. The French Revolution, far from following the American model, was mired in public executions and an unprecedented reign of terror, to the horror of many Americans. Not everyone, however, shared this perception of the events in that country. James Madison, for one, found it "mortifying... that [the President] should have anything to apprehend from the success of liberty in another country, since he owes his preeminence to the success of it in his own," sentiments with which Jefferson was in full accord.[744]

Relations with France became even more troublesome with the arrival of Edmond-Charles Genêt, the new French envoy to the United States, whose actions led to an escalation of the domestic political dissension between Anglophiles and Francophiles.[745] Genêt's advent on the American scene was viewed with consternation in London, lest he bring new and enticing commercial proposals from France for the U.S. government. Hammond and his superiors in London need not have been concerned. Genêt turned out to be a liability for France. Charming, handsome, and mercurial, he quickly made himself a thorn in the side of the Washington administration. Encouraged by Genêt, pro-French societies were springing up all over the country.[746]

Among Genêt's more provocative activities was commissioning armed privateer vessels and recruiting crews for them in American ports to capture British and neutral vessels. Genêt's actions were thus creating a serious challenge to the President's policy of neutrality and were also the cause of repeated protests lodged by Britain with the administration.[747]

Already walking a tightrope between the belligerent powers, Washington perceived that the French were putting the American government in a dangerous quandary.[748] In the face of challenges to U.S. sovereignty, Washington felt compelled to take forceful action to reassert U.S. jurisdiction over all such matters. The dilemma was that whatever action he took ran the risk of incurring the ire of either Britain or France and provoking a military confrontation with one of them.

What was needed, therefore, was an innovative solution unassailable by either side. Obviously, our first President was trying to think outside the box. In a bold vision centuries ahead of his time, Washington the warrior could see no reason why some disputes between nations could not lend themselves to judicial intervention, to be decided fairly and impartially based on the rule of law. If so, then it should be possible for foreign relations and international commerce to be maintained without costly military engagements. What was at stake, therefore, was whether the U.S. could redefine the rights of neutral countries in the realm of commerce under the law of nations.[749]

The President carefully weighed his options. His solution was a master stroke: He wisely permitted the illegitimacy of the French practices in American ports to be declared through the newly-established U.S. judicial process, thus keeping his administration out of any direct involvement in the matter. Deciding to couch these issues as constituting legal disputes between the parties, Washington looked to the judiciary to step into the fray. He hoped that the federal courts would take this opportunity to provide the more neutral and open forum for foreigners that the Constitution and the Judiciary Act had envisioned for them. To his dismay, however, several federal district courts (in Pennsylvania, Maryland, New York and South Carolina) all disavowed jurisdiction over prize cases. When the issue finally percolated up to the United States Supreme Court, however, the justices – all of whom had been hand-picked by Washington – rose to the occasion and did not disappoint. In a far-reaching opinion, they held in *Glass v. Sloop Betsey* that foreign consuls had no jurisdiction on American soil and only the federal courts of the United States had the power to determine whether restitution for seized ships was proper.[750] The Court also decided that foreign nations did not have the right to erect courts of admiralty on U.S. territory "unless special arrangements had been made in a treaty." As France and the United States were bound by no such treaty provision, the justices declared that "the admiralty jurisdiction, which has been exercised in the United States by the Consuls of France . . . is not of right."[751]

The Supreme Court thus became a powerful instrument in enforcing the Proclamation of Neutrality and in the prevention of French actions against the British in American waters and ports. Washington's decision had solved a thorny issue for the U.S. government, and in the process had focused worldwide attention on the dignity and credibility of America's highest tribunal.

If the administration expected a favorable response from London to its Proclamation of Neutrality, it was in for a surprise. Britain embarked on a series of actions that could only drive America into France's arms. On June 8, 1793, an order-in-council authorized British naval commanders to seize any neutral ships carrying foodstuffs destined for France. This was designed to strangle the trade with the French Indies, ensuring British victory in the Caribbean. For the United States, which had enjoyed active trade with the French West Indies, this was hardly good news.[752]

An even more severe version of the order was issued on November 6, essentially authorizing British captains to seize *any* American ship. It commanded British ships to "stop and detain all ships laden with the produce of any colony belonging to France, or carrying provisions or other supplies for the use of such colony, and shall bring the same, with their cargoes, to legal adjudication in our [British] courts of admiralty." To ensure that the Royal Navy could surprise and seize American and other neutral merchant vessels, the announcement of the revised order was delayed until late December. Thomas Pinckney, the U.S. ambassador in London, received word of the revised order nearly fifty days after it had already gone into effect.[753]

The revised order-in-council wreaked havoc with American merchant shipping in the West Indies. Under its mandate, the Royal Navy seized more than 220 American civilian vessels in the Caribbean. The capture of these merchant ships caused outrage in the U.S., which turned to full-blown fury when reports reached the country of abusive treatment of American seamen by the Royal Navy. Many believed Britain was systematically taking American ships out of action in preparation for war with the United States. At about the same time, the British government notified the American minister in London that it intended to maintain its garrisons in the northwest posts indefinitely, even if the United States gave full satisfaction for its outstanding British debts. On March 25, 1794, Washington forwarded these reports to Congress. Already incensed by the British naval aggression, the House of Representatives began discussing preparations for war and quickly passed a month-long embargo against any ships in U.S. ports departing for foreign lands. Intended to weaken the British in the West Indies, the embargo was ratified by the Senate. The House then passed a non-intercourse bill, designed to ban all imports from Britain until it abandoned its frontier posts and compensated Americans for the seized ships. Hamilton, who had strongly opposed the passage of this legislation, took it upon himself to reassure Britain that the law would have little effect on British shipping.[754]

Hamilton's personal sentiments notwithstanding, public ire was aroused to such a fever pitch that if the President did not move quickly to defuse the passions, war with Britain would become inevitable. To avert armed conflict, Washington turned decisively to a diplomatic solution. He needed to send a new mission to Great Britain and considered Hamilton for this role.

In many ways, pro-British Hamilton was a suitable candidate for this mission. He was on friendly terms with the British ambassador, and his known sympathies for England could lead to a positive reception in London. He was also eager to preserve the peace if possible. Unless absolutely necessary, he had written Washington during the Caribbean crisis, "the country ought not to set itself afloat on an ocean so fluctuating, so dangerous, and so uncertain" as war.[755] On the other hand, Hamilton's affiliation with the English cause was well-known to the American public. With feelings running high against Britain, [756] and recognizing the political brouhaha that might ensue from his appointment, Hamilton wisely asked that his name be dropped from the list of potential envoys. He then urged the President to take "vigorous and effectual measures" to prepare for war.[757] A rush to military engagement, however, was exactly what Washington was laboring to avoid. The President continued to mull over possible candidates for this crucial and delicate assignment, but he rebuffed any attempt to influence his choice. Carefully weighing his options, in the end he selected John Jay. Jay had extensive experience in diplomatic negotiations. During the Revolutionary War, he had represented the Continental Congress in attempting to persuade Spain to recognize the new United States and to provide financial assistance to the new federal government. Then, in 1782, Congress had recalled Jay from the Spanish court and reassigned him to Paris to join John Adams and Benjamin Franklin in negotiating the 1783 Treaty of Peace with Britain. As the Chief Justice of the U.S. Supreme Court, Jay had a sufficiently impressive title to justify his presence in the rank-conscious Court of St. James. He was also sympathetic to some of the British grievances against the United States, having some years earlier quietly expressed the opinion that all legal impediments to the recovery of British debts should be removed.[758] While his position on some of the pending issues between the U.S. and Britain may have been controversial at home, it would lead the British government to believe that Jay would be flexible and reasonable in bilateral negotiations.[759]

On April 16, Washington nominated Jay to the Senate as envoy extraordinary, and Jay felt duty-bound to accept. Washington's nomination contained an implied assurance that, although Jay had demonstrated friendliness toward Britain in the past, his mission was not to achieve peace at any price: "I have thought proper to nominate, and do hereby nominate, John Jay, as Envoy Extraordinary of the United States, to his Britannic Majesty.... Going immediately from the United States, such an Envoy will carry with him a full knowledge of the existing temper and sensibility of our country, and will thus be taught to vindicate our rights with firmness, and to cultivate peace with sincerity."[760]

The Senate was skeptical, and strongly resistant to the nomination. The Anti-Federalist opponents of the proposed mission tried several parliamentary maneuvers to block the appointment. They asked Washington for the records of Jay's prior term as Secretary of Foreign Affairs. They then proposed a bill requiring Washington "to inform Senate of the whole business with which the proposed Envoy is to be charged." The next move consisted of yet another bill which required "that any communications to be made to the Court of Great Britain may be made through our Minister now at that Court, with equal facility and effect, and at much less expense, than by an Envoy Extraordinary; and that such an appointment is at present inexpedient and unnecessary." When all efforts failed, the Senate finally confirmed John Jay by a vote of 18 to 8.[761]

The appointment of Jay to this vital assignment was no less controversial outside Congress than within it. Predictably, his position on the subject of British debts raised hackles. The virulently anti-administration publication the *Aurora* suggested that the President had nominated his Chief Justice for the mission in order to avoid impeachment.[762]

Preparing Jay for his work in London was itself a challenge. With months of delay in communication between Britain and United States, Jay would have little opportunity to obtain further instructions after getting a better feel for the posture and attitude of his counterparts in

London. On a matter of such consequence for the country, Washington was careful to send Jay off with as detailed a set of instructions as possible.

The U.S. would accept no terms that would violate established obligations to France. The U.S. would agree to no commercial treaty unless it gave American merchant vessels access to the British West Indies. Regarding the seizure of American merchant vessels in the Caribbean, "compensation for all the injuries sustained" by seizures was to be "pressed strenuously," but it was acknowledged that full compensation might not be forthcoming. British refusal to make amends for those seizures would not, in and of itself, be a deal-breaker. Jay was to try to persuade the British to permit the disputes over debts owed to British creditors to be handled by the United States judiciary. Jay, however, was to keep discussions of the "vexations and spoliations" in the Caribbean separate from discussions of the outstanding obligations under the 1783 treaty. Therefore, he was not authorized to agree to indemnification by the United States government for the debts owed to British subjects in exchange for compensation for the vessels seized and seamen impressed in the Caribbean. On the issue of attacks by Native Americans against American settlers, despite the administration having credible evidence of British complicity in the violence, Jay would level no accusations but only stress that Britain had an obligation to restrain its agents from inciting violence against the United States.[763]

If Jay managed to secure some agreement regarding compensation for seized cargo and ongoing violations of the treaty of 1783, he was then authorized to discuss the terms of a possible treaty of commerce. Because Washington fully expected that the country would be in a position to negotiate a more favorable treaty in the future, Jay was not to accept a treaty lasting longer than fifteen years. As to the other terms of a potential commercial treaty, Jay was provided a list of suggested terms covering a panoply of topics including increased fishing rights, protection for merchant vessels, and restrictions on trade with Native American tribes in the event of a conflict between the United States and those tribes. Jay went off to London with nineteen issues of great importance to the United States. If, however, Britain proved wholly intractable, then Jay was authorized to meet with representatives of Russia, Denmark, and Sweden to "sound those ministers upon the probability of an alliance with their nations to support [the principles of armed neutrality]." He was to take these steps if, but only if, they would not jeopardize a reasonable chance of reaching an accommodation with Britain.[764]

The non-intercourse bill introduced earlier in Congress to bar commerce with Great Britain would now be an embarrassment to Jay and inhibit his diplomatic efforts as he set sail for England. At the behest of the administration, the bill was narrowly defeated in the Senate, and no new anti-British legislation was introduced.[765] Jay departed New York with his son Peter on May 12, 1794, and arrived in London exactly one month later. Revolutionary France had declared war on England the previous year, and the government was preoccupied with preparations for the defense of the country against a possible French invasion. Jay reviewed these events in order to estimate their impact on his mission. He noted that France and Spain might be close to reconciling, and that Sweden, Denmark, and France had been attempting to revive the old principles of armed neutrality.[766] He hoped that England's concern about these developments may make the British government more amenable to an accommodation with the United States. He would have probably been even more optimistic about the upcoming meetings if he had known that there was a sense in London that the Americans could not have made a better choice than John Jay to represent their interests, which, incidentally, was also a gratifying confirmation of the President's judgment.

The man with whom Jay would be negotiating was William Grenville, the son of George Grenville, the hard-nosed First Lord of the Admiralty who, in a speech to Parliament in 1766, said, "Protection and obedience are reciprocal. Great Britain protects America, America is bound to yield obedience." That infamous justification for the imposition of various revenue-raising measures on the colonies was still well remembered in America. The young William Grenville was reputed to have a steel-trap mind and to be a formidable negotiator. At thirty-five, he was already possessed of a string of public credentials few in Great Britain could rival. Elected to Parliament at twenty-three, he was now a leader in the House of Lords. He was also a member of the King's Privy Council and served as the Secretary for Foreign Affairs in the ministry of William Pitt, his cousin. Jay must have hoped that William Grenville was cut of a different cloth from his father. As it turned out, young Grenville, while dealing from a position of strength, nevertheless demonstrated a willingness to devise an acceptable commercial treaty between the two countries. He also proved to be a gracious social host to Jay, whom he introduced to many other leaders of the government, even arranging an audience with the King. Even more significant, it was a clear indication of the importance Britain attached to the meetings with the special envoy from the United States that, considering the exigencies of the European war and the consequent demands on the time of the Foreign Secretary, Lord Grenville chose to handle the negotiations personally with Jay.

The meetings began on a cordial note with reciprocal recitation of good intentions. Great Britain had no wish to go to war against the United States. The U.S. was Britain's best customer, and Britain could not afford to divert its navy against another enemy. The U.S. was also an important supplier of foodstuff to the British West Indies, and loss of American supplies, or a lengthy continuation of the existing embargo, would be damaging to Britain. To prove good faith and provide an auspicious start to the negotiations, Grenville agreed to suspend the order-in-council then in effect authorizing the seizure of American ships. He also agreed to suspend any hostile action that may be occurring or planned against the U.S. government on the western frontier. Both parties agreed to observe a ceasefire during the pendency of the negotiations.[767]

These were good beginnings. Once past these initial pronouncements, however, the negotiations followed a tough, often uncompromising, and quite stressful path for the U.S. envoy, lasting about five months. The final draft of the treaty settled a host of festering and troublesome issues, the most important being that it removed the threat of imminent war in Article One, which declared "firm, inviolable and universal peace" between the two nations,[768] and Article Two, which called for the removal of British troops from the western frontier of the United States by June 1, 1796.[769] Other articles provided for the establishment of joint boundary commissions to determine the proper northwestern and northeastern boundaries of the United States. The rights to compensation of British creditors and others injured through the actions of French privateers in U.S. ports, the issue of the repayment of British debts and compensation for other British losses, and the rights of Americans to compensation for injuries sustained as a result of Britain's seizure of U.S. vessels were all given guarantees of payment by the respective governments. In each case, a joint commission would be established to determine which claims could not be dealt with through the normal judicial processes in each country, and thus be entitled to seek redress through the governmental guarantees.[770]

The United States was also given the right to trade with the British West Indies using American ships. This important British concession – without which Jay was not to conclude any commercial treaty with Great Britain – was, however, limited as to tonnage and as to goods manufactured only in the U.S. and the British West Indies. This provision was to remain in effect for only two years, after which it would be re-examined and renegotiated. If a suitable agreement could not then be reached, the first ten articles of the treaty (relating to the continuation of peace between the U.S. and Britain) would remain in effect, but the remaining articles (those relating primarily to commerce) would lapse. Another article structured the terms of U.S. trade with and through the British East Indies, essentially formalizing the existing trading conditions for those islands. (Jay was particularly pleased with this provision, which he described as "a manifestation and proof of good will toward us.") Each nation would also receive most-favored-nation trade status. The document provided mildly enhanced protection for America's merchant ships and partially clarified the procedures governing the seizure of ships carrying contraband to the enemy. As there were technical definitional difficulties relating to the term "contraband," the final draft provided a separate mechanism for compensation of U.S. merchants whose cargo had been seized. Greater protection for merchant vessels was also provided, obliging privateers to provide security of £3,000-£6,000 before receiving their commissions. Any damages caused by a privateer or his crew contrary to the spirit of the treaty could be collected from those amounts, as could legal fees. Other articles required each nation to accept the warships of the other into its ports and to turn foreign privateers away from its ports. Each nation was compelled to accept the other's privateers and prizes into its ports.[771] While these last were inconsistent with the terms of the existing treaty of the U.S. with France, the document did, however, provide that "nothing in this treaty contained shall . . .

be construed or operate contrary to former and existing public treaties with other sovereigns or states." Two important items notably absent from the draft treaty were (a) the reimbursement for property taken by the British during the Revolution, and (b) a prohibition on the impressment of U.S. citizens into the Royal Navy.[772]

The treaty that was hammered out was far from ideal, and Jay himself bluntly admitted, "I have no reason to believe or conjecture that one more favorable to us is attainable."[773] Jay signed it on November 18, 1794, and sent two original copies to Philadelphia by a British ship. When the ship was captured en route by the French, the documents were destroyed. Thus, the President did not receive a copy until almost four months later, on March 7, 1795.[774]

Washington knew the treaty would disappoint the members of Congress and perhaps enrage the public. In sending it to the Senate for consideration, he therefore asked that all discussion about it be carried out behind closed doors and under an injunction of secrecy. On June 19, after eleven days of debate over the treaty, the Senate passed a motion requesting Washington "to cause to be laid before the Senate the reports of John Jay while in the Office of Foreign Affairs, the correspondence of the Commander-in-Chief," and Mitchell's map of North America. The Senate then debated whether it should require that certain articles of the treaty be renegotiated before it approved it, expressing serious objection to the provisions relating to trade with the West Indies. The Senate then recommended to the President "to proceed, without delay, to further friendly negotiations with his Majesty, on the subject of the said trade, and on the terms and conditions in question." In the end, the Senate's conditional consent to the treaty barely passed by a vote along party lines, 20 in favor (the minimum number required) to 10 against.

Washington was not permitted to consider the merits of the treaty in the secrecy and calm he would have preferred. Soon after the Senate gave its conditional approval of the treaty, Stevens Thomson Mason, a senator from Virginia and a friend and ally of Thomas Jefferson, sent "his copy of the treaty to Pierre Adet, the newly arrived minister from France, who thereupon turned it over to Bache."[775] Benjamin Bache was the editor of the virulently Anti-Federalist and anti-Washington newspaper, the

Aurora. By early July copies of the treaty were readily available to all. As Washington lamented, "The Treaty . . . has . . . made its public entry into the Gazettes of this city."[776]

On July 4, 1795, a mob in Philadelphia burned not only copies of the treaty but also effigies of Jay. Outpourings of public hostility toward Jay were so strong that he claimed he could walk from one end of the country to the other by the light of his effigies burning. Washington was equally in distress about public reaction to the treaty. Responding to domestic protests against it, Washington reminded the nation of their prior faith in him and asserted his intention to make an independent judgment. "While I feel the most lively gratitude for the many instances of approbation from my country," he wrote, "I can no otherwise deserve it than by obeying the dictates of my conscience." Washington was certain that he would be castigated if he signed the treaty. "I am," he wrote to Edmund Randolph, the Secretary of State, "preparing my mind for... the obloquy which disappointment and malice are preparing to heap upon me," noting that the United States would remain in a precarious situation whether he accepted or rejected the treaty. "In time when passion shall have yielded to sober reason, the current may possibly turn; but in the meanwhile this government in relation to France and England may be compared to a ship between the rocks of Scylla and Charybdis. If the Treaty is ratified, the partisans of the French (or rather of war and confusion) will excite them to hostile measures, or at least to unfriendly sentiments; if it is not, there is no foreseeing all the consequences which may follow as it respects Great Britain."[777]

Given the vigorous domestic opposition to the treaty, the uncertain international fallout from whatever decision he might make, it is little wonder that Washington delayed making a decision for many weeks.

Great Britain, in the meantime, did little to make approval of the treaty less difficult. On the contrary, it renewed the order-in-council that had enraged the American public, authorizing the Royal Navy once again to begin seizing certain American merchant vessels. Britain's action would make Washington's support of the treaty even more damaging to his administration. On July 13, Randolph informed Hammond that "the President cannot persuade himself that he ought to ratify during the existence of the order."[778]

Toward the end of July, while Washington was away at Mount Vernon, his home in Philadelphia was beset by protestors. On July 22, 1795, Washington directed an aide to inform the Cabinet that the President intended to ratify the treaty if, but only if, the Provision Orders were not then in operation, and only to the extent already agreed upon by the Senate. He believed that it was "better to ratify it in the manner the Senate have advised (and with the reservation already mentioned), than to suffer matters to remain as they are, unsettled."[779] The President signed Jay's Treaty in August. "The Anglomen have in the end got their treaty through," Jefferson remarked with bitterness and foreboding, "and so far have triumphed over the cause of republicanism."[780]

As Washington had predicted, with the passage of time passions began to cool and reason to prevail; funding for the treaty was allocated by the House of Representatives despite substantial opposition. A war had been averted, providing more time for the flourishing economy to develop deeper roots. Westward migration, slowed to a trickle by actions of Britain and its Indian allies, was now revived in earnest, and business began to boom in American ports. In the process, the line separating the Federalists from the Anti-Federalists, which had started at the time of the ratification of the Constitution, now solidified into the two-party system defining American politics ever since.

Jay himself had little respite upon his return to the United States. During his absence from the country, he had been elected Governor of New York.

Nor did Washington have much time to enjoy the relative peace of Mount Vernon. Hammond, the British ambassador to the United States, had been recalled to London to discuss matters "relative to the treaty on the supposition of it being ratified." On July 31, Attorney General Edmund Randolph and Secretary of War Timothy Pickering wrote to him requesting that he return to Philadelphia. "I learn that Mr. Hammond has received letters of recall," Randolph wrote, "and that he expects to depart in three weeks. I am disposed to believe, from accidental intimations, that before his departure some useful and perhaps very important arrangements may be made to facilitate the compliance with the condition on which the advice of the Senate for ratifying the treaty was suspended, and possibly for expediting the execution of that part of it which respects the posts..."[781]

Another matter weighed on Pickering's mind, however, one that made Washington's presence urgent. "On the subject of the treaty I confess that I feel extreme solicitude; and for a *special reason* which can be communicated to you only in person. I entreat therefore that you will return with all convenient speed to the seat of Government," he wrote. Pickering urged Washington to make no important political decisions until he arrived in Philadelphia. All of this was quite puzzling, and the mystery was only deepened by Pickering's caution that the letter was for Washington's "own eye alone."[782]

When, on August 11th, Washington arrived in Philadelphia, Pickering unburdened himself of his secret "special reason." Certain French dispatches had been intercepted by the British, and they showed that Edmund Randolph, in conversations with Joseph Fauchet, the French ambassador to the United States, had referred to the President as being out of touch. The letter also lent itself to the inference that Randolph had asked Fauchet for a bribe in exchange for his opposition to Jay's Treaty. Washington responded to this troubling information with caution. Randolph had been the sole remaining voice in his Cabinet against ratification, and now doubts were cast upon his motive and integrity. A scandal in the administration at this juncture would only diminish Washington's ability to push through an unpopular measure without inciting widespread violence and disorder. If he wished to sign the treaty, he would have to do so before word of Randolph's purported action leaked. The day after he learned of Fauchet's dispatches, Washington surprised his Cabinet by rising to announce "I will ratify the treaty." Randolph's signature as Secretary of State was acquired on the treaty, and his resignation later quietly accepted. As for Randolph's alleged behavior, most biographers believe that, although he may have been indiscreet, there is no credible evidence of treachery or treason by him.[783]

What does history say about Jay's Treaty? It had always been Washington's ultimate goal to secure for the United States a desperately-needed period of peace with Great Britain, during which the country could develop both its sense of national cohesion and its military and economic strength. These objectives had been realized by the treaty, but that had come at a steep price for the President domestically. One could have wished for more favorable terms, or that the public could have shown greater cognizance of what had been accomplished. Nevertheless, time would prove that the value of Jay's Treaty to the country was inestimable. In the eyes of respected historians, for George Washington to have affixed his signature to Jay's Treaty was "one of his wisest and bravest acts in a life filled with wisdom and bravery."[784]

Chapter Fifteen

THE EUROPEAN THEATER – SPAIN

America is made on an inspired plan. Europe is a first idea, a crude production, before the maker knew his trade, or had made up his mind as to what he wanted.

Thomas Jefferson

It was September 3, 1783, and His Most Catholic Majesty Carlos III, King of Spain, was in uncommonly good humor. The rebellion of the Americans had succeeded beyond all expectations, and the English bulldog given a well-deserved and long-overdue bloody nose. It was sweet revenge for the King, who had seen his ambitious colonization projects in North America dealt one setback after another at the hand of the English Crown.

In the sixteenth and seventeenth centuries, Spain had been a major world power, financing its foreign forays by wresting large shiploads of gold and silver from its conquered lands, particularly from its South

American colonies. Then, like the other great maritime nations of the age, Spain was bent on establishing new settlements and expanding old ones in various parts of the globe, bringing it into inevitable collision with rival forces. During his long reign (1759-1788), Carlos III devoted substantial resources to colonizing the American continents for Spain. In North America, he established dominion over Florida, Louisiana, and the Mississippi Valley region, and founded the communities of San Diego, Los Angeles, Santa Barbara, and the San Fernando Valley on the Pacific coast. His aggressive expansion into the New World raised the ire of the English king, George III, who had similar designs in the same regions.[785] In the never-ending conflicts among the great powers of the day, the crowned heads of Europe indulged in personal rivalries and needed little provocation to array their armies against other monarchs as though the continents were their private chessboards. By the time America had declared its independence, Spain had already suffered a series of defeats in the international arena, including the loss of significant portions of its North American colonies to Great Britain.

The onset of the American Revolution gave King Carlos III a rare opportunity to turn the tables on King George III. Carlos cagily permitted his Bourbon cousin, King Louis XVI of France, to cajole him into joining the American Revolution on the side of Britain's rebellious former colonies, the bait being the chance to humble the English king and drive his army out of the regions of North America to which Spain laid prior claim. France even committed itself to continue fighting until the British were thrown out of Gibraltar and the island recaptured for Spain.

And so, on that particular day in 1783, Carlos III had good reason to be jubilant, and to celebrate the American victory in the Revolutionary War as his own. At a time of declining Spanish power on the world stage, this had been an opportunity for Carlos to regain a measure of its old glory for Spain. He had used the American Revolution solely to advance his own territorial ambitions and had done little to be of direct help to the American cause. He had in fact come close to achieving every item on his American wish list. Spain had succeeded in conquering all of British West Florida, capturing Fort Bute and Natchez on the Mississippi, and Mobile and Pensacola on the Gulf. The Mississippi

River was now totally under the control of Spain, literally turning the Gulf of Mexico into a Spanish lake.[786]

As for Louis XVI, it was true that France had struck a humiliating blow at its archenemy, Great Britain, but aside from gaining trading rights off the coast of India and an exchange of some Caribbean islands, there was not much cause for celebration, even though it was France that had been unstinting in providing arms and ammunition, ground troops, and naval support to the United States. To help the new and impoverished republic, France had dug so deep into its pockets that it bankrupted its own government in the process. By the end of the war, France had provided the staggering sum of one billion livres in financial assistance to America, depleting France's treasury. This in turn ultimately led to the French revolution, in the course of which Louis XVI and Marie Antoinette were beheaded by guillotine, ending the monarchy of the House of Bourbon.[787]

Compared to France's involvement, Spain's support of the United States in the Revolutionary War could not have been more grudging and half-hearted. Concerned about the potential of a strong America at the back door of its empire, Spain had delayed its recognition of the new United States until the very last moment, and then only after Britain had already done so.[788] Then, after the war, to protect its North American territories from the aggressive and expansion-minded west-bound hordes of domestic and foreign immigrants who had little or no loyalty to Spain, its government used every opportunity to try to restrict the boundaries of the United States to a landlocked region with no direct access to the Great Lakes, the Mississippi River, or the Gulf of Mexico.[789] At the behest of the Spaniards, the French foreign ministry sent a secret mission to meet with Lord Shelburne during the negotiations for the Peace Treaty of 1783 with the intent of convincing Britain's first Prime Minister to keep the Americans out of the vast western open spaces and to preserve that land as the playground of the colonizing European powers. Shelburne was not impressed. He saw the new United States as a major potential trading partner for Britain and had little enthusiasm for participating in Spain's machinations in its quest to recover its lost glory.

If one were to write a script on how *not* to win friends and influence people in the new western territories of America, Spain's actions would follow its precepts faithfully. It put in place draconian land laws and immigration policies designed to thwart and control the new arrivals into its territories. Every settled region in Louisiana and West Florida was under military rule headed by a Spanish army officer. From him, the chain of command extended successively to the governor of Louisiana, then to the governor of Havana, before eventually reaching the multi-layered departments in Madrid. The administration of colonial affairs, meant to protect Spanish possessions in North America, was in fact accomplishing the exact opposite. As the residents of America's western territories saw it, Spain had devised a set of cumbersome and rigid policies for the oversight of its dominions, administered by a frustratingly slow-moving bureaucracy shackled by religious and social intolerance and prejudice. Not surprisingly, most westerners had only disdain for the high-handed edicts emanating from Madrid and made no secret of their desire for the U.S. government to intervene on their behalf against Spain.[790]

Once the Revolutionary War was over, Spain quickly chose to demonstrate that its national interests did not run parallel with those of the United States. It closed the ports of Havana and New Orleans to Americans, and barred them from access to the Mississippi River.[791] As British subjects, Americans had enjoyed free access to the navigation of the Mississippi River ever since Britain had acquired that right from France in 1763. After the British were driven out of the region during the Revolutionary War, Spain had continued to permit Americans the use of the river, leading them to expect that their right to the navigation of the Mississippi was perpetual.[792] All too soon, however, they found out that their license was of brief duration, to their frustration and fury.[793] By closing access to this vital waterway, Spain was sowing the seeds of wholesale failure for the farming communities of the west. The Allegheny Mountains constituted a formidable barrier to trade between the farmers in the west and cities on the east coast, and the only alternative for the farmers was to look to markets in New Orleans and Mobile, using flatboats on the Mississippi River to float their wheat, tobacco, flour, hides, and other produce there. Without access to the waterway, they would be deprived of the ability to sell their products and would have no cash with which to buy the goods desperately needed for life on the frontier such as metal implements, cloth, gunpowder, and the like sold by itinerant peddlers. For these frontier communities, access to the Mississippi River was a make-or-break issue.[794]

Spain had actually been warned by its own agents in the United States against taking western Americans for granted or underestimating their potential as warriors. It was, therefore, determined to create a buffer between its possessions and the potentially dangerous and land-hungry Americans, and looked to the neighboring Indian nations to provide the desired protection against the American westward drive.

Throughout the first half of the eighteenth century, Florida was under Spanish control until Britain gained possession of it in 1763. Simultaneously with entering into the peace treaty with the United States at the end of the Revolutionary War, Britain had concluded a separate treaty with Spain, also signed on September 3, 1783. It transferred to Spain the possession of East and West Florida without designating their boundaries or making any mention of the navigation of the Mississippi River. During the intervening decades between the two pacts, Britain had pushed Florida's borders northward, but as the 1783 treaty did not delineate the exact boundary between the United States and Florida, sovereignty over the northern parts of Florida remained contested. Spain claimed that the treaty gave it possession of Florida at the northernmost point formerly claimed by Britain. This would have placed the boundary between Florida and the U.S. at roughly the 32nd parallel.[795] The United States argued that the Treaty of Paris, which had also provided for the free navigation of the Mississippi River throughout its course for Americans and Britons, had merely returned to Spain the territory it held in 1763, and that Spain could not claim sovereignty over the northern end of Florida. (The inclusion of the British as co-beneficiaries of the American right to use the Mississippi was the brainchild of John Jay during the negotiations leading to the Treaty of Paris, designed to inject the military heft of Great Britain on the same side as the U.S. into any discussion over the use of the Mississippi.) Britain may have ceded territorial rights to the United States that it did not possess; nevertheless, the Americans insisted, the true boundary lay at the 31st parallel.[796]

Clearly, there was a built-in conflict between the U.S. and Spain over control of a broad band of territory from the Mississippi through the heart of the southern Indian country. If Spain desired to have a buffer between its North American territories and the United States, none of the treaties provided for it. Spain, however, was undeterred. It continued to claim that its land stretched from the Great Lakes through Ohio down to Georgia and included all of Florida to the 32nd parallel. In effect, Spain was trying to keep the Americans hundreds of miles away from the Mississippi River.[797]

A related issue concerned dealings with Native American tribes inhabiting the boundary between the U.S. and the territories of Florida and Louisiana. The U.S. contended that Spain stirred up resentments against it, armed the Indians, and incited attacks on American settlers.[798] Washington bluntly stated that the Spaniards "employ the Indians against us."[799] Spain also dispatched a large group of agitators and rabble-rousers into the United States with instructions to encourage the western separatist movement and to support its leaders. Even though the actions of these agents were, in practice, clumsy and ineffective, Spain persevered in its attempts to undermine the federal government well into Washington's Presidency.[800]

The United States had thus emerged from the Revolution facing irreconcilable claims with Spain, but efforts to secure peaceful relations with the former ally had been hardly promising.[801] Later U.S. efforts to try to settle the unresolved questions with Spain ran into a brick wall. Spanish ministers kept American representatives cooling their heels for months at a time, complained that the U.S. negotiators lacked sufficient rank to merit presence at the Spanish court, or that an American diplomat had been indiscreet, all the while holding fast to the Spanish position on the basic issues separating the two governments.[802]

Americans were aware that the United States possessed no ability to oust Spain through the use of force. The country had virtually no military preparedness while Spain was still a major world power. As he had done in the relations with Britain, President Washington was determined to avoid an open break with Spain, but he operated out of a conviction that time was on America's side. Spanish garrisons in Louisiana and East and West Florida were under-manned, and the population of the Kentucky

District of Virginia was already equal to that of Spanish Louisiana. As late as 1787, the Spanish governor of Louisiana had admitted that only five hundred soldiers manned the garrisons on the Louisiana-U.S. border. A European crisis, Washington believed, would provide the right opportunity for the U.S. to negotiate from a position of strength and press Madrid into a satisfactory settlement. Washington also believed that, given time and population growth, the U.S. access to the navigation of the Mississippi would be inevitable. "Whenever the new states become so populous and so extended to the westward, as really to need it," Washington wrote, "there will be no power which can deprive them of the use of the Mississippi." So the President adopted a strategic posture vis-à-vis Spain of "watchful waiting" – a minuet of stalls and delays carefully orchestrated by the American government to appear cooperative and not recalcitrant – designed to buy time for the United States.[803]

Until that critical time when the U.S. demand for navigation rights could no longer be contained, Washington was more concerned with the behavior of western settlers, whose fury at Spain had the potential of drawing the U.S. into an unwanted war. He counseled patience to the westerners in the Spanish regions. Nevertheless, they were the difficult and unpredictable element in Washington's plans; they appeared in no mood to wait patiently for the fruits of diplomacy. The collapse of the earlier negotiations initiated at the behest of the Continental Congress had already served to inflame western demands for access to the Mississippi, and there was angry talk of Westerners taking matters into their own hands.[804] That summer, Jefferson wrote to Governor Shelby of Kentucky, asking him to take appropriate steps to prevent further incitements.[805] The governor stonewalled for months and finally demanded to know by what authority the President requested any action from him.[806]

Despite the openly aroused passions, Washington firmly stuck to his strategic policy of avoiding violent conflict, "endeavoring to keep things quiet," and biding his time before insisting on concessions from Spain.[807]

By the time Washington assumed the Presidency, the Spanish Crown had passed from Carlos III to his son in 1788. Carlos IV was a weak and indecisive man totally dominated by his wife, Queen Luisa. A love affair between the Queen and an ambitious and handsome young member of the royal guards by the name of Manuel de Godoy led to his appointment by the King, at his wife's urging, to successively higher ranks. He was given the title of the Duke of Alcudia, raised to the rank of field marshal, and appointed foreign minister. The next promotion was for Godoy to become supreme in the Council of State. Under Godoy's direction, Spain made a series of foreign policy moves and entanglements that led to disastrous losses and defeats for its government. It was Manuel de Godoy, known by the honorific "Prince of Peace," that Washington out-maneuvered and out-negotiated to avert not only a war with Spain and its surrogates, the southwestern Indian nations, but also the creation of an independent state supported by Spain in the western territories, and to wrest a spectacularly favorable settlement of the pending issues between the two countries.[808]

In 1793, while Spain was engulfed in the wars precipitated by the French Revolution, Godoy tried to enlist the United States in a military alliance in return for access to the Mississippi and agreement on the Florida boundaries.[809] The proposal was a non-starter, as Washington operated out of a deeply-held conviction that the United States was best served by staying out of the ever-shifting European alliances. Godoy was using the customary diplomatic channels and mouthing the appropriate words, but it was all subterfuge. Indulging his penchant for intrigue, he was tantalized by the prospect of going down in history as the minister who created a vast independent state in the west supported by Spain. His orders to Spain's representatives in Philadelphia were to do all they could to inflame the resentments of the inhabitants of the western territories of the United States. An expanded network of Spanish agents was then infiltrated into the western lands to make contact with secessionist activists, to strengthen Spanish alliances with southwestern Indian tribes, and to establish garrisons wherever possible. Spanish representatives also dangled before western immigrants the ultimate bait – they would enjoy full access to the navigation of the Mississippi, free land grants, freedom of religion, and all the rights of Spanish subjects, and all they had to do was to take an oath of allegiance to the Spanish crown.

Spain's activities in the west were hardly designed to escape attention. "Spain is playing a game," Washington quoted a letter from a Kentucky resident, "which, if not counteracted, will depopulate that country and carry most of the future immigrants to her territory."[810] The previous January, Washington had named William Carmichael, the U.S. chargé d'affaires in Madrid, and William Short, the chargé in Paris, as joint commissioners to negotiate the navigation rights on the Mississippi River.[811] To gain time for his schemes and for his agents to do their undercover work in the American west, Godoy sent a note through diplomatic channels in 1794, complaining that Short and Carmichael lacked sufficient stature to function as negotiators at the Spanish court.[812] What was required was a minister of such character and eminence as "became a residence near the royal person."[813]

To an exasperated Washington, the message was a transparent ploy, designed to throw the American government off balance, thereby delaying any substantive bilateral negotiations. It was also blatantly disrespectful of the United States of America. "The conduct of Spain toward us is unaccountable and injurious" was Washington's remarkable understatement.[814] Nevertheless, he chose to comply. He sounded out Thomas Jefferson and Patrick Henry for the position of envoy to Spain, but they both refused the commission.[815] Then on November 21, 1794, Washington nominated Thomas Pinckney, the American minister in London, for the post in Madrid. The scion of an influential and wealthy Southern family, Pinckney, educated at Oxford, had distinguished himself in the Revolutionary War and had served as the governor of North Carolina. A seasoned diplomat, he was articulate, charming and elegant in manner, and a good negotiator. The Senate confirmed his appointment the next day. William Short, the U.S. chargé in Madrid who had done much to lay the groundwork for a possible treaty with Spain, would remain there to assist Pinckney as the new envoy extraordinary.[816]

When Pinckney received the notice of his appointment to the Spanish court, John Jay was still in London negotiating with Lord Grenville, trying to hammer out the treaty between the United States and Great Britain for which he had taken leave from his duties as Chief Justice of the U.S. Supreme Court. Pinckney, fully aware of the urgency of Jay's work, delayed his own departure for Madrid until Jay's treaty negotiations were concluded.[817]

Arriving at the Spanish court, Pinckney was aware that the unfolding of recent events in Europe was affecting the dynamics of the tense relationship Spain maintained with the United States. The revolution in France and the blood bath it had loosed on that country's royalty and aristocracy dominated European news. News of the flight of King Louis XVI to Varennes, followed by his capture and beheading by guillotine, moved like a shockwave to monarchies throughout the capitals of Europe. The new French government's aggressive stance against other European powers led to wholesale new military alliances and realignments. In that volatile environment, several former enemies joined forces against France. Spain, whose interests in the New World and at sea frequently placed it in conflict with Britain, now found itself allied with its old enemy.[818] In a series of treaties signed in 1793, Spain, Russia, Britain, and Prussia – strange bedfellows indeed – agreed to take all possible active measures against France to force it to the peace table.[819]

Washington hoped this new crisis in Europe would provide the opening he had been seeking to press Spain into a reasonable negotiating posture. That, alas, was not to be. Even more ominous, the new alliance of Britain and Spain brought together the two countries most intent on keeping the new American republic weak and unstable. The only cause for optimism was Washington's conviction that the makeshift alliance between Britain and Spain was hardly a match made in heaven. In fact, it did not take long for Spain to realize that its new ally was prosecuting the war against France only to gain new territories for itself. By 1795, Spain was eager to slough off its British connection and make peace with France. Predictably, the coalition soon began to collapse.[820]

John Jay's mission as the new U.S. special envoy to the Court of St. James had also created deep concern in Madrid: If an alliance between Britain and the United States should result, it would pose a serious threat to Spanish holdings in the Americas. Already in conflict with France, Spain could not afford to fight on another front simultaneously.[821] Spain's difficulty was America's opportunity – it was indeed the moment Washington had counted on.[822] His instructions to Pinckney were quite specific; the most imperative issues were the navigation rights on the Mississippi

River and the establishment of the boundary line between the U.S. and the Spanish territories of Louisiana and Florida at the 31st -parallel.[823]

Compared to the years of slow, fruitless diplomacy practiced by American representatives in an unyielding Spanish court, Pinckney's mission found a more accommodating reception in Madrid upon his arrival there in June 1795. By October, however, after a promising start on several fronts, the negotiations stalled on the "right of deposit" – the freedom of Americans to use the port of New Orleans to unload their cargos for sale or transshipment to ocean-going vessels. Without it, the right to navigate the Mississippi River would be all but meaningless. Godoy declared that the right of deposit was absolutely nonnegotiable. Pinckney, armed with explicit instructions from the President, did not hesitate. He unceremoniously petitioned the Spanish government to return his passport, intending to terminate all discussions and return to his post in England. Godoy, aware the U.S. had signed Jay's Treaty but with no knowledge of its terms, feared that Spain's worst nightmare, namely a U.S. Britain alliance, might come to pass. Pinckney's dramatic gesture had the desired effect. Godoy quickly capitulated on the right of deposit.[824]

The Spanish-American Treaty was signed in the City of San Lorenzo on October 27, 1795, by Thomas Pinckney on behalf of the United States and Don Manuel de Godoy himself on behalf of Spain.[825]

The Treaty of San Lorenzo was a major triumph for the United States. In its first article, it established a "firm and inviolable peace" between the U.S. and Spain.[826] While this recitation was rather pro forma, the second article contained a radical concession. It determined the boundaries between the United States and the Spanish colonies in America in almost exact concordance with the American demand, to extend from the Mississippi along the 31st parallel to the "middle of the River Apalachicola or Catahouche, thence along the middle thereof to its junction with the Flint, thence straight to the head of St. Mary's River, and thence down the middle thereof to the Atlantic Ocean," running along the line between Florida and Georgia from the Atlantic to the Mississippi. Recognizing that foreign troops and garrisons remained on either side of the new boundary, the treaty provided six months for each party to remove its soldiers and property from the other's territory.[827] To delineate the agreed-upon boundary line, Spain and the United States would each appoint one commissioner and one surveyor.[828] Spain retained the colony of Louisiana, although it was somewhat diminished by the terms of the treaty which set the western boundary between the U.S. and Spanish Louisiana at the middle of the Mississippi River.[829] Spain essentially conceded that almost all of present-day Mississippi and Alabama were within the United States.[830]

The treaty granted the United States the right to navigate the entire Mississippi River from its source to the ocean, as well as the right for Americans to trade and "deposit their merchandize and effects in the Port of New Orleans" without any discriminatory duties or taxes for three years. After that time, the right to use the port of New Orleans was renewable at the discretion of the Spanish king. If American use of New Orleans proved prejudicial, Spain was to grant the use of another equivalent port.[831]

From the U.S. perspective, there was a possible problem with the articles concerning the Mississippi. The treaty contemplated that Spain and the United States would possess the sole and exclusive right to navigate the Mississippi, subject to the right of Spain to extend navigation privileges to an additional nation at a later date. This created a direct conflict with Article III of Jay's Treaty between the U.S. and Britain which provided that "the Mississippi shall...be entirely open to both parties." Pinckney brought this conflict to Godoy's attention in his notes on an early draft of the treaty, but the conflict was not removed from the final draft.[832]

The thorny issue of the Spanish encouragement of attacks by Native American tribes on western settlers was favorably resolved. Under Article V, both nations agreed to avoid inciting Native American tribes, and each nation was to restrain violence by tribes within its borders against the other nation.[833]

Another conflict of more recent origin was the seizure by Spain, during its period of alliance with Britain, of U.S. ships and possible mistreatment of some U.S. crews while in Spanish captivity. Spain's policy in this respect ran counter to the "free ships, free goods" stance of the United States which provided that all non-contraband articles on neutral ships were to be free from seizure. To resolve outstanding claims by American citizens for goods and vessels taken by Spanish privateers during the Franco-Spanish conflict, therefore, the treaty provided for the establishment of an administrative commission composed of one Spaniard, one citizen of the United States, and one mutually agreed-upon candidate. The determinations and awards of this commission would be final and non-appealable.[834]

On trade relations, the treaty provided that the two nations would "give to their mutual commerce all the extension and favor which the advantage of both countries may require." Although Spain was a frequent trading partner, it was much less commercially significant than Britain or France. (In 1792, U.S. export trade with Britain was roughly eight times that with Spain, and the French trade nearly four times that with Spain.) The failure to establish formal reciprocal most-favored-nation trade status was not, therefore, a stumbling block to the approval of the treaty by the United States.[835]

Each nation also agreed that, within its own waters, it would protect the vessels of the other nation. This provision did not require the United States to protect Spanish vessels on the high seas, but merely to assure the safety of Spanish vessels off the coast and in the ports of the United States. Each nation further promised to allow the vessels of the other safe harbor from pirates and enemies in its ports and rivers.[836]

Other articles provided reciprocal property and legal rights to both nations' citizens and merchants, barred citizens of either nation from working as privateers against the other, and enacted safeguards against accidental seizure of the other's goods or citizens in the event of war. In providing for "liberty of navigation and commerce" between the two countries, the treaty defined contraband with sufficient specificity, unlike Jay's Treaty, to exclude cloths and provisions.[837]

On Thursday, March 3, 1796, the U.S. Senate approved the Treaty of San Lorenzo after only two days of deliberations and recommended its ratification by the President. This treaty, which was introduced in the Senate only a few months after the ratification of Jay's Treaty, must have come as welcome relief to the Senators. The treaty with Great Britain, while averting a war and resolving certain outstanding disputes between the two countries, had divided the nation, being in many ways a testament to Great Britain's vastly superior military and economic power. The American treaty with Spain, by contrast, through superior timing and negotiating skills, had secured for the United States the opportunity of winning almost every privilege it had sought. Spain, on the other hand, received few advantages for which it had hoped, including the guarantee of security it had desired for its American holdings, Florida and Louisiana. Nor did Spain have a chance to secure an alliance with this country, as the President wisely elected to avoid such involvements at that early stage in the country's development. In refusing to guarantee Spain's American holdings, the treaty followed Washington's policy of remaining detached from the "insidious wiles" and "political vicissitudes" of the European powers. In the realm of trade, the U.S. had also made no major commitment to Spain, in line with Washington's preference that commerce should be allowed to follow "the natural course of things."[838]

In his farewell address, Washington held up the Treaty of San Lorenzo as an object lesson in the dangers of political and geographic factionalism. Recalling western settlers' perception that the federal government would not fight for their rights nor protect their interests, the President cautioned against future attempts to rouse regional angst in the United States. "The inhabitants of our Western country... have seen," he wrote, "in the negotiation by the Executive, and in the unanimous ratification by the Senate, of the treaty with Spain, and in the universal satisfaction at that event, throughout the United States, a decisive proof how unfounded were the suspicions propagated among them of a policy in the General Government and in the Atlantic states unfriendly to their interests in regard to the Mississippi."[839]

The Treaty of San Lorenzo was the capstone of Washington's foreign policy initiatives and of his belief that international tensions could be defused through the establishment of bilateral commercial treaties. The treaty went into effect at about the same time as the President's farewell address.

EPILOGUE

His boundless energies, spent in a lifetime of faithfully performing his duties and responsibilities, finally got George Washington into trouble.

Thursday, December 12, 1799, found him doing what he loved – running his flourishing farming and manufacturing enterprises. Still enjoying good health at sixty-seven, he was looking forward to the dawn of a new century less than three weeks away. He began his daily rounds at Mount Vernon and continued for five hours as the sky darkened and the weather turned from rain to snow, ice, and high winds. By the time he was finished, his clothes were thoroughly soaked, and he was chilled to the bone. Characteristically paying little attention to physical discomfort, he stayed in his wet clothes through dinner. He soon developed a cold and sore throat but went out again on Friday to attend to several matters, then returned home to deal with the unceasing deluge of his personal correspondence. He wrote his last letter to Alexander Hamilton, approving the plans for the establishment of the United States Military Academy at West Point, which had been the subject of much discussion between them. He ended his letter with an assurance of "very great esteem and regard."[840]

By Saturday morning, with little warning, Washington's condition had become critical. Tobias Lear, his longtime aide, hastily sent for the President's physician who arrived within the hour and then summoned another doctor for consultation. Martha Washington's physician also arrived a short time later. Bloodletting to remove toxins was standard medical practice, and the three men utilized the procedure repeatedly. As the day turned into night, the doctors had extracted nearly forty percent of Washington's blood and resorted to other desperate and unpleasant measures. The treatments only worsened his condition. He had contracted an infection of the epiglottis, the thin membrane at the base of the tongue, blocking his airway and making breathing increasingly difficult. Antibiotics being unknown at the time, the first President of the United States slowly choked to an excruciating death over the next harrowing twenty hours.

Washington had always said that he had no wish "beyond the humble and happy lot of living and dying a private citizen" on his own farm. He assumed – and told friends over the years – that upon retirement he would "gently drift down the stream of life" until he slept with his fathers. It was not, however, a gentle death that overtook him on December 14, 1799. Far from it. Yet observers noted that even in unbearable pain, George Washington retained that dignity and calmness of conduct which had distinguished him through life, until he took his very last agonizing breath.[841]

* * *

"In him were the courage of a soldier, the intrepidity of a chief, the fortitude of a hero," declared Gouverneur Morris, who had known Washington well. In a highly emotional eulogy in New York City on December 31, 1799, Morris recited an impossibly long catalog of Washington's achievements in the service of his country, then confidently predicted that the President's spirit will live forever in the hearts and minds of all Americans, and that his name will bring tears of gratitude and love to their eyes.[842]

Over the centuries, others have linked Washington's name with the dreams and aspirations of all mankind. Unlike other heads of state of his era, Washington had worked tirelessly for the betterment of the lives of his people. With a passionate belief in the greater United States, he had brought unsurpassed energy and vitality to the Presidency and defined, enlarged, and elevated the office. A contemporary journalist gave voice to the plaintive lament of countless Americans when he wrote, "Many a private man might make a great president, but will there ever be a President who will make so great a man as Washington?"[843] Thomas Jefferson echoed the same sentiments when he wrote that "never did nature and fortune combine more perfectly to make a man great."[844]

Perhaps no accolade could be more poignant than the one from an English aristocrat and military hero, the Duke of Wellington. When he defeated Napoleon at the Battle of Waterloo, a grateful nation rewarded him with one of the most magnificent and valuable estates in all of England, Stratfield Saye House. Years later, an American general by the name of James Wilson related that when he first visited Stratfield Saye House, he was surprised to see a Gilbert Stuart portrait of George Washington prominently displayed in the main drawing room. The Iron Duke's son explained why:

> *"It was placed there by my father, who esteemed Washington as perhaps the purest and noblest character of modern times – possibly of all time."*[845]

Image Credits

The Life of George Washington: The Farmer (detail), Claude Regnier lithograph after Junius Brutus Stearns painting, courtesy Library of Congress, Washington, DC.

George Washington in the Uniform of a Colonel in the Virginia Regiment (detail), Charles Willson Peale, courtesy Washington-Custis-Lee Collection, Washington and Lee University, Lexington, Virginia.

George Washington (The Constable-Hamilton portrait) (detail), Gilbert Stuart, courtesy Crystal Bridges Museum of American Art, Bentonville, Arkansas, 2005.27. Photo courtesy of the Museum of Fine Arts, Houston.

The Courtship of Washington, 1758, Jean Leon Gerome Ferris, courtesy Virginia Museum of History & Culture, Richmond, Virginia.

Portrait of Martha Washington, John Chester Buttre engraving after John Wollaston painting, courtesy Albright Knox Art Gallery, Buffalo, New York.

"The house grew as gracefully as the man" (detail), Jim Lane, "George Washington the Architect," *Art Now and Then*, June 24, 2012 http://art-now-and-then.blogspot.com/2012/06/george-washington-architect.html.

Lawrence Washington, possibly Gustavus Hesselius, courtesy of Wikimedia Commons.

Thomas Fairfax, 6th Lord Fairfax of Cameron, Artist Unknown, courtesy of Wikimedia Commons.

Daniel Parke II, John Closterman, courtesy Virginia Museum of History & Culture, Richmond, Virginia.

Hardwicke Papers: Additional Manuscripts. 36217 f. 165-168, dorse (f.168v.), (detail), © The British Library Board/The Image Works.

"First page of the contents of volume I, George Washington's bookplate," in his copy of Adam Smith's *Wealth of Nations*, Paul R. Wagner, "Books from the Library of George Washington now in the Princeton University Library," *Princeton University Library Chronicle* XXXII, 2 (Winter, 1971), 111-15.

Transcription of *Washington and Custis Family Account Book* page, courtesy Special Collections and Archives, James G. Leyburn Library, Washington and Lee University.

Thomas Jefferson, Gilbert Stuart, courtesy of National Gallery of Art, Washington, DC.

Alexander Hamilton, John Trumbull, courtesy National Gallery of Art, Washington, DC.

James Madison, Gilbert Stuart, courtesy National Gallery of Art, Washington, DC.

John Jay, Gilbert Stuart, photograph by A. W. Elson, courtesy Library of Congress, Washington, DC.

Robert Morris, Charles Willson Peale, photograph by Detroit Publishing Company, courtesy Library of Congress, Washington, DC.

Phillis Wheatley (in the frontispiece to her book *Poems on Various Subjects*), Scipio Moorhead, courtesy Library of Congress, Washington, DC.

The First Cabinet, T. Phillibrown after Alonzo Chappel, courtesy Lilly Library, Indiana University, Bloomington, Indiana.

"Bank of the United States, in Third Street Philadelphia," Plate 17 from *The City of Philadelphia as it appeared in the Year 1800*, Published by W. Birch, Springland Cot. near Neshaminy Bridge on the Bristol Road; Pennsylvania, Decr. 31st 1800.

Pennsylvania Railroad travel poster: Building the First White House (detail), N.C. Wyeth, courtesy Wisconsin Historical Society, WHS-68040, Madison, Wisconsin.

Maria Luisa of Parma, Anton Raphael Mengs, courtesy Wikimedia Commons.

BIBLIOGRAPHY

American State Papers, Commerce and Navigation

U.S. Congress. *American State Papers. Documents, Legislative and Executive, of the Congress of the United States from the First Session of the First... to the Second Session of the Seventeenth... March 3, 1789-March 3, 1823.* Commerce and Navigation. Washington: Gales and Seaton, 1832-1834.

American State Papers, Foreign Relations

U.S. Congress. *American State Papers: Documents, Legislative and Executive, of the Congress of the United States, from the First Session of the First Congress to the Thirty-Fifth Congress... March 3, 1789-March 3, 1859.* Foreign Relations. Washington, 1832-1859. 6 volumes.

Annals of Congress

U.S. Congress. *The Debates and Proceedings in the Congress of the United States with an Appendix Containing Important State Papers and Public Documents, and all the Laws of a Public Nature, with Copious Index 1st Congress to 18th Congress, 1st session...March 3, 1789-May 27, 1824*; Compiled from Authentic Sources. Washington: Gales and Seaton; 1834-1856. 42 volumes.

House Journal

U.S. Congress. House of Representatives. *Journal of the House of Representatives of the United States.* Washington; 1826- to date.

Senate Journal

U.S. Congress. Senate. *Journal of the Senate of the United States.* Washington; 1820-to date.

Senate Executive Journal

U.S. Congress. Senate. *Journal of the Executive Proceedings of the Senate.* Washington: Government Printing Office; 1789-to date.

Statutes-at-Large

The United States Statutes at Large, Containing the Laws and Concurrent Resolutions, Proclamations, Treaties and International Agreements, and Reorganization Plans[titles vary]. Washington: Government Printing Office; 1789-to date; Volume 1.

Abbot, W. W, et al., eds. *The Papers of George Washington.* Charlottesville: University of Virginia Press, 1987.

Achenbach, Joel. *The Grand Idea: George Washington's Potomac and the Race to the West.* New York: Pantheon Books-Random House, 2007.

Alden, John Richard. *Robert Dinwiddie: Servant of the Crown.* Williamsburg, VA: The Colonial Williamsburg Foundation, 1973.

Anderson, William G. *The Price of Liberty: The Public Debt of the American Revolution.* Charlottesville: University of Virginia Press, 1983.

Arnebeck, Bob. *Through a Fiery Trial: Building Washington, 1790-1800.* New York: Madison Books, 1991.

Baack, Ben. "Forging a Nation State: The Continental Congress and the Financing of the War of American Independence." *Economic History Review* vol. 54, no.4 (2001).

Baldwin, Simeon E. "American Business Corporations before 1789." *The American Historical Review*, Vol. 8, No. 3 (April, 1903).

Baumol, William J., Litan, Robert E., Schramm, Carl J. *Good Capitalism, Bad Capitalism, and the Economics of Growth and Prosperity.* New Haven: Yale University Press, 2007.

Bayley, Rafael A. *The National Loans of the United States, from July 4, 1776, to June 30, 1880.* Washington: Government Printing Office, 1882.

Beeman, Richard. *Plain, Honest Men: The Making of the American Constitution.* New York: Random House, 2009.

Beer, George Louis. *British Colonial Policy, 1754-1765.* New York: The MacMillan Company, 1907.

Bemis, Samuel Flagg. *Jay's Treaty: A Study in Commerce and Diplomacy.* New Haven: Yale University Press, 1962.

Berg, Scott. *Grand Avenues: The Story of the French Visionary Who Designed Washington, D.C.* New York: Pantheon Books, 2007.

Bernstein, R. B. *Thomas Jefferson*. New York: Oxford University Press, 2003.

Black, Jeremy. *George III, America's Last King*. New Haven: Yale University Press, 2006.

Blackstone, William. *Commentaries on the Laws of England*, 4 volumes. Oxford, 1768.

—— and Chase, George. *Commentaries on the Laws of England in Four Books*. New York: Banks & Brothers, 1894.

Bordewich, Fergus M. *Washington: The Making of the American Capital*. New York: Harper Collins, 2008.

Bowen, Clarence Winthrop, ed. *The History of the Centennial Celebration of George Washington as First President of the United States*. New York: D. Appleton and Company, 1892.

Bowling, Kenneth R. *The Creation of Washington, D.C.: The Idea and Location of the American Capital*. Fairfax, VA: George Mason University Press, 1991.

Boyd, Julian P., et al., eds. *The Papers of Thomas Jefferson*. Princeton: Princeton University Press, 1950.

Brady, Patricia. *Martha Washington: An American Life*. New York: Viking-Penguin, 2005.

Breen, T.H. *Tobacco Culture: The Mentality of the Great Tidewater Planters on the Eve of Revolution*. Princeton: Princeton University Press, 1985.

Brooke, John. *King George III*. London: Constable & Company, Ltd., 1972.

Brookhiser, Richard. *James Madison*. New York: Basic Books, 2011.

Bryan, Helen. *Martha Washington: First Lady of Liberty*. New York: John Wiley & Sons, 2002.

Budka, Metchie J. E., ed. *Under Their Vine and Fig Tree: Travels through America in 1797-1799, 1805, with Some Further Account of Life in New Jersey*, Collections of the New Jersey Historical Society. Elizabeth, NJ: Grassman Publishing Company, 1965.

Burstein, Andrew and Isenberg, Nancy. *Madison and Jefferson*. New York: Random House, 2010.

Butterfield, L. H., ed. *Letters of Benjamin Rush*. Princeton: Princeton University Press, 1951.

Carson, Hampton L. *The History of the Supreme Court of the United States, With Biographies of All the Chief and Associate Justices*. Philadelphia: P.W. Zeigler & Co., 1902.

Casto, William R. *The Supreme Court in the Early Republic: The Chief Justiceships of John Jay and Oliver Ellsworth*. Columbia, SC, University of South Carolina Press, 1995.

Cerami, Charles A. *Dinner at Mr. Jefferson's: Three Men, Five Great Wines, and the Evening That Changed America*. Hoboken, NJ: John Wiley & Sons, 2008.

——. *Young Patriots: The Remarkable Story of Two Men, Their Impossible Plan, and the Revolution That Created the Constitution*. Naperville, IL: Sourcebooks, Inc., 2005.

Chernow, Ron. *Alexander Hamilton*. New York: The Penguin Press, 2004.

——. *Washington: A Life*. New York: The Penguin Press, 2010.

Christman, Margaret C.S. *The First Federal Congress, 1789-1791*. Washington: Smithsonian Institution Press, 1989.

Clark, Allen C. *Origin of the Federal City*. Reprinted from *Records of the Columbia Historical Society*, Volume 35-36, 1935.

Clark, E. Harrison. *All Cloudless Glory: The Life of George Washington, Volume* 1, *From Youth to Yorktown*. Washington: Regnery Publishing, 1995.

——. *All Cloudless Glory: The Life of George Washington, Volume* 2, *Making a Nation*. Washington: Regnery Publishing, 1996.

Clarke, M. St. Clair, and Hall, D.A., eds. *Legislative and Documentary History of the Bank of the United States*. 1832; reprint, New York: Augustus M. Kelley, 1967.

Coleman, Peter J. *Debtors and Creditors in America: Insolvency, Imprisonment for Debt, and Bankruptcy, 1607-1900*. Washington: Beard Books, 1999.

Conway, Moncure Daniel. *Omitted Chapters of History Disclosed in the Life and Papers of Edmund Randolph*. New York: G.P. Putnam's Sons, 1889.

Cook, Don. *The Long Fuse: How England Lost the American Colonies, 1760-1785*. New York: Atlantic Monthly Press, 1995.

Corfield, Penelope J. "Class by Name and Number in Eighteenth-Century Britain" in Penelope J. Corfield, ed., *Language, History and Class*. Oxford: Blackwell Publishers, 1991.

Cowen, David Jack. *The Origins and Economic Impact of the First Bank of the United States, 1791-1797*, Financial Sector of the American Economy. New York: Garland Publishing, 2000.

Dallas, Alexander James. *Reports of cases ruled and adjudged in the several courts of the United States, and of Pennsylvania: held at the seat of the federal government*. Philadelphia: Printed for the reporter at the Aurora Office, 1798.

Davis, Joseph Stancliffe. *Essays in the Earlier History of American Corporations*, Volume II. Cambridge: Harvard University Press, 1917.

Decatur, Stephen and Lear, Tobias. *Private Affairs of George Washington: From the Records and Accounts of Tobias Lear, Esquire, his Secretary*. Boston: Houghton Mifflin Company, 1933.

De Soto, Hernando. *The Mystery of Capital: Why Capitalism Triumphs in the West and Fails Everywhere Else*. New York: Basic Books, 2000.

Dewey, Davis Rich. *Financial History of the United States*. 1903; reprint, New York: Augustus M. Kelley, 1968.

Dickerson, Oliver Morton. *American Colonial Government, 1696-1765: A Study of the British Board of Trade in Its Relations to the American Colonies, Political, Industrial, Administrative*. Cleveland, Ohio: The Arthur H. Clark Company, 1912.

Dunaway, Wayland Fuller. *History of the James River and Kanawha Company*. New York: Columbia University, 1922.

Durant, Will and Ariel. *The Story of Civilization*. New York: Simon and Schuster, 1967.

Ebenstein, Alan. *Hayek's Journey: The Mind of Friedrich Hayek*. New York: Palgrave Macmillan, 2003.

Elkins, Stanley and McKitrick, Eric. *The Age of Federalism*. New York: Oxford University Press, 1993.

Ellis, Joseph J. *American Sphinx: The Character of Thomas Jefferson*. New York: Vintage Books, 1998.

——. *Founding Brothers: The Revolutionary Generation*. New York: Vintage Books-Random House, 2002.

——. *His Excellency: George Washington*. New York: Knopf, 2004.

Ernst, Joseph Albert. *Money and Politics in America, 1755-1775: A Study in the Currency Act of 1764 and the Political Economy of Revolution*. Chapel Hill: University of North Carolina Press, 1973.

Farrand, Max, ed. *The Records of the Federal Convention of 1787*, 4 vols. New Haven, CT: Yale University Press, 1911.

Ferguson, E. James, et al., eds. *The Papers of Robert Morris, 1781-1784*. Pittsburgh: University of Pittsburgh Press, 1973-1999.

——. *The Power of the Purse: A History of American Public Finance, 1776-1790*. Chapel Hill: The University of North Carolina Press, 1961.

Ferling, John E. *The First of Men: A Life of George Washington*. Knoxville, TN: University of Tennessee Press, 1988.

——. *A Leap in the Dark: The Struggle to Create the American Republic*. Oxford: Oxford University Press, 2003.

Fitzpatrick, John C., ed. *The Diaries of George Washington: 1748-1799, Volume I*. Boston and New York: Houghton Mifflin Company, 1925.

—— ed. *The Writings of George Washington from the Original Manuscript Sources, 1745-1799*. Washington: United States Government Printing Office, 1931-1940.

Flexner, James Thomas. *George Washington and the New Nation, 1783-1793*. Boston: Little, Brown and Company, 1970.

——. *George Washington in the American Revolution, 1775-1783*. Boston: Little, Brown and Company, 1968.

——. *George Washington: The Forge of Experience, 1732-1775*. Boston: Little, Brown and Company, 1965.

Flippin, Percy Scott. *The Royal Government in Virginia, 1624-1775*. New York: Columbia University, 1919.

Ford, Paul Leicester, ed. *The Writings of Thomas Jefferson*. New York: G. P. Putnam's Sons, 1894,

Ford, Worthington Chauncey, ed. *The Writings of George Washington*, 14 vols. New York: G.P. Putnam's Sons, 1892.

Freeman, Douglas Southall. *George Washington: A Biography*, vol. 1, *Young Washington*. New York: Charles Scribner's Sons, 1949.

——. *George Washington: A Biography*, vol. 2, *Young Washington*. New York: Charles Scribner's Sons, 1949.

———. *George Washington: A Biography*, vol. 3, *Planter and Patriot*. New York: Charles Scribner's Sons, 1951.

———. *George Washington: A Biography*, vol. 6, *Patriot and President*. New York: Charles Scribner's Sons, 1954.

Friedman, Lawrence M. *A History of American Law*. New York: Simon & Schuster, 2007.

Friedman, Leon and Israel, Fred L. *The Justices of the United States Supreme Court 1789-1969: Their Lives and Major Opinions*, 4 vols. New York: R. R. Bowker, 1969.

Gerber, Scott Douglas, ed. *Seriatim: The Supreme Court Before John Marshall*. New York: New York University Press, 1998.

Gordon, John Steele. *Hamilton's Blessing: The Extraordinary Life and Times of Our National Debt*. New York: Walker and Company, 2010.

Greenfield, Edward W. "Some New Aspects of the Life of Daniel Parke." *The Virginia Magazine of History and Biography*, Vol. 54, No. 4 (October 1946).

Grizzard, Frank E., Jr. *George Washington: A Biographical Companion*. Buena Vista, VA: Mariner Publishing, 2002.

Gutheim, Frederick and Lee, Antoinette J. *Worthy of the Nation: Washington, DC, from L'Enfant to the National Capital Planning Commissioner*. Baltimore: Johns Hopkins University Press, 2006.

Hamilton, John C., ed. The *Works of Alexander Hamilton Comprising His Correspondence, and His Political and Official Writings, Exclusive of the Federalist, Civil and Military*. New York: John F. Trow, 1850-51.

Hammond, Bray. *Banks and Politics in America: From the Revolution to the Civil War*. Princeton: Princeton University Press, 1985.

Harper, Lawrence A. *The English Navigation Laws: A Seventeenth-Century Experiment in Social Engineering*. New York: Octagon Books, 1964.

Henderson, Archibald. *The Conquest of the Old Southwest*. New York: The Century Co., 1920.

Hening, William Waller. *The Statutes at Large: Being a Collection of all the Laws of Virginia, from the First Session of the Legislature in the Year 1619*. Richmond, VA: N.P., 1819-23.

Herring, George C. *From Colony to Superpower: U.S. Foreign Relations since 1776*. Oxford: Oxford University Press, 2008.

Jackson, Donald and Twohig, Dorothy, eds. *The Diaries of George Washington*. Charlottesville: University Press of Virginia, 1976-79.

Jakle, John A. *Images of the Ohio Valley: A Historical Geography of Travel, 1740-1860*. New York: Oxford University Press, 1977.

Johnson, Emory R., et al. *History of Domestic and Foreign Commerce of the United States*. New York: B. Franklin, 1964.

Johnston, Rebecca. "William Byrd Title Book (Concluded)." *The Virginia Magazine of History and Biography*, Vol. 50, No. 3 July 1942.

Kagan, Robert. *Dangerous Nation*. New York: Alfred A. Knopf, 2006.

Kammen, Michael. *Empire and Interest: The American Colonies and the Politics of Mercantilism*. Philadelphia: J. B. Lippincott Company, 1970.

Kapsch, Robert J. *The Potomac Canal: George Washington and the Waterway West*. Morgantown, WV: West Virginia University Press, 2007.

Kirk, Paul W., Jr., ed. *The Great Dismal Swamp*. Charlottesville: University Press of Virginia, 1979.

Kite, Sarah Elizabeth. *L'Enfant and Washington*. Baltimore: Johns Hopkins University Press, 1929.

Kluger, Richard. *Seizing Destiny: How America Grew from Sea to Shining Sea*. New York: Alfred Knopf, 2007

Landes, David S. *The Wealth and Poverty of Nations: Why Some Are So Rich and Some So Poor*. New York: W.W. Norton & Company, 1999.

Lee, Alfred McClung. *The Daily Newspaper in America, with a Biography of Printers*. New York: Macmillan Company, 1947.

Lewis, George E. *The Indiana Company, 1763-1798: A Study in Eighteenth Century Frontier Land Speculation and Business Venture*. Glendale, CA: The Arthur H. Clark Company, 1941.

Littlefield, Douglas R. "The Potomac Company: A Misadventure in Financing an Early American Internal Improvement Project." *The Business History Review*, Vol. 58, No. 4 (Winter 1984).

Looney, J. Jefferson, ed. *The Papers of Thomas Jefferson: Retirement Series*. Princeton: Princeton University Press, 2010.

Lucas, Stephen E. "Genre Criticism and Historical Context: The Case of George Washington's First Inaugural Address." *Southern Speech Communication Journal*, Vol. 51, No. 4 (1986).

Maclay, Edgar S., ed. *Journal of William Maclay*. New York: D. Appleton and Company, 1890.

Maier, Pauline. "The Revolutionary Origins of the American Corporation." *The William and Mary Quarterly*, Third Series, Vol. 50, No. 1, Law and Society in Early America (Jan., 1993).

Mann, Bruce H. *Republic of Debtors: Bankruptcy in the Age of American Independence*. Cambridge: Harvard University Press, 2002.

Marcus, Maeva, et al., eds. *The Documentary History of the Supreme Court of the United States, 1789-1800*. New York: Columbia University Press, 1985.

McCullough, David. *John Adams*. New York: Simon & Schuster, 2001.

McCusker, John J. *Money and Exchange in Europe and America, 1600-1775: A Handbook*. Chapel Hill, NC: University of North Carolina Press, 1978.

—— and Russell R. Menard. *The Economy of British America, 1607-1789*. Chapel Hill, NC: The University of North Carolina Press, 1985.

McDonald, Forrest, ed. *Confederation and Constitution, 1781-1789*. Columbia: University of South Carolina Press, 1968.

——. *The Presidency of George Washington*. Lawrence, KS: University Press of Kansas: 1974.

Middlekauff, Robert. *The Glorious Cause: The American Revolution, 1763-1789.* Oxford: Oxford University Press, 2005.

Mittelberger, Gottlieb. *Gottlieb Mittelberger's Journey to Pennsylvania in the Year 1750 and Return to Germany in the Year 1754*, trans. Carl Eben. Philadelphia: John Jos McVey, 1898.

Morris, Richard B. *The Forging of the Union, 1781-1789.* New York: Harper & Row, 1987.

Myers, Margaret G. *A Financial History of the United States.* New York: Columbia University Press, 1970.

Nettels, Curtis P. *The Emergence of a National Economy: 1775-1815*, vol. 2 *of The Economic History of the United States.* New York: Holt, Rinehart & Winston, 1962.

Oberholtzer, Ellis Paxson. *Robert Morris, Patriot and Financier.* New York: The Macmillan Company, 1903.

Osborne, John Ball. "The First President's Interest in Washington as Told by Himself." *Records of the Columbia Historical Society.* Vol. 4 (1901).

Osgood, Herbert L. *The American Colonies in the Eighteenth Century.* New York: Columbia University Press, 1924.

Parker, Matthew. *The Sugar Barons: Family, Corruption, Empire, and War in the West Indies.* New York: Walker and Company, 2011.

Perez, L. Jeffrey. "'Bonds of Friendship and Mutual Interest': Virginia's Waterways Improvement Companies." Ph.D. diss., College of William and Mary, 2000.

Perkins, Edwin J. *American Public Finance and Financial Services, 1700-1815.* Columbus: Ohio State University Press, 1994.

Phillipson, Nicholas. *Adam Smith: An Enlightened Life.* New Haven, CT: Yale University Press, 2010.

Pinckney, Charles Cotesworth. *Life of General Thomas Pinckney.* Cambridge, MA: Riverside Press, 1895.

Pogue, Dennis J. and White, Esther C. *George Washington's Gristmill at Mount Vernon,* David Bruce Smith Book Series. Mount Vernon, VA: Mount Vernon Ladies' Association, 2005.

Rakove, Jack N. *James Madison and the Creation of the American Republic*, 3rd ed., Library of Am. Biography Series. New York: Pearson Longman, 2007.

Randall, E. O. "Washington's Ohio Lands." *Ohio Archaeological and Historical Quarterly*, vol. 19, no. 3 (July 1910).

Rappleye, Charles. *Robert Morris: Financier of the American Revolution.* New York: Simon & Schuster, 2010.

Reuter, Frank T. *Trials and Triumphs: George Washington's Foreign Policy.* Fort Worth, TX: Texas Christian University Press, 1983.

Ritcheson, Charles R. *Aftermath of Revolution: British Policy toward the United States, 1783-1795.* Dallas, TX: Southern Methodist University Press, 1969.

Royster, Charles. *The Fabulous History of the Dismal Swamp Company: A Story of George Washington's Times.* New York: Alfred A. Knopf, 1999.

Rutland, Robert A., et al., eds. *The Papers of James Madison*. Charlottesville: University Press of Virginia, 1977–.

Sheridan, Richard B. "The British Credit Crisis of 1772 and the American Colonies." *The Journal of Economic History*, vol. 20, no. 2 (June 1960).

Simms, Brendan. *Three Victories and a Defeat: The Rise and Fall of the First British Empire, 1714-1783*. New York: Basic Books, 2009.

Simpson, Bland. *The Great Dismal: A Carolinian Swamp Memoir*. Chapel Hill, NC: University of North Carolina Press, 1998.

Sloan, Herbert E. *Principle and Interest: Thomas Jefferson and the Problem of Debt*. New York: Oxford University Press, 1995.

Smith, Adam; Campbell, R. H. and Skinner, A. S., eds. *Adam Smith, An Inquiry into the Nature and Causes of the Wealth of Nations*, The Glasgow Edition of the Works and Correspondence of Adam Smith. 1979, exact photographic reproduction; Indianapolis, IN: Liberty Press/Liberty Classics, 1981.

Smith, Charles Daniel. *The Early Career of Lord North, the Prime Minister*. Cranbury, NJ: Associated University Presses, 1979.

Smith, Page. *The Shaping of America: A People's History of the Young Republic*. New York: Penguin, 1980.

Smith, Richard Norton. *Patriarch: George Washington and the New American Nation*. New York: Houghton Mifflin, 1993.

Sokoloff, Kenneth L. "Inventive Activity in Early Industrial America: Evidence from Patent Records, 1790-1846." *The Journal of Economic Activity*, Vol. 48, No. 4 (December 1988).

Sparks, Jared. *The Life of Gouverneur Morris, With Selections from his Correspondence and Miscellaneous Papers*. Boston: Gray and Bowen, 1832.

Stahr, Walter. *John Jay, Founding Father*. New York: Hambledon & Continuum, 2006.

Studenski, Paul and Krooss, Herman E. *Financial History of the United States*. New York: McGraw-Hill Company, 1952.

Sumner, William Graham. *The Financier and the Finances of the American Revolution*. 1891; reprint, New York: Burt Franklin, 1970.

Swank, James M. *Introduction to a History of Ironmaking and Coal Mining in Pennsylvania*. Philadelphia: Published by author, 1878.

Sylla, Richard. "Experimental Federalism: The Economics of American Government, 1789-1914," in Stanley L. Engerman and Robert E. Gallman, eds., *The Cambridge Economic History of the United States: Volume 2, The Long Nineteenth Century*. Cambridge: Cambridge University Press, 2000.

Syrett, Harold C., ed. *The Papers of Alexander Hamilton*. New York: Columbia University Press, 1961-87.

Thomas, Isaiah. *History of Printing in America, with a Biography of Printers*. 1810 Albany, NY: Joel Munsell, Printer for the American Antiquarian Society, 1874.

Thomas, Peter D. G. *George III: King and Politicians, 1760-1770*. Manchester: Manchester University Press, 2002.

Trench, Charles Chenevix. *The Royal Malady*. London: Longmans, Green and Company, Ltd, 1964.

Ver Steeg, Clarence L. *Robert Morris, Revolutionary Financier*. New York: Octagon Books, 1972.

Volwiler, Albert T. *George Croghan and the Westward Movement, 1741-1782*.1926; reprint, New York: AMS Press, Inc., 1971.

Warren, Charles. *Bankruptcy in United States History*. Cambridge, MA: Harvard University Press, 1935.

——. *The Supreme Court in United States History*. Boston: Little, Brown & Company, 1923.

Washburne, George Adrian. *Imperial Control of the Administration of Justice in the Thirteen American Colonies, 1684-1776*. Clark, NJ: The Lawbook Exchange, 2006.

Webb, Stephen Saunders. *Marlborough's America*, The Lewis Walpole Series in Eighteenth-Century Culture and History. New Haven: Yale University Press, 2013.

Wexler, Natalie. "In the Beginning: The First Three Chief Justices." *University of Pennsylvania Law Review*, Vol. 154, No. 6, pp. 1373-1419 (Jun., 2006).

Wilson, Rufus Rockwell, ed. *Burnaby's Travels through North America: Reprinted from the Third Edition of 1798*. New York: A. Wessels Company, 1904.

Wood, Gordon S. *Empire of Liberty: A History of the Early Republic, 1789-1815*. New York: Oxford University Press, 2009.

——. *The Radicalism of the American Revolution*. New York: Alfred A. Knopf-Random House, 1992.

Wright, Robert E. *One Nation Under Debt: Hamilton, Jefferson and the History of What We Owe*. New York: McGraw-Hill, 2008.

NOTES

1. William Tindall, *Standard History of the City of Washington* (Knoxville, TN: H. W. Crew & Co., 1914), 37.

2. *See*, e.g., John Ferling, *Jefferson and Hamilton: The Rivalry That Forged a Nation* (New York: Bloomsbury Press, 2013), 231; "finance and commerce [were] matters clearly beyond Washington's ken and outside his area of interest," Forrest McDonald, *The Presidency of George Washington* (Lawrence, KS: The University Press of Kansas, 1974), 41; or George Washington's "sense of futility" when faced with the country's fiscal records in Joseph J. Ellis, *His Excellency: George Washington* (New York: Borzoi-Alfred A. Knopf-Random House, 2004), 203-04.

3. Mustafa Kemal Atatürk (1881-1938), President of Turkey, 1923.

4. Sir Winston Churchill (1874-1965), Prime Minister of United Kingdom, 1940-1945, 1951-1955.

5. Harold Geneen (1910-1997), former chairman, ITT.

6. George Will, *One Man's America: The Pleasures and Provocations of Our Singular Nation* (New York: Crown Forum-Random House, 2008), 227.

7. Walter Stahr, *John Jay: Founding Father* (New York: Hambledon & Continuum, 2006), 385.

8. "Thomas Jefferson to Walter Jones, 2 January 1814," in Julian P. Boyd, et al., eds., *The Papers of Thomas Jefferson* (Princeton: Princeton University Press, 1950–), Retirement Series, 7:100-04; John White, "A Medal of Honor for George Washington," *Wall Street Journal,* January 28, 2012, A-13.

9. Fergus M. Bordewich, *Washington: The Making of the American Capital,* (New York: Harper Collins, 2008), 15; Douglas Southall Freeman, *George Washington: A Biography,* vol. 6, *Patriot and President* (New York: Charles Scribner's Sons, 1954), 190-92; Clarence Winthrop Bowen, ed., *The History of the Centennial Celebration of George Washington as First President of the United States* (New York: D. Appleton and Company, 1892), 14-16.

10. Clarence Winthrop Bowen, ed., *The History of the Centennial Celebration of George Washington as First President of the United States* (New York: D. Appleton and Company, 1892), 28-36; Douglas Southall Freeman, *George Washington: A Biography,* vol. 6, *Patriot and President* (New York: Charles Scribner's Sons, 1954), 6:167-84.

11. "From George Washington to Henry Knox, 1 April 1789," W. W. Abbot, et al., eds., *The Papers of George Washington* (Charlottesville: University of Virginia Press, 1987–), Presidential Series 2:2-3; Clarence Winthrop Bowen, ed., *The History of the Centennial Celebration of George Washington as First President of the United States* (New York: D. Appleton and Company, 1892), 20-21; "From George Washington to Edward Rutledge, 5 May 1789," W. W. Abbot, et al., eds., *The Papers of George Washington* (Charlottesville: University of Virginia Press, 1987–), Presidential Series, 2:217-18; [April 1789], Donald Jackson and Dorothy Twohig, eds., *The Diaries of George Washington* (Charlottesville: University Press of Virginia, 1976-79), 5:445.

12. Dispatch of Rudolph Van Dorsten, Secretary of Legation of Netherland, to the Recorder of the States-General, dated in New York on May 4, 1789, as cited in Stephen Decatur and Tobias Lear, *Private Affairs of George Washington: From the Records and Accounts of Tobias Lear, Esquire, his Secretary* (Boston: Houghton Mifflin Company, 1933) 9; Edgar S. Maclay, ed., *Journal of William Maclay* (New York: D. Appleton and Company, 1890), 9.

13. Lauren Collins, "Big Pin," *The New Yorker,* October 5, 2009, p. 24; George Washington "To Comte D'Estaing, May 15, 1784," John C. Fitzpatrick, ed., The *Writings of George Washington from the Original Manuscript Sources, 1745-1799* (Washington: United States Government Printing Office, 1931-1940), 27:401-02.

14. Edgar S. Maclay, ed., *Journal of William Maclay* (New York: D. Appleton and Company, 1890), 9; Seth Ames, ed., *Works of Fisher Ames* (Boston: Little, Brown and Company: 1854), 1:34.

15. Douglas Southall Freeman, *George Washington: A Biography,* vol. 2, *Young Washington* (New York: Charles Scribner's Sons, 1949), 267.

16. George Washington, "To Edward Rutledge, May 5, 1789," John C. Fitzpatrick, ed., *The Writings of George Washington from the Original Manuscript Sources, 1745-1799* (Washington: United States Government Printing Office, 1931-1940), 30:309.

17. "Benjamin Rush to Thomas Ruston, October 29, 1775," L. H. Butterfield, ed., *Letters of Benjamin Rush* (Princeton: Princeton University Press, 1951), 2:91-94.

18. Brendan Simms, *Three Victories and a Defeat: The Rise and Fall of the First British Empire, 1714-1783* (New York: Basic Books, 2009), 666-67.

19. Letter of George III to Lord North, June 22, 1779, in Jeremy Black, *George III, America's Last King,* (New Haven: Yale University Press, 2006), 233, 240.

20. Nicholas Phillipson, *Adam Smith: An Enlightened Life* (New Haven, CT: Yale University Press, 2010), 229, quoting Adam Smith in R.H. Campbell and A. S. Skinner, eds., *Adam Smith: An Inquiry into the Nature and Causes of the Wealth of Nations,* The Glasgow Edition of the Works and Correspondence of Adam Smith (Oxford: Oxford University Press, 1976), 2:604-5.

21. Clarence L. Ver Steeg, *Robert Morris, Revolutionary Financier* (New York: Octagon Books, 1972), 48.
22. Don Cook, *The Long Fuse: How England Lost the American Colonies, 1760-1785* (New York: Atlantic Monthly Press, 1995), 342.
23. James C. Rees and Stephen Spignesi, *George Washington's Leadership Lessons: What the Father of Our Country Can Teach Us About Effective Leadership and Character* (Hoboken, NJ: John Wiley & Sons, Inc., 2007), 95.
24. Charles Chenevix Trench, *The Royal Malady* (London: Longmans, Green and Company, Ltd, 1964), 32; Don Cook, *The Long Fuse: How England Lost the American Colonies, 1760-1785* (New York: Atlantic Monthly Press, 1995), 348.
25. Brendan Simms, *Three Victories and a Defeat: The Rise and Fall of the First British Empire, 1714-1783* (New York: Basic Books, 2009), 663.
26. Don Cook, *The Long Fuse: How England Lost the American Colonies, 1760-1785* (New York: Atlantic Monthly Press, 1995), 17-18, 348; Brendan Simms, *Three Victories and a Defeat: The Rise and Fall of the First British Empire, 1714-1783* (New York: Basic Books, 2009), 665-66.
27. Don Cook, *The Long Fuse: How England Lost the American Colonies, 1760-1785* (New York: Atlantic Monthly Press, 1995), 5-7, 373-75; Charles Chenevix Trench, *The Royal Malady* (London: Longmans, Green and Company, Ltd, 1964), 32.
28. John Fiske, *The Critical Period of American History, 1783-1789* (Boston: Houghton, Mifflin and Company, 1895), 130; Thomas Paine, *The Crisis, XIII: Thoughts on the Peace, and Probable Advantages* (Philadelphia), April 19, 1783.
29. Richard B. Morris, *The Forging of the Union 1781-1789* (New York: Harper & Row, 1987), 14; Don Cook, *The Long Fuse: How England Lost the American Colonies, 1760-1785* (New York: Atlantic Monthly Press, 1995), 1-2; Robert Kagan, *Dangerous Nation* (New York: Alfred A. Knopf, 2006), 4, citing Norman A. Graebner, *Foundations of American Foreign Policy: A Realist Appraisal from Franklin to McKinley* (Wilmington, DE: Scholarly Resources, 1985), xxxii.
30. The census of 1790 showed the U.S. population at 3.9 million, from 2.3 million immediately after the war, see *Heads of Families at the First Census of the United States Taken in the Year 1790* (Washington: Government Printing Office, 1908).
31. Robert Middlekauff, *The Glorious Cause: The American Revolution, 1763-1789,* (Oxford: Oxford University Press, 2005), 590; John Brooke, *King George III,* (London: Constable & Company, Ltd., 1972), 219-20; Don Cook, *The Long Fuse: How England Lost the American Colonies, 1760-1785* (New York: Atlantic Monthly Press, 1995), 348-49.
32. Brendan Simms, *Three Victories and a Defeat: The Rise and Fall of the First British Empire, 1714-1783* (New York: Basic Books, 2009), 683; Charles R. Ritcheson, *Aftermath of Revolution: British Policy toward the United States, 1783-1795* (Dallas, TX: Southern Methodist University Press, 1969), 3-4.
33. Don Cook, *The Long Fuse: How England Lost the American Colonies, 1760-1785* (New York: Atlantic Monthly Press, 1995), 361-62.
34. George C. Herring, *From Colony to Superpower: U.S. Foreign Relations since 1776* (Oxford: Oxford University Press, 2008), 29; Charles R. Ritcheson, *Aftermath of Revolution: British Policy toward the United States, 1783-1795* (Dallas, TX: Southern Methodist University Press, 1969), 5.

35. Charles R. Ritcheson, *Aftermath of Revolution: British Policy toward the United States, 1783-1795* (Dallas, TX: Southern Methodist University Press, 1969), 4-5; Richard B. Morris, *The Forging of the Union 1781-1789* (New York: Harper & Row, 1987), 75; Don Cook, *The Long Fuse: How England Lost the American Colonies, 1760-1785* (New York: Atlantic Monthly Press, 1995), 362-63.

36. Walter Stahr, *John Jay, Founding Father,* (New York: Hambledon& Continuum, 2006), 165-66.

37. John Ferling, *A Leap in the Dark: The Struggle to Create the American Republic* (Oxford: Oxford University Press, 2003), 253-54.

38. Don Cook, *The Long Fuse: How England Lost the American Colonies, 1760-1785* (New York: Atlantic Monthly Press, 1995), 365-75.

39. George Washington, "Address to Congress on Resigning his Commission," December 23, 1783, John C. Fitzpatrick, ed., The *Writings of George Washington from the Original Manuscript Sources, 1745-1799* (Washington: United States Government Printing Office, 1931-1940), 27:284-85; John Ferling, *A Leap in the Dark: The Struggle to Create the American Republic* (Oxford: Oxford University Press, 2003), 255.

40. "From George Washington to Lafayette, 1 February 1784," W. W. Abbot, et al., eds., *The Papers of George Washington* (Charlottesville: University of Virginia Press, 1987-), Confederation Series, 1:87-89.

41. Charles R. Ritcheson, *Aftermath of Revolution: British Policy toward the United States, 1783-1795* (Dallas, TX: Southern Methodist University Press, 1969), vii-viii.

42. Charles R. Ritcheson, *Aftermath of Revolution: British Policy toward the United States, 1783-1795* (Dallas, TX: Southern Methodist University Press, 1969), viii.

43. Charles R. Ritcheson, *Aftermath of Revolution: British Policy toward the United States, 1783-1795* (Dallas, TX: Southern Methodist University Press, 1969), vii, citing *American Quarterly Review*, September 1827, 267-306.

44. John Lord Sheffield, *Observations on the Commerce of the American States* (London: J. Debrett, 1784), 267; Ronald Hoffman, ed., *The Economy of Early America: The Revolutionary Period, 1763-1790* (Charlottesville, VA: University Press of Virginia, 1988), 283, 319; Curtis P. Nettels, *The Emergence of a National Economy, 1775-1815* (New York: Holt, Rinehart and Winston, 1962), 60; Richard B. Morris, *The Forging of the Union 1781-1789* (New York: Harper & Row, 1987), 130-32; George C. Herring, *From Colony to Superpower: U.S. Foreign Relations since 1776* (Oxford: Oxford University Press, 2008), 37; Robert Kagan, *Dangerous Nation* (New York: Alfred A. Knopf, 2006), 54; Charles R. Ritcheson,. *Aftermath of Revolution: British Policy toward the United States, 1783-1795* (Dallas, TX: Southern Methodist University Press, 1969), 21.

45. Robert Kagan, *Dangerous Nation* (New York: Alfred A. Knopf, 2006), 53.

46. George C. Herring, *From Colony to Superpower: U.S. Foreign Relations since 1776* (Oxford: Oxford University Press, 2008), 35, 41-43; A. L. Burt, *The United States, Great Britain, and British North America: From the Revolution to the Establishment of Peace After the War of 1812* (New York: Russell & Russell, 1961), 94-107; Robert Kagan, *Dangerous Nation* (New York: Alfred A. Knopf, 2006), 54; Charles R. Ritcheson, *Aftermath of Revolution: British Policy toward the United States, 1783-1795* (Dallas, TX: Southern Methodist University Press, 1969), 166-67.

47. "Thomas Jefferson to Nathanael Greene, Jan. 12, 1785," Paul Leicester Ford, ed., *The Writings of Thomas Jefferson* (New York: G. P. Putnam's Sons, 1894), 4:25; "From Thomas Jefferson to William Carmichael, 5 May 1786," Julian P. Boyd, et al., eds., *The Papers of Thomas Jefferson* (Princeton: Princeton University Press, 1950–), 9:448-49; George C. Herring, *From Colony to Superpower: U.S. Foreign Relations since 1776* (Oxford: Oxford University Press, 2008), 38; Richard B. Morris, *The Forging of the Union 1781-1789* (New York: Harper & Row, 1987), 205; Robert Kagan, *Dangerous Nation* (New York: Alfred A. Knopf, 2006), 55.

48. George Washington, "Circular to the States," June 8, 1783, John C. Fitzpatrick, ed., *The Writings of George Washington from the Original Manuscript Sources, 1745-1799* (Washington: United States Government Printing Office, 1931-1940), 26:483-96.

49. George C. Herring, *From Colony to Superpower: U.S. Foreign Relations since 1776* (Oxford: Oxford University Press, 2008), 22, 28, 38; Robert Kagan, *Dangerous Nation* (New York: Alfred A. Knopf, 2006), 54-56.

50. George C. Herring, *From Colony to Superpower: U.S. Foreign Relations since 1776* (Oxford: Oxford University Press, 2008), 44; Charles R. Ritcheson, *Aftermath of Revolution: British Policy toward the United States, 1783-1795* (Dallas, TX: Southern Methodist University Press, 1969), 158-59; Robert Kagan, *Dangerous Nation* (New York: Alfred A. Knopf, 2006), 56.

51. Robert Kagan, *Dangerous Nation* (New York: Alfred A. Knopf, 2006), 53-56; Charles R. Ritcheson, *Aftermath of Revolution: British Policy toward the United States, 1783-1795* (Dallas, TX: Southern Methodist University Press, 1969), 38-45.

52. Forrest McDonald, ed., *Confederation and Constitution, 1781-1789* (Columbia: University of South Carolina Press, 1968), 3; Curtis P. Nettels, *The Emergence of a National Economy, 1775-1815* (New York: Holt, Rinehart and Winston, 1962), 20; Robert Middlekauff, *The Glorious Cause: The American Revolution, 1763-1789,* (Oxford: Oxford University Press, 2005), 595; E. James Ferguson, *The Power of the Purse; a History of American Public Finance, 1776-1790* (Chapel Hill: The University of North Carolina Press, 1961), 221.

53. Forrest McDonald, ed., *Confederation and Constitution, 1781-1789* (Columbia: University of South Carolina Press, 1968), 45.

54. Gordon S. Wood, *Empire of Liberty: A History of the Early Republic, 1789-1815* (New York: Oxford University Press, 2009), 13; George C. Herring, *From Colony to Superpower: U.S. Foreign Relations since 1776* (Oxford: Oxford University Press, 2008), 34; John J. McCusker and Russell R. Menard, *The Economy of British America, 1607-1789* (Chapel Hill, NC: The University of North Carolina Press, 1985), 373-74; George Washington "To the Secretary for Foreign Affairs [John Jay]," May 18, 1786, John C. Fitzpatrick, ed., The *Writings of George Washington from the Original Manuscript Sources, 1745-1799* (Washington: United States Government Printing Office, 1931-1940), 28:430-32; "To Thomas Jefferson from John Jay, 14 December 1786," Julian P. Boyd, et al., eds., *The Papers of Thomas Jefferson* (Princeton: Princeton University Press, 1950–), 10:596-99; John Ferling, *A Leap in the Dark: The Struggle to Create the American Republic* (Oxford: Oxford University Press, 2003), 256.

55. "From George Washington to James Madison, 5 November 1786," W. W. Abbot, et al., eds., *The Papers of George Washington* (Charlottesville: University of Virginia Press, 1987–), Confederation Series, 4:331-32.

56. "From George Washington to William Pearce, 6 October 1793," W. W. Abbot, et al., eds., *The Papers of George Washington* (Charlottesville: University of Virginia Press, 1987–), Presidential Series 14:172-73; Robert William Fogel, *The Escape from Hunger and Premature*

Death, 1700-2100: Europe, America, and the Third World (Cambridge: Cambridge University Press, 2004), 2; "From George Washington to Henry Knox, 20 February 1784," W. W. Abbot, et al., eds., *The Papers of George Washington* (Charlottesville: University of Virginia Press, 1987–), Confederation Series, 1:136-38.

57. The term "critical period" was first coined by historian John Fiske in 1888, *see* John Fiske, *The Critical Period of American History, 1783-1789* (Boston: Houghton, Mifflin and Company, 1895), v-vii.

58. Don Cook, *The Long Fuse: How England Lost the American Colonies, 1760-1785* (New York: Atlantic Monthly Press, 1995), 374.

59. George Washington "to David Humphreys, July 25, 1785," John C. Fitzpatrick, ed., The *Writings of George Washington from the Original Manuscript Sources, 1745-1799* (Washington: United States Government Printing Office, 1931-1940), 28:203; James Thomas Flexner, *George Washington: The Forge of Experience, 1732-1775* (Boston: Little Brown and Company, 1965), 1:305; Joel Achenbach, *The Grand Idea: George Washington's Potomac and the Race to the West* (New York: Pantheon Books-Random House, 2007), 22.

60. Douglas Southall Freeman, *George Washington: A Biography,* vol. 1, *Young Washington* (New York: Charles Scribner's Sons, 1949), xi; James Thomas Flexner, *George Washington: The Forge of Experience, 1732-1775* (Boston: Little Brown and Company, 1965), 31.

61. Jacob Abbott, *History of King Charles the First of England* (New York: Harper & Brothers, 1848), 277-83.

62. Douglas Southall Freeman, *George Washington: A Biography,* Vol. 1, *Young Washington* (New York: Charles Scribner's Sons, 1949), 447-86.

63. Rufus Rockwell Wilson, ed., *Burnaby's Travels through North America: Reprinted from the Third Edition of 1798* (New York: A. Wessels Company, 1904), 197-98, 205.

64. Douglas Southall Freeman, *George Washington: A Biography,* Vol. 1, *Young Washington* (New York: Charles Scribner's Sons, 1949), 501-10.

65. Douglas Southall Freeman, *George Washington: A Biography,* Vol. 1, *Young Washington* (New York: Charles Scribner's Sons, 1949), 186-90.

66. George Washington, "Youthful Survey of Hell Hole on Mount Vernon Tract," in John C. Fitzpatrick, ed., *The Diaries of George Washington: 1748-1799, Volume I* (Boston and New York: Houghton Mifflin Company, 1925).

67. Metchie J. E. Budka, ed., *Under Their Vine and Fig Tree: Travels through America in 1797-1799, 1805, with Some Further Account of Life in New Jersey,* Collections of the New Jersey Historical Society (Elizabeth, NJ: Grassman Publishing Company, 1965), 14:102; John C. Fitzpatrick, ed., *The Diaries of George Washington: 1748-1799, Volume I* (Boston and New York: Houghton Mifflin Company, 1925), 2-12.

68. John C. Fitzpatrick, ed., *The Diaries of George Washington: 1748-1799, Volume I* (Boston and New York: Houghton Mifflin Company, 1925), 2-12; Metchie J. E. Budka, ed., *Under Their Vine and Fig Tree: Travels through America in 1797-1799, 1805, with Some Further Account of Life in New Jersey,* Collections of the New Jersey Historical Society (Elizabeth, NJ: Grassman Publishing Company, 1965), 14:102.

69. "George Washington's Professional Surveys, 22 July 1749-25 October 1752," W.W. Abbot et al., eds., *The Papers of George Washington* (Charlottesville: University Press of Virginia, 1987–), Colonial Series, 1:8-37.

70. Douglas Southall Freeman, *George Washington: A Biography,* Vol. 1, *Young Washington* (New York: Charles Scribner's Sons, 1949), 234.
71. "George Washington's Professional Surveys, 22 July 1749-25 October 1752," Abbot et al., *Papers of George Washington* (Charlottesville: University Press of Virginia, 1987–), Colonial Series, 1:8-37.
72. "George Washington's Professional Surveys, 22 July 1749-25 October 1752," W. W. Abbot, et al., eds., *The Papers of George Washington* (Charlottesville: University of Virginia Press, 1987–), Colonial Series, 1:8-37; Edward Redmond, "George Washington: Surveyor and Mapmaker," *Annals of the Association of American Geographers,* 23, no. 3, (1941), 147.
73. "George Washington's Professional Surveys, 22 July 1749-25 October 1752," W. W. Abbot, et al., eds., *The Papers of George Washington* (Charlottesville: University of Virginia Press, 1987–), Colonial Series 1:8-37; Douglas Southall Freeman, *George Washington: A Biography,* Vol. 1, *Young Washington* (New York: Charles Scribner's Sons, 1949), 243-44. The original of Washington's field notes for the survey of one of the tracts he acquired is still in existence, and on display at the Library of Congress in Washington, D.C., as part of the George Washington Collection.
74. *See,* e.g., Douglas Southall Freeman, *George Washington: A Biography,* Vol. 1, *Young Washington* (New York: Charles Scribner's Sons, 1949), 239.
75. James M. Swank, *Introduction to a History of Ironmaking and Coal Mining in Pennsylvania,* (Philadelphia: Published by author, 1878), 11; Douglas Southall Freeman, *George Washington: A Biography,* Vol. 1, *Young Washington* (New York: Charles Scribner's Sons, 1949), 38-41.
76. Nathaniel Wright Stephenson and Waldo Hilary Dunn, *George Washington* (Oxford: Oxford University Press, 1940), 1:33-34.
77. John C. Fitzpatrick, ed., *The Diaries of George Washington: 1748-1799, Volume I* (Boston and New York: Houghton Mifflin Company, 1925), 86-92.
78. James Thomas Flexner, *George Washington: The Forge of Experience, 1732-1775* (Boston: Little Brown and Company, 1965), 46; Douglas Southall Freeman, *George Washington: A Biography,* Vol. 1, *Young Washington* (New York: Charles Scribner's Sons, 1949), 194.
79. Herbert L. Osgood, *The American Colonies in the Eighteenth Century,* (New York: Columbia University Press, 1924), 4:225; see, for example, Charles Royster, *The Fabulous History of the Dismal Swamp Company: A Story of George Washington's Times,* (New York: Alfred A. Knopf, 1999), 52; also the Portrait of Robert Dinwiddie; original in the National Portrait Gallery, London.
80. James Thomas Flexner, *George Washington: The Forge of Experience, 1732-1775* (Boston: Little Brown and Company, 1965), 47-48; Isaac Norris to Robert Charles, April 19, 1754, quoted in Charles Royster, *The Fabulous History of the Dismal Swamp Company: A Story of George Washington's Times,* (New York: Alfred A. Knopf, 1999), 55; Freeman, *George Washington,* 1:236; Royster, *Fabulous History,* 53, quoting letter of Robert Dinwiddie to Thomas Cresap, January 23, 1752, R. A. Brock, ed., *The Official Records of Robert Dinwiddie, Lieutenant-Governor of the Colony of Virginia, 1751-1758* (Richmond: Virginia Historical Society, 1883), 1:17-18.
81. Douglas Southall Freeman, *George Washington: A Biography,* Vol. 1, *Young Washington* (New York: Charles Scribner's Sons, 1949), 274-76.

82. "From George Washington to Robert Dinwiddie," 29 May 1754, W. W. Abbot, et al., eds., *The Papers of George Washington* (Charlottesville: University of Virginia Press, 1987–), Colonial Series, 1:107.
83. David Preston, *Braddock's Defeat* (New York: Oxford University Press, 2015), 26.
84. James Thomas Flexner, *George Washington: The Forge of Experience, 1732-1775* (Boston: Little Brown and Company, 1965), 86-92; Joel Achenbach, *The Grand Idea: George Washington's Potomac and the Race to the West* (New York: Pantheon Books-Random House, 2007), 16-18.
85. George Washington, *The Journal of Major George Washington, sent by the Hon. Robert Dinwiddie, Esq.; His Majesty's Lieutenant-Governor, and Commander in Chief of Virginia, to the Commandant of the French Forces on Ohio* (1754; reprint, Williamsburg, VA: The Colonial Williamsburg Foundation, 1959).
86. "Instructions from Robert Dinwiddie, 14 August 1755," W. W. Abbot, et al., eds., *The Papers of George Washington* (Charlottesville: University of Virginia Press, 1987–), Colonial Series, 2:4-6; Douglas Southall Freeman, *George Washington: A Biography,* vol. 2, *Young Washington* (New York: Charles Scribner's Sons, 1949), 113.
87. George Louis Beer, *British Colonial Policy 1754-1765,* (New York: The MacMillan Company, 1907), 174-78; Douglas Southall Freeman, *George Washington: A Biography,* Vol. 1, *Young Washington* (New York: Charles Scribner's Sons, 1949), 423-24; James Thomas Flexner, *George Washington: The Forge of Experience, 1732-1775* (Boston: Little Brown and Company, 1965), 175; "From George Washington to John Robinson, 1 September 1758," W. W. Abbot, et al., eds., *The Papers of George Washington* (Charlottesville: University of Virginia Press, 1987–), Colonial Series, 5:432; Joseph J. Ellis, *His Excellency George Washington,* (New York: Knopf, 2004), 39.
88. Douglas Southall Freeman, *George Washington: A Biography,* vol. 2, *Young Washington* (New York: Charles Scribner's Sons, 1949), 2:301-02; 3:1-3, 10-13.
89. Charles Royster, *The Fabulous History of the Dismal Swamp Company: A Story of George Washington's Times,* (New York: Alfred A. Knopf, 1999), 113-14.
90. "From George Washington to Robert Cary and Co., 28 September 1760," W. W. Abbot, et al., eds., *The Papers of George Washington* (Charlottesville: University of Virginia Press, 1987–), Colonial Series, 6:460; James Thomas Flexner, *George Washington: The Forge of Experience, 1732-1775* (Boston: Little Brown and Company, 1965), 281-82.
91. T.H. Breen, *Tobacco Culture: The Mentality of the Great Tidewater Planters on the Eve of Revolution* (Princeton: Princeton University Press, 1985), 84-86.
92. Richard Sheridan, "The British Credit Crisis of 1772 and the American Colonies," *The Journal of Economic History* 20 (June 1960), 172; T.H. Breen, *Tobacco Culture: The Mentality of the Great Tidewater Planters on the Eve of Revolution* (Princeton: Princeton University Press, 1985), 127.
93. James Thomas Flexner, *George Washington: The Forge of Experience, 1732-1775* (Boston: Little Brown and Company, 1965), 283.
94. Richard Norton Smith, *Patriarch: George Washington and the New American Nation* (New York: Houghton Mifflin, 1993), 11; Charles Royster, *The Fabulous History of the Dismal Swamp Company: A Story of George Washington's Times,* (New York: Alfred A. Knopf, 1999), 72.
95. Dorothy Troth Muir, *Potomac Interlude: The Story of Woodlawn Mansion and the Mount Vernon Neighborhood, 1846-1943* (Washington, DC: Mount Vernon Print Shop, 1943), 18; James Thomas Flexner, *George Washington: The Forge of Experience, 1732-1775* (Boston: Little

Brown and Company, 1965), 283-84; "From George Washington to Robert Cary & Company, 1 June 1774," W. W. Abbot, et al., eds., *The Papers of George Washington* (Charlottesville: University of Virginia Press, 1987-), Colonial Series, 10:83.
96. [Diary entry: 27 March 1760], Donald Jackson and Dorothy Twohig, eds., *The Diaries of George Washington* (Charlottesville: University Press of Virginia, 1976-79), 1:257-58. A recent archeology project at Mount Vernon has unearthed fragments of the heating ducts under the greenhouse floor.
97. [April 1760], Donald Jackson and Dorothy Twohig, eds., *The Diaries of George Washington* (Charlottesville: University Press of Virginia, 1976-79), 1:260-75.
98. Eric Jay Dolin, *Leviathan: The History of Whaling in America* (New York: W.W. Norton & Company, Inc., 2007), 75-77, 109-11.
99. George Washington, *Manuscript Ledger Book 1*, 1750-72, George Washington Papers, Library of Congress, 88-300; James Thomas Flexner, *George Washington: The Forge of Experience, 1732-1775* (Boston: Little Brown and Company, 1965), 283-84.
100. George Washington, *Manuscript Ledger Book 1*, 1750-72, George Washington Papers, Library of Congress, 326;James Thomas Flexner, *George Washington: The Forge of Experience, 1732-1775* (Boston: Little Brown and Company, 1965), 283-84; Joe Holley, "With a Sailor's Eye, He Provided a New View of George Washington," *The Washington Post,* April 13, 2008, C-8.
101. Dennis J. Pogue and Esther C. White, *George Washington's Gristmill at Mount Vernon,* David Bruce Smith Book Series (Mount Vernon, VA: Mount Vernon Ladies' Association, 2005), 14-15, 45-52.
102. Dennis J. Pogue and Esther C. White, *George Washington's Gristmill at Mount Vernon,* David Bruce Smith Book Series (Mount Vernon, VA: Mount Vernon Ladies' Association, 2005), 5-6.
103. "Particulars of the Life and Character of General Washington, Extracted from a Letter in Lloyd's Evening post of August 17, Signed An Old Soldier," *The Gentleman's Magazine,* vol. 48(August 1778), reprinted in William S. Baker, *Early Sketches of George Washington* (Philadelphia: J. B. Lippincott Company, 1894), 50; Rupert Hughes, *George Washington* (New York, 1926-1930), 2:213; all as cited in James Thomas Flexner, *George Washington: The Forge of Experience, 1732-1775* (Boston: Little Brown and Company, 1965), 284, 315; Donald Jackson and Dorothy Twohig, eds., *The Diaries of George Washington* (Charlottesville: University Press of Virginia, 1976-79), 1 xxv-xxxvi.
104. J. P. Hale, ed., "Visit to Washington," *The West Virginia Historical Magazine Quarterly,* vol. 1, no. 1 (1901), 60-64; Metchie J. E. Budka, ed., *Under Their Vine and Fig Tree: Travels through America in 1797-1799, 1805, with Some Further Account of Life in New Jersey,* Collections of the New Jersey Historical Society (Elizabeth, NJ: Grassman Publishing Company, 1965), 100-01.
105. "George Washington's Last Will and Testament, 9 July 1799," W. W, Abbot, et al., eds., *The Papers of George Washington* (Charlottesville: University of Virginia Press, 1987-), Retirement Series, 4:479-511.
106. Henry Wiencek, *An Imperfect God: George Washington, His Slaves, and the Creation of America* (New York: Farrar, Straus and Giroux, 2003), 185; "Fairfax County Resolves, 18 July 1774," W. W, Abbot, et al., eds., *The Papers of George Washington* (Charlottesville: University of Virginia Press, 1987-), Colonial Series, 10:119-28; "From George Washington to Robert Morris, 12 April 1786," W. W, Abbot, et al., eds., *The Papers of George Washington*

(Charlottesville: University of Virginia Press, 1987-), Confederation Series, 4:15-17; John Bernard, Mrs. Bayle Bernard, Laurence Hutton and Brander Matthews, Retrospections of America, 1797-1811 (New York: Harper & Brothers, 1887), 91.

107. "From George Washington to George William Fairfax, 10 November 1785," W. W. Abbot, et al., eds., *The Papers of George Washington* (Charlottesville: University of Virginia Press, 1987-), Confederation Series, 3:348-51.

108. George Washington "To George William Fairfax," July 10, 1783, John C. Fitzpatrick, ed., *The Writings of George Washington from the Original Manuscript Sources, 1745-1799* (Washington: United States Government Printing Office, 1931-1940), 27:57-60.

109. Kenneth R. Bowling and Helen E. Veit, eds., *The Diary of William Maclay and Other Notes on Senate Debates* (Baltimore: Johns Hopkins University Press, 1988), 258.

110. Woodrow Wilson, *George Washington* (New York and London: Harper & Brothers, 1905), 105.

111. 1710-1720, from John J. McCusker, "Table Eg1-59 Population, by race and by colony or locality: 1610-1780," Susan B. Carter, et al., eds., *Historical Statistics of the United States, Millennial Edition On Line*, Cambridge University Press 2006; "From George Washington to Lord Dunmore, 15 June 1772," W. W. Abbot, et al., eds., *The Papers of George Washington* (Charlottesville: University of Virginia Press, 1987–), Colonial Series 9:55-57; Charles Royster, *The Fabulous History of the Dismal Swamp Company: A Story of George Washington's Times* (New York: Borzoi-Alfred A. Knopf-Random House, 1999), 62.

112. George E. Lewis, *The Indiana Company 1763-1798* (Glendale, CA: The Arthur H. Clark Company, 1941), 20-23; John A. Jakle, *Images of the Ohio Valley: A Historical Geography of Travel, 1740-1860,* (New York: Oxford University Press, 1977), 3-4; Lord Hillsborough, President of the Board of Trade, "Report of the Lords Commissioners for Trade and Plantations, on the Petition of the Honorable Thomas Walpole and his Associates for a Grant of Lands on the River Ohio in North America," April 15, 1772, in Albert Henry Smyth, *The Writings of Benjamin Franklin* (New York: The Macmillan Company, 1906), 5:474.

113. Albert T. Volwiler, *George Croghan and the Westward Movement 1741-1782* (1926; reprint, New York: AMS Press, Inc., 1971), 233-35; George E. Lewis, *The Indiana Company 1763-1798* (Glendale, CA: The Arthur H. Clark Company, 1941), 21.

114. James Thomas Flexner, *George Washington: The Forge of Experience, 1732-1775* (Boston: Little Brown and Company, 1965), 289, 291; Joel Achenbach, *The Grand Idea: George Washington's Potomac and the Race to the West* (New York: Simon & Schuster, 2004), 7; "From George Washington to John Parke Custis, 1 February 1778," W. W. Abbot, et al., eds., *The Papers of George Washington* (Charlottesville: University of Virginia Press, 1987–), Revolutionary War Series 13:435-37.

115. Bland Simpson, *The Great Dismal: A Carolinian Swamp Memoir* (University of North Carolina Press: 1998), 41-46; Paul W. Kirk, Jr., ed., *The Great Dismal Swamp* (Charlottesville: University Press of Virginia, 1979), 4.

116. Charles Royster, *The Fabulous History of the Dismal Swamp Company: A Story of George Washington's Times*, (New York: Alfred A. Knopf, 1999), 81-83.

117. Paul W. Kirk, Jr., ed., *The Great Dismal Swamp* (Charlottesville: University Press of Virginia, 1979), 59; Charles Royster, *The Fabulous History of the Dismal Swamp Company: A Story of George Washington's Times*, (New York: Alfred A. Knopf, 1999), 12; Frank E. Grizzard, Jr., *George Washington: A Biographical Companion*, (Buena Vista, VA: Mariner Publishing,

2002), 86-87; "To the Great Dismal Swamp, 15 October 1763," and "15 Octobr. 1763," Donald Jackson and Dorothy Twohig, eds., *The Diaries of George Washington* (Charlottesville: University Press of Virginia, 1976-79), 1:319-26.

118. John C. Fitzpatrick, ed., *The Diaries of George Washington 1748-1799* (Boston: Houghton Mifflin, 1925), 1:188-94; "To the Great Dismal Swamp, 15 October 1763," and "15 Octobr. 1763," Donald Jackson and Dorothy Twohig, eds., *The Diaries of George Washington* (Charlottesville: University Press of Virginia, 1976-79), 1:319-26.

119. Percy Scott Flippin, *The Royal Government in Virginia 1624-1775* (New York: Columbia University, 1919), 218.

120. "Dismal Swamp Land Company Articles of Agreement, 3 November 1763," W. W. Abbot, et al., eds., *The Papers of George Washington* (Charlottesville: University of Virginia Press, 1987–), Colonial Series 7:269-74; Herbert L. Osgood, *The American Colonies in the Eighteenth Century* (New York: Columbia University Press, 1924), 4:236; Percy Scott Flippin, *The Royal Government in Virginia 1624-1775* (New York: Columbia University, 1919), 213, citing H.R. McIlwaine and John Pendleton Kennedy, eds., *Journal of the House of Burgesses of Virginia, 1659/60-1776* (Richmond: Virginia State Library Board, 1905-1915), 9:274; John Robinson died in 1766; Daniel J. Boorstin, *The Americans: The Colonial Experience* (New York: Random House, 1958), 112; Charles Royster, *The Fabulous History of the Dismal Swamp Company: A Story of George Washington's Times*, (New York: Alfred A. Knopf, 1999), 84-5, 112-15, 136-43; Gerald Newman and Leslie Ellen Brown, eds., *Britain in the Hanoverian Age, 1714-1837: An Encyclopedia*, Volume 1481 of Garland Reference Library of the Humanities (London: Taylor & Francis, 1997), 37; Merrow Egerton Sorley, *Lewis of Warner Hall: The History of a Family…* (1935; reprint, Baltimore: Genealogical Publishing Co., 1964), 137-39; Amy Waters Yarsinke, *The Elizabeth River* (Charleston, SC: The History Press, 2007), 229; Royster, Fabulous History, 29-31, 38; Mary Selden Kennedy, *Seldens of Virginia and Allied Families*, (New York: Frank Allaben Genealogical Company, 1911), 1:610-11; Hayes, *Road to Monticello*, 30; Maeva Marcus, et al., eds., *The Documentary History of the Supreme Court of the United States, 1789-1800* (New York: Columbia University Press, 2003), 7:232 n. 3.

121. "Dismal Swamp Land Company Articles of Agreement," W. W. Abbot, et al., eds., *The Papers of George Washington* (Charlottesville: University of Virginia Press, 1987–), Colonial Series 7:269-74; Charles Royster, *The Fabulous History of the Dismal Swamp Company: A Story of George Washington's Times*, (New York: Alfred A. Knopf, 1999), 81-83.

122. Bland Simpson, *The Great Dismal: A Carolinian Swamp Memoir* (University of North Carolina Press: 1998), 43-46; Frank E. Grizzard, Jr., *George Washington: A Biographical Companion*, (Buena Vista, VA: Mariner Publishing, 2002), 87.

123. Charles Royster, *The Fabulous History of the Dismal Swamp Company: A Story of George Washington's Times*, (New York: Alfred A. Knopf, 1999), 81, 216-17.

124. George Washington "To William Crawford, June 9, 1781," John C. Fitzpatrick, ed., *The Writings of George Washington from the Original Manuscript Sources, 1745-1799* (Washington: United States Government Printing Office, 1931-44), 22:194.

125. Bland Simpson, *The Great Dismal: A Carolinian Swamp Memoir* (University of North Carolina Press: 1998), 41-46; Charles Royster, *The Fabulous History of the Dismal Swamp Company: A Story of George Washington's Times*, (New York: Alfred A. Knopf, 1999), 257-58.

126. Charles Royster, *The Fabulous History of the Dismal Swamp Company: A Story of George Washington's Times*, (New York: Alfred A. Knopf, 1999), 292-93.

127. "From Thomas Jefferson to Hugh Williamson, 6 February 1785," Julian P. Boyd, et al., eds., *The Papers of Thomas Jefferson* (Princeton: Princeton University Press, 1950–), 7:641-42; "To Thomas Jefferson from Hugh Williamson, 11 December 1784," Boyd, et al., *Papers of Thomas Jefferson*, 7:569-70.
128. William Waller Hening, *The Statutes at Large: Being a Collection of all the Laws of Virginia, from the First Session of the Legislature in the Year 1619* (Richmond, VA: N.P. 119-23), 12:478-94; Walter Clark, *The State Records of North Carolina*, vol. 25 (Goldsboro, NC: Trustees of the Public Libraries, 1906), 83-93.
129. Charles Royster, *The Fabulous History of the Dismal Swamp Company: A Story of George Washington's Times*, (New York: Alfred A. Knopf, 1999), 340-41.
130. Frank E. Grizzard, Jr., *George Washington: A Biographical Companion*, (Buena Vista, VA: Mariner Publishing, 2002), 87; Bland Simpson, *The Great Dismal: A Carolinian Swamp Memoir* (University of North Carolina Press: 1998), 41-46; Daniel Owen Sayers, *The Diasporic World of the Great Dismal Swamp*, 1630-1860 (Ann Arbor, MI: ProQuest, 2008), 81-82; Waverly Traylor, *The Great Dismal Swamp in Myth and Legend* (Pittsburgh: RoseDog Books, 2010), 211-12, 217.
131. Frank E. Grizzard, Jr., *George Washington: A Biographical Companion*, (Buena Vista, VA: Mariner Publishing, 2002), 86-87.
132. Frank E. Grizzard, Jr., *George Washington: A Biographical Companion*, (Buena Vista, VA: Mariner Publishing, 2002), 86.
133. "From George Washington to Patrick Henry, 24 June 1785," W. W. Abbot, et al., eds., *The Papers of George Washington* (Charlottesville: University of Virginia Press, 1987-), Confederation Series 3:80.
134. Bland Simpson, *The Great Dismal: A Carolinian Swamp Memoir* (University of North Carolina Press: 1998), 46.
135. William Thomas Hutchinson, *The Bounty Lands of the American Revolution in Ohio*, (New York: Arno Press, 1979), 2-4, 15.
136. "From George Mercer to George Washington, 16 September 1759," W. W. Abbot, et al., eds., *The Papers of George Washington* (Charlottesville: University of Virginia Press, 1987-), Colonial Series 6:343.
137. *The National Cyclopaedia of American Biography* (New York: James T. White & Company, 1906), 13:390; Charles Royster, *The Fabulous History of the Dismal Swamp Company: A Story of George Washington's Times*, (New York: Alfred A. Knopf, 1999), 132.
138. C.W. Butterfield, *An Historical Account of the Expedition against Sandusky under Col. William Crawford in 1782* (1873; reprint, Canal Winchester, OH: Badgley Publishing Company, 2009), 387-92.
139. Douglas Southall Freeman, *George Washington: A Biography*, vol. 3, *Planter and Patriot* (New York: Charles Scribner's Sons, 1951), 237, 296-303; "Resolutions of the Officers of the Virginia Regiment of 1754, 23 November 1772," W. W. Abbot, et al., eds., *The Papers of George Washington* (Charlottesville: University of Virginia Press, 1987–), Colonial Series, 9:128-31.
140. [Diary entries: 28 October 1770, and November 1770 (1)], Donald Jackson and Dorothy Twohig, eds., *The Diaries of George Washington* (Charlottesville: University Press of Virginia, 1976-79), 2:304, 318-19.
141. *The National Cyclopaedia of American Biography* (New York: James T. While & Company, 1906), 13:390.

142. James A. Hagemann, *Lord Dunmore: Last Royal Governor of Virginia, 1771-1776* (Hampton, VA: Wayfarer Enterprises, 1974), 5-6; Charles Ramsdell Lingley, *The Transition in Virginia from Colony to Commonwealth* (New York: Columbia University, 1910), 61; Earl of Dunmore to Earl of Hillsborough, March 1772, Colonial Office 5/154, ff. 35-36, Public Record Office, London, cited in Charles Royster, *The Fabulous History of the Dismal Swamp Company: A Story of George Washington's Times*, (New York: Alfred A. Knopf, 1999), 181, 183; Jerrilyn Greene Marston, *King and Congress: The Transfer of Political Legitimacy, 1774-1776* (Princeton: Princeton University Press, 1987), 277.

143. [February 1760] Donald Jackson and Dorothy Twohig, eds., *The Diaries of George Washington* (Charlottesville: University Press of Virginia, 1976-79), 1:240-41; "From George Washington to the Officers and Soldiers of the Virginia Regiment of 1754, 23 December 1772," W. W. Abbot, et al., eds., *The Papers of George Washington* (Charlottesville: University of Virginia Press, 1987–), Colonial Series 9:143-48.

144. Charles Royster, *The Fabulous History of the Dismal Swamp Company: A Story of George Washington's Times*, (New York: Alfred A. Knopf, 1999), 216, 221.

145. *See*, An Act for adjusting and settling the titles of claimers to unpatented lands under the present and former government, previous to the establishment of the commonwealth's land office, in William Waller Hening, *The Statutes at Large: Being a Collection of all the Laws of Virginia, from the First Session of the Legislature in the Year 1619* (Richmond, VA: N.P., 1819-23), 10:35-49.

146. *See*, e.g., "To George Washington from John Page, 14 February 1774," W. W. Abbot, et al., eds., *The Papers of George Washington* (Charlottesville: University of Virginia Press, 1987–), Colonial Series, 9:477-78; E. O. Randall, "Washington's Ohio Lands," *Ohio Archaeological and Historical Quarterly*, vol. 19, no. 3, (July 1910), 303-18.

147. William Waller Hening, *The Statutes at Large: Being a Collection of all the Laws of Virginia, from the First Session of the Legislature in the Year 1619* (Richmond, VA: N.P., 1819-23), 10:564-66, 11:309-12, 326-28; E. O. Randall, "Washington's Ohio Lands," *Ohio Archaeological and Historical Quarterly*, vol. 19, no. 3, (July 1910): 306.

148. E. O. Randall, "Washington's Ohio Lands," *Ohio Archaeological and Historical Quarterly*, vol. 19, no. 3, (July 1910), 304, 307; William Waller Hening, *The Statutes at Large: Being a Collection of all the Laws of Virginia, from the First Session of the Legislature in the Year 1619* (Richmond, VA: N.P., 1819-23), 10:564-66, 11:326-28. *See also* "On Appointment of a Surveyor for the Virginia Military District," *American State Papers, Public Lands* (Washington, DC: Gales & Seaton, 1860), 5:342.

149. "An Act to Enable the Officers and Soldiers of the Virginia Line on the Continental Establishment, to Obtain Titles to Certain Lands Lying Northwest of the River Ohio, between the Little Miami and Sciota," (August 10, 1790), in Richard Peters, et al., eds., *The Public Statutes at Large of the United States of America…* (Boston: Little and Brown, 1845-1873) 1:182-84.

150. "From George Washington to Richard Clough Anderson, 30 July 1798," W. W. Abbot, et al., eds., *The Papers of George Washington* (Charlottesville: University of Virginia Press, 1987–), Retirement Series, 2:474-75; E. O. Randall, "Washington's Ohio Lands," *Ohio Archaeological and Historical Quarterly*, vol. 19, no. 3, (July 1910), 308-09.

151. John C. Fitzpatrick, ed., *The Last Will and Testament of George Washington and Schedule of his Property, to which is Appended the Last Will and Testament of Martha Washington*, (Mount

Vernon, VA: Mount Vernon Ladies Association, 1947). *See also* Eugene E. Prussing, *The Estate of George Washington, Deceased*(Boston: Little, Brown and Company, 1927).

152. E. O. Randall, "Washington's Ohio Lands," *Ohio Archaeological and Historical Quarterly*, vol. 19, no. 3, (July 1910), 310-318; Journal of the House, 9th Cong. 1st sess., March 14, 1806; "An Act Authorizing Patents to Issue for Lands Located and Surveyed by Virtue of Certain Virginia Resolution Warrants," 2 *Stat.* 437 (March 3, 1807); see, e.g., "An Act to Make Land Warrants Assignable, and for Other Purposes," 10 *Stat.* 3-4 (March 22, 1852); Senate Bill No. 1238 (60th Cong., 1st sess.), House Bill No. 5489 (60th Cong., 1st session.)

153. Douglas Southall Freeman, *George Washington: A Biography,* Vol. 1, *Young Washington* (New York: Charles Scribner's Sons, 1949), 372-73.

154. Douglas Southall Freeman, *George Washington: A Biography,* Vol. 1, *Young Washington* (New York: Charles Scribner's Sons, 1949), 341-43, 372-73.

155. James M. Swank, *Introduction to a History of Ironmaking and Coal Mining in Pennsylvania,* (Philadelphia: Published by author, 1878), 11.

156. John C. Fitzpatrick, ed., *The Diaries of George Washington: 1748-1799, Volume I* (Boston and New York: Houghton Mifflin Company, 1925), 408; William E. Burns, *Daily Life Through History: Science and Technology in Colonial America* (Westport, CT: Greenwood Press, 2005), 73; James M. Swank, *Introduction to a History of Ironmaking and Coal Mining in Pennsylvania,* (Philadelphia: Published by author, 1878), 111-12.

157. Paul Leland Haworth, *George Washington: Farmer,* (Indianapolis, IN: The Bobbs-Merrill Company, 1915), 23-24.

158. Douglas Southall Freeman, *George Washington: A Biography,* vol. 6, *Patriot and President* (New York: Charles Scribner's Sons, 1954), 18.

159. *See* generally: Douglas Southall Freeman, *George Washington: A Biography,* vol. 3, *Planter and Patriot* (New York: Charles Scribner's Sons, 1951), 3:308-09, 324-25, 343; 6:17-18; E. Harrison Clark, *All Cloudless Glory: The Life of George Washington,* vol. 1, *From Youth to Yorktown* (Washington, DC: Regnery Publishing, 1995), 180-81; E. Harrison Clark, *All Cloudless Glory: The Life of George Washington,* vol. 2, *Making a Nation* (Washington, DC: Regnery Publishing, 1996), 74-77.

160. Hernando De Soto, *The Mystery of Capital: Why Capitalism Triumphs in the West and Fails Everywhere Else* (New York: Basic Books, 2000), 9; Richard Kluger, *Seizing Destiny: How America Grew from Sea to Shining Sea,* (New York: Alfred Knopf, 2007), 185-189.

161. *See*, generally: James Thomas Flexner, *George Washington and the New Nation (1783-1793)* (Boston: Little, Brown and Company, 1970), 58-61; Douglas Southall Freeman, *George Washington: A Biography,* vol. 2, *Young Washington* (New York: Charles Scribner's Sons, 1949), 2:75-77; E. Harrison Clark, *All Cloudless Glory: The Life of George Washington,* vol. 2, *Making a Nation* (Washington, DC: Regnery Publishing, 1996), 75, 77.

162. G. Frederick Wright and Frederick Bennett Wright, eds., "Washington's Canoe Trip Down the Potomac Related in a Letter to Colonel Innes," *Records of the Past* 9 (1910), 74-79; Robert J. Kapsch, *The Potomac Canal: George Washington and the Waterway West* (Morgantown, WV: West Virginia University Press, 2007), 14.

163. "From George Washington to Charles Carter, August 1754," W. W. Abbot, et al., eds., *The Papers of George Washington* (Charlottesville: University of Virginia Press, 1987–), Colonial Series 1:196-98; "Notes on the Navigation of the Potomac River above the Great Falls, July-August 1754," Abbot, et al., *Papers of George Washington*, Colonial Series 1:179.

164. Robert J. Kapsch, *The Potomac Canal: George Washington and the Waterway West* (Morgantown, WV: West Virginia University Press, 2007), 15.
165. Robert J. Kapsch, *The Potomac Canal: George Washington and the Waterway West* (Morgantown, WV: West Virginia University Press, 2007), 23-25; T. Gibson Hobbs, Jr., *The Canal on the James: An Illustrated Guide to the James River and Kanawha Canal*, Nancy Blackwell Marion, comp., Mary Molyneux Abrams and Thomas G. Ledford, eds. (Blackwell Press: Lynchburg, VA, 2009), 3-4; "From George Washington to a Participant in the Potomac River Enterprise, [c. 1762]," W. W. Abbot, et al., eds., *The Papers of George Washington* (Charlottesville: University of Virginia Press, 1987–), Colonial Series 7:175-56.
166. L. Jeffrey Perez, "'Bonds of Friendship and Mutual Interest': Virginia's Waterways Improvement Companies," (Ph.D. diss., College of William and Mary, 2000), 3-5.
167. "From George Washington to Thomas Jefferson, 29 March 1784," W. W. Abbot, et al., eds., *The Papers of George Washington* (Charlottesville: University of Virginia Press, 1987–), Confederation Series 1:237-40; Robert J. Kapsch, *The Potomac Canal: George Washington and the Waterway West* (Morgantown, WV: West Virginia University Press, 2007), 46-8; "To George Washington from Normand Bruce, 13 November 1784," W. W. Abbot, et al., eds., *The Papers of George Washington* (Charlottesville: University of Virginia Press, 1987–), Confederation Series 2:126-33; "From Thomas Jefferson to George Washington, 15 March 1784, W. W. Abbot, et al., eds., *The Papers of George Washington* (Charlottesville: University of Virginia Press, 1987–), Confederation Series 1:215-18.
168. James Thomas Flexner, *George Washington and the New Nation, 1783-1793* (Boston: Little, Brown and Company, 1970), 75; Robert J. Kapsch, *The Potomac Canal: George Washington and the Waterway West* (Morgantown, WV: West Virginia University Press, 2007), 50-52; William Waller Hening, *The Statutes at Large: Being a Collection of all the Laws of Virginia, from the First Session of the Legislature in the Year 1619* (Richmond, VA: N.P., 1819-23), 11: 450-61, 510-25; Douglas R. Littlefield, "The Potomac Company: A Misadventure in Financing an Early American Internal Improvement Project," *The Business History Review*, Vol. 58, No. 4 (Winter 1984), 562-85.
169. L. Jeffrey Perez, "'Bonds of Friendship and Mutual Interest': Virginia's Waterways Improvement Companies," (Ph.D. diss., College of William and Mary, 2000), 67-70; Douglas R. Littlefield, "The Potomac Company: A Misadventure in Financing an Early American Internal Improvement Project," *The Business History Review*, Vol. 58, No. 4 (Winter 1984), 566-69; Wayland Fuller Dunaway, *History of the James River and Kanawha Company* (New York: Columbia University, 1922), 26-27; James Thomas Flexner, *George Washington and the New Nation, 1783-1793* (Boston: Little, Brown and Company, 1970), 76-77.
170. "From George Washington to Thomas Johnson and Thomas Sim Lee, 18 May 1785," W. W. Abbot, et al., eds., *The Papers of George Washington* (Charlottesville: University of Virginia Press, 1987–), Confederation Series 2:562-66; "George Washington's Last Will and Testament, 9 July 1799," W. W. Abbot, et al., eds., *The Papers of George Washington* (Charlottesville: University of Virginia Press, 1987–), Retirement Series 4:477-92.
171. Robert J. Kapsch, *The Potomac Canal: George Washington and the Waterway West* (Morgantown, WV: West Virginia University Press, 2007), 56-7; Corra Bacon-Foster, *Early Chapters in the Development of the Patomac Route to the West* (Washington: Columbia Historical Society, 1912), 66-72; "From George Washington to James Rumsey, 5 June 1785," W. W.

Abbot, et al., eds., *The Papers of George Washington* (Charlottesville: University of Virginia Press, 1987–), Confederation Series 3:40-2.

172. "From George Washington to William Grayson, 22 August 1785," W. W. Abbot, et al., eds., *The Papers of George Washington* (Charlottesville: University of Virginia Press, 1987-), Confederation Series 3:193-95.

173. "From George Washington to Samuel Holden Parsons, 15 July 1788," W. W. Abbot, et al., eds., *The Papers of George Washington* (Charlottesville: University of Virginia Press, 1987-), Confederation Series 6:379-80.

174. Wayland Fuller Dunaway, *History of the James River and Kanawha Company* (New York: Columbia University, 1922), 29-30.

175. Wayland Fuller Dunaway, *History of the James River and Kanawha Company* (New York: Columbia University, 1922), 23-24; William Waller Hening, *The Statutes at Large: Being a Collection of all the Laws of Virginia, from the First Session of the Legislature in the Year 1619* (Richmond, VA: N.P., 1819-23),) 11:525-26; "To Thomas Jefferson from James Madison, 9 January 1785," Julian P. Boyd, et al., eds., *The Papers of Thomas Jefferson* (Princeton: Princeton University Press, 1950-), 7:588-99; Ron Chernow, *Washington: A Life* (New York: The Penguin Press, 2010), 501-02; "From George Washington to Edmund Randolph, 30 July 1785," W. W. Abbot, et al., eds., *The Papers of George Washington* (Charlottesville: University of Virginia Press, 1987–), Confederation Series 3:163-65.

176. "George Washington's Last Will and Testament, 9 July 1799," W. W. Abbot, et al., eds., *The Papers of George Washington* (Charlottesville: University of Virginia Press, 1987-), Retirement Series 4:477-92.

177. L. Jeffrey Perez, "'Bonds of Friendship and Mutual Interest': Virginia's Waterways Improvement Companies," (Ph.D. diss., College of William and Mary, 2000), 199-222.

178. "From George Washington to George Plater, 25 October 1784," W. W. Abbot, et al., eds., *The Papers of George Washington* (Charlottesville: University of Virginia Press, 1987-), Confederation Series 2:106-10.

179. Joel Achenbach, *The Grand Idea: George Washington's Potomac and the Race to the West* (New York: Simon & Schuster, 2004), 129.

180. Joel Achenbach, *The Grand Idea: George Washington's Potomac and the Race to the West* (New York: Pantheon Books-Random House, 2007), 19, citing M. L. Weems, *The Life of George Washington; With Curious Anecdotes*, (Philadelphia: J. B. Lippincott & Co., 1858), 47-48.

181. Anne Bezanson, *Prices and inflation during the American Revolution: Pennsylvania, 1770-1790* (Philadelphia: University of Pennsylvania Press, 1951), cited in Clarence L. Ver Steeg, *Robert Morris, Revolutionary Financier* (New York: Octagon Books, 1972), 49.

182. Lucia Naldi, et al., "Entrepreneurial Orientation, Risk Taking, and Performance in Family Firms," *Family Business Review* 20, no. 1 (2007): 33.

183. "From George Washington to Burwell Bassett, 19 June 1775," W. W. Abbot, et al., eds., *The Papers of George Washington* (Charlottesville: University of Virginia Press, 1987-), Revolutionary War Series, 1:12-14.

184. William Blackstone and George Chase, *Commentaries on the Laws of England in Four Books* (New York: Banks & Brothers, 1894), 892.

185. Joseph J. Ellis, *His Excellency George Washington*, (New York: Knopf, 2004), 35; Ron Chernow, *Washington: A Life* (New York: The Penguin Press, 2010), 98.

186. Frank E. Grizzard, Jr., *George! A Guide to All Things Washington* (Buena Vista & Charlottesville, VA: Mariner Publishing, 2005), 333-35; Douglas Southall Freeman, *George Washington: A Biography*, vol. 2, *Young Washington* (New York: Charles Scribner's Sons, 1949), 298.

187. John J. McCusker, *Money and Exchange in Europe and America, 1600-1775: A Handbook* (Chapel Hill: University of North Carolina Press, 1978), 209-14; "Editorial Note," W. W. Abbot, et al., eds., *The Papers of George Washington* (Charlottesville: University of Virginia Press, 1987–), Colonial Series, 6:201-09; "Editorial Note," Abbot, et al., *Papers of George Washington*, Colonial Series, 7:81-84; "III. Guardian Accounts, 12 April 1762," Abbot, et al., *Papers of George Washington*, Colonial Series, 7:86-93.

188. "Editorial Note," W. W. Abbot, et al., eds., *The Papers of George Washington* (Charlottesville: University of Virginia Press, 1987–), Colonial Series, 6:201-09; "IV-C. Martha Parke Custis's Estate Account, c. November 1761," Abbot, et al., *Papers of George Washington*, Colonial Series, 6:275-76; "Editorial Note," Abbot, et al., *Papers of George Washington*, Colonial Series, 7:81-84; "I. Washington's Appointment as Guardian, 21 October 1761," Abbot, et al., *Papers of George Washington*, Colonial Series, 7: 84; "III. Guardian Accounts, 12 April 1762," Abbot, et al., *Papers of George Washington*, Colonial Series, 7:86-93.

189. Ron Chernow, *Washington: A Life* (New York: The Penguin Press, 2010), 162.

190. Linda E. Speth, "More Than Her 'Thirds': Wives and Widows in Colonial Virginia," *Women, Family, and Community in Colonial America: Two Perspectives* (1983; reprint, New York: Routledge, 2011), 7-11; Joan R. Gundersen and Gwen Victor Gampel, "Married Women's Legal Status in Eighteenth-Century New York and Virginia," *The William and Mary Quarterly*, Vol. 39, No. 1 (Jan., 1982), 114-34; "Editorial Note," W. W. Abbot, et al., eds., *The Papers of George Washington* (Charlottesville: University of Virginia Press, 1987–), Colonial Series, 6:201-09; "Editorial Note," Abbot, et al., *Papers of George Washington*, Colonial Series, 7:81-84.

191. Matthew Parker, *The Sugar Barons: Family, Corruption, Empire, and War in the West Indies*, (New York: Walker and Company, 2011), 209-18; Douglas Southall Freeman, *George Washington: A Biography*, vol. 2, *Young Washington* (New York: Charles Scribner's Sons, 1949), 279-302; Stephen Saunders Webb, *Marlborough's America*, The Lewis Walpole Series in Eighteenth-Century Culture and History (New Haven: Yale University Press, 2013), 91-92, 393.

192. Edward W. Greenfield, "Some New Aspects of the Life of Daniel Parke," *The Virginia Magazine of History and Biography*, Vol. 54, No. 4 (October 1946), 306-15; Matthew Parker, *The Sugar Barons: Family, Corruption, Empire, and War in the West Indies*, (New York: Walker and Company, 2011), 209.

193. Natalie A. Zacek, *Settler Society in the English Leeward Islands, 1670-1776* (Cambridge: Cambridge University Press, 2010), 16.

194. Matthew Parker, *The Sugar Barons: Family, Corruption, Empire, and War in the West Indies*, (New York: Walker and Company, 2011), 211-15; Stephen Saunders Webb, *Marlborough's America*, The Lewis Walpole Series in Eighteenth-Century Culture and History (New Haven: Yale University Press, 2013), 267-83, 392-93; William A. Pettigrew, *Freedom's Debt: The Royal African Company and the Politics of the Atlantic Slave Trade, 1672-1752* (Chapel Hill, NC: University of North Carolina Press, 2013), 135.

195. Stephen Saunders Webb, *Marlborough's America*, The Lewis Walpole Series in Eighteenth-Century Culture and History (New Haven: Yale University Press, 2013), 267-89.

196. Rebecca Johnston, "William Byrd Title Book (Concluded)," *The Virginia Magazine of History and Biography,* Vol. 50, No. 3 (July 1942), 238-63; Douglas Southall Freeman, *George Washington: A Biography,* vol. 2, *Young Washington* (New York: Charles Scribner's Sons, 1949), 281-85.
197. Helen Bryan, *Martha Washington: First Lady of Liberty* (New York: John Wiley & Sons, 2002), 43-45; Edward W. Greenfield, "Some New Aspects of the Life of Daniel Parke," *The Virginia Magazine of History and Biography,* Vol. 54, No. 4 (October 1946), 309, Douglas Southall Freeman, *George Washington: A Biography,* vol. 2, *Young Washington* (New York: Charles Scribner's Sons, 1949), 281-83; Anonymous, *Antigua and the Antiguans: A Full Account of the Colony and its Inhabitants,* (London: Saunders and Otley, 1844), 339; George Adrian Washburne, *Imperial Control of the Administration of Justice in the Thirteen American Colonies, 1684-1776* (Clark, NJ: The Lawbook Exchange, 2006), 139-40.
198. Rebecca Johnston, "William Byrd Title Book (Concluded)," *The Virginia Magazine of History and Biography,* Vol. 50, No. 3 (July 1942), 238-63; Douglas Southall Freeman, *George Washington: A Biography,* vol. 2, *Young Washington* (New York: Charles Scribner's Sons, 1949), 284-86.
199. Douglas Southall Freeman, *George Washington: A Biography,* vol. 2, *Young Washington* (New York: Charles Scribner's Sons, 1949), 286-87; George Adrian Washburne, *Imperial Control of the Administration of Justice in the Thirteen American Colonies, 1684-1776* (Clark, NJ: The Lawbook Exchange, 2006), 140.
200. James Thomas Flexner, *George Washington: The Forge of Experience, 1732-1775* (Boston: Little, Brown and Company, 1965), 188-90.
201. Douglas Southall Freeman, *George Washington: A Biography,* vol. 2, *Young Washington* (New York: Charles Scribner's Sons, 1949), 287-89.
202. Rebecca Johnston, "William Byrd Title Book (Concluded)," *The Virginia Magazine of History and Biography,* Vol. 50, No. 3 (July 1942), 238-63;Douglas Southall Freeman, *George Washington: A Biography,* vol. 2, *Young Washington* (New York: Charles Scribner's Sons, 1949), 287-89.
203. George Adrian Washburne, *Imperial Control of the Administration of Justice in the Thirteen American Colonies, 1684-1776* (Clark, NJ: The Lawbook Exchange, 2006), 139-42.
204. George Adrian Washburne, *Imperial Control of the Administration of Justice in the Thirteen American Colonies, 1684-1776* (Clark, NJ: The Lawbook Exchange, 2006), 140-41; Douglas Southall Freeman, *George Washington: A Biography,* vol. 2, *Young Washington* (New York: Charles Scribner's Sons, 1949), 299.
205. W. L. Grant and James Munro, eds., *Acts of the Privy Council of England,* Colonial Series vol. IV, A. D. 1745-1766 (London: His Majesty's Stationery Office, 1911), 288-90.
206. Helen Bryan, *Martha Washington: First Lady of Liberty* (New York: John Wiley & Sons, 2002), 80.
207. "I. Queries to John Mercer, 20 April 1759," W. W. Abbot, et al., eds., *The Papers of George Washington* (Charlottesville: University of Virginia Press, 1987–), Colonial Series, 6:210-13.
208. A quote from Tobias Lear, Washington's longtime secretary, in Patricia Brady, *Martha Washington: An American Life* (New York: Viking-Penguin, 2005), 151.
209. "I. Queries to John Mercer, 20 April 1759," W. W. Abbot, et al., eds., *The Papers of George Washington* (Charlottesville: University of Virginia Press, 1987–), Colonial Series, 6:210-13;

"II. John Mercer's Answers, c.20-26 April 1759," Abbot, et al., *Papers of George Washington*, Colonial Series, 6:213-15.

210. In the meantime, Patsy Custis died in 1773, and Jacky Custis married sixteen-year-old Nelly Calvert in 1774.

211. Douglas Southall Freeman, *George Washington: A Biography*, vol. 2, *Young Washington* (New York: Charles Scribner's Sons, 1949), 286-90, 298-301, Douglas Southall Freeman, *George Washington: A Biography*, vol. 3, *Planter and Patriot* (New York: Charles Scribner's Sons, 1951), 21, 225-27; "From George Washington to Johnathan Boucher, 9 July 1771," W. W. Abbot, et al., eds., *The Papers of George Washington* (Charlottesville: University of Virginia Press, 1987–), Colonial Series, 8:494-98; "From George Washington to Robert Stewart, 27 April 1763," Abbot et al., *Papers of George Washington,* Colonial Series, 7:205-07.

212. Douglas Southall Freeman, *George Washington: A Biography,* vol. 3, *Planter and Patriot* (New York: Charles Scribner's Sons, 1951), 209.

213. James Thomas Flexner, *George Washington: The Forge of Experience, 1732-1775* (Boston: Little Brown and Company, 1965), 286, 293.

214. E. O. Randall, "Washington's Ohio Lands," *Ohio Archaeological and Historical Quarterly*, 19 (1910): 304-18.

215. James Thomas Flexner, *George Washington in the American Revolution (1775-1783)* (Boston: Little, Brown and Company, 1968), 517.

216. "George Washington's Last Will and Testament, 9 July 1799," W. W. Abbot, et al., eds., *The Papers of George Washington* (Charlottesville: University of Virginia Press, 1987-), Retirement Series 4:479-511.

217. "Schedule of Property," W. W. Abbot, et al., eds., *The Papers of George Washington* (Charlottesville: University of Virginia Press, 1987-), Retirement Series, 4:512-27.

218. Walter Stahr, *John Jay, Founding Father,* (New York: Hambledon& Continuum, 2006), 195, citing "The John Jay Freedom Box" in *Christie's Magazine,* January-February 2001.

219. Patrick Hruby, "George Washington's Annotated Constitution Fetches Almost $10 Million," *The Washington Times,* June 22, 2012.

220. "George Washington's Last Will and Testament, 9 July 1799," W. W. Abbot, et al., eds., *The Papers of George Washington* (Charlottesville: University of Virginia Press, 1987-), Retirement Series 4:479-511.

221. Andrew G. Gardner, "How Did Washington Make His Millions?" *Colonial Williamsburg*, Vol. XXXV, No. 1 (Winter 2013).

222. "Current-dollar and 'real' GDP," National Economic Accounts, *Bureau of Economic Analysis*, http://www.bea.gov/national/index.htm#gdp (accessed 3/12/15); *cf. Wall Street Journal*, March 16, 2001

223. William Blackstone, *Commentaries on the Laws of England*, 4 volumes, (Oxford, 1768), 1:246, 270-71; Will and Ariel Durant, *The Story of Civilization* (New York: Simon and Schuster, 1967), 10:686, 737; Gordon S. Wood, *The Radicalism of the American Revolution* (New York: Alfred A. Knopf-Random House, 1992), 214.

224. Don Cook, *The Long Fuse: How England lost the American Colonies, 1760-1785,* (New York: The Atlantic Monthly Press, 1995), 5; Will and Ariel Durant, *The Story of Civilization* (New York: Simon and Schuster, 1967), 10:701; Jeremy Black, *George III, America's Last King* (New Haven: Yale University Press, 2006); 418; C. E. Vulliamy, *Royal George: A Study of King George III, His Experiment in Monarchy, His Decline and Retirement; With a View of Society,*

Politics and Historic Events during His Reign (London: D. Appleton-Century Company, Incorporated, 1937).
225. "The King to Lord Shelburne, November 10th, 1782," Sir John Fortescue, ed., *The Correspondence of King George the Third: From 1760 to December 1783,* Volume VI (London: MacMillan and Co., 1928), 154.
226. Don Cook, *The Long Fuse: How England lost the American Colonies, 1760-1785,* (New York: The Atlantic Monthly Press, 1995), xii.
227. Charles Daniel Smith, *The Early Career of Lord North, the Prime Minister* (Cranbury, NJ: Associated University Presses, 1979), 13.
228. Charles Daniel Smith, *The Early Career of Lord North, the Prime Minister* (Cranbury, NJ: Associated University Presses, 1979), 13, 26, 57-58; W. Baring Pemberton, *Lord North* (London: Longmans, Green & Co., 1938), 2.
229. Peter D. G. Thomas, *George III, King and Politician, 1760-1770,* (Manchester: Manchester University Press, 2002), 231.
230. *Notes and Queries,* 1st ser. 7 (February 26, 1853): 207, cited in Charles Daniel Smith, *The Early Career of Lord North, the Prime Minister* (Cranbury, NJ: Associated University Presses, 1979), 37, n. 8; John Brooke, ed., *King George III* (New York: McGraw Hill Book Company, 1972), 263; Charles Daniel Smith, *The Early Career of Lord North, the Prime Minister* (Cranbury, NJ: Associated University Presses, 1979), 30.
231. "*Recreative Review of Eccentricities of Literature and Life,* vol. II, (London: j. Wallis, 1822), 14; "Lord North," *Number 10 Downing Street: The Official site of the British Prime Minister's Office,* 2011, http://www.number10.gov.uk/history-and-tour/lord-north/ (6 January 2012); Wroxton College," *Fairleigh Dickinson University,* 2012, http://view.fdu.edu/default.aspx?id=326 (28 March 2012).
232. Andreas A. M. Kinneging, *Aristocracy, Antiquity, and History: Classicism in Political Thought,* (New Brunswick, NJ: Transaction Publishers, 1997), 33; Will and Ariel Durant, *The Story of Civilization* (New York: Simon and Schuster, 1967), 10:684, citing M. Dorothy George, *England in Transition* (London: George Routledge & Sons Ltd, 1931), 219; J.V. Beckett, *The Aristocracy in England, 1600-1914 (Oxford University Press: 1986), 17-42,* while the focus here is on the English society, it should be borne in mind that not only did the class system exist in other European countries, but that in a variety of ways the English may have in fact been more enlightened for the times; Michael Kammen, *Empire and Interest: The American Colonies and the Politics of Mercantilism* (Philadelphia: J. B. Lippincott Company, 1970), 124; Don Cook, *The Long Fuse: How England lost the American Colonies, 1760-1785,* (New York: The Atlantic Monthly Press, 1995), 16; Benjamin M. Friedman, *The Moral Consequences of Economic Growth* (New York: Vintage Books, 2005), 222.
233. Thomas William Heyck, *The Peoples of the British Isles: A New History,* Volume II: From 1688 to 1870 (Chicago: Lyceum Books, 2008), 47; Sylvia Nasar, *Grand Pursuit: The Story of Economic Genius* (New York: Simon & Schuster, 2011), xii, note 7; Charles Daniel Smith, *The Early Career of Lord North, the Prime Minister* (Cranbury, NJ: Associated University Presses, 1979), 45-46.
234. *See,* generally, Gordon S. Wood, *The Radicalism of the American Revolution* (New York: Alfred A. Knopf-Random House, 1992), 280-286, Will and Ariel Durant, *The Story of Civilization* (New York: Simon and Schuster, 1967), 10:733.

235. John Richard Alden, *Robert Dinwiddie: Servant of the Crown* (Williamsburg: The Colonial Williamsburg Foundation, 1973), 13-16; Gordon S. Wood, *The Radicalism of the American Revolution* (New York: Alfred A. Knopf-Random House, 1992), 229; Will and Ariel Durant, *The Story of Civilization* (New York: Simon and Schuster, 1967), 10:730-33.
236. Charles Chenevix Trench, *The Royal Malady,* (London: Longmans, Green & Company, Ltd., 1964), 26-27, 275 citing Sir George Baker's Diary; John Brooke, ed., *King George III* (New York: McGraw-Hill Book Co., 1972), 322; Will and Ariel Durant, *The Story of Civilization* (New York: Simon and Schuster, 1967), 10:684-87; *See,* generally, Charles Seymour and Donald Paige Frary, *How the World Votes: The Story of Democratic Development in Elections* (Springfield, Mass.: C.A. Nichols Company, 1918), 64-112; Richard Brookhiser, *Alexander Hamilton, American* (New York: Touchstone-Simon & Schuster, 1999), 13-14, citing F.R. Angier et al., *The Making of the West Indies* (Trinidad: Longman Caribbean, 1960), 107.
237. Charles Daniel Smith, *The Early Career of Lord North, the Prime Minister* (Cranbury, NJ: Associated University Presses, 1979), 85-86; Charles Chenevix Trench, *The Royal Malady,* (London: Longmans, Green & Company, Ltd., 1964), 401-02.
238. George Louis Beer, *British Colonial Policy 1754-1765* (New York: The MacMillan Company, 1907), 231-232; Don Cook, *The Long Fuse: How England lost the American Colonies, 1760-1785,* (New York: The Atlantic Monthly Press, 1995), 58-59; John Richard Alden, *Robert Dinwiddie: Servant of the Crown* (Williamsburg: The Colonial Williamsburg Foundation, 1973), 17.
239. Don Cook, *The Long Fuse: How England lost the American Colonies, 1760-1785,* (New York: The Atlantic Monthly Press, 1995), 15.
240. John Richard Alden, *Robert Dinwiddie: Servant of the Crown* (Williamsburg: The Colonial Williamsburg Foundation, 1973), 13-17.
241. Charles Royster, *The Fabulous History of the Dismal Swamp Company: A Story of George Washington's Times* (New York: Borzoi-Alfred A. Knopf-Random House, 1999), 52-53.
242. Herbert L. Osgood, *The American Colonies in the Eighteenth Century,* (New York: Columbia University Press, 1924), 226-230; Percy Scott Flippin, *The Royal Government in Virginia 1624-1775* (New York: Longmans, Green & Co., 1919), 78.
243. Kenneth P. Bailey, *The Ohio Company of Virginia and the Westward Movement 1748-1792: A Chapter in the History of the Colonial Frontier* (Glendale, CA: The Arthur H. Clark Co., 1939), 36; Charles Royster, *The Fabulous History of the Dismal Swamp Company: A Story of George Washington's Times,* (New York: Alfred A. Knopf, 1999), 69.
244. Percy Scott Flippin, *The Royal Government in Virginia 1624-1775* (New York: Columbia University, 1919), 58.
245. Charles Royster, *The Fabulous History of the Dismal Swamp Company: A Story of George Washington's Times,* (New York: Alfred A. Knopf, 1999), 69, 132.
246. William Blackstone, *Commentaries on the Laws of England,* 4 volumes, (Oxford, 1768), 2:36-37.
247. George Louis Beer, *British Colonial Policy 1754-1765,* (New York: The MacMillan Company, 1907), 190, 231.
248. Percy Scott Flippin, *The Royal Government in Virginia 1624-1775* (New York: Columbia University, 1919), 60-62.
249. Bryan Little, "Norborne Berkeley: Gloucestershire Magnate," *The Virginia Magazine of History and Biography,* V. 63; N. 4 (Oct. 1955), pp. 400-405; Charles Royster, *The Fabulous*

History of the Dismal Swamp Company: A Story of George Washington's Times, (New York: Alfred A. Knopf, 1999), 132-33.

250. Charles Royster, *The Fabulous History of the Dismal Swamp Company: A Story of George Washington's Times*, (New York: Alfred A. Knopf, 1999), 158, 180-81; Robert A. Williams, *The American Indian in Western Legal Thought: The Discourses of Conquest* (New York: Oxford University Press, 1990), 274; Merrill Jensen, *The Founding of a Nation: A history of the American Revolution, 1763-1776* (Indianapolis, IN: Hackett Publishing Company, 1968), 392-93; Archibald Henderson, *The Conquest of the Old Southwest* (New York: The Century Co., 1920), 206-11.

251. Archibald Henderson, *The Conquest of the Old Southwest* (New York: The Century Co., 1920), 206-11, 238-42; Charles Royster, *The Fabulous History of the Dismal Swamp Company: A Story of George Washington's Times*, (New York: Alfred A. Knopf, 1999), 213.

252. John R. Alden, *A History of the American Revolution*, (New York: Da Capo-Perseus, 1969), 122; Robert McNutt McElroy, *Kentucky in the Nation's History* (New York: Moffat, Yard and Company, 1909, 42; Archibald Henderson, *The Conquest of the Old Southwest* (New York: The Century Co., 1920), 206-08; "The Remonstrance of the General Assembly of Virginia, to the Delegates of the United American States in Congress Assembled," William Waller Hening, *The Statutes at Large: Being a Collection of all the Laws of Virginia, from the First Session of the Legislature in the Year 1619* (Richmond, VA: N.P., 1819-23), 10:557-58.

253. Percy Scott Flippin, *The Royal Government in Virginia 1624-1775* (New York: Columbia University, 1919), 223-29.

254. History does not record whether Adair in turn had to kick back to Albemarle a portion of his own take, or whether there was kinship or other special relationship between the two men, exempting Adair from having to do so.

255. Charles Royster, *The Fabulous History of the Dismal Swamp Company: A Story of George Washington's Times*, (New York: Alfred A. Knopf, 1999), 32, 182.

256. A.J. Poitras, *Capitalist Rising:The Short History of a Long Insurgency* (New York: Vantage Press, 2007), 162-63; Francis Cherunilam, *International Economics*, 4th ed., (New Delhi: Tata McGraw-Hill, 2006), 120-21; John Findling and Frank Thackeray, *What Happened? An Encyclopedia of Events that Changed America Forever*, 17th Century (Santa Barbara, CA: ABC-CLIO, LLC, 2011), 7.

257. Joseph Albert Ernst, *Money and Politics in America, 1755-1775: A Study in the Currency Act of 1764 and the Political Economy of Revolution* (Chapel Hill: University of North Carolina Press, 1973), 89;Michael G. Kammen, *Empire and Interest: The American Colonies and the Politics of Mercantilism* (Philadelphia: Lippincott, 1970), 48.

258. Between 1651 and 1774 Parliament passed a series of laws affecting the American colonies, including the Molasses Act of 1733, Sugar Act of 1764, Currency Act of 1764, Stamp Act of 1765, Quartering Act of 1765, Declaratory Act of 1766, Townshend Revenue Act of 1767, Tea Act of 1773, Boston Port Act of 1774, Massachusetts Government Act of 1774, Quartering Act of 1774, Administration of Justice Act of 1774, and Quebec Act of 1774. These last five became known as the Intolerable Acts, also Repressive Acts and/or Coercive Acts.

259. Richard S. Grossman, *Wrong: Nine Economic Policy Disasters and What We Can Learn from Them* (New York: Oxford University Press, 2013), 26.

260. Thomas Arkle Clark, ed., *Speech of Edmund Burke, Esq. on Moving His Resolutions for Conciliation with the Colonies, March 22, 1775* (New York: Charles Scribner's Sons, 1908), 16.
261. Will and Ariel Durant, *The Story of Civilization* (New York: Simon and Schuster, 1967), 10:607.
262. E. A. Smith, *George IV* (New Haven: Yale University Press, 1999), 48-49; Charles Chenevix Trench, *The Royal Malady* (London: Longmans, Green & Company, Ltd., 1964), 11, 63-64.
263. Andrew Burstein and Nancy Isenberg, *Madison and Jefferson* (New York: Random House, 2010), 193-94.
264. Francis Jennings, *The Creation of America: Through Revolution to Empire* (Cambridge: Cambridge University Press, 2000), 50.
265. Douglas Southall Freeman, *George Washington: A Biography*, vol. 1, *Young Washington* (New York: Charles Scribner's Sons, 1949), 111.
266. John Carswell, *The South Sea Bubble* (1960; reprint, Gloucester: Alan Sutton, revised edition, 1993); John G. Sperling, *South Sea Company: An Historical Essay and Bibliographical Finding List* (Boston: Baker Library, Harvard Graduate School of Business Administration, 1962); Charles P. Kindleberger and Robert Z. Aliber, *Manias, Panics, and Crashes: A History of Financial Crises*, 5th ed.(Hoboken, NJ: John Wiley & Sons, 1996), 54, 58-59; Christopher Reed, "The Damn'd South Sea", *Harvard Magazine*, vol. 101, no. 5 (May/June 1999).
267. Michael Kammen, *Empire and Interest: The American Colonies and the Politics of Mercantilism* (Philadelphia: J. B. Lippincott Company, 1970), 55.
268. Julian Hoppit, "The Myths of the South Sea Bubble," *Transactions of the Royal Historical Society*, Sixth Series, Vol. 12 (2002), 141-65; President and Fellows of Harvard College, "South Sea Bubble Short History," *Sunk in Lucre's Sordid Charms: South Sea Bubble Resources in the Kress Collection at Baker Library*, 2010, Harvard Business School, http://www.library.hbs.edu/hc/ssb/history.html; Michael Kammen, *Empire and Interest: The American Colonies and the Politics of Mercantilism* (Philadelphia: J. B. Lippincott Company, 1970), 55.
269. Charles P. Kindleberger and Robert Z. Aliber, *Manias, Panics, and Crashes: A History of Financial Crises*, 5th ed.(Hoboken, NJ: John Wiley & Sons, 1996), 59; Edward Chancellor, "Plenty of Blame To Go Around," review of *I.O.U.: Why Everyone Owes Everyone and No One Can Pay* by John Lanchester, *The Wall Street Journal*, January 26, 2010, A-15.
270. Joseph Albert Ernst, *Money and Politics in America, 1755-1775: A Study in the Currency Act of 1764 and the Political Economy of Revolution* (Chapel Hill: University of North Carolina Press, 1973), 90-91; T. H. Breen, *Tobacco Culture: The Mentality of the Great Tidewater Planters on the Eve of Revolution* (Princeton: Princeton University Press, 1985), 126-27.
271. Nick Robins, *The Corporation that Changed the World: How the East India Company Shaped the Modern Multinational* (London: Pluto Press, 2006), 87-98.
272. Peter D. G. Thomas, *George III: King and Politicians, 1760-1770* (Manchester: Manchester University Press, 2002), 35-37, 159-65.
273. Will and Ariel Durant, *The Story of Civilization* (New York: Simon and Schuster, 1967), 10:715.
274. Richard B. Sheridan, "The British Credit Crisis of 1772 and the American Colonies," *The Journal of Economic History*, vol. 20, no. 2 (June 1960), 167, 172; Charles Royster, *The Fabulous History of the Dismal Swamp Company: A Story of George Washington's Times* (New York: Borzoi-Alfred A. Knopf-Random House, 1999), 185.

275. Will and Ariel Durant, *The Story of Civilization* (New York: Simon and Schuster, 1967), 10:714-17; Peter D. G. Thomas, *George III: King and Politicians, 1760-1770* (Manchester: Manchester University Press, 2002), 35-37, 159-65; Charles Royster, *The Fabulous History of the Dismal Swamp Company: A Story of George Washington's Times*, (New York: Alfred A. Knopf, 1999), 200.
276. Michael Kammen, *Empire and Interest: The American Colonies and the Politics of Mercantilism* (Philadelphia: J. B. Lippincott Company, 1970), 139.
277. Will and Ariel Durant, *The Story of Civilization* (New York: Simon and Schuster, 1967), 10:732; C. M. Andrews, "Anglo-French Commercial Rivalry, 1700-1750," *American Historical Review*, vol. xx, no. 3, 554; Michael Kammen, *Empire and Interest: The American Colonies and the Politics of Mercantilism* (Philadelphia: J. B. Lippincott Company, 1970), 102; Percy Scott Flippin, *The Royal Government of Virginia, 1624-1775* (New York: Columbia University, 1919), 49-50.
278. Percy Scott Flippin, *The Royal Government in Virginia 1624-1775* (New York: Columbia University, 1919), 50-51, citing *Journal of the House of Burgesses*, 1770-1772, 283; Will and Ariel Durant, *The Story of Civilization* (New York: Simon and Schuster, 1967), 10:708, citing William E. Lecky, *History of England in the Eighteenth Century* (London: Longmans, Green and Co., 18178-90), 3:300.
279. Stephen R. Bowen, *Merchant Kings: When Companies Ruled the World, 1600-1900* (New York: St. Martin's Press, 2009), 5.
280. Percy Scott Flippin, *The Royal Government in Virginia 1624-1775* (New York: Columbia University, 1919), 36-43; Oliver Morton Dickerson, *American Colonial Government, 1696-1765: A Study of the British Board of Trade in Its Relations to the American Colonies, Political, Industrial, Administrative* (Cleveland, Ohio: The Arthur H. Clark Company, 1912), 24-26.
281. Percy Scott Flippin, *The Royal Government in Virginia 1624-1775* (New York: Columbia University, 1919), *44-46, 51*; *see also*, generally, Oliver Morton Dickerson, *American Colonial Government, 1696-1765: A Study of the British Board of Trade in Its Relations to the American Colonies, Political, Industrial, Administrative* (Cleveland, Ohio: The Arthur H. Clark Company, 1912).
282. George Louis Beer, *British Colonial Policy: 1754-1765* (New York: MacMillan Company, 1907), 203; Percy Scott Flippin, *The Royal Government in Virginia 1624-1775* (New York: Columbia University, 1919), 52-55.
283. Percy Scott Flippin, *The Royal Government in Virginia 1624-1775* (New York: Columbia University, 1919), 46, 52-54.
284. Percy Scott Flippin, *The Royal Government in Virginia 1624-1775* (New York: Columbia University, 1919), 48-49, 52-54.
285. Joseph Albert Ernst, *Money and Politics in America, 1755-1775: A Study in the Currency Act of 1764 and the Political Economy of Revolution* (Chapel Hill: University of North Carolina Press, 1973), Lawrence A. Harper, *The English Navigation Laws: A Seventeenth-Century Experiment in Social Engineering* (New York: Octagon Books, 1964), 244-46.
286. Emory R. Johnson, et al., *History of Domestic and Foreign Commerce of the United States* (New York: B. Franklin, 1964), 45; Richard B. Morris, *The Era of the American Revolution* (New York: Harper & Row, 1965), 7; John C. Fitzpatrick, ed., *The Writings of George Washington from the Original Manuscript Sources* (Washington: U.S. Government Printing Office, 1931-40), 2:348, 357, 363, 383, 405, 419; Lawrence A. Harper, *The English Navigation Laws: A*

Seventeenth-Century Experiment in Social Engineering (New York: Octagon Books, 1964), 244-46; Arthur Pierce Middleton, *Tobacco Coast: A Maritime History of Chesapeake Bay in the Colonial Era* (Newport News, VA: Mariners' Museum, 1953), 105.

287. Emory R. Johnson, et al., *History of Domestic and Foreign Commerce of the United States* (New York: B. Franklin, 1964), 35, 43; Lawrence A. Harper, *The English Navigation Laws: A Seventeenth-Century Experiment in Social Engineering* (New York: Octagon Books, 1964), 57, 245-46.

288. Edwin J. Perkins, *The Economy of Colonial America* (New York: Columbia University Press, 1988), 24.

289. Emory R. Johnson, et al., *History of Domestic and Foreign Commerce of the United States* (New York: B. Franklin, 1964), 45.

290. Emory R. Johnson, et al., *History of Domestic and Foreign Commerce of the United States* (New York: B. Franklin, 1964), 45; Michael Kammen, *Empire and Interest: The American Colonies and the Politics of Mercantilism* (Philadelphia: J. B. Lippincott Company, 1970), 80; Charles Royster, *The Fabulous History of the Dismal Swamp Company: A Story of George Washington's Times*, (New York: Alfred A. Knopf, 1999), 200.

291. Percy Scott Flippin, *The Royal Government in Virginia 1624-1775* (New York: Columbia University, 1919), 278.

292. Emory R. Johnson, et al., *History of Domestic and Foreign Commerce of the United States* (New York: B. Franklin, 1964), 36, 40-46.

293. T. H. Breen, "Subjecthood and Citizenship: The Context of James Otis's Radical Critique of John Locke," *The New England Quarterly*, vol. 71, no. 3 (Sep., 1998), 378-403.

294. T.H. Breen, *Tobacco Culture: The Mentality of the Great Tidewater Planters on the Eve of Revolution* (Princeton: Princeton University Press, 1985), xix-xx, 23-24, 140.

295. H.V. Bowen, *The Business of Empire: The East India Company and Imperial Britain, 1756-1833* (Cambridge: Cambridge University Press, 2006), 1.

296. Percy Scott Flippin, *The Royal Government in Virginia 1624-1775* (New York: Columbia University, 1919), 56.

297. Charles Chenevix Trench, *The Royal Malady,* (London: Longmans, Green & Company, Ltd., 1964), 75, citing "Parliamentary History," xvi 91-103.

298. Don Cook, *The Long Fuse: How England Lost the American Colonies, 1760-1785* (New York: Atlantic Monthly Press, 1995), 6.

299. George Louis Beer, *British Colonial Policy 1754-1765,* (New York: The MacMillan Company, 1907), 296, 306.

300. David S. Heidler and Jeanne T. Heidler, *Daily Life in the Early American Republic, 1790-1820,* Daily Life Through History series (Westport, CT: Greenwood Press, 2004), 51.

301. Percy Scott Flippin, *The Royal Government in Virginia 1624-1775* (New York: Columbia University, 1919), 58-59; Michael Kammen, *Empire and Interest: The American Colonies and the Politics of Mercantilism* (Philadelphia: J. B. Lippincott Company, 1970), 114.

302. James Thomas Flexner, *George Washington: The Forge of Experience (1732-1775)* (Boston: Little, Brown and Company, 1965), 309-10; George Louis Beer, *British Colonial Policy 1754-1765,* (New York: The MacMillan Company, 1907), 182-88; John Bigelow, ed., *The Complete Works of Benjamin Franklin, vol. III* (New York and London: G. P. Putnam's Sons, 1887), 418.

303. One writer calculated that the colonists owed the English trading houses and merchants £4,930,656, including interest: Richard Sheridan, "The British Credit Crisis of 1772 and the American Colonies," *The Journal of Economic History*, vol. 20, no. 2 (June 1960), 161-86.
304. Michael Kammen, *Empire and Interest: The American Colonies and the Politics of Mercantilism* (Philadelphia: J. B. Lippincott Company, 1970), 5, 7, 48.
305. Alan Ebenstein, *Hayek's Journey: The Mind of Friedrich Hayek* (New York: Palgrave Macmillan, 2003), 99-100.
306. Percy Scott Flippin, *The Royal Government in Virginia 1624-1775* (New York: Columbia University, 1919), 270.
307. George Louis Beer, *British Colonial Policy 1754-1765,* (New York: The MacMillan Company, 1907), 229-30; Don Cook, *The Long Fuse: How England lost the American Colonies, 1760-1785,* (New York: The Atlantic Monthly Press, 1995), 52.
308. Charles R. Ritcheson, *Aftermath of Revolution: British Policy toward the United States 1783-1795,* (Dallas: Southern Methodist University Press: 1969), ix.
309. George Louis Beer, *British Colonial Policy 1754-1765,* (New York: The MacMillan Company, 1907), 14; Herbert L. Osgood, *The American Colonies in the Eighteenth Century,* (New York: Columbia University Press, 1924), 233; Don Cook, *The Long Fuse: How England lost the American Colonies, 1760-1785,* (New York: The Atlantic Monthly Press, 1995), 3; Leslie V. Brock, *The Currency of the American Colonies, 1700-1764: A Study in Colonial Finance and Imperial Relations* (New York: Arno Press, 1975), 474; E. James Ferguson, "Currency Finance: An Interpretation of Colonial Money Practices," *The William and Mary Quarterly,* vol. 10, no. 2 (April, 1953), 174.
310. Peter D. G. Thomas, *George III: King and Politicians, 1760-1770* (Manchester: Manchester University Press, 2002), 35; Don Cook, *The Long Fuse: How England lost the American Colonies, 1760-1785,* (New York: The Atlantic Monthly Press, 1995), 33-34, 45, 67; Nicholas Phillipson, *Adam Smith: An Enlightened Life,* (New Haven: Yale University Press, 2010), 213.
311. "From George Washington to Robert Dinwiddie, 22 April 1756," W. W. Abbot, et al., eds., *The Papers of George Washington* (Charlottesville: University of Virginia Press, 1987–), Colonial Series, 3:33-35; Don Cook, *The Long Fuse: How England lost the American Colonies, 1760-1785,* (New York: The Atlantic Monthly Press, 1995), 36-38; George Louis Beer, *British Colonial Policy 1754-1765,* (New York: The MacMillan Company, 1907), 11-15, 263.
312. George Louis Beer, *British Colonial Policy 1754-1765,* (New York: The MacMillan Company, 1907), 10, 213.
313. Don Cook, *The Long Fuse: How England lost the American Colonies, 1760-1785,* (New York: The Atlantic Monthly Press, 1995), 59; George Louis Beer, *British Colonial Policy 1754-1765,* (New York: The MacMillan Company, 1907), 8.
314. George Louis Beer, *British Colonial Policy 1754-1765,* (New York: The MacMillan Company, 1907), 287.
315. That this approach was not restricted to Britain in its relationship with its colonies, but that it was the prevailing policy for all colonizing powers of the time, *see:* Paul S. Reinsch, *Colonial Government,* (New York: The Macmillan Company, 1916), 60-61. Percy Scott Flippin, *The Royal Government in Virginia 1624-1775* (New York: Columbia University, 1919), 37-42.
316. Don Cook, *The Long Fuse: How England lost the American Colonies, 1760-1785,* (New York: The Atlantic Monthly Press, 1995), 37-38; Dorothy Deneen Volo and James M. Volo,

Daily Life during the American Revolution, Daily Life through History Series (Westport, CT: Greenwood Press, 2003), 18-19.

317. Forrest McDonald, *The Presidency of George Washington* (Lawrence, KS: University Press of Kansas: 1974), 6.

318. Richard Beeman, *Plain, Honest Men: The Making of the American Constitution* (New York: Random House, 2009), 22.

319. The other seven institutions of higher learning were Harvard, Yale, St. John's College, College of New Jersey (subsequently Princeton), King's College (subsequently Columbia), College of Philadelphia (subsequently University of Pennsylvania), and Queen's College (subsequently Rutgers).

320. In 1908, The Harvard Graduate School of Business Administration, the world's first MBA program, was established: "Our History," *Harvard Business School*, http://www.hbs.edu/about/history.html; Philip Delves Broughton, *Ahead of the Curve: Two Years at Harvard Business School* (New York: Penguin Group, 2008), 46; Richard B. Morris, *Seven Who Shaped Our Destiny: The Founding Fathers as Revolutionaries* (New York: Harper & Row, 1973); Gordon S. Wood, *Empire of Liberty: A History of the Early Republic, 1789-1815* (New York: Oxford University Press, 2009), 23; "Thomas Jefferson to Thomas Mann Randolph, Jr., May 30, 1790," Julian P. Boyd et al., eds., *The Papers of Thomas Jefferson* (Princeton: Princeton University Press, 1950-), 16:449.

321. *Dictionary of the United States Secretaries of the Treasury, 1789-1995* (Westport, CT: Greenwood Press, 1996), 14-16.

322. Alan Ebenstein, *Hayek's Journey: The Mind of Friedrich Hayek* (New York: Palgrave Macmillan, 2003), 50.

323. Nicholas Phillipson, *Adam Smith: An Enlightened Life* (New Haven: Yale University Press, 2010), 192-195.

324. "From George Washington to Samuel Chamberline, 3 April 1788," W. W. Abbot, et al., eds., *The Papers of George Washington* (Charlottesville: University of Virginia Press, 1987-), Confederation Series, 6:190-91.

325. James Gilreath and Douglas L. Wilson, eds., *Thomas Jefferson's Library: A Catalog with the Entries in His Own Order* (1989; reprint, Clark, NJ: The Lawbook Exchange, Ltd., 2008), 35, 52-57; Edwin Wolf 2nd and Kevin J. Hayes, *The Library of Benjamin Franklin*, Memoirs of the American Philosophical Society Held at Philadelphia for Promoting Useful Knowledge Vol. 257 (Philadelphia: American Philosophical Society and Library Company of Philadelphia, 2006), 506-507, 586, 733; Andrew Burstein and Nancy Isenberg, *Madison and Jefferson* (New York: Random House, 2010), 51, 169; E. James Ferguson, et al., eds., *The Papers of Robert Morris, 1781-1784* (Pittsburgh: University of Pittsburgh Press, 1973-1999), 6:43-44.

326. *See*, generally, W. M. Spellman, *John Locke*, British History in Perspective Series (New York: St. Martin's Press, 1997).

327. Alexander Somerville, *Free Trade and the League: A Biographic History* (Manchester: James Ainsworth, 1853), 1:79-97.

328. *See*, generally, C. Mossner, *The Life of David Hume*, 2nd edition (Oxford: Oxford University Press, 1980).

329. W. Baring Pemberton, *Lord North* (London: Longmans, Green & Co. Ltd., 1938), 195.

330. "Letter from Adam Smith, LL.D., to William Strahan, Esq., Nov. 9, 1776," in T. H. Green and T. H. Grose, eds., *Essays Moral, Political and Literary by David Hume* (London: Longmans, Green, and Co., 1898), 9-14.
331. Adam Smith, *An Inquiry into the Nature and Causes of the Wealth of Nations*, ed. R. H. Campbell & A. S. Skinner (Oxford, 1976); Nicholas Phillipson, *Adam Smith: An Enlightened Life* (New Haven, CT: Yale University Press, 2010), 208-12, 214, 217-18, 222-24, 229, 231, 235, 254, 260-61.
332. *Catalogue of the Library of the Late Bishop John Fletcher Hurst: Part I, Washington—Franklin* (New York: The Anderson Auction Co., 1904), 4; Jeremy Dibbell, "George Washington," Legacy Libraries, *LibraryThing*, http://www.librarything.com/work/13183/details/47673119; Clarence L. Ver Steeg, *Robert Morris, Revolutionary Financier* (New York: Octagon Books, 1972), 133; Charles Rappleye, *Robert Morris: Financier of the American Revolution* (New York: Simon & Schuster, 2010), 284-85, 292-93; [13 May 1787 – 18 September 1787], Donald Jackson and Dorothy Twohig, eds., *The Diaries of George Washington* (Charlottesville: University of Virginia Press, 1979), 5:155-56, 158-60, 162, 168-86.
333. John C. Fitzpatrick, *The Diaries of George Washington 1748-1799* (Boston: Houghton Mifflin Company, 1925), 1:86-92.
334. George Washington "To the President of Congress, May 8, 1781," in John C. Fitzpatrick, ed., *The Writings of George Washington from the Original Manuscript Sources* (Washington, DC: U.S. Government Printing Office, 1931-44), 22:60-61.
335. Clarence L. Ver Steeg, *Robert Morris, Revolutionary Financier* (New York: Octagon Books, 1972), 133.
336. Robert Morris "To John Jay, 13 July 1781," Ferguson, et al., *Papers of Robert Morris*, 1:287-91.
337. Charles Rappleye, *Robert Morris: Financier of the American Revolution* (New York: Simon & Schuster, 2010), 374.
338. Robert Morris "To the President of Congress (John Hanson), February 11th 1782," E. James Ferguson, et al., eds., *The Papers of Robert Morris, 1781-1784* (Pittsburgh: University of Pittsburgh Press, 1973-1999), 4:205-14.
339. Now enshrined as Independence Hall.
340. Max Farrand, *The Records of the Federal Convention of 1787*, 3 volumes (New Haven: Yale University Press, 1911), 2:641-43.
341. Gordon S. Wood, *The Radicalism of the American Revolution* (New York: Alfred A. Knopf-Random House, 1992), 209.
342. George F. Will, *One Man's America* (New York: Three River Press, 2008), 336.
343. Richard Beeman, *Plain, Honest Men: The Making of the American Constitution* (New York: Random House, 2009), 362.
344. Richard B. Morris, *The Forging of the Union, 1781-1789* (New York: Harper & Row, 1987) 270.
345. Donald Jackson and Dorothy Twohig, eds., *The Diaries of George Washington* (Charlottesville: University Press of Virginia, 1976-79), 5:155-56, 158-60, 162, 165, 168-86.
346. Emmette S. Redford & Charles B. Hagan, *American Government and the Economy*, (New York: MacMillan, 1965), 106, 109.
347. George Washington to Henry Knox, August 19, 1787, in Fitzpatrick, *Writings of George Washington*, 29:261.

348. Stephen E. Lucas, "Genre Criticism and Historical Context: The Case of George Washington's First Inaugural Address," *Southern Speech Communication Journal* 51 (1986), 354-70; Gordon S. Wood, *The Radicalism of the American Revolution* (New York: Alfred A. Knopf-Random House, 1992), 209, citing Monroe to Jefferson, 12 July 1788, Julian P. Boyd, et al., eds., *The Papers of Thomas Jefferson* (Princeton: Princeton University Press, 1950–), 13:352. North Carolina (November 21, 1789) and Rhode Island (May 29, 1790) were the last to ratify the Constitution.

349. Gordon S. Wood, *Empire of Liberty: A History of the Early Republic, 1789-1815* (New York: Oxford University Press, 2009), 36-37 citing Benjamin Rush to Elias Boudinot, "Observations on the Federal Procession in Philadelphia, 9 July 1788," L. H. Butterfield, ed., *Letters of Benjamin Rush* (Princeton: Princeton University Press, 1951), 1:470-75, and "Address to the President", December 1796, *Annals of Congress*, 4th Congress, 2nd session, 1612-42.

350. James Thomas Flexner, *George Washington and the New Nation (1783-1793) (*Boston: Little, Brown and Company, 1970), 182-83, 190, 195-96.

351. "To George Washington from the Board of Treasury [June 9, 10, 11, 15; July 23; August 14, 21, 1789]," W. W. Abbot, et al., eds., *The Papers of George Washington* (Charlottesville: University of Virginia Press, 1987–), Presidential Series 2:456, 457-60, 465-72, 3:1-31, 265-89, 426-62, 503-07

352. W. W. Abbot, et al., eds., *The Papers of George Washington* (Charlottesville: University of Virginia Press, 1987-), Presidential Series 3:21-27.

353. "Plan of American Finance, October 1789," John C. Fitzpatrick, ed., *The Writings of George Washington from the Original Manuscript Sources, 1745-1799* (Washington: United States Government Printing Office, 1931-1940), 30:454-55.

354. Richard B. Morris, *The Forging of the Union 1781-1789* (New York: Harper & Row, 1987), 288; George Washington "To Chevalier de Chastellux October 12, 1783," John C. Fitzpatrick, ed., The *Writings of George Washington from the Original Manuscript Sources, 1745-1799* (Washington: United States Government Printing Office, 1931-1940), 27:189; Washington "To Governor George Clinton, December 28, 1783," Fitzpatrick, *Writings of George Washington*, 27:287-88.

355. George Washington "To Nathaniel Gorham, July 21, 1788," in John C. Fitzpatrick, ed., The *Writings of George Washington from the Original Manuscript Sources, 1745-1799* (Washington: United States Government Printing Office, 1931-1940), 30:23-24.

356. "From George Washington to Thomas Jefferson, 31 August 1788," W. W. Abbot, et al., eds., *The Papers of George Washington* (Charlottesville: University of Virginia Press, 1987–), Confederation Series 6:491-95; "From George Washington to Marquis de Lafayette, 29 January 1789," in Abbot, et al., *Papers of George Washington*, Presidential Series, 1:262-64; Charles Cerami, *Young Patriots: The Remarkable Story of Two Men, Their Impossible Plan, and the Revolution that Created the* Constitution (Naperville, IL: Sourcebooks, Inc., 2005), 43.

357. "From George Washington to David Stuart, 30 November 1785," W. W. Abbot, et al., eds., *The Papers of George Washington* (Charlottesville: University of Virginia Press, 1987-), Confederation Series, 3:423-24.

358. "From George Washington to John Armstrong, 25 April 1788," W. W. Abbot, et al., eds., *The Papers of George Washington* (Charlottesville: University of Virginia Press, 1987-), Confederation Series, 6:224-27.

359. "From George Washington to George William Fairfax, 30 June 1785," W. W. Abbot, et al., eds., *The Papers of George Washington* (Charlottesville: University of Virginia Press, 1987-), Confederation Series, 3:87-92; "From George Washington to Marquis de Lafayette, August 15, 1786," Abbot, et al., *Papers of George Washington*, Confederation Series 4:216.
360. "From George Washington to David Stuart, 30 November 1785," W. W. Abbot, et al., eds., *The Papers of George Washington* (Charlottesville: University of Virginia Press, 1987–), Confederation Series, 3:423-24; George Washington "To Theodorick Bland," April 4, 1783" John C. Fitzpatrick, ed., The *Writings of George Washington from the Original Manuscript Sources, 1745-1799* (Washington: United States Government Printing Office, 1931-1940), 26:293-96.
361. Hernando De Soto, *The Mystery of Capital: Why Capitalism Triumphed in the West and Fails Everywhere Else* (New York: Basic Books: 2000), 16.
362. Gordon S. Wood, *Empire of Liberty: A History of the Early Republic, 1789-1815* (New York: Oxford University Press, 2009), 7; "Circular to the States, June 8, 1783," John C. Fitzpatrick, ed., The *Writings of George Washington from the Original Manuscript Sources, 1745-1799* (Washington: United States Government Printing Office, 1931-1940), 26:483-96; "From George Washington to Lafayette, 29 January 1789," W. W. Abbot, et al., eds., *The Papers of George Washington* (Charlottesville: University of Virginia Press, 1987–), Presidential Series, 1:262-64; "From George Washington to Daniel Hinsdale, 8 April 1789," Abbot, et al., *Papers of George Washington*, Presidential Series, 2:41-42; "From George Washington to William Irvine, 31 October 1788," Abbot, et al., *Papers of George Washington*, Presidential Series, 1:86.
363. First Annual Address, "From George Washington to the United States Senate and House of Representatives," January 8, 1790," W. W. Abbot, et al., eds., *The Papers of George Washington* (Charlottesville: University of Virginia Press, 1987–), Presidential Series 4:543-49.
364. E. Harrison Clark, *All Cloudless Glory: The Life of George Washington,* vol. 2, *Making a Nation* (Washington, DC: Regnery Publishing, 1996), 127-28.
365. "[Proposed Address to Congress, April ?, 1789]," John C. Fitzpatrick, ed., The *Writings of George Washington from the Original Manuscript Sources, 1745-1799* (Washington: United States Government Printing Office, 1931-1940), 30:296-308; Nathaniel E. Stein, "The Discarded Inaugural Address of George Washington," *Manuscripts*, X (1958) 2-17; Stephen E. Lucas, "Genre Criticism and Historical Context: The Case of George Washington's First Inaugural Address," *The Southern Speech Communication Journal* 51, no. 4 (1986); "Undelivered First Inaugural Address: Fragments, 30 April 1789," W. W. Abbot, et al., eds., *The Papers of George Washington* (Charlottesville: University of Virginia Press, 1987–), Presidential Series, 2:158-73.
366. "Farewell Address, September 19, 1796," John C. Fitzpatrick, ed., *The Writings of George Washington from the Original Manuscript Sources, 1745-1799* (Washington: United States Government Printing Office, 1931-1940), 35:214-38.
367. First Annual Address, "To the United States Senate and House of Representatives, 8 January 1790," W. W. Abbot, et al., eds., *The Papers of George Washington* (Charlottesville: University of Virginia Press, 1987–), Presidential Series 4:543-49; Clark, *All Cloudless Glory*, 2:127-28.
368. E. Harrison Clark, *All Cloudless Glory: The Life of George Washington,* vol. 2, *Making a Nation* (Washington, DC: Regnery Publishing, 1996), 127-28.

369. Richard Beeman, *Plain, Honest Men: The Making of the American Constitution* (New York: Random House, 2009), 6; "Memorandum on a Discussion of the President's Retirement, 5 May 1792," Robert A. Rutland, et al., eds., *The Papers of James Madison* (Charlottesville: University Press of Virginia, 1977-), 14:299-304.
370. Richard Brookhiser, *James Madison* (New York: Basic Books, 2011), 31.
371. "Editorial Note [New York, 30 April 1789]," W. W. Abbot, et al., eds., *The Papers of George Washington* (Charlottesville: University of Virginia Press, 1987-), Presidential Series 2:152-57.
372. Rosemarie Zagarri, ed., *David Humphreys' Life of General Washington: with George Washington's Remarks* (Athens, GA: University of Georgia Press, 2006), 73-76, 78-79, 86-87.
373. Joseph J. Ellis, *American Sphinx: The Character of Thomas Jefferson* (New York: Vintage Books, 1998), 200-201; Andrew Burstein and Nancy Isenberg, *Madison and Jefferson* (New York: Random House, 2010), xvi-xx, 19-20, 56, 167-68, 207, 224-25; Richard Brookhiser, *James Madison* (New York: Basic Books, 2011), 10-12, 18, 29; Ron Chernow, *Alexander Hamilton* (New York: The Penguin Press, 2004), 311, 320, 322; Charles A. Cerami, *Dinner at Mr. Jefferson's: Three Men, Five Great Wines, and the Evening that Changed America* (Hoboken, NJ: John Wiley & Sons, 2008), 81-83, 91-92.
374. *Federalist No. 51*: "The Structure of the Government Must Furnish the Proper Checks and Balances between the Different Departments," *New York Packet,* February 8, 1788.
375. Virginia Convention Speech, June 6, 1788 in, Ralph Ketcham, ed., *Selected Writings of James Madison,* The American Heritage Series (Indianapolis: Hackett Publishing Company, 2006), 142-53.
376. Jack N. Rakove, *James Madison and the Creation of the American Republic,* 3rd ed., Library of Am. Biography Series (New York: Pearson Longman, 2007), 84.
377. Kenneth R. Bowling, *The Creation of Washington, D.C.: The Idea and Location of the American Capital* (Fairfax, VA: George Mason University Press, 1991), 143; Andrew Burstein and Nancy Isenberg, *Madison and Jefferson* (New York: Random House, 2010), 224-25, 228; Richard Brookhiser, *James Madison* (New York: Basic Books, 2011), 98.
378. Kenneth R. Bowling, *The Creation of Washington, D.C.: The Idea and Location of the American Capital* (Fairfax, VA: George Mason University Press, 1991), 143; Andrew Burstein and Nancy Isenberg, *Madison and Jefferson* (New York: Random House, 2010), 167, 171, 179-80, 224-25, 228; Richard Brookhiser, *James Madison* (New York: Basic Books, 2011), 98; "From Thomas Jefferson to John Adams, August 30, 1787," Julian P. Boyd, et al., eds., *The Papers of Thomas Jefferson* (Princeton: Princeton University Press, 1950-), 12:67-69; "From Thomas Jefferson to James Madison, December 20, 1787," Boyd, et al., *Papers of Thomas Jefferson,* 12:438-443; "From Thomas Jefferson to Benjamin Rush, 23 September 1800," Boyd, et al., *Papers of Thomas Jefferson,* 32:166-69; Gordon S. Wood, *Empire of Liberty: A History of the Early Republic, 1789-1815* (New York: Oxford University Press, 2009), 11; "From Thomas Jefferson to Edward Carrington, 16 January 1787," in Boyd, et al., *Papers of Thomas Jefferson,* 11:48-50.
379. "Thomas Jefferson to John Taylor, 28 May 1816," Julian P. Boyd, et al., eds., *The Papers of Thomas Jefferson* (Princeton: Princeton University Press, 1950–), Retirement Series, 10:86-90; R. B. Bernstein, *Thomas Jefferson* (New York: Oxford University Press, 2003), xii, 12-14; Henry Childs Merwin, *Thomas Jefferson,* Riverside Biographical Series (Boston: Houghton, Mifflin and Company, 1901), 91-92; Joseph J. Ellis, *American Sphinx: The Character of Thomas Jefferson* (New York: Vintage Books, 1998), 200-201; 135-36, 162-63, 185-86; Herbert E.

Sloan, *Principle and Interest: Thomas Jefferson and the Problem of Debt* (New York: Oxford University Press, 1995), 3-4, 26.

380. Thomas Jefferson, *Notes on the State of Virginia*, 8th ed. (Boston: David Carlisle, 1801), 244-45; Clay S. Jenkinson, *Becoming Jefferson's People: Re-Inventing the American Republic in the Twenty-First Century* (Marmarth, ND: Marmarth Press, 2005), 27; "From Thomas Jefferson to Benjamin Rush, 23 September 1800," in Julian P. Boyd, et al., eds., *The Papers of Thomas Jefferson* (Princeton: Princeton University Press, 1950–), 32:166-69.

381. Gaillard Hunt and James Brown Scott, eds., *The Debates in the Federal Convention of 1787 which Framed the Constitution of the United States of America* (New York: Oxford University Press, 1920), 38; Andrew Burstein and Nancy Isenberg, *Madison and Jefferson* (New York: Random House, 2010), xix, 161-62; Gordon S. Wood, *Empire of Liberty: A History of the Early Republic, 1789-1815* (New York: Oxford University Press, 2009), 65.

382. Gordon S. Wood, *Empire of Liberty: A History of the Early Republic, 1789-1815* (New York: Oxford University Press, 2009), 53 and n. 4, citing "Agrippa Letters," in Paul L. Ford, ed. *Essays on the Constitution of the United States* (Brooklyn, 1892), 64-65.

383. Stephen E. Lucas, "Genre Criticism and Historical Context: The Case of George Washington's First Inaugural Address," *Southern Speech Communication Journal* 51, no. 4 (1986), 206; George Washington, First Inaugural Address, April 30, 1789, John H. Rhodehamel, ed., *George Washington: Writings* (Des Moines, IA: The Library of America, 1997), 733.

384. U. S. Constitution, Article II, Section 3; Lawrence H. Chamberlain, "The President, Congress, and Legislation," *Political Science Quarterly*, Vol. 61, No. 1, (March 1946), 42-60; Richard E. Neustadt, "Presidency and Legislation: Planning the President's Program," *The American Political Science Review*, Vol. 49, No. 4 (December 1955), 980-1021; Mark Byrnes, "The Presidency and Domestic Policy," *OAH Magazine of History*, Vol. 11, No. 4, The Presidency, (Summer 1997), 21-27; James P. Pfeiffner, "The President's Legislative Agenda," *Annals of the American Academy of Political and Social Science*, Vol. 499, Congress and the Presidency: Invitation to Struggle (September 1988), 22-35; John R. Johannes, "The President Proposes and Congress Disposes — But Not Always: Legislative Initiative on Capitol Hill," *The Review of Politics*, Vol. 36, No. 3 (July 1974), 356-370; Richard B. Morris, "The Constitution and Launching the Government," *Presidential Studies Quarterly*, Vol. 18, No. 1 (Winter 1988), pp. 41-45..

385. "From James Madison to Jared Sparks, May 30, 1827" letter, Library of Congress, *The James Madison Papers, 1723-1836*, Series 1: General Correspondence.

386. John Clement Fitzpatrick, *George Washington Himself: A Common-Sense Biography Written from His Manuscripts* (Indianapolis: The Bobbs-Merrill Company, 1933), 529.

387. James Thomas Flexner, *George Washington and the New Nation, 1783-1793* (Boston: Little, Brown and Company, 1970), 162.

388. Jared Sparks, 1789-1866, was a Unitarian Minister, editor of the *Writings of Washington*, and later President of Harvard University. *See*, generally, Herbert B. Adams, *The Life and Writings of Jared Sparks*, 2 vols. (Boston: Houghton, Mifflin and Co., 1893).

389. "From James Madison to Jared Sparks, May 30, 1827" letter, Library of Congress, *The James Madison Papers, 1723-1836*, Series 1: General Correspondence; Stuart Leibiger, *Founding Friendship*, (Charlottesville: University Press of Virginia, 1999), 104.

390. "[Proposed Address to Congress, April ?, 1789]," John C. Fitzpatrick, ed., The *Writings of George Washington from the Original Manuscript Sources, 1745-1799* (Washington: United States Government Printing Office, 1931-1940), 30:296-308. In 1987, the University Press of

Virginia released an updated version of *The Papers of George Washington*, in which the text of the proposed inaugural address is included in the *Presidential Series* of the multi-volume work. The prodigious effort of the editors of both editions to collect, analyze, and correctly order the existing fragments is commendable, and has been of extraordinary utility to Washington scholars everywhere.

391. "[Proposed Address to Congress, April ?, 1789]," John C. Fitzpatrick, ed., The *Writings of George Washington from the Original Manuscript Sources, 1745-1799* (Washington: United States Government Printing Office, 1931-1940), 30:296; "From George Washington to the United States Senate and House of Representatives," January 8, 1790," "8 December 1790," "25 October 1791," "3 December 1793," W. W. Abbot, et al., eds., *The Papers of George Washington* (Charlottesville: University of Virginia Press, 1987–), Presidential Series 4:543-49, 7:45-49. 9:110-17, 14:462-69; "Address to the United States Senate and House of Representatives, 6 November 1792," Abbot, et al., *Papers of George Washington*, Presidential Series, 11:342-51; "Sixth Annual Address to Congress, November 19, 1794," "Seventh Annual Address, December 8, 1795," "Eighth Annual Address to Congress, December 7, 1796," Fitzpatrick, *Writings of George Washington*, 34:28-37, 386-393, 35:310-320; E. Harrison Clark, *All Cloudless Glory: The Life of George Washington*, vol. 2, *Making a Nation* (Washington, DC: Regnery Publishing, 1996), 127.

392. E. Harrison Clark, *All Cloudless Glory: The Life of George Washington*, vol. 2, *Making a Nation* (Washington, DC: Regnery Publishing, 1996), 127-28.

393. Prof. Gerhard Rempel, Western New England College, "Mercantilism," http://www1.udel.edu/History-old/figal/Hist104/assets/pdf/readings/08mercantilism.pdf

394. Joseph Albert Ernst, *Money and Politics in America, 1755-1775: A Study in the Currency Act of 1764 and the Political Economy of Revolution*, (Chapel Hill: University of North Carolina Press, 1973), 89; Michael G. Kammen, *Empire and Interest: The American Colonies and the Politics of Mercantilism*, (Philadelphia: Lippincott, 1970), 5, 48, 110.

395. Adam Smith, R. H. Campbell and A. S. Skinner, *An Inquiry into the Nature and Causes of the Wealth of Nations*, Glasgow Edition (1976; reprint, Indianapolis: Liberty Press, 1981), 2:595.

396. Adam Smith, R. H. Campbell and A. S. Skinner, *An Inquiry into the Nature and Causes of the Wealth of Nations*, Glasgow Edition (1976; reprint, Indianapolis: Liberty Press, 1981), 2:582.

397. Forrest McDonald, *The Presidency of George Washington* (Lawrence, KS: The University Press of Kansas, 1974), 25.

398. Alfred Marshall, *Principles of Economics*, 3rd edition (London: MacMillan and Co., 1907), 1.

399. David Faust, *The Limits of Scientific Reasoning* (Minneapolis: University of Minnesota Press, 1984), 7; Heinrich Klüver, introduction to *The Sensory Order: An Inquiry into the Foundations of Theoretical Psychology*, by F. A. Hayek (1952; reprint, Chicago: University of Chicago Press, 2012), xviii.

400. Interview with Columbia University economist Jeffrey Sachs by Anthony Liversidge in *Omni* 13, no. 9 (1991), 79.

401. Sendhil Mullainathan, "Investing in the Dark," *The New York Times*, July 12, 2015, BU-11.

402. Kenneth Roman, "The Man Who Sharpened Gillette," review of *Doing What Matters*, by James M. Kilts, *The Wall Street Journal*, September 4, 2007.

403. Alan Ebenstein, *Hayek's Journey The Mind of Friedrich Hayek* (New York: Palgrave Macmillan, 2003), 13, 21, citing Carl Menger, *Principles of Economics* (Grove City, PA: Libertarian Press, 1994), 78, 107.

404. Michael Faraday (1791-1867), the scientist who did seminal work on gravitational forces, quoted in Michael Guillen, *Five Equations that Changed the World: The Power and Poetry of Mathematics* (New York: Hyperion Publishers, 1995), 133-59.

405. "From George Washington to Marquis de Lafayette, 29 January 1789," W. W. Abbot, et al., eds., *The Papers of George Washington* (Charlottesville: University of Virginia Press, 1987–), Presidential Series, 1:262-643.

406. "Undelivered First Inaugural Address: Fragments," W. W. Abbot, et al., eds., *The Papers of George Washington* (Charlottesville: University of Virginia Press, 1987-), Presidential Series, 2:158-73.

407. "Undelivered First Inaugural Address: Fragments," W. W. Abbot, et al., eds., *The Papers of George Washington* (Charlottesville: University of Virginia Press, 1987–), Presidential Series, 2:158-73; "From George Washington to the United States Senate and House of Representatives," January 8, 1790," Abbot, et al., *Papers of George Washington*, Presidential Series 4:543-49; "From George Washington to the United States Senate and House of Representatives 25 October 1791," Abbot, et al., *Papers of George Washington*, Presidential Series, 9:110-17; "From George Washington to the United States Senate and House of Representatives, 3 December 1793," Abbot, et al., *Papers of George Washington*, Presidential Series, 14:462-69.

408. "Undelivered First Inaugural Address: Fragments," W. W. Abbot, et al., eds., *The Papers of George Washington* (Charlottesville: University of Virginia Press, 1987-), Presidential Series, 2:158-73.

409. "Undelivered First Inaugural Address: Fragments," W. W. Abbot, et al., eds., *The Papers of George Washington* (Charlottesville: University of Virginia Press, 1987–), Presidential Series, 2:158-73; "Farewell Address, September 19, 1796," John C. Fitzpatrick, ed., The *Writings of George Washington from the Original Manuscript Sources, 1745-1799* (Washington: United States Government Printing Office, 1931-1940), 35:214-38.

410. John Stuart Mill (1806-1873). Joseph A. Schumpeter, *History of Economic Analysis* (1954; reprint, London: Taylor & Francis e-Library, 2006), 554-57.

411. Sylvia Nasar, *Grand Pursuit: The Story of Economic Genius* (New York: Simon & Schuster, 2011), 10; *see, e.g.*, "John Chamberlain, Columnist, Dies at 91," *The New York Times*, April 13, 1995.

412. *See*, "… an extraordinarily myopic view of the world," John Mills, *A Critical History of Economics* (New York: Palgrave Macmillan, 2002), 176.

413. Justin Fox, review of *Grand Pursuit: The Story of Economic Genius* by Sylvia Nasar, in *The New York Times Book Review*, October 9, 2011, 22.

414. Joseph Alois Schumpeter (1883-1950): *Theory of Economic Development*, 1911; *Economic Doctrine and Method*, 1914; *Business Cycle*, 1939; *Capitalism, Socialism and Democracy*, 1942; *History of Economic Analysis*, 1954; They were, in addition to Schumpeter, Ludwig von Mises (1880-1973), Friedrich A. von Hayek (1899-1992), and Fritz Machlup (1902-1983). *See:*Ebenstein, *Hayek's Journey*, 105.

415. Friedrich A. Hayek, *The Road to Serfdom* (Chicago: University of Chicago Press, 1944), 240; Alan Ebenstein, *Hayek's Journey: The Mind of Friedrich Hayek* (New York: Palgrave Macmillan, 2003), 111-12.
416. Gordon S. Wood, *The Radicalism of the American Revolution* (New York: Alfred A. Knopf-Random House, 1992), 232.
417. John J. McCusker and Russell R. Menard, *The Economy of British America, 1607-1789* (Chapel Hill, NC and London: The University of North Carolina Press for the Omohundro Institute of Early American History and Culture, 1985), 373-74.
418. David Armitage, *The Declaration of Independence: A Global History* (Cambridge: Harvard University Press, 2007), 103 *et seq.*; "Undelivered First Inaugural Address: Fragments," W. W. Abbot, et al., eds., *The Papers of George Washington* (Charlottesville: University of Virginia Press, 1987-), Presidential Series, 2:158-73.
419. James Madison, "*The Federalist*Number 40, [18 January] 1788," Robert A. Rutland, et al., eds., *The Papers of James Madison* (Chicago: The University of Chicago Press, 1977-), 10:384-90.
420. *See, e.g.,* David S. Landes, *The Wealth and Poverty of Nations: Why Some are so Rich and Some so Poor* (New York: W.W. Norton & Company, 1999); William J. Baumol, Robert E. Litan, Carl J. Schramm, *Good Capitalism Bad Capitalism and the Economics of Growth and Prosperity,* (New Haven: Yale University Press, 2007); Saras D. Sarasvathy, 2001, "What Makes Entrepreneurs Entrepreneurial?" working paper, available at SSRN; Saras D. Sarasvathy, "Effectual Reasoning in Expert Entrepreneurial Decisions: Existence and Bounds," Academy of Management 2001 Meeting Best Paper Proceedings, ENT D1-D6, 2001; Saras D. Sarasvathy with S. Venkataraman, "Strategy and Entrepreneurship: Outlines of an Untold Story," in *The Blackwell Handbook of Strategic Management*, eds. Michael A. Hitt, R. Edward Freeman, and Jeffrey S. Harrison (Wiley-Blackwell, 2001).
421. Gordon S. Wood, *The Radicalism of the American Revolution* (New York: Alfred A. Knopf-Random House, 1992), 232.
422. Richard Sylla, "Comparing the UK and US Financial Systems, 1790-1830," Working Paper, 2006, cited in David J. Cowen, Richard Sylla, and Robert E. Wright, "The U.S. Panic of 1792: Financial Crisis Management and the Lender of Last Resort," NBER DAE Summer Institute, July 2006; Louis Johnston and Samuel H. Williamson, "What Was the U.S. GDP Then?" *Measuring Worth*, 2011, http://www.measuringworth.org/usgdp/.
423. *See*, e.g., David Hackett Fischer, "Editor's Note" in Colin G. Calloway, *The Scratch of a Pen: 1763 and the Transformation of North America,* Pivotal Moments in American History series (New York: Oxford University Press, 2006), xi.
424. *See*, generally, Dan Jones, *Magna Carta: The Birth of Liberty* (New York: Viking, 2015).
425. "From James Madison to Thomas Jefferson, 14 March 1794," Robert A. Rutland, et al., eds., *The Papers of James Madison* (Charlottesville: University Press of Virginia, 1977-), 15-284-85; "From George Washington to William Triplett, 25 September 1786," W. W. Abbot, et al., eds., *The Papers of George Washington* (Charlottesville: University of Virginia Press, 1987–), Confederation Series, 4:268-74; "From George Washington to William Shotwell, 7 April 1789," Abbot, et al., *Papers of George Washington,* Presidential Series, 2:38-39.
426. Clinton Rossiter, *1787: The Grand Convention* (New York: Macmillan, 1966), 24; James Thomas Flexner, *George Washington and the New Nation, 1783-1793* (Boston: Little Brown and Company, 1970), 105.

427. "From Alexander Hamilton to George Clinton, 14 February 1783," Harold C. Syrett, ed., *The Papers of Alexander Hamilton* (New York: Columbia University Press, 1961-87), 3:255-57.
428. "Benjamin West to Rufus King, May 3, 1797," in Robert E. Spiller, et al., A Literary History of the United States (New York: Macmillan, 1963), 200.
429. *See also:* F. Fukuyama, "Culture and Economic Development: Cultural Concerns", in *International Encyclopedia of the Social and Behavioral Sciences,* editors-in-chiefNeil J. Smelser and Paul B. Baltes, (Oxford: Elsevier Science, Ltd., 2001), 3130; P.H.H. Vries, "The Role of Culture and Institutions in Economic History: Can Economics Be of Any Help?", NEHA-Jaarboek 64 (2001), 37, 41; David S. Landes, *The Wealth and Poverty of Nations: Why Some Are So Rich and Some So Poor* (New York: W. W. Norton & Company, 1998), 516; Thomas Sowell, *Conquests and Cultures: An International History* (New York: Basic Books-Perseus Books, 1999), x; Stephen Kalberg, introduction to Max Weber, *The Protestant Ethic and the Spirit of Capitalism,* trans. Stephen Kalberg (New York: Routledge, 2012), l-li; Richard Swedberg, *The Max Weber Dictionary: Key Words and Central Concepts* (Stanford, CA: Stanford University Press, 2005), 56-57; Albert O. Hirschman, *The Strategy of Economic Development* (New Haven: Yale University Press, 1958), 9; James S. Buchanan and Howard S. Ellis, *Approaches to Economic Development* (New York: The Twentieth Century Fund, 1955), 406; Simon Kuznets, *Modern Economic Growth: Rate Structure and Spread* (New Haven: Yale University Press, 1966), 491; Thomas Sowell, *Wealth, Poverty and Politics: An International Perspective* (New York: Basic Books-Perseus, 2015), 53-92.
430. John Mills, *A Critical History of Economics* (New York: Palgrave McMillan), 2002, 175-76.
431. Dennis O'Neil "What is Culture?" *Human Culture: An Introduction to the Characteristics of Culture and the Methods used by Anthropologists to Study It,* 2006, https://www2.palomar.edu/anthro/culture/culture_1.htm.
432. Penelope J. Corfield, "Class by Name and Number in Eighteenth-Century Britain," in Penelope J. Corfield, ed., *Language, History and Class* (Oxford: Blackwell Publishers, 1991), 101-30; Timothy McInerney, "The Better Sort: Nobility and Human Variety in Eighteenth-Century Great Britain," in *Journal of Eighteenth-Century Studies,* Vol. 38, No. I (2015), 50; Thomas William Heyck, *A History of the People of the British Isles: From 1688-1914* (Chicago: Lyceum Books, 2002) 47-51.
433. Penelope J. Corfield, "Class by Name and Number in Eighteenth-Century Britain," in Penelope J. Corfield, ed., *Language, History and Class* (Oxford: Blackwell Publishers, 1991), 119, citing Henry Fielding, *The History of the Life of the Late Mr. Jonathan Wild the Great* (1743; reprint, London: Everyman, 1976), 41-42; Gordon S. Wood, *The Radicalism of the American Revolution,* (New York: Alfred A. Knopf, 1992), 27.
434. "Alexander Hamilton to John Jay, November 26, 1775," Harold C. Syrett, ed., *The Papers of Alexander Hamilton* (New York: Columbia University Press, 1961-87), 1:176-77; "Thomas Jefferson's Hints to Americans Traveling in Europe, 19 June 1788," Julian P. Boyd, et al., eds., *The Papers of Thomas Jefferson* (Princeton: Princeton University Press, 1950–), 13:268; February 4, 1772 entry, L. H. Butterfield, ed., *Diary and Autobiography of John Adams* (Cambridge, MA: Belknap Press, 1961), 2:53; "Nathanael Greene to Samuel Ward, 9 October 1772," Richard Showman, et al., eds., *The Papers of General Nathanael Greene* (Chapel Hill: University of North Carolina Press, 1976–), 1:47.

435. Kevin P. Phillips, *Wealth and Democracy: A Political History of the American Rich* (New York: Broadway Books, 2002), 4-5; Wood, *Radicalism*, 12.
436. James Thomas Flexner, *George Washington and the New Nation, 1783-1793* (Boston: Little, Brown and Company, 1970), 182-83.
437. Britain itself began making a serious effort to change this culture with the ministry of William Gladstone in the second half of the 19th century.
438. Frank E. Grizzard, Jr., ed., *John Milton Mackie's The Administration of President Washington* (Buena Vista, VA: Mariner Publishing, 2006), xii.
439. "Thomas Jefferson to Walter Jones, 2 January 1814," J. Jefferson Looney, ed., *The Papers of Thomas Jefferson:Retirement Series* (Princeton: Princeton University Press, 2010), 7:100-04.
440. "Undelivered First Inaugural Address: Fragments," W. W. Abbot, et al., eds., *The Papers of George Washington* (Charlottesville: University of Virginia Press, 1987–), Presidential Series, 2:158-73; H.G. Good, "George Washington and Education," *Educational Research Bulletin*, vol. 11, no. 2, (Jan. 20, 1932), 39-44.
441. Richard Brookhiser, George Washington on Leadership (New York Basic Books-Perseus, 2008), 194-95; Ralph Ketcham, *Presidents above Party: The First American Presidency, 1789-1829* (Chapel Hill, NC: University of North Carolina Press, 1984), 56-112.
442. "Vices of the Political System of the United States, April 1787," Robert A. Rutland, et al., eds., *The Papers of James Madison* (Charlottesville: University Press of Virginia, 1977-), 9:345-58.
443. William Blackstone, *Commentaries on the Laws of England,* (Oxford: Clarendon Press, 1768), 2:36-37.
444. "Undelivered First Inaugural Address: Fragments," W. W. Abbot, et al., eds., *The Papers of George Washington* (Charlottesville: University of Virginia Press, 1987-), Presidential Series, 2:158-73.
445. Richard E. James, "Putting Fear Back Into the Law and Debtors Back Into Prison: Reforming the Debtors' Prison System", *Washburn Law Journal* 42, no. 1 (2002): 143, 147; Lawrence M. Friedman, *A History of American Law* (New York: Simon & Schuster, 2007), 199-202, and citing Peter J. Coleman, *Debtors and Creditors in America: Insolvency, Imprisonment for Debt, and Bankruptcy, 1607-1900* (Washington: Beard Books, 1999), 207; Bruce H. Mann, *Republic of Debtors: Bankruptcy in the Age of American Independence* (Cambridge: Harvard University Press, 2002), 3.
446. Bruce H. Mann, *Republic of Debtors: Bankruptcy in the Age of American Independence* (Cambridge: Harvard University Press, 2002), 3-18, 77-105, 193-228, 257, 354; *see also,* "History of Eastern State Penitentiary, Philadelphia" at www.EasternState.org; Joel Achenbach, *The Grand Idea: George Washington's Potomac and the Race to the West,* (New York: Simon & Schuster, 2004), 88, and quoting John Bach McMaster, *A History of the People of the United States, from the Revolution to the Civil War,* vol. 1 (New York: D. Appleton, 1893), 99.
447. Bruce H. Mann, *Republic of Debtors: Bankruptcy in the Age of American Independence* (Cambridge: Harvard University Press, 2002), 103-05.
448. *See*, e.g., Bruce H. Mann, *Republic of Debtors: Bankruptcy in the Age of American Independence* (Cambridge: Harvard University Press, 2002), 50.
449. Gottlieb Mittelberger, *Gottlieb Mittelberger's Journey to Pennsylvania in the Year 1750 and Return to Germany in the Year 1754,* trans. Carl Eben (Philadelphia: John Jos McVey, 1898), 26-29; Henry W. Farnam, *Chapters in the History of Social Legislation in the United States to*

1860 (1938; reprint, Union, NJ: Lawbook Exchange, 2000), 61-63; Lawrence M. Friedman, *A History of American Law* (New York: Simon & Schuster, 2007), 44.

450. Lawrence M. Friedman, *A History of American Law* (New York: Simon & Schuster, 2007), 44; *see* also Christine Daniels, "'Liberty to Complaine': Servant Petitions in Maryland, 1652-1797," in Christopher L. Tomlins and Bruce H. Mann, eds., *The Many Legalities of Early America* (Chapel Hill, NC: For the Omohundro Institute of Early American History and Culture by University of North Carolina Press, 2001), 222; Gordon S. Wood, *The Americanization of Benjamin Franklin* (New York: Penguin Press, 2004), 17-24.

451. *See*, e.g., Lawrence M. Friedman, *A History of American Law* (New York: Simon & Schuster, 2007), 45; Daniels, "Liberty to Complaine", 226-27; and Gottlieb Mittelberger, *Gottlieb Mittelberger's Journey to Pennsylvania in the Year 1750 and Return to Germany in the Year 1754*, trans. Carl Eben (Philadelphia: John Jos McVey, 1898), 29; Sharon V. Salinger, "Send no More Women: Female Servants in Eighteenth-century Philadelphia," *The Pennsylvania Magazine of History and Biography* 107, no. 1 (1983): 29-48.

452. Bruce H. Mann, *Republic of Debtors: Bankruptcy in the Age of American Independence* (Cambridge: Harvard University Press, 2002), 5; "From George Washington to George Mason, 5 April 1769," W. W. Abbot, et al., eds., *The Papers of George Washington* (Charlottesville: University of Virginia Press, 1987–), Colonial Series, 8:177-81; George Washington "To Joseph Jones, March 18, 1783," John C. Fitzpatrick, ed., The *Writings of George Washington from the Original Manuscript Sources, 1745-1799* (Washington: United States Government Printing Office, 1931-1940), 26:232-34; *see* also George Washington "To Theodorick Bland, April 4, 1783," Fitzpatrick, *Writings of George Washington*, 26:293-96.

453. James Thomas Flexner, *George Washington: The Forge of Experience, 1732-1775* (Boston: Little Brown and Company, 1965), 252-53; "From George Washington to William Aylett, 6 March 1775," W. W. Abbot, et al., eds., *The Papers of George Washington* (Charlottesville: University of Virginia Press, 1987–), Colonial Series, 10:288; Bruce H. Mann, *Republic of Debtors: Bankruptcy in the Age of American Independence* (Cambridge: Harvard University Press, 2002), 68; George Washington "To Edmund Randolph, July 22, 1795, John C. Fitzpatrick, ed., The *Writings of George Washington from the Original Manuscript Sources, 1745-1799* (Washington: United States Government Printing Office, 1931-1940), 34:205; "From George Washington to Bryan Fairfax, 4 July 1774," Abbot, et al., *Papers of George Washington*, Colonial Series, 10:109-10; Peter J. Coleman, *Debtors and Creditors in America: Insolvency, Imprisonment for Debt, and Bankruptcy, 1607-1900* (Washington: Beard Books, 1999), 117.

454. Lawrence M. Friedman, *A History of American Law* (New York: Simon & Schuster, 2007), 202, citing 1 Am. Jurist 45 (1829).

455. U.S. Constitution, Art. I, sect. 8, cl. 8 (giving Congress the power "to establish uniform laws on the Subject of Bankruptcy throughout the United States); Records of the Federal Convention, September 3, 1787; Charles Warren, *Bankruptcy in United States History* (Cambridge, MA: Harvard University Press, 1935), 4-5; James Madison, *Federalist* no. 42.

456. *U.S. House Journal*, 1792, 2nd Cong., 2nd sess., 10 December; Charles Warren, *Bankruptcy in United States History* (Cambridge, MA: Harvard University Press, 1935), 16.

457. Charles Warren, *Bankruptcy in United States History* (Cambridge, MA: Harvard University Press, 1935), 16-18; Bruce H. Mann, *Republic of Debtors: Bankruptcy in the Age of American Independence* (Cambridge: Harvard University Press, 2002), 125, 206, 208; William

Maclay, *Sketches of Debate in the First Senate of the United States, in 1789-90-91* George W. Harris, ed., (Harrisburg, PA: Lane S. Hart, printer, 1880), 3477.

458. Bruce H. Mann, *Republic of Debtors: Bankruptcy in the Age of American Independence* (Cambridge: Harvard University Press, 2002), 6-82.

459. Ellis Paxson Oberholtzer, *Robert Morris, Patriot and Financier* (New York: The Macmillan Company, 1903), 66-341.

460. "[Diary entry: 27 November 1798]," Donald Jackson and Dorothy Twohig, eds., *The Diaries of George Washington* (Charlottesville: University Press of Virginia, 1976-79), 6:324-26; Oberholtzer, *Robert Morris*, 351; George Washington Parke Custis, *Recollections and Private Memoirs of Washington* (New York: Derby & Jackson, 1860), 327-29.

461. "From George Washington to Mary White Morris, 21 September 1799," W. W. Abbot, et al., eds., *The Papers of George Washington* (Charlottesville: University of Virginia Press, 1987-), Retirement Series, 4:317-18.

462. Bruce H. Mann, *Republic of Debtors: Bankruptcy in the Age of American Independence* (Cambridge: Harvard University Press, 2002), 192-96.

463. Charles Warren, *Bankruptcy in United States History* (Cambridge, MA: Harvard University Press, 1935), 13; U.S. *House Journal*, Dec. 11, 1798, 5th Cong, 3d sess.; Jan. 15, 1799, 5th Cong., 3d sess.; "An Act to Establish An Uniform System of Bankruptcy Throughout the United States," Apr. 4, 1800, 2 Stat. 19, repealed Dec. 19, 1803, 2 Stat. 248.

464. "Farewell Address, September 19, 1796," John C. Fitzpatrick, ed., The *Writings of George Washington from the Original Manuscript Sources, 1745-1799* (Washington: United States Government Printing Office, 1931-1940), 35:214-38; *see*, Charles Warren, *Bankruptcy in United States History* (Cambridge, MA: Harvard University Press, 1935), Foreword.

465. U.S. Constitution, 13th amendment; Lawrence M. Friedman, *A History of American Law* (New York: Simon & Schuster, 2007), 45-46; Peter J. Coleman, *Debtors and Creditors in America: Insolvency, Imprisonment for Debt, and Bankruptcy, 1607-1900* (Washington: Beard Books, 1999), xi; Becky A. Vogt, "Note: State v. Allison: Imprisonment for Debt in South Dakota," *South Dakota Law Review*, vol. 46 (2001), 334, 345-46.

466. William Blackstone, *Commentaries on the Laws of England*, 4 volumes, (Oxford, 1768), 1:472-481.

467. William Blackstone, *Commentaries on the Laws of England*, 4 volumes, (Oxford, 1768), 1:472-485.

468. Joseph Stancliffe Davis, *Essays in the Earlier History of American Corporations*, Volume II (Cambridge: Harvard University Press, 1917), 5, 258-60.

469. Joseph Stancliffe Davis, *Essays in the Earlier History of American Corporations*, Volume II (Cambridge: Harvard University Press, 1917), 5; Bubble Act 1720, 6 Geo I, c 18.

470. However, the Susquehanna Company appears to have been permitted to be active without one during the same period. Simeon E. Baldwin, "American Business Corporations before 1789," *The American Historical Review*, Vol. 8, No. 3 (April, 1903), 450-51.

471. Simeon E. Baldwin, "American Business Corporations before 1789," *The American Historical Review*, Vol. 8, No. 3 (April, 1903), 451-65; Richard Sylla, "The Political Economy of Early U.S. Financial Development," Stephen Haber, Douglass C. North, and Barry R. Weingast, eds., *Political Institutions and Financial Development* (Stanford, CA: Stanford University Press, 2008), 75-76.

472. Joseph Stancliffe Davis, *Essays in the Earlier History of American Corporations*, Volume II (Cambridge: Harvard University Press, 1917), 2:5-6; William H. Sewell, Jr., *Work and Revolution in France: The Language of Labor from the Old Regime to 1848,* (Cambridge: Cambridge University Press, 1980), 86-103.

473. Gordon S. Wood, *The Radicalism of the American Revolution* (New York: Alfred A. Knopf-Random House, 1992), 320; Franklin B. Sawvel, ed., *The Complete Anas of Thomas Jefferson* (New York: The Round Table Press, 1903), 36-37.

474. Simeon E. Baldwin, "American Business Corporations before 1789," *The American Historical Review*, Vol. 8, No. 3 (April, 1903), 463-465; Joseph Stancliffe Davis, *Essays in the Earlier History of American Corporations*, Volume II (Cambridge: Harvard University Press, 1917), 2:257-291, 320-321; Thomas C. Cochran, "The Business Revolution," *The American Historical Review*, Vol. 79, No. 5 (Dec., 1974), 1450-52, 1456-60.

475. Pauline Maier, "The Revolutionary Origins of the American Corporation," *The William and Mary Quarterly*, Third Series, Vol. 50, No. 1, Law and Society in Early America (Jan., 1993), 75-78; Davis, *Essays in the History*, 2:152, 320-23; Robert E. Wright, *One Nation Under Debt: Hamilton, Jefferson and the History of What We Owe* (New York, McGraw-Hill, 2008), 149-50.

476. Pauline Maier, "The Revolutionary Origins of the American Corporation," *The William and Mary Quarterly*, Third Series, Vol. 50, No. 1, Law and Society in Early America (Jan., 1993), 83; Joseph Stancliffe Davis, *Essays in the Earlier History of American Corporations*, Volume II (Cambridge: Harvard University Press, 1917), 2:7-8, 14-15.

477. Joseph S. Davis, "Charters for American Business Corporations in the Eighteenth Century," *Publications of the American Statistical Association*, Vol. 15, No. 116 (December 1916), 432.

478. "Address to the United States Senate and House of Representatives, 6 November 1792," W. W. Abbot, et al., eds., *The Papers of George Washington* (Charlottesville: University of Virginia Press, 1987–), Presidential Series, 11:342-51; HR, 13 July 1790, *Annals of Congress*, 1st Cong., 2nd sess., 1834, 2:1737; Isaiah Thomas, *History of Printing in America, with a Biography of Printers,* 1810 (Albany, NY: Joel Munsell, Printer for the American Antiquarian Society, 1874), 148, 199; Alfred McClung Lee, *The Daily Newspaper in America, with a Biography of Printers* (New York: Macmillan Company, 1947), 711-14.

479. *See,* for example, *Pennsylvania Gazette,* August 22, 1787; George Washington "To Edward Rutledge, May 5, 1789, John C. Fitzpatrick, ed., The *Writings of George Washington from the Original Manuscript Sources, 1745-1799* (Washington: United States Government Printing Office, 1931-1940), 30:308-10; George Washington "To David Stuart, January 8, 1797, Fitzpatrick, *Writings of George Washington*, 35:357-60.

480. See, e.g., *Gazette of the United States,* 25 July 1792.

481. *National Gazette,* 6 February 1792, 27 February 1792; Lewis Leary, *The Rascal Freneau: A Study in Literary Failure* (New York, NY: Octagon Books, 1971), 83; 199; *National Gazette*, 2 April 1792, 29 March 1792, 5 April 1792, and 5 June 1793.

482. George Washington "To Edmund Randolph, August 26, 1792," John C. Fitzpatrick, ed., The *Writings of George Washington from the Original Manuscript Sources, 1745-1799* (Washington: United States Government Printing Office, 1931-1940), 32:135-37; *National Gazette*, February 2, 1793.

483. George Washington "To Secretary of State, 23 August 1792," John C. Fitzpatrick, ed., *The Writings of George Washington from the Original Manuscript Sources, 1745-1799* (Washington: United States Government Printing Office, 1931-1940), 32:128-32.

484. George Washington "To Governor Henry Lee, July 21, 1793," John C. Fitzpatrick, ed., The *Writings of George Washington from the Original Manuscript Sources, 1745-1799* (Washington: United States Government Printing Office, 1931-1940), 33:22-24; George Washington "To Secretary of the Treasury, August 26, 1792," Fitzpatrick, *Writings of George Washington*, 32:132-34; George Washington "To Secretary of State, August 23, 1792," in Fitzpatrick, *Writings of George Washington*, 32:128-32.

485. *See*, e.g., *Gazette of the United States*, 25 July 1792.

486. *Aurora*, September 9, 21, October 21, 1795; December 23, 1796; 6 March 1797; Joseph Tartakovsky, "In Praise of Political Insults," *The Wall Street Journal*, July 2, 2008.

487. *Aurora*, 6 March 1797.

488. George Washington "To Reverend William Gordon, October 15, 1797," John C. Fitzpatrick, ed., The *Writings of George Washington from the Original Manuscript Sources, 1745-1799* (Washington: United States Government Printing Office, 1931-1940), 36:48-51; George Washington "To Henry Lee, July 21, 1793," Fitzpatrick, *Writings of George Washington*, 33:22-24; George Washington "To Oliver Wolcott, July 6, 1796," Fitzpatrick, *Writings of George Washington*, 35:125-26.

489. George Washington "To Gouverneur Morris, October 20, 1792," John C. Fitzpatrick, ed., *The Writings of George Washington from the Original Manuscript Sources, 1745-1799* (Washington: United States Government Printing Office, 1931-1940), 32:188-90.

490. "An Act for the Punishment of Certain Crimes against the United States [Sedition Act]," § 1, *United StatesStatutes at Large*, 14 July 1798, 1:596-97.

491. Geoffrey R. Stone, *Perilous Times: Free Speech in Wartime: From the Sedition Act of 1798 to the War on Terrorism* (New York: W. W. Norton, 2004), 63; James Morton Smith, *Freedom's Fetters: The Alien and Sedition Laws and American Civil Liberties* (New York: Cornell University Press, 1956), 185-87; George Henry Payne, *Historyof Journalism in the United States* (New York: D. Appleton & Co., 1920), 181, 185-86; John Spencer Bassett, *The American Nation, A History: The Federalist System, 1789-1801* (New York: Harper & Brother, 1906), 261-64.

492. Smith, *Freedom's Fetters*, 200; Jeffrey L. Pasley, *The Tyranny of Printers: Newspaper Politics in the Early American Republic* (Charlottesville: University of Virginia Press, 2001), 102; Sedition Act.

493. The data are from Committee to Protect Journalists (http://www.cpj.org/), and Reporters without Borders (http://en.rsf.org/), two organizations that track the worldwide developments in this area of human activity. Reporters without Borders publishes an annual index of media freedom for every country in the world. In 2002, the U.S. ranked 17th (out of 179 countries); in 2014, it is in 46th place.

494. Thomas Barlow's January 1783 letter to Elias Boudinot in National Archives, Papers of the Continental Congress, No. 78, IV, folios 369-72.

495. "Vices of the Political System of the United States, April 1787," Robert A. Rutland, et al., eds., *The Papers of James Madison* (Charlottesville: University Press of Virginia, 1977-), 9:345-58.

496. "From Thomas Jefferson to James Madison, 31 July 1788," Julian P. Boyd, et al., eds., *The Papers of Thomas Jefferson* (Princeton: Princeton University Press, 1950-), 13:440-43.

497. George Washington "To Thomas Coleman Martin, October 3, 1797, May 15, 1798, June 17, 1798," John C. Fitzpatrick, ed., The *Writings of George Washington from the Original Manuscript Sources, 1745-1799* (Washington: United States Government Printing Office, 1931-1940), 36:37-39, 261-62, 296-97; George Washington "To Samuel Chamberline, April 3, 1788," in Fitzpatrick, *Writings of George Washington*, 29:455-56..
498. U.S. *Senate Journal*, 1790. 1st Cong., 2nd sess., 8 January, 102-04.
499. U.S. *House Journal*, 1789, 1st Cong., 1st sess., 17 August, 80-81; U.S. *House Journal*, 1790, 1st Cong., 2nd sess., 25 January, 145-46; U.S. *House Journal*, 1790, 1st Cong., 2nd sess., 16 February, 159-60; Act of April 10, 1790, ch. 7, 1 *Stat*. 109-12.
500. "From George Washington to the United States Senate and House of Representatives, 8 January 1790," W. W. Abbot, et al., eds., *The Papers of George Washington* (Charlottesville: University of Virginia Press, 1987-), Presidential Series 4:543-49.
501. Act of February 21, 1793, ch. 11, 1 *Stat*. 318-23.
502. B. Zorina Khan, *The Democratization of Invention: Patents and Copyrights in American Economic Development, 1790-1920* (New York: Cambridge University Press, 2005), 28, 54; Kenneth L. Sokoloff, "Inventive Activity in Early Industrial America: Evidence from Patent Records, 1790-1846," *The Journal of Economic Activity*, Vol. 48, No. 4 (December 1988), 813-50.
503. United States Patent Office, *The Story of the American Patent System, 1790-1952*, (Washington: U. S. Government Printing Office, 1940), 2; Benjamin Franklin, *Autobiography*, in *Benjamin Franklin's Autobiographical Writings*, ed. Carl Van Doren (New York: Viking Press, 1945), 720-21; Dennis J. Pogue and Esther C. White, *George Washington's Gristmill at Mount Vernon* (Mount Vernon: Mount Vernon Ladies Association, 2005), 8-10.
504. Kenneth R. Bowling, *The Creation of Washington, D.C.: The Idea and Location of the American Capital* (Fairfax, VA: George Mason University Press, 1991), 3.
505. John Ball Osborne, "The First President's Interest in Washington as Told by Himself," *Records of the Columbia Historical Society* 4 (1901), 177; Margaret C.S. Christman, *The First Federal Congress, 1789-1791* (Washington: Smithsonian Institution Press, 1989), 182; Fergus M. Bordewich, *Washington: The Making of the American Capital*, (New York: Harper Collins, 2008), 42; Kenneth R. Bowling, *The Creation of Washington, D.C.: The Idea and Location of the American Capital* (Fairfax, VA: George Mason University Press, 1991), 129-38, 161-81; "Editorial Note: Fixing the Seat of Government on the Potomac," Julian P. Boyd, et al., eds., *The Papers of Thomas Jefferson* (Princeton: Princeton University Press, 1950–), 17:452-60.
506. Kenneth R. Bowling, *The Creation of Washington, D.C.: The Idea and Location of the American Capital* (Fairfax, VA: George Mason University Press, 1991), 37, 88-89.
507. Fergus M. Bordewich, *Washington: The Making of the American Capital*, (New York: Harper Collins, 2008), 42-43; Andrew Burstein and Nancy Isenberg, *Madison and Jefferson* (New York: Random House, 2010), 219-20; Richard Norton Smith, *Patriarch: George Washington and the New American Nation* (Boston: Houghton Mifflin, 1993), 41.
508. Richard Norton Smith, *Patriarch: George Washington and the New American Nation* (New York: Houghton Mifflin, 1993), 41; Page Smith, *The Shaping of America: A People's History of the Young Republic* (New York: Penguin, 1980), 156; Charles Rappleye, *Robert Morris: Financier of the American Revolution* (New York: Simon & Schuster, 2010), 476-77.
509. Charles Rappleye, *Robert Morris: Financier of the American Revolution* (New York: Simon & Schuster, 2010), 476-77.

510. Kenneth R. Bowling, *The Creation of Washington, D.C.: The Idea and Location of the American Capital* (Fairfax, VA: George Mason University Press, 1991), 179-80.

511. Charles Rappleye, *Robert Morris: Financier of the American Revolution* (New York: Simon & Schuster, 2010), 476-77; Kenneth R. Bowling, *The Creation of Washington, D.C.: The Idea and Location of the American Capital* (Fairfax, VA: George Mason University Press, 1991), 179-80.

512. Kenneth R. Bowling, *The Creation of Washington, D.C.: The Idea and Location of the American Capital* (Fairfax, VA: George Mason University Press, 1991), 180.

513. Page Smith, *The Shaping of America: A People's History of the Young Republic* (New York: Penguin, 1980), 156; Margaret C.S. Christman, *The First Federal Congress, 1789-1791* (Washington: Smithsonian Institution Press, 1989), 184.

514. Albert S. Bolles, *The Financial History of the United States, from 1774 to 1789: Embracing the Period of the American Revolution*, 2nd ed., Library of American Civilization Series (New York: D. Appleton and Co., 1884), 7-8; David Hackett Fischer, *Washington's Crossing* (New York: Oxford University Press, 2004), 274; E. James Ferguson, *The Power of the Purse: A History of American Public Finance, 1776-1790* (Chapel Hill: University of North Carolina Press, 1961), 3-145; Edwin J. Perkins, *American Public Finance and Financial Services 1700-1815* (Columbus: Ohio State University Press, 1994), 103; John Steele Gordon, *Hamilton's Blessing: The Extraordinary Life and Times of Our National Debt* (New York: Walker and Company, 2010), 11-12; William G. Anderson, *The Price of Liberty: The Public Debt of the American Revolution* (Charlottesville: University of Virginia Press, 1983); Richard B. Morris, *The Forging of the Union 1781-1789* (New York: Harper & Row, 1987), 34-42; Ben Baack, "Forging a Nation State: The Continental Congress and the Financing of the War of American Independence." *Economic History Review* vol. 54, no.4 (2001), 639-56; Curtis P. Nettels, *The Emergence of a National Economy: 1775-1815*, vol. 2 of *The Economic History of the United States* (New York: Holt, Rinehart & Winston, 1962), 115; Robert E. Wright, *One Nation Under Debt: Hamilton, Jefferson, and the History of What We Owe* (New York: McGraw-Hill, 2008), 132; Paul Studenski and Herman E. Krooss, *Financial History of the United States* (New York: McGraw-Hill Company, 1952), 27; Margaret G. Myers, *A Financial History of the United States* (New York: Columbia University Press, 1970), 50-51.

515. Edwin J. Perkins, *American Public Finance and Financial Services 1700-1815* (Columbus: Ohio State University Press, 1994), 95-6; E. James Ferguson, *The Power of the Purse: A History of American Public Finance, 1776-1790* (Chapel Hill: University of North Carolina Press, 1961), 9-10, 26-29, 46-47; Ben Baack, "Forging a Nation State: The Continental Congress and the Financing of the War of American Independence." *Economic History Review* vol. 54, no.4 (2001), 641-44; Paul Studenski and Herman E. Krooss, *Financial History of the United States* (New York: McGraw-Hill Company, 1952), 27-28; Davis Rich Dewey, *Financial History of the United States* (1903; reprint, New York: Augustus M. Kelley, 1968), 36-37; William Graham Sumner, *The Financier and the Finances of the American Revolution* (1891; reprint, New York: Burt Franklin, 1970), 40-41; Margaret G. Myers, *A Financial History of the United States* (New York: Columbia University Press, 1970), 24-28; William G. Anderson, *The Price of Liberty: The Public Debt of the American Revolution* (Charlottesville: University of Virginia Press, 1983); 3.

516. E. James Ferguson, *The Power of the Purse: A History of American Public Finance, 1776-1790* (Chapel Hill: University of North Carolina Press, 1961), 30-32, 44-46, 65-67; Edwin

J. Perkins, *American Public Finance and Financial Services 1700-1815* (Columbus: Ohio State University Press, 1994), 96-98; William G. Anderson, *The Price of Liberty: The Public Debt of the American Revolution* (Charlottesville: University of Virginia Press, 1983); 10-11; John Steele Gordon, *Hamilton's Blessing: The Extraordinary Life and Times of Our National Debt* (New York: Walker and Company, 2010), 11; Mildred F. Otenasek, *Alexander Hamilton's Financial Policies* (New York: Arno Press, 1977), 10-11; George Washington "To John Jay, April 23, 1779," John C. Fitzpatrick, ed., The *Writings of George Washington from the Original Manuscript Sources, 1745-1799* (Washington: United States Government Printing Office, 1931-1940), 14:89-91; Davis Rich Dewey, *Financial History of the United States* (1903; reprint, New York: Augustus M. Kelley, 1968), 39-41; William Graham Sumner, *The Financier and the Finances of the American Revolution* (1891; reprint, New York: Burt Franklin, 1970), 78-81; Richard B. Morris, *The Forging of the Union 1781-1789* (New York: Harper & Row, 1987), 36.

517. E. James Ferguson, *The Power of the Purse: A History of American Public Finance, 1776-1790* (Chapel Hill: University of North Carolina Press, 1961), 40-42, 126-28; Richard B. Morris, *The Forging of the Union 1781-1789* (New York: Harper & Row, 1987), 34; Rafael A. Bayley, *The National Loans of the United States, from July.4, 1776, to June 30, 1880* (Washington: Government Printing Office, 1882), 5-18; William G. Anderson, *The Price of Liberty: The Public Debt of the American Revolution* (Charlottesville: University of Virginia Press, 1983), 3-12; Margaret G. Myers, *A Financial History of the United States* (New York: Columbia University Press, 1970), 35; "Benjamin Franklin to John Adams, February 12, 1782," Francis Wharton, ed., *The Revolutionary Diplomatic Correspondence of the United States,* 6 volumes (Washington: Government Printing Office, 1889), 5:159.

518. Rafael A. Bayley, *The National Loans of the United States, from July.4, 1776, to June 30, 1880* (Washington: Government Printing Office, 1882), 12.

519. William G. Anderson, *The Price of Liberty: The Public Debt of the American Revolution* (Charlottesville: University of Virginia Press, 1983); 5-6; E. James Ferguson, *The Power of the Purse: A History of American Public Finance, 1776-1790* (Chapel Hill: University of North Carolina Press, 1961), 128-29; Richard B. Morris, *The Forging of the Union 1781-1789* (New York: Harper & Row, 1987), 34; Paul Studenski and Herman E. Krooss, *Financial History of the United States* (New York: McGraw-Hill Company, 1952), 29-30; Davis Rich Dewey, *Financial History of the United States* (1903; reprint, New York: Augustus M. Kelley, 1968), 47-48.

520. William G. Anderson, *The Price of Liberty: The Public Debt of the American Revolution* (Charlottesville: University of Virginia Press, 1983), 6-12; E. James Ferguson, *The Power of the Purse: A History of American Public Finance, 1776-1790* (Chapel Hill: University of North Carolina Press, 1961), 35-40, 51; Richard B. Morris, *The Forging of the Union 1781-1789* (New York: Harper & Row, 1987), 35-36; Davis Rich Dewey, *Financial History of the United States* (1903; reprint, New York: Augustus M. Kelley, 1968), 45-47; William Graham Sumner, *The Financier and the Finances of the American Revolution* (1891; reprint, New York: Burt Franklin, 1970), 85-86.

521. E. James Ferguson, *The Power of the Purse: A History of American Public Finance, 1776-1790* (Chapel Hill: University of North Carolina Press, 1961), 39-40, 53-55, 285; William G. Anderson, *The Price of Liberty: The Public Debt of the American Revolution* (Charlottesville: University of Virginia Press, 1983); 37-88.

522. John Steele Gordon, *Hamilton's Blessing: The Extraordinary Life and Times of Our National Debt* (New York: Walker and Company, 2010), 12; Robert E. Wright, *One Nation Under Debt: Hamilton, Jefferson and the History of What We Owe* (New York, McGraw-Hill, 2008), 61, 130; William G. Anderson, *The Price of Liberty: The Public Debt of the American Revolution* (Charlottesville: University of Virginia Press, 1983); 41; Edwin J. Perkins, *American Public Finance and Financial Services 1700-1815* (Columbus: Ohio State University Press, 1994), 101; E. James Ferguson, *The Power of the Purse: A History of American Public Finance, 1776-1790* (Chapel Hill: University of North Carolina Press, 1961), 179-80; John Watts Kearny, *Sketch of American Finances, 1789-1835* (1887; reprint, New York: Greenwood Press, 1968), 11.

523. Clarence L. Ver Steeg, *Robert Morris, Revolutionary Financier* (New York: Octagon Books, 1972), 133.

524. Robert Morris "To John Jay, July 13, 1781," E. James Ferguson, et al., eds., *Papers of Robert Morris: 1781-1784* (Pittsburgh: University of Pittsburgh Press, 1973-1999), 1:287-91.

525. Robert Morris "To the President of Congress (John Hanson), February 11, 1782," E. James Ferguson, et al., eds., *Papers of Robert Morris: 1781-1784* (Pittsburgh: University of Pittsburgh Press, 1973-1999), 4:205.

526. John Steele Gordon, *Hamilton's Blessing: The Extraordinary Life and Times of Our National Debt* (New York: Walker and Company, 2010), 12, 18-19.

527. Robert E. Wright, *One Nation Under Debt: Hamilton, Jefferson and the History of What We Owe* (New York, McGraw-Hill, 2008), 128-29.

528. Richard Sylla, "Experimental Federalism: The Economics of American Government, 1789-1914," in Stanley L. Engerman and Robert E. Gallman, eds., *The Cambridge Economic History of the United States: Volume 2, The Long Nineteenth Century* (Cambridge: Cambridge University Press, 2000), 498. *See also* Robert E. Wright, *One Nation Under Debt: Hamilton, Jefferson and the History of What We Owe* (New York, McGraw-Hill, 2008), 132; Curtis P. Nettels, *The Emergence of a National Economy: 1775-1815*, vol. 2 *of The Economic History of the United States* (New York: Holt, Rinehart & Winston, 1962), 115; Wood, *Empire of Liberty*, 95.

529. "Report Relative to a Provision for the Support of Public Credit, [9 January 1790]," Harold C. Syrett, ed., *The Papers of Alexander Hamilton* (New York: Columbia University Press, 1961-87), 6:65-110; Robert E. Wright, *One Nation Under Debt: Hamilton, Jefferson and the History of What We Owe* (New York, McGraw-Hill, 2008), 130-31.

530. "Report Relative to a Provision for the Support of Public Credit, [9 January 1790]," Harold C. Syrett, ed., *The Papers of Alexander Hamilton* (New York: Columbia University Press, 1961-87), 6:106; Peter McNamara, *Political Economy and Statesmanship: Smith, Hamilton, and the Foundation of the Commercial Republic* (DeKalb, Ill.: Northern Illinois University Press 1998), 121-28; Robert E. Wright, *One Nation Under Debt: Hamilton, Jefferson and the History of What We Owe* (New York, McGraw-Hill, 2008), 130-34; William G. Anderson, *The Price of Liberty: The Public Debt of the American Revolution* (Charlottesville: University of Virginia Press, 1983); 41-45, 51-52; Curtis P. Nettels, *The Emergence of a National Economy: 1775-1815*, vol. 2 *of The Economic History of the United States* (New York: Holt, Rinehart & Winston, 1962), 112-17; Edwin J. Perkins, *American Public Finance and Financial Services 1700-1815* (Columbus: Ohio State University Press, 1994), 215-19; John Steele Gordon, *Hamilton's Blessing: The Extraordinary Life and Times of Our National Debt* (New York: Walker

and Company, 2010), 26; Richard Sylla, "Experimental Federalism: The Economics of American Government, 1789-1914," in Stanley L. Engerman and Robert E. Gallman, eds., *The Cambridge Economic History of the United States: Volume 2, The Long Nineteenth Century* (Cambridge: Cambridge University Press, 2000), 498-500.

531. "Report Relative to a Provision for the Support of Public Credit, [9 January 1790]," Harold C. Syrett, ed., *The Papers of Alexander Hamilton* (New York: Columbia University Press, 1961-87), 6:78; Robert E. Wright, *One Nation Under Debt: Hamilton, Jefferson and the History of What We Owe* (New York, McGraw-Hill, 2008), 132; Edwin J. Perkins, *American Public Finance and Financial Services 1700-1815* (Columbus: Ohio State University Press, 1994), 214-17; Curtis P. Nettels, *The Emergence of a National Economy: 1775-1815*, vol. 2 *of The Economic History of the United States* (New York: Holt, Rinehart & Winston, 1962), 112-13.

532. Forrest McDonald, *The Presidency of George Washington* (Lawrence, KS: The University Press of Kansas, 1974), 39; "[Diary entry: 2 January 1790]," Donald Jackson and Dorothy Twohig, eds., *The Diaries of George Washington* (Charlottesville: University Press of Virginia, 1976-79), 6:1; "Report Relative to a Provision for the Support of Public Credit, [9 January 1790]," Harold C. Syrett, ed., *The Papers of Alexander Hamilton* (New York: Columbia University Press, 1961-87), 6:65-110.

533. Charles A. Beard, *Economic Origins of Jeffersonian Democracy* (New York: The MacMillan Company, 1915), 215-16; Harry Ammon, *James Monroe: The Quest for National Identity* (Charlottesville: University Press of Virginia, 1990), 85-86; Robert E. Wright, *One Nation Under Debt: Hamilton, Jefferson and the History of What We Owe* (New York, McGraw-Hill, 2008), 135-37.

534. Curtis P. Nettels, *The Emergence of a National Economy: 1775-1815*, vol. 2 *of The Economic History of the United States* (New York: Holt, Rinehart & Winston, 1962), 114, 127-28; Robert E. Wright, *One Nation Under Debt: Hamilton, Jefferson and the History of What We Owe* (New York, McGraw-Hill, 2008), 136-39; Edwin J. Perkins, *American Public Finance and Financial Services 1700-1815* (Columbus: Ohio State University Press, 1994), 212, 222-24; William G. Anderson, *The Price of Liberty: The Public Debt of the American Revolution* (Charlottesville: University of Virginia Press, 1983); 46-48.

535. Forrest McDonald, *Alexander Hamilton*, quoted in Robert E. Wright, *One Nation Under Debt: Hamilton, Jefferson and the History of What We Owe* (New York, McGraw-Hill, 2008), 141.

536. Robert E. Wright, *One Nation Under Debt: Hamilton, Jefferson and the History of What We Owe* (New York, McGraw-Hill, 2008), 137.

537. "General Orders, May 21, 1783," John C. Fitzpatrick, ed., The *Writings of George Washington from the Original Manuscript Sources, 1745-1799* (Washington: United States Government Printing Office, 1931-1940), 26:446-47; George Washington "To Joseph Jones, March 18, 1783," Fitzpatrick, *Writings of George Washington*, 26:232-34.

538. George Washington "To Lund Washington, March 19, 1783," John C. Fitzpatrick, ed., *The Writings of George Washington from the Original Manuscript Sources, 1745-1799* (Washington: United States Government Printing Office, 1931-1940), 26:245-46.

539. E. James Ferguson, *The Power of the Purse: A History of American Public Finance, 1776-1790* (Chapel Hill: University of North Carolina Press, 1961), 299-305; Edwin J. Perkins, *American Public Finance and Financial Services 1700-1815* (Columbus: Ohio State University

Press, 1994), 225-31; Robert E. Wright, *One Nation Under Debt: Hamilton, Jefferson and the History of What We Owe* (New York, McGraw-Hill, 2008), 141.
540. Curtis P. Nettels, *The Emergence of a National Economy: 1775-1815*, vol. 2 *of The Economic History of the United States* (New York: Holt, Rinehart & Winston, 1962), 114-15; Richard Sylla, "Experimental Federalism: The Economics of American Government, 1789-1914," in Stanley L. Engerman and Robert E. Gallman, eds., *The Cambridge Economic History of the United States: Volume 2, The Long Nineteenth Century* (Cambridge: Cambridge University Press, 2000), 499.
541. John Ball Osborne, "The First President's Interest in Washington as Told by Himself," *Records of the Columbia Historical Society* 4 (1901), 177.
542. "From Thomas Jefferson to George Rogers Clark, 4 December 1783," Julian P. Boyd, et al., eds., *The Papers of Thomas Jefferson* (Princeton: Princeton University Press, 1950-), 6:371.
543. Benjamin Goodhue, Congressman from Massachusetts, quoted in Margaret C.S. Christman, *The First Federal Congress, 1789-1791* (Washington: Smithsonian Institution Press, 1989), 188.
544. Bob Arnebeck, *Through a Fiery Trial: Building Washington, 1790-1800* (New York: Madison Books, 1991), 17; Fergus M. Bordewich, *Washington: The Making of the American Capital,* (New York: Harper Collins, 2008), 27-2.
545. "To George Washington from James Madison, 11 August 1788," W. W. Abbot, et al., eds., *The Papers of George Washington* (Charlottesville: University of Virginia Press, 1987–), Confederation Series, 6:437-39; "From George Washington to James Madison, 17[-18] August 1788," Abbot, et al., *Papers of George Washington*, Confederation Series, 6:454-55.
546. "From George Washington to Arthur Young, 5 December 1791," W. W. Abbot, et al., eds., *The Papers of George Washington* (Charlottesville: University of Virginia Press, 1987–), Presidential Series, 9:253-58; Kenneth R. Bowling, *The Creation of Washington, D.C.: The Idea and Location of the American Capital* (Fairfax, VA: George Mason University Press, 1991), 13, *see*, also, 106-26.
547. Kenneth R. Bowling, *The Creation of Washington, D.C.: The Idea and Location of the American Capital* (Fairfax, VA: George Mason University Press, 1991), 138.
548. Fergus M. Bordewich, *Washington: The Making of the American Capital,* (New York: Harper Collins, 2008), 44-49; Joseph J. Ellis, *Founding Brothers: The Revolutionary Generation* (New York: Vintage Books-Random House, 2002), 72-74; Jacob E. Cooke, "The Compromise of 1790," *The William and Mary Quarterly*, Third Series, Vol. 27, No. 4 (Oct., 1970), 525-26, 541-42.
549. Edwin J. Perkins, *American Public Finance and Financial Services 1700-1815* (Columbus: Ohio State University Press, 1994), 223-24; Edgar S. Maclay, ed., *Journal of William Maclay* (New York: D. Appleton and Company, 1890), 327-29; Curtis P. Nettels, *The Emergence of a National Economy: 1775-1815,* vol. 2 *of The Economic History of the United States* (New York: Holt, Rinehart & Winston, 1962), 115.
550. Edwin J. Perkins, *American Public Finance and Financial Services 1700-1815* (Columbus: Ohio State University Press, 1994), 216-18, 220-21.
551. "From George Washington to David Stuart, 15 June 1790," W. W. Abbot, et al., eds., *The Papers of George Washington* (Charlottesville: University of Virginia Press, 1987–), Presidential Series, 5:523-28; "From George Washington to David Stuart, 28 March 1790," Abbot, et al., *Papers of George Washington*, Presidential Series, 5:286-88..

552. "From George Washington to David Stuart, 15 June 1790," W. W. Abbot, et al., eds., *The Papers of George Washington* (Charlottesville: University of Virginia Press, 1987-), Presidential Series, 5:523-28.
553. E. James Ferguson, *The Power of the Purse: A History of American Public Finance, 1776-1790* (Chapel Hill: University of North Carolina Press, 1961), 321-22; Curtis P. Nettels, *The Emergence of a National Economy: 1775-1815*, vol. 2 *of The Economic History of the United States* (New York: Holt, Rinehart & Winston, 1962), 115.
554. Robert E. Wright, *One Nation Under Debt: Hamilton, Jefferson and the History of What We Owe* (New York, McGraw-Hill, 2008), 131.
555. Robert E. Wright, *One Nation Under Debt: Hamilton, Jefferson and the History of What We Owe* (New York, McGraw-Hill, 2008), 145-63; Richard Sylla, "Experimental Federalism: The Economics of American Government, 1789-1914," in Stanley L. Engerman and Robert E. Gallman, eds., *The Cambridge Economic History of the United States: Volume 2, The Long Nineteenth Century* (Cambridge: Cambridge University Press, 2000), 500.
556. John Steele Gordon, *Hamilton's Blessing: The Extraordinary Life and Times of Our National Debt* (New York: Walker and Company, 2010), 36; Richard Sylla, "Experimental Federalism: The Economics of American Government, 1789-1914," in Stanley L. Engerman and Robert E. Gallman, eds., *The Cambridge Economic History of the United States: Volume 2, The Long Nineteenth Century* (Cambridge: Cambridge University Press, 2000), 500; Robert E. Wright, *One Nation Under Debt: Hamilton, Jefferson and the History of What We Owe* (New York, McGraw-Hill, 2008), 12, 151.
557. "From George Washington to the United States Senate and House of Representatives, 8 December 1790," W. W. Abbot, et al., eds., *The Papers of George Washington* (Charlottesville: University of Virginia Press, 1987–), Presidential Series, 7:45-49; "From George Washington to the United States Senate and House of Representatives, 25 October 1791," Abbot et al., *Papers of George Washington*, Presidential Series, 9:110-17; "Noah Webster to James Greenleaf, October 13, 1791," Harry R. Warfel, ed., *Letters of Noah Webster* (New York: Library Publishers, 1953), 103.
558. Junius P. Rodriguez, *The Louisiana Purchase: A Historical and Geographical Encyclopedia* (Santa Barbara, CA: ABC-CLIO, 2002), 25-26; The Baring Archive Ltd., "Exhibition: The Louisiana Purchase" *Baring Archive*, https://www.baringarchive.org.uk/exhibitions/louisiana_purchase/3.
559. Fergus M. Bordewich, *Washington: The Making of the American Capital*, (New York: Harper Collins, 2008), 50-51; Kenneth R. Bowling, *The Creation of Washington, D.C.: The Idea and Location of the American Capital* (Fairfax, VA: George Mason University Press, 1991), 198-202, 204-05; Margaret C.S. Christman, *The First Federal Congress, 1789-1791* (Washington: Smithsonian Institution Press, 1989), 184-86; Richard Norton Smith, *Patriarch: George Washington and the New American Nation* (New York: Houghton Mifflin, 1993), 42; Edgar S. Maclay, ed., *Journal of William Maclay* (New York: D. Appleton and Company, 1890), 327-29.
560. "From George Washington to La Luzerne, 10 August 1790," W. W. Abbot, et al., eds., *The Papers of George Washington* (Charlottesville: University of Virginia Press, 1987-), Presidential Series, 6:229-30.
561. Act of July 16, 1790, ch. 28, 1 *Stat.* 130.

562. Fergus M. Bordewich, *Washington: The Making of the American Capital*, (New York: Harper Collins, 2008), 55.

563. Kenneth R. Bowling, *The Creation of Washington, D.C.: The Idea and Location of the American Capital* (Fairfax, VA: George Mason University Press, 1991), 209-11; Bob Arnebeck, *Through a Fiery Trial: Building Washington, 1790-1800* (New York: Madison Books, 1991), 26-29.

564. Bob Arnebeck, *Through a Fiery Trial: Building Washington, 1790-1800* (New York: Madison Books, 1991), 26-29; Kenneth R. Bowling, *The Creation of Washington, D.C.: The Idea and Location of the American Capital* (Fairfax, VA: George Mason University Press, 1991), 210-12.

565. Scott Berg, *Grand Avenues: The Story of the French Visionary Who Designed Washington, D.C.* (New York: Pantheon Books, 2007), 17-55; Frederick Gutheim and Antoinette J. Lee, *Worthy of the Nation: Washington, DC, from L'Enfant to the National Capital Planning Commissioner* (Baltimore: Johns Hopkins University Press, 2006), 12-15; Sarah Elizabeth Kite, *L'Enfant and Washington* (Baltimore: Johns Hopkins University Press, 1929), 2-4.

566. Scott Berg, *Grand Avenues: The Story of the French Visionary Who Designed Washington, D.C.* (New York: Pantheon Books, 2007), 57-60, 64-67.

567. "To George Washington from Pierre L'Enfant, 11 September 1789," W. W. Abbot, et al., eds., *The Papers of George Washington* (Charlottesville: University of Virginia Press, 1987–), Presidential Series, 4:15-19; Frederick Gutheim and Antoinette J. Lee, *Worthy of the Nation: Washington, DC, from L'Enfant to the National Capital Planning Commissioner* (Baltimore: Johns Hopkins University Press, 2006), 14-15; "From George Washington to David Stuart, 20 November 1791," Abbot, et al., *Papers of George Washington*, Presidential Series, 9:209-14.

568. "Memorandum from Thomas Jefferson, 29 August 1790," and "Memorandum from James Madison, 29 August 1790," W. W. Abbot, et al., eds., *The Papers of George Washington* (Charlottesville: University of Virginia Press, 1987–), Presidential Series, 6:368-72; "II. Jefferson's Report to Washington on Meeting Held at Georgetown, [14 September 1790]," Julian P. Boyd, et al., eds., *The Papers of Thomas Jefferson* (Princeton: Princeton University Press, 1950–), 17:461-63; "From George Washington to the United States Senate and House of Representatives, 24 January 1791," Abbot, et al., *Papers of George Washington*, Presidential Series, 7:277-78; Kenneth R. Bowling, *The Creation of Washington, D.C.: The Idea and Location of the American Capital* (Fairfax, VA: George Mason University Press, 1991), 213; Act of March 3, 1791, ch. 17, 1 *Stat.* .214-15.

569. Bob Arnebeck, *Through a Fiery Trial: Building Washington, 1790-1800* (New York: Madison Books, 1991), 38, Scott Berg, *Grand Avenues: The Story of the French Visionary Who Designed Washington, D.C.* (New York: Pantheon Books, 2007), 3-7.

570. Scott Berg, *Grand Avenues: The Story of the French Visionary Who Designed Washington, D.C.* (New York: Pantheon Books, 2007), 3-15; Fergus M. Bordewich, *Washington: The Making of the American Capital*, (New York: Harper Collins, 2008), 81-82.

571. "X. Pierre Charles L'Enfant to Thomas Jefferson, 4 April 1791," Julian P. Boyd, et al., eds., *The Papers of Thomas Jefferson* (Princeton: Princeton University Press, 1950-), 20:83-84; "XII. Thomas Jefferson to Pierre Charles L'Enfant, 10 April 1791," Boyd, et al., *Papers of Thomas Jefferson*, 20:86-87.

572. Frederick Gutheim and Antoinette J. Lee, *Worthy of the Nation: Washington, DC, from L'Enfant to the National Capital Planning Commissioner* (Baltimore: Johns Hopkins University

Press, 2006), 16; Scott Berg, *Grand Avenues: The Story of the French Visionary Who Designed Washington, D.C.* (New York: Pantheon Books, 2007), 12-13.

573. Frederick Gutheim and Antoinette J. Lee, *Worthy of the Nation: Washington, DC, from L'Enfant to the National Capital Planning Commissioner* (Baltimore: Johns Hopkins University Press, 2006), 391.

574. "Memorandum from Thomas Jefferson, 29 August 1790," W. W. Abbot, et al., eds., *The Papers of George Washington* (Charlottesville: University of Virginia Press, 1987-), Presidential Series, 6:368-70.

575. Frederick Gutheim and Antoinette J. Lee, *Worthy of the Nation: Washington, DC, from L'Enfant to the National Capital Planning Commissioner* (Baltimore: Johns Hopkins University Press, 2006), 3; Kenneth R. Bowling, *The Creation of Washington, D.C.: The Idea and Location of the American Capital* (Fairfax, VA: George Mason University Press, 1991), 208.

576. "[Diary entry: 28 March 1791]," Donald Jackson and Dorothy Twohig, eds., *The Diaries of George Washington* (Charlottesville: University Press of Virginia, 1976-79), 6:103-04.

577. Fergus M. Bordewich, *Washington: The Making of the American Capital,* (New York: Harper Collins, 2008), 81-82.

578. Scott Berg, *Grand Avenues: The Story of the French Visionary Who Designed Washington, D.C.* (New York: Pantheon Books, 2007), 78-79; "Memorandum of Pierre-Charles L'Enfant," 26 March 1791," W. W. Abbot, et al., eds., *The Papers of George Washington* (Charlottesville: University of Virginia Press, 1987-), Presidential Series, 8:5-9.

579. "[Diary entry: 29 March 1791]," Donald Jackson and Dorothy Twohig, eds., *The Diaries of George Washington* (Charlottesville: University Press of Virginia, 1976-79), 6:104-05; John E. Ferling, *The First of Men: A Life of George Washington* (Knoxville, TN: University of Tennessee Press, 1988), 398-99.

580. Allen C. Clark, *Origin of the Federal City* (reprinted from *Records of the Columbia Historical Society*, Volume 35-36, 1935), 61-62.

581. Fergus M. Bordewich, *Washington: The Making of the American Capital,* (New York: Harper Collins, 2008), 74-76; Allen C. Clark, *Origin of the Federal City* (reprinted from *Records of the Columbia Historical Society*, Volume 35-36, 1935), 42-49; Kenneth R. Bowling, *The Creation of Washington, D.C.: The Idea and Location of the American Capital* (Fairfax, VA: George Mason University Press, 1991), 222; Bob Arnebeck, *Through a Fiery Trial: Building Washington, 1790-1800* (New York: Madison Books, 1991), 43-44.

582. "From George Washington to Thomas Jefferson, 31 March 1791," W. W. Abbot, et al., eds., *The Papers of George Washington* (Charlottesville: University of Virginia Press, 1987–), Presidential Series, 8:28-30; Scott Berg, *Grand Avenues: The Story of the French Visionary Who Designed Washington, D.C.* (New York: Pantheon Books, 2007), 83-84.

583. *See,* e.g., Alexander Garvin, *The Planning Game: Lessons from Great Cities* (New York: W. W. Norton & Company, 2013).

584. Allen C. Clark, *Origin of the Federal City* (reprinted from *Records of the Columbia Historical Society*, Volume 35-36, 1935), 43-44.

585. Scott Berg, *Grand Avenues: The Story of the French Visionary Who Designed Washington, D.C.* (New York: Pantheon Books, 2007), 102-13; Bob Arnebeck, *Through a Fiery Trial: Building Washington, 1790-1800* (New York: Madison Books, 1991), 52-53; Richard Norton Smith, *Patriarch: George Washington and the New American Nation* (New York: Houghton Mifflin, 1993), 105.

586. "From Thomas Jefferson to Pierre Charles L'Enfant, [2] March 1791," Julian P. Boyd, et al., eds., *The Papers of Thomas Jefferson* (Princeton: Princeton University Press, 1950-), 19:355-56.

587. "III. Pierre Charles L'Enfant to Thomas Jefferson, 11 March 1791," Julian P. Boyd, et al., eds., *The Papers of Thomas Jefferson* (Princeton: Princeton University Press, 1950-), vol. 20:76-78.

588. C.M. Harris, "Washington's 'Federal City,' Jefferson's 'Federal Town,'" *Washington History* 12:1 (Spring/Summer 2000), 49-53; "Memorandum of Pierre-Charles L'Enfant," 26 March 1791, W. W. Abbot, et al., eds., *The Papers of George Washington* (Charlottesville: University of Virginia Press, 1987–), Presidential Series, 8:5-9; "Memorandum from Thomas Jefferson, 29 August 1790," Abbot, et al., *Papers of George Washington*, Presidential Series, 6:368-70; Scott Berg, *Grand Avenues: The Story of the French Visionary Who Designed Washington, D.C.* (New York: Pantheon Books, 2007), 73-74.

589. Pamela Scott, "L'Enfant's Washington Described: The City in the Public Press, 1791-1795," *Washington History* 3:1 (Spring/Summer 1991), 96-111. Referring to the seat of the federal government as a "district" first became a habit among delegates to the 1783 Continental Congress, in their debates on the question of whether to locate the on the Delaware River. The usage caught on, and the idea of a federal "district" became embedded in debates about the location, design, and construction of the new city, Madison and Jefferson's preference for the term "territory" notwithstanding. Frederick Gutheim and Antoinette J. Lee, *Worthy of the Nation: Washington, DC, from L'Enfant to the National Capital Planning Commissioner* (Baltimore: Johns Hopkins University Press, 2006), 9; Fergus M. Bordewich, *Washington: The Making of the American Capital,* (New York: Harper Collins, 2008), 83.

590. Isabella Liston to My Dear Uncle, 6 September 1796, in Bradford Perkins, ed., "A Diplomats Wife in Philadelphia: Letters of Henrietta Liston, 1796-1800," *The William and Mary Quarterly*, 3rd ser. 11:4 (October 1954), 592-632.

591. Ron Chernow, *Washington: A Life* (New York: The Penguin Press, 2010), 770.

592. Fergus M. Bordewich, *Washington: The Making of the American Capital,* (New York: Harper Collins, 2008), 212-13; Richard Norton Smith, *Patriarch: George Washington and the New American Nation* (New York: Houghton Mifflin, 1993), 304.

593. *See*, for example, Joe Nocera, "Russian Justice," *New York Times*, May 23, 2011, A-25.

594. Diana Rodriguez and Linda Ehrichs, eds., *Global Corruption Report 2007: Corruption in Judicial Systems* (Cambridge: Cambridge University Press, 2007), xvi-xxviii and 3-159.

595. *See*, e.g., "From George Washington to Cyrus Griffin, 18 August 1789," W.W. Abbot, et al., eds., *The Papers of George Washington* (Charlottesville: University of Virginia Press, 1987-), Presidential Series, 3:491.

596. Richard S. Arnold, "Judicial Politics under President Washington," 38 *Arizona Law Review* 473 (1996), 478.

597. *See* Maeva Marcus, et al., eds., *The Documentary History of the Supreme Court of the United States, 1789-1800* (New York: Columbia University Press, 1985), 1:xli (quoting George Washington to the Chief Justice and Associate Justices of the Supreme Court of the United States, April 30, 1790).

598. Transparency International, *Corruption Perceptions Index 2017* (Berlin: Transparency International, 2018), 3-10.

599. *See* for example, William J. Baumol, Robert E. Litan, and Carl J. Schramm, *Good Capitalism Bad Capitalism, and the Economics of Growth and Prosperity*, (Yale University Press, 2007) 93-131, 154-56.
600. William R. Casto, *The Supreme Court in the Early Republic: The Chief Justiceship of John Jay and Oliver Ellsworth*, (Columbia, SC, University of South Carolina Press, 1995), 55.
601. *See*, e.g., *New York Daily Advertiser*, February 3, 1791; *Gazette of the United States* (New York), February 3, 1790; Charles Warren, *The Supreme Court in United States History* (Boston: Little, Brown & Company, 1923), 1:58.
602. Timothy R. Smith, "When Congress Acts as its Founders Intended," *The Washington Post*, November 3, 2013, H6.
603. Peter Irons, *A People's History of the Supreme Court* (New York: Penguin Books, 1999), 85; Maeva Marcus, et al., eds., *The Documentary History of the Supreme Court of the United States, 1789-1800* (New York: Columbia University Press, 1985), 6:1.
604. *See*, e.g., *New York Daily Advertiser*, February 3, 1791; *Gazette of the United States* (New York), February 3, 1790; Charles Warren, *The Supreme Court in United States History* (Boston: Little, Brown & Company, 1923), 1:58.
605. Robert Lowry Clinton, "The Supreme Court before John Marshall," *Journal of Supreme Court History*, 27 (2002), 222-39.
606. *West v. Barnes*, 2 *Dallas* 401.
607. Maeva Marcus, et al., eds., *The Documentary History of the Supreme Court of the United States, 1789-1800* (New York: Columbia University Press, 1985), 6:6.
608. William R. Casto, *The Supreme Court in the Early Republic: The Chief Justiceship of John Jay and Oliver Ellsworth* (Columbia, SC, University of South Carolina Press, 1995), 247.
609. *See* generally, Scott Douglas Gerber, ed., *Seriatim: The Supreme Court Before John Marshall* (New York: New York University Press, 1998), 1-26; William R. Casto, *The Supreme Court in the Early Republic: The Chief Justiceship of John Jay and Oliver Ellsworth* (Columbia, SC, University of South Carolina Press, 1995), 1-4.
610. *Marbury v. Madison*, 5 U.S. 137 (1803); *McCulloch v. Maryland*, 17 U.S. 316 (1819).
611. Gordon Wood, *Empire of Liberty : A History of the Early Republic, 1789-1815* (New York: Oxford University Press, 2009), 449, citing "Thomas Jefferson to Phillip Mazzei, November 1785," Julian P. Boyd, et al., eds., *The Papers of Thomas Jefferson* (Princeton: Princeton University Press, 1950–), 9:67-72.
612. *See*, e.g., "From George Washington to John Rutledge, 29 September 1789, W. W. Abbot, et al., eds., *The Papers of George Washington* (Charlottesville: University of Virginia Press, 1987–), Presidential Series, 4:114-15.
613. *See*, e.g., *Ware v. Hylton*, 3 *Dallas* 1796 (striking down a Virginia law that allowed Virginians to satisfy debts owed to British citizens by making payments to Virginia itself).
614. Max Farrand, ed., *The Records of the Federal Convention of 1787* (New Haven, CT: Yale University Press, 1911), 1:119.
615. For an example of the public outcry against inferior courts, see Luther Martin's "Genuine Information," in *Documentary History of the Ratification of the Constitution*, Merrill Jensen, ed. (Madison: State Historical Society of Wisconsin, 1976), 15:379.
616. Max Farrand, ed., *The Records of the Federal Convention of 1787* (New Haven, CT: Yale University Press, 1911), 1:46.

617. Max Farrand, ed., *The Records of the Federal Convention of 1787* (New Haven, CT: Yale University Press, 1911), 1:125-27.
618. *See*, e.g., Robert Yates, "The Letters of Sydney," in *Essays on the Constitution Published During Its Discussion by the People, 1787-1788,* Paul Leicester Ford, ed. (Brooklyn: Historical Printing Club, 1892), 295.
619. Judiciary Act of 1789, 1 Stat. 73 (1789).
620. Judiciary Act of 1789, sec. 1, 2 and 3; "David Sewall to Caleb Strong, 2 May 1789," Maeva Marcus, et al., eds., *The Documentary History of the Supreme Court of the United States, 1789-1800* (New York: Columbia University Press, 1985), 4:384.
621. U.S. Constitution, art. II, section 2, cl. 2.
622. *See*, e.g., "From George Washington to Robert H. Harrison, 28 September 1789," in W. W. Abbot, et al., eds., *The Papers of George Washington* (Charlottesville: University of Virginia Press, 1987–), Presidential Series, 4:99-100 ("Your friends, and your fellow citizens, anxious for the respect of the Court to which you are appointed, will be happy to learn your acceptance — and no one among them will be more so than myself."); "From George Washington to Edmund Randolph, 28 September 1789," Abbot, et al., *Papers of George Washington*, Presidential Series, 4:106-07; "From George Washington to John Rutledge, 29 September 1789," Abbot, et al., *Papers of George Washington*, Presidential Series 4:114-15; "From George Washington to the United States Senate, 24 September 1789," Abbot, et al., *Papers of George Washington*, Presidential Series, 4:75-80.
623. "From George Washington to Robert H. Harrison, 28 September 1789," W. W. Abbot, et al., eds., *The Papers of George Washington* (Charlottesville: University of Virginia Press, 1987-), Presidential Series, 4:99-100.
624. Hampton L. Carson, *The History of the Supreme Court of the United States, With Biographies of All the Chief and Associate Justices* (Philadelphia: P.W. Zeigler & Co., 1902), 1:154; John Adams to Stephen Higginson (Sept. 21, 1789) Maeva Marcus, et al., eds., *The Documentary History of the Supreme Court of the United States, 1789-1800* (New York: Columbia University Press, 1985), 1:663.
625. Leon Friedman, "John Rutledge," *The Justices of the United States Supreme Court 1789-1969: Their Lives and Major Opinions*, ed. Leon Friedman and Fred L. Israel, 4 vols. (New York: R. R. Bowker, 1969), 1:39-41; Gustavus Myers, *History of the Supreme Court of the United States* (Chicago: Charles H. Kerr & Co., 1912), 147; Robert G. McCloskey, "James Wilson," Friedman and Israel, *Justices of the United States Supreme Court*, 89-90; Fred L. Israel, "John Blair, Jr.," Friedman and Israel, *Justices of the United States Supreme Court*, 111; Hampton L. Carson, *The History of the Supreme Court of the United States, With Biographies of All the Chief and Associate Justices* (Philadelphia: P.W. Zeigler & Co., 1902), 1:155; John Jay, *The Federalist* no. 2-5; General Order from George Washington, 6 November 1775 [appointing Robert Hanson Harrison Esqr as Washington's Aide-de-Camp], John C. Fitzpatrick, ed., *The Writings of George Washington from the Original Manuscript Sources 1745-1799* (Washington, DC: Government Printing Office, 1931-1940), 4:68; Rutledge served as President of the South Carolina Republic, then as Governor of South Carolina. Leon Friedman, "John Rutledge," Friedman and Israel, *Justices of the United States Supreme* Court, 1:37-38; Iredell served as the Attorney General for North Carolina. Carson, *History of the Supreme Court*, 1:154; Wilson, for example, was a delegate to the Confederation Congress, Charles Page Smith. *James Wilson, Founding Father: 1742-1798* (Chapel Hill, NC: University of North Carolina Press, 1956),

187-214; Natalie Wexler, "In the Beginning: The First Three Chief Justices," 154 *University of Pennsylvania Law Review*, 1373, 1379-80 (2006), 1374.

626. William R. Casto, *The Supreme Court in the Early Republic: The Chief Justiceship of John Jay and Oliver Ellsworth* (Columbia, SC, University of South Carolina Press, 1995), 65 (citing *New-York Journal*, April 16, 1789 (New York, NY) Maeva Marcus, et al., eds., *The Documentary History of the Supreme Court of the United States, 1789-1800* (New York: Columbia University Press, 1985), 1:611 -12); *see* also Richard S. Arnold, "Judicial Politics under President Washington," 38 *Arizona Law Review* 473 (1996), 478; George Washington to James Madison (Aug.20 - Sept.11, 1789) in Marcus, et al., *Documentary History*, 1:651-52, n. 3 ("Richard Henry Lee, the brother of Arthur Lee, suggested that Arthur's 'opposition to the Constitution [was the] cause for rejecting his abilities, and long public services from this system…'").

627. See Henry J. Abraham, *Justices and Presidents: A Political History of Appointments to the Supreme Court*, 3rd ed. (New York: Oxford University Press, 1992), 72; James Perry, "Supreme Court Appointments, 1789-1801: Criteria, Presidential Style, and the Press of Events," 6 *Journal Early Republic* 371 (1986); William R. Casto, *The Supreme Court in the Early Republic: The Chief Justiceship of John Jay and Oliver Ellsworth* (Columbia, SC, University of South Carolina Press, 1995), 56, 66; Arnold, "Judicial Politics," 488; Wexler, "In the Beginning," 1373, 1379-80; "To James Madison from Joseph Jones, 24 June 1789," Robert A. Rutland, et al., eds., *The Papers of James Madison* (Charlottesville: University Press of Virginia, 1977-), 12:258-60; Joseph J. Ellis, *Founding Brothers: The Revolutionary Generation* (New York: Vintage Books-Random House, 2002), 156; *See*, e.g., Christopher Gore to Rufus King, 6 August 1789, (expressing Gore's assumption that Massachusetts would have no more than one native son on the bench) Maeva Marcus, et al., eds., *The Documentary History of the Supreme Court of the United States, 1789-1800* (New York: Columbia University Press, 1985), 1:641-42.

628. *Federal Gazette* (Philadelphia), February 21, 1789; one Pennsylvanian suggested by the *Gazette* was James Wilson; *Massachusetts Gazette* (Boston), July 29, 1788, both of the candidates proposed in the article (Cushing and Dana) served on the Massachusetts Supreme Judicial Court.

629. The initial nominations submitted to the Senate by President Washington included Robert Harrison of Maryland, who declined the nomination as he was in ill health and died shortly thereafter. The President then appointed James Iredell to the bench in Harrison's place on February 8, 1790, which was confirmed by the Senate on February 10. Iredell, at thirty-eight, was the youngest of Washington's nominees.

630. Nomination by George Washington (September 24, 1789) Maeva Marcus, et al., eds., *The Documentary History of the Supreme Court of the United States, 1789-1800* (New York: Columbia University Press, 1985), 1:9; see also Richard S. Arnold, "Judicial Politics under President Washington," 38 *Arizona Law Review* 473 (1996), 473, noting that Washington also nominated eleven district judges, eleven U.S. Attorneys and eleven U.S. Marshals.

631. Letter of Ralph Izard to Edward Rutledge, (September 26, 1789), Maeva Marcus, et al., eds., *The Documentary History of the Supreme Court of the United States, 1789-1800* (New York: Columbia University Press, 1985), 1:668-69.

632. *See*, e.g., Benjamin Rush to John Adams, 22 April 1789, at Massachusetts Historical Society, Boston, Adams Manuscript Trust ("His [Wilson's] Abilities & knowledge in framing the constitution, & his zeal in promoting its establishment, have exposed him to a

most virulent persecution from the antifederalists in this state."). Maeva Marcus, et al., eds., *The Documentary History of the Supreme Court of the United States, 1789-1800* (New York: Columbia University Press, 1985), 1:613.

633. Fisher Ames to John Lowell, 28 July 1789, Massachusetts Historical Society, Boston, Adams Manuscript Trust, Maeva Marcus, et al., eds., *The Documentary History of the Supreme Court of the United States, 1789-1800* (New York: Columbia University Press, 1985), 1:640-41.

634. "To George Washington from David Humphreys, 28 October 1789," W. W. Abbot, et al., eds., *The Papers of George Washington* (Charlottesville: University of Virginia Press, 1987-), Presidential Series, 4:252-53.

635. Judiciary Act, sec. 4.

636. Scott Douglas Gerber, ed., *Seriatim: The Supreme Court Before John Marshall* (New York: New York University Press, 1998), 217.

637. Charles Warren, *The Supreme Court in United States History* (Boston: Little, Brown & Company, 1923), 1:62; James Iredell to Hannah Iredell, 8 September 1791, North Carolina State Department of Archives and History, Raleigh, North Carolina, Charles E. Johnson Collection, Maeva Marcus, et al., eds., *The Documentary History of the Supreme Court of the United States, 1789-1800* (New York: Columbia University Press, 1985), 2:208-09; *see*, also, James Iredell to Hannah Iredell, 16 September 1791, and 19 September 1791, Marcus, et al., *Documentary History*, 2:210.

638. "From George Washington to the United States Supreme Court Justices, 3 April 1790," W. W. Abbot, et al., eds., *The Papers of George Washington* (Charlottesville: University of Virginia Press, 1987–), Presidential Series, 5:313-14.

639. *See*, e.g., Nathaniel Peaslee Sargeant to John Adams, 25 April 1789, Massachusetts Historical Society, Boston, Adams Collection; also Kenneth B. Umbriet, *Our Eleven Chief Justices: A History of the Supreme Court in Terms of Their Personalities* (New York: Harper & Brothers, 1938), 42, Maeva Marcus, et al., eds., *The Documentary History of the Supreme Court of the United States, 1789-1800* (New York: Columbia University Press, 1985), 4:380.

640. See, e.g., *Maryland Journal* (Baltimore), May 17, 1791; *Columbian Centinel*(Boston), May 11, 1791.

641. "Neutrality Proclamation, 22 April 1793," W. W. Abbot, et al., eds., *The Papers of George Washington* (Charlottesville: University of Virginia Press, 1987-), Presidential Series, 12:472-74.

642. "Opinions of the Heads of the Departments," July 12, 1793, Maeva Marcus, et al., eds., *The Documentary History of the Supreme Court of the United States, 1789-1800* (New York: Columbia University Press, 1985), 6:743 and Thomas Jefferson's July 12, 1793 letter to Chief Justice John Jay, Marcus, et al., *Documentary History*, 6:7444.

643. *See*, e.g., Letter from Thomas Jefferson to the Justices of the Supreme Court (July 18, 1793), Maeva Marcus, et al., eds., *The Documentary History of the Supreme Court of the United States, 1789-1800* (New York: Columbia University Press, 1985), 6:747; Notes on Neutrality Questions (July 12, 1793), Julian P. Boyd, et al., eds., *The Papers of Thomas Jefferson* (Princeton: Princeton University Press, 1950–), 26:106.

644. Thomas Jefferson to the Justices of the Supreme Court, 18 July 1793, Maeva Marcus, et al., eds., *The Documentary History of the Supreme Court of the United States, 1789-1800* (New York: Columbia University Press, 1985), 6:747.

645. William R. Casto, *The Supreme Court in the Early Republic: The Chief Justiceship of John Jay and Oliver Ellsworth* (Columbia, SC, University of South Carolina Press, 1995), 79, and n.

20; Thomas Jefferson to John Jay, 12 July 1793, Maeva Marcus, et al., eds., *The Documentary History of the Supreme Court of the United States, 1789-1800* (New York: Columbia University Press, 1985), 6:744; letter from Thomas Jefferson to the Justices of the Supreme Court (July 18, 1793), Marcus, et al., *Documentary History*, 6:747.

646. August 8, 1793 letter from the Justices of the Supreme Court to George Washington, Maeva Marcus, et al., eds., *The Documentary History of the Supreme Court of the United States, 1789-1800* (New York: Columbia University Press, 1985), 6:755.

647. "Farewell Address, September 19, 1796," John C. Fitzpatrick, ed., The *Writings of George Washington from the Original Manuscript Sources, 1745-1799* (Washington: United States Government Printing Office, 1931-1940), 35:214-38; *see* Douglas J. Sylvester, "International Law as Sword or Shield? Early American Foreign Policy and the Law of Nations," 32 *N.Y.U. J. Int'l L. & Pol.* 1 (1999).

648. Scott Douglas Gerber, ed., *Seriatim: The Supreme Court Before John Marshall* (New York: New York University Press, 1998), 6, 9-11.

649. "Alexandria, Feb. 17," *The Federal Gazette, and Philadelphia Evening Post*, 23 Feb. 1791, 2;"Baltimore, Feb. 15," *The Federal Gazette, and Philadelphia Evening Post*, 22 Feb. 1791, 3; *see*, also,"Baltimore, Feb. 11," *The Pennsylvania Mercury, and Universal Advertiser*, 22 February 1791, issue 669, 3; for the celebration in Boston, which included a federal discharge of cannon in the morning and "a number of gentlemen" dining at Concert Hall after a number of patriotic toasts, *see*: "Domestic Occurrences. Boston, Feb. 12," *The Federal Gazette, and Philadelphia Evening Post*, 23 Feb. 1791, 2; "Philadelphia, 22nd February," *The Federal Gazette, and Philadelphia Evening Post*, 22 Feb. 1791, 2; Edward Lawler, Jr., "The President's House in Philadelphia: The Rediscovery of a Lost Landmark," *The Pennsylvania Magazine of History and Biography*, vol. 126, no. 1 (Jan., 2002), 5-95; Edward Lawler, Jr., "The President's House Revisited," *The Pennsylvania Magazine of History and Biography*, vol. 129, no. 4 (Oct., 2005), 371-410.

650. "Philadelphia, February 23. The President's Birth Day," *Dunlap's American Daily Advertiser*, 23 Feb. 1791, issue 4080, 3.

651. "Tuesday; President; Assemblies," *The General Advertiser and Political, Commercial, Agricultural, and Literary Journal*, 24 Feb. 1791, issue 126, 3.

652. "Philadelphia, 24th February," *The Federal Gazette, and Philadelphia Evening Post*, 24 Feb. 1791, 3; *The Pennsylvania Mercury, and Universal Advertiser*, 24 Feb. 1791, issue 670, 3; Dixon Wecter, *The Saga of American Society: A record of Social Aspiration* (New York: Charles Scribner's Sons, 1937), 301.

653. "From George Washington to the United States Senate, 22 February 1791," W. W. Abbot, et al., eds., *The Papers of George Washington* (Charlottesville: University of Virginia Press, 1987-), Presidential Series7:417-18.

654. "Final Version of the Second Report on the Further Provision Necessary for Establishing Public Credit (Report on a National Bank), 13 December 1790," Harold C. Syrett, ed., *The Papers of Alexander Hamilton* (New York: Columbia University Press, 1955-1987), 7:305-42.

655. "Alexander Hamilton to Robert Morris, 30 April, 1781," Harold C. Syrett, ed., *The Papers of Alexander Hamilton* (New York: Columbia University Press, 1961-87), 2:604-35.

656. "Final Version of the Second Report on the Further Provision Necessary for Establishing Public Credit (Report on a National Bank), 13 December 1790," Harold C. Syrett, ed., *The Papers of Alexander Hamilton* (New York: Columbia University Press, 1955-1987), 7:305-42.

657. "Final Version of the Second Report on the Further Provision Necessary for Establishing Public Credit (Report on a National Bank), 13 December 1790," Harold C. Syrett, ed., *The Papers of Alexander Hamilton* (New York: Columbia University Press, 1955-1987), 7:305-42; Adam Smith; R. H. Campbell and A. S. Skinner, eds., *Adam Smith, An Inquiry into the Nature and Causes of the Wealth of Nations*, The Glasgow Edition of the Works and Correspondence of Adam Smith (1979, exact photographic reproduction; Indianapolis, IN: Liberty Press/Liberty Classics, 1981), 324.

658. Curtis P. Nettels, *The Emergence of a National Economy: 1775-1815*, vol. 2 of The Economic History of the United States (New York: Holt, Rinehart & Winston, 1962), 118; John Steele Gordon, *Hamilton's Blessing: The Extraordinary Life and Times of Our National Debt* (1997, reprint; New York: Walker Publishing Co., 2010), 30; Edwin J. Perkins, *American Public Finance and Financial Services, 1700-1815* (Columbus, OH: Ohio State University Press, 1994), 236-7; David Jack Cowen, *The Origins and Economic Impact of the First Bank of the United States, 1791-1797*, Financial Sector of the American Economy (New York: Garland Publishing, 2000), 13-14; "Final Version of the Second Report on the Further Provision Necessary for Establishing Public Credit (Report on a National Bank), 13 December 1790," Harold C. Syrett, ed., *The Papers of Alexander Hamilton* (New York: Columbia University Press, 1955-1987), 7:305-4.

659. Richard Sylla, "Experimental Federalism: The Economics of American Government, 1789-1914," in Stanley L. Engerman and Robert E. Gallman, eds., *The Cambridge Economic History of the United States: Volume 2, The Long Nineteenth Century* (Cambridge: Cambridge University Press, 2000), 500; David Jack Cowen, *The Origins and Economic Impact of the First Bank of the United States, 1791-1797*, Financial Sector of the American Economy (New York: Garland Publishing, 2000), 12; Ron Chernow, *Alexander Hamilton* (New York: The Penguin Press, 2004), 349; M. St. Clair Clarke and D.A. Hall, eds., *Legislative and Documentary History of the Bank of the United States* (1832; reprint, New York: Augustus M. Kelley, 1967), 24.

660. "Enclosure: Opinion on the Constitutionality of an Act to Establish a Bank, 23 February 1791," W. W. Abbot, et al., eds., *The Papers of George Washington* (Charlottesville: University of Virginia Press, 1987–), Presidential Series, 7:425-52; Edwin J. Perkins, *American Public Finance and Financial Services, 1700-1815* (Columbus, OH: Ohio State University Press, 1994), 238, 245

661. Curtis P. Nettels, *The Emergence of a National Economy: 1775-1815*, vol. 2 of The Economic History of the United States (New York: Holt, Rinehart & Winston, 1962), 117-9; John Steele Gordon, *Hamilton's Blessing: The Extraordinary Life and Times of Our National Debt* (1997, reprint; New York: Walker Publishing Co., 2010), 31.

662. John C. Hamilton, ed., The *Works of Alexander Hamilton Comprising His Correspondence, and His Political and Official Writings, Exclusive of the Federalist, Civil and Military* (New York: John F. Trow, 1850-51), 3:14.

663. "Final Version of the Second Report on the Further Provision Necessary for Establishing Public Credit (Report on a National Bank), 13 December 1790," Harold C. Syrett, ed., *The Papers of Alexander Hamilton* (New York: Columbia University Press, 1955-1987), 7:305-42.

664. "Legislative," *The Federal Gazette, and Philadelphia Evening Post*, 22 Feb. 1791, 2; "From George Washington to the United States Senate, 22 February 1791," W. W. Abbot, et al., eds., *The Papers of George Washington* (Charlottesville: University of Virginia Press, 1987-), Presidential Series 7:417-18.

665. M. St. Clair Clarke and D.A. Hall, eds., *Legislative and Documentary History of the Bank of the United States* (1832; reprint, New York: Augustus M. Kelley, 1967), 37.
666. Curtis P. Nettels, *The Emergence of a National Economy: 1775-1815,* vol. 2 of The Economic History of the United States (New York: Holt, Rinehart & Winston, 1962), 126-9; Bray Hammond, *Banks and Politics in America: From the Revolution to the Civil War* (Princeton: Princeton University Press, 1985), 116-8; David Jack Cowen, *The Origins and Economic Impact of the First Bank of the United States, 1791-1797*, Financial Sector of the American Economy (New York: Garland Publishing, 2000), 17-8; Robert E. Wright, *One Nation Under Debt: Hamilton, Jefferson, and the History of What We Owe* (New York: McGraw-Hill, 2008), 149; Bourne to Zephaniah Andrews, February 3, 1791, quoted in Kenneth Russell Bowling, "Politics in the First Congress, 1789-1791" (Ph.D. thesis, University of Wisconsin, 1968), 235.
667. *Annals of Congress*, 1st Cong., 2nd sess., 1944-52.
668. Gordon S. Wood, *The Radicalism of the American Revolution: How a Revolution Transformed a Monarchichal Society into a Democratic One Unlike any that had Ever Existed* (New York: Alfred A. Knopf, 1992), 421, n. 31 citing Frank Bourgin, *The Great Challenge: The Myth of Laissez-Faire in the Early Republic* (New York: George Braziller, 1989), 44.
669. *Annals of Congress*, 1st Cong., 2nd sess., 1944-52.
670. *Annals of Congress*, 1st Cong., 2nd sess., 1944-52.
671. *Annals of Congress*, 1st Cong., 2nd sess., 2012.
672. "From George Washington to Alexander Hamilton, 16 February 1791," W. W. Abbot, et al., eds., *The Papers of George Washington* (Charlottesville: University of Virginia Press, 1987-), Presidential Series 7:357.
673. Halsted L. Ritter, *Washington as a Business Man* (New York: Sears Publishing Company, 1931), 10-12, 30, 59-67, 74-84, 89-90, 99-115; James Thomas Flexner, *George Washington: The Forge of Experience, 1732-1775* (Boston: Little, Brown and Company, 1965), 272-88.
674. "III-B. Schedule B: General Account of the Estate," c. October 1759, W. W. Abbot, et al., eds., *The Papers of George Washington* (Charlottesville: University of Virginia Press, 1987-), Colonial Series, 6:252-61.
675. Adam Smith, *An Inquiry into the Nature and Causes of the Wealth of Nations*, R. H. Campbell and A. S. Skinner, eds., Glasgow edition of the works and correspondence of Adam Smith (1979, reprint; Indianapolis: Liberty Classics, 1981), 1:297.
676. "From George Washington to Wakelin Welch, 1 July 1786," W. W. Abbot, et al., eds., *The Papers of George Washington* (Charlottesville: University of Virginia Press, 1987-), Confederation Series 4:144-46.
677. "George Washington's Last Will and Testament, 9 July 1799," W. W. Abbot, et al., eds., *The Papers of George Washington* (Charlottesville: University of Virginia Press, 1987–), Retirement Series, 4:477-92.
678. *Annals of Congress*, 1st Cong., 2nd sess., 2011; Ron Chernow, *Alexander Hamilton* (New York: The Penguin Press, 2004), 351; David Jack Cowen, *The Origins and Economic Impact of the First Bank of the United States, 1791-1797*, Financial Sector of the American Economy (New York: Garland Publishing, 2000), 20.
679. "To George Washington from Beverley Randolph, 4 January 1791," W. W. Abbot, et al., eds., *The Papers of George Washington* (Charlottesville: University of Virginia Press, 1987-), Presidential Series, 7:176-81.

680. Edgar S. Maclay, ed., *Journal of William Maclay:United States Senator from Pennsylvania 1789-1791* (New York: D. Appleton and Company, 1890), 345, 373.
681. "Shepard's-Town, Feb. 1," *The Federal Gazette, and Philadelphia Evening Post*, 22 Feb. 1791, 3.
682. "For the Federal Gazette," *The Federal Gazette, and Philadelphia Evening Post*, 22 Feb. 1791, 2.
683. "Enclosure: Opinion on the Constitutionality of the Bank, 12 February 1791," W. W. Abbot, et al., eds., *The Papers of George Washington* (Charlottesville: University of Virginia Press, 1987–), Presidential Series, 7:333.
684. "Thomas Jefferson to John Adams, 24 January 1814," in J. Jefferson Looney, ed., *The Papers of Thomas Jefferson: Retirement Series* (Princeton: Princeton University Press, 2010), 7:146-51.
685. Bray Hammond, *Banks and Politics in America: From the Revolution to the Civil War* (Princeton: Princeton University Press, 1985), 116-17; "To George Washington from Thomas Jefferson, 15 February 1791," W. W. Abbot, et al., eds., *The Papers of George Washington* (Charlottesville: University of Virginia Press, 1987–), Presidential Series 7:348-53.
686. "To George Washington from Thomas Jefferson, 15 February 1791," W. W. Abbot, et al., eds., *The Papers of George Washington* (Charlottesville: University of Virginia Press, 1987–), Presidential Series, 7:348-53.
687. *Annals of Congress*, 1st Cong., 2nd sess., 400-03.
688. John Richard Alden, *George Washington: A Biography* (Baton Rouge: Louisiana State University Press, 1996), 246; David Jack Cowen, *The Origins and Economic Impact of the First Bank of the United States, 1791-1797*, Financial Sector of the American Economy (New York: Garland Publishing, 2000), 15.
689. "From George Washington to Alexander Hamilton, February 16, 1791," W. W. Abbot, et al., eds., *The Papers of George Washington* (Charlottesville: University of Virginia Press, 1987–), Presidential Series, 7:357..
690. Moreau de St. Méry, *Moreau de St. Méry's American Journey,* translated and edited by Kenneth Roberts and Anna M. Roberts (Garden City, NY: Doubleday, 1947), 135.
691. "From Alexander Hamilton to George Washington, [21 February 1791]," Harold C. Syrett, ed., *The Papers of Alexander Hamilton* (New York: Columbia University Press, 1961-87), 8:57-58.
692. "Undelivered First Inaugural Address: Fragments, 30 April 1789," W. W. Abbot, et al., eds., *The Papers of George Washington* (Charlottesville: University of Virginia Press, 1987-), Presidential Series, 2:158-73.
693. David Jack Cowen, *The Origins and Economic Impact of the First Bank of the United States, 1791-1797*, Financial Sector of the American Economy (New York: Garland Publishing, 2000), 6-7; "To George Washington from Alexander Hamilton, 23 February 1791, W. W. Abbot, et al., eds., *The Papers of George Washington* (Charlottesville: University of Virginia Press, 1987–), Presidential Series, 7:422.
694. John C. Hamilton, ed., The Works of Alexander Hamilton Comprising His Correspondence, and His Political and Official Writings, Exclusive of the Federalist, Civil and Military (New York: John F. Trow, 1850-51), 111-12.
695. M. St. Clair Clarke and D.A. Hall, eds., *Legislative and Documentary History of the Bank of the United States* (1832; reprint, New York: Augustus M. Kelley, 1967), 96.

696. "Enclosure: Opinion on the Constitutionality of an Act to Establish a Bank, 23 February 1791," W. W. Abbot, et al., eds., *The Papers of George Washington* (Charlottesville: University of Virginia Press, 1987-), Presidential Series, 7:425-52; "From George Washington to Alexander Hamilton, 23 February 1791, W. W. Abbot, et al., eds., *The Papers of George Washington* (Charlottesville: University of Virginia Press, 1987-), Presidential Series7:452.

697. Curtis P. Nettels, *The Emergence of a National Economy: 1775-1815,* vol. 2 of The Economic History of the United States (New York: Holt, Rinehart & Winston, 1962), 118-19.

698. "Final Version of the Second Report on the Further Provision Necessary for Establishing Public Credit (Report on a National Bank), 13 December 1790," Harold C. Syrett, ed., *The Papers of Alexander Hamilton* (New York: Columbia University Press, 1955-1987), 7:305-42.

699. "Enclosure: Notes on the Advantages of a National Bank, [27 March 1791]," Harold C. Syrett, ed., *The Papers of Alexander Hamilton* (New York: Columbia University Press, 1961-87), 8:218-23.

700. Curtis P. Nettels, *The Emergence of a National Economy: 1775-1815,* vol. 2 of The Economic History of the United States (New York: Holt, Rinehart & Winston, 1962), 118-19.

701. Robert E. Wright, *One Nation Under Debt: Hamilton, Jefferson and the History of What We Owe* (New York, McGraw-Hill, 2008), 149; Richard Sylla, "Experimental Federalism: The Economics of American Government, 1789-1914," in Stanley L. Engerman and Robert E. Gallman, eds., *The Cambridge Economic History of the United States: Volume 2, The Long Nineteenth Century* (Cambridge: Cambridge University Press, 2000), 500; Thomas M. Doerflinger, *A Vigorous Spirit of Enterprise: Merchants and Economic Development in Revolutionary Philadelphia* (Chapel Hill, NC: Published for the Institute of Early American History and Culture, Williamsburg, VA, by the University of North Carolina Press. 1986), 312; Edwin J. Perkins, *American Public Finance and Financial Services 1700-1815* (Columbus: Ohio State University Press, 1994), 245-46.

702. "From Alexander Hamilton to Robert Morris, 30 April 1781," Harold C. Syrett, ed., *The Papers of Alexander Hamilton* (New York: Columbia University Press, 1961-87), 2:604-35.

703. Robert E. Wright, *One Nation Under Debt: Hamilton, Jefferson and the History of What We Owe* (New York, McGraw-Hill, 2008), 157-60.

704. "To Thomas Jefferson from James Madison, 10 July 1791," Julian P. Boyd, et al., eds., *The Papers of Thomas Jefferson* (Princeton: Princeton University Press, 1950-), 20:616-17.

705. David Jack Cowen, *The Origins and Economic Impact of the First Bank of the United States, 1791-1797,* Financial Sector of the American Economy (New York: Garland Publishing, 2000),

706. Curtis P. Nettels, *The Emergence of a National Economy: 1775-1815,* vol. 2 of The Economic History of the United States (New York: Holt, Rinehart & Winston, 1962), 48.

707. "From George Washington to Gouverneur Morris, 28 July 1791," W. W. Abbot, et al., eds., *The Papers of George Washington* (Charlottesville: University of Virginia Press, 1987-), Presidential Series, 8:381-84.

708. "From Thomas Jefferson to James Madison, 1 October 1792," Julian P. Boyd, et al., eds., *The Papers of Thomas Jefferson* (Princeton: Princeton University Press, 1950-), 24:432-33.

709. George Washington "To Gouverneur Morris, March 25, 1793," John C. Fitzpatrick, ed., *The Writings of George Washington from the Original Manuscript Sources, 1745-1799* (Washington: United States Government Printing Office, 1931-44), 32:402-03.

710. "Fifth Annual Address to Congress, December 3, 1793", John C. Fitzpatrick, ed., The *Writings of George Washington from the Original Manuscript Sources, 1745-1799* (Washington: United States Government Printing Office, 1931-1940), 33:163-69.

711. "Farewell Address [First Draft] [May 15, 1796]," John C. Fitzpatrick, ed., *The Writings of George Washington from the Original Manuscript Sources, 1745-1799* (Washington: United States Government Printing Office, 1931-1940), 35:51-61.

712. "George Washington to Charles Carroll, 1 May 1796, "in Worthington Chauncey Ford, ed., *The Writings of George Washington* (New York: G.P. Putnam's Sons, 1892), 13:187-88.

713. Samuel Flagg Bemis, "Jay's Treaty and the Northwest Boundary Gap," *The American Historical Review*, vol.27 (April 1922), 465-66; Treaty of Paris, 1783, Article VII; International Treaties and Related Records, 1778-1974; General Records of the United States Government, Record Group 11; National Archives; George Washington to Congress, 7 December 1796, in *American State Papers: Foreign Relations* (Buffalo, New York: W.S. Hein, 1998), 1:30; Gouverneur Morris to George Washington, 29 May 1790, in Jared Sparks, *The Life of Gouverneur Morris, With Selections from his Correspondence and Miscellaneous Papers,* (Boston: Gray and Bowen, 1832), 2:25.

714. Treaty of Paris, Articles IV, V and VI.

715. Emory G. Evans, "Planter Indebtedness and the Coming of the Revolution in Virginia," *William and Mary Quarterly*, vol. 19 (1962), 511; *see*, e.g., Georgia Confiscation Act of 1782, in *First Laws of the State of Georgia,* John D. Cushing, comp. (Wilmington, DE: Michael Glazier, Inc., 1981), 245.

716. Charles R. Ritcheson, *Aftermath of Revolution: British Policy toward the United States 1783-1795* (Dallas, TX: Southern Methodist University Press, 1969), 147-63.

717. Gouverneur Morris to George Washington, 29 May 1790, Jared Sparks, *The Life of Gouverneur Morris, With Selections from his Correspondence and Miscellaneous Papers,* (Boston: Gray and Bowen, 1832), 2:23-26; Duke of Leeds to Gouverneur Morris, September 10, 1790, in Sparks, *Life of Gouverneur Morris*, 2:40, and Gouverneur Morris to George Washington, September 18, 1790, in Sparks, *Life of Gouverneur Morris*, 2:40-47.

718. "7 October 1789," Donald Jackson and Dorothy Twohig, eds., *The Diaries of George Washington* (Charlottesville: University Press of Virginia, 1976-79), 5:454-55; Samuel Flagg Bemis, *Jay's Treaty: A Study in Commerce and Diplomacy*, (New Haven: Yale University Press, 1962), 66.

719. "7 October 1789," Donald Jackson and Dorothy Twohig, eds., *The Diaries of George Washington* (Charlottesville: University Press of Virginia, 1976-1979), 5:454-55; Richard Brookhiser, *Gentleman Revolutionary: Gouverneur Morris, the Rake who Wrote the Constitution* (New York: Free Press-Simon & Schuster, 2003), xvii.

720. George Washington "To Gouverneur Morris, 13 October 1789," John C. Fitzpatrick, ed., *The Writings of George Washington from the Original Manuscript Sources, 1745-1799* (Washington: United States Government Printing Office, 1931-1940), 30:439-42.

721. Anne Cary Morris, ed., *The Diary and Letters of Gouverneur Morris, Minister of the United States to France; Member of the Constitutional Convention, etc.,* (New York: Charles Scribner's Sons, 1888), 1:26, 309-48; Samuel Flagg Bemis, *Jay's Treaty: A Study in Commerce*

and Diplomacy, (New Haven: Yale University Press, 1962), 68; see also Alexander Hamilton to George Washington, 30 September 1790 in John C. Hamilton, ed., *The Works of Alexander Hamilton: Comprising His Correspondence, and His Political and Official Writings* (New York: John F. Trow, 1850-51), 4:73.

722. Thomas J. Schaeper, *Edward Bancroft: Scientist, Author, Spy* (New Haven: Yale University Press, 2011), xiv; "7 October 1789," Donald Jackson and Dorothy Twohig, eds., *The Diaries of George Washington* (Charlottesville: University Press of Virginia, 1976-79), 5:455; *see* also, "Edward Bancroft (@ Edwd.Edwards), Estimable Spy," *Central Intelligence Agency,* May 8, 2007.

723. Alexander DeConde, *Entangling Alliance: Politics and Diplomacy under George Washington,* (Durham, NC: Duke University Press, 1958), 68-70; Samuel Flagg Bemis, *Jay's Treaty: A Study in Commerce and Diplomacy,* (New Haven: Yale University Press, 1962), 70-85; Gouverneur Morris to George Washington, 18 September 1790, Jared Sparks, *The Life of Gouverneur Morris, With Selections from his Correspondence and Miscellaneous Papers,* (Boston: Gray and Bowen, 1832), 2:42.

724. Gouverneur Morris to George Washington, 29 May 1790, Jared Sparks, *The Life of Gouverneur Morris, With Selections from his Correspondence and Miscellaneous Papers,* (Boston: Gray and Bowen, 1832), 2:20-23; Gouverneur Morris to the Duke of Leeds, 24 September 1790, Sparks, *Life of Gouverneur Morris,* 2:20-23, 47-48; Gouverneur Morris to George Washington, 24 September 1790, Sparks, *Life of Gouverneur Morris,* 2:49-51.

725. Gouverneur Morris to George Washington, 29 May 1790, Jared Sparks, *The Life of Gouverneur Morris, With Selections from his Correspondence and Miscellaneous Papers,* (Boston: Gray and Bowen, 1832), 2:21-24; Treaty of Paris, Art. 7; Thomas Jefferson to George Hammond, 15 December 1791, *American State Papers: Foreign Relations*, 1:190.

726. Bernard Mayo, ed., *Instructions to the British Ministers to the United States* (Washington: U.S. Government Printing Office, 1941), 2-19.

727. S.W. Jackman, "A Young Englishman Reports on the New Nation: Edward Thornton to James Bland Burges, 1791-1793," *The William and Mary Quarterly*, Vol. 18, No. 1 (January 1961), 86; Charles R. Ritcheson, *Aftermath of Revolution: British Policy toward the United States, 1783-1795* (Dallas, TX: Southern Methodist University Press, 1969), 140-44; George Hammond to Thomas Jefferson, 30 November 1791, *American State Papers: Foreign Relations,* 1:189.

728. Charles R. Ritcheson, *Aftermath of Revolution: British Policy toward the United States, 1783-1795* (Dallas, TX: Southern Methodist University Press, 1969), 141-44.

729. George Hammond to Thomas Jefferson, 5 March 1792, *American State Papers: Foreign Relations*, 1:193-200; Thomas Jefferson to George Hammond, 29 May 1792, *American State Papers: Foreign Relations*, 1:201-37.

730. Thomas Jefferson to George Hammond, 29 May 1792, *American State Papers: Foreign Relations*, 1:202-45.

731. Robert E. Wright, *One Nation Under Debt* (New York: McGraw Hill, 2008), 154.

732. Charles R. Ritcheson, *Aftermath of Revolution: British Policy toward the United States, 1783-1795* (Dallas, TX: Southern Methodist University Press, 1969), 273.

733. George Washington "To Governor Henry Lee, May 6, 1793, John C. Fitzpatrick, ed., *The Writings of George Washington from the Original Manuscript Sources, 1745-1799* (Washington: United States Government Printing Office, 1931-1940), 32:448-50.

734. Charles R. Ritcheson, *Aftermath of Revolution: British Policy toward the United States, 1783-1795* (Dallas, TX: Southern Methodist University Press, 1969), 274.
735. Charles R. Ritcheson, *Aftermath of Revolution: British Policy toward the United States, 1783-1795* (Dallas, TX: Southern Methodist University Press, 1969), 242.
736. U.S. Constitution, art. I, sec. 8, cl. 11; George Washington "To Catherine Macaulay Graham, January 9, 1790," John C. Fitzpatrick, ed., *The Writings of George Washington from the Original Manuscript Sources, 1745-1799* (Washington: United States Government Printing Office, 1931-1940), 30:496.
737. Richard W. Van Alstyne, *Empire and Independence: The International History of the American Revolution,* (New York: John Wiley and Sons, 1965), 163; George Washington "To the Secretary of State, April 12, 1793, John C. Fitzpatrick, ed., The *Writings of George Washington from the Original Manuscript Sources, 1745-1799* (Washington: United States Government Printing Office, 1931-1940), 32:415-16.
738. *See*, e.g., Thomas Pinckney to Thomas Jefferson, 25 November 1793, in *American State Papers: Foreign Relations*, 1:24.
739. George Washington to Cabinet, 18 April 1793, in John C. Hamilton, ed., The *Works of Alexander Hamilton Comprising His Correspondence, and His Political and Official Writings, Exclusive of the Federalist, Civil and Military* (New York: John F. Trow, 1850-51), 4:359-61; John Ferling, *A Leap in the Dark: The Struggle to Create the American Republic* (New York: Oxford University Press, 2003).
740. George Washington, Neutrality Proclamation, 22 April 1793, in George Washington to Cabinet, 18 April 1793, John C. Hamilton, ed., The *Works of Alexander Hamilton Comprising His Correspondence, and His Political and Official Writings, Exclusive of the Federalist, Civil and Military* (New York: John F. Trow, 1850-51), 4:361-62.
741. Richard B. Morris, "The Constitution and Launching the Government," *Presidential Studies Quarterly,* (Winter 1981), 41-45.
742. *See*, e.g., Thomas Pinckney to Thomas Jefferson, 25 November 1793, in *American State Papers: Foreign Relations*, 1:31.
743. "Rules on Neutrality, 3 August 1793," Julian P. Boyd, et al., eds., *Papers of Thomas Jefferson* (Princeton: Princeton University Press, 1950-), 26:608-10.
744. "From James Madison to Thomas Jefferson, 19 June 1793," Robert A. Rutland, et al., eds., *The Papers of James Madison* (Charlottesville: University Press of Virginia, 1977-), 15:33-34.
745. David McCullough, *John Adams* (New York: Simon & Schuster, 2001), 444; William R. Casto, *The Supreme Court in the Early Republic: The Chief Justiceship of John Jay and Oliver Ellsworth* (Columbia, SC, University of South Carolina Press, 1995), 77.
746. David McCullough, *John Adams* (New York: Simon & Schuster, 2001), 445, quoting John Adams to Thomas Jefferson, June 30, 1813.
747. "Editorial Note: The Recall of Edmond Charles Genet," Julian P. Boyd, et al., eds., *The Papers of Thomas Jefferson* (Princeton: Princeton University Press, 1950–), 26:685-92; William R. Casto, *The Supreme Court in the Early Republic: The Chief Justiceship of John Jay and Oliver Ellsworth* (Columbia, SC, University of South Carolina Press, 1995), 77.
748. George Washington to Alexander Hamilton, 29 July 1795, John C. Hamilton, ed., The *Works of Alexander Hamilton Comprising His Correspondence, and His Political and Official Writings, Exclusive of the Federalist, Civil and Military* (New York: John F. Trow, 1850-51), 6:25-26.

749. William R. Casto, *The Supreme Court in the Early Republic: The Chief Justiceship of John Jay and Oliver Ellsworth* (Columbia, SC, University of South Carolina Press, 1995), 74-76; Maeva Marcus, et al., eds., *The Documentary History of the Supreme Court of the United States, 1789-1800* (New York: Columbia University Press, 1985), 6:297-99.
750. *Glass v. Sloop Betsey,* 3 Dallas 6 (1794).
751. Maeva Marcus, et al., eds., *The Documentary History of the Supreme Court of the United States, 1789-1800* (New York: Columbia University Press, 1985), 6:310.
752. Instructions to the Commanders, in *American State Papers: Foreign Relations*, 1:240; Josiah Newcomb, "New Light on Jay's Treaty," *The American Journal of International Law* 4 (October, 1934): 685; Thomas Pinckney to Edmund Randolph, 9 January 1794, in *American State Papers: Foreign Relations*, 1:430-31.
753. Order-in-Council, November 6, 1793, in *American State Papers: Foreign Relations*, 1:430-31 (copy enclosed with Pinckney's January 9, 1794 letter to Randolph); Thomas Pinckney to Thomas Jefferson, 26 December 1793, in *American State Papers: Foreign Relations*, 1:430.
754. Fulwar Skipwith to Washington, 1, 7 March 1794, in *American State Papers: Foreign Relations*, 1:428-29; Samuel Flagg Bemis, *Jay's Treaty: A Study in Commerce and Diplomacy*, (New Haven: Yale University Press, 1962), 106-07, 113; U.S. Congress, *House Journal*, 3d Cong., 1st sess., March 25, March 31, and April 25, 1794; U.S. Congress, *Senate Journal*, 3d Cong., 1st sess., March 26, 1794.
755. Alexander Hamilton to George Washington, 14 April 1794, John C. Hamilton, ed., The *Works of Alexander Hamilton Comprising His Correspondence, and His Political and Official Writings, Exclusive of the Federalist, Civil and Military* (New York: John F. Trow, 1850-51), 4:524.
756. George Washington to James Monroe, 9 April 1794, Worthington Chauncey Ford, *The Writings of George Washington* (New York: G.P. Putnam's Sons, 1892), 12:415-16.
757. Hamilton to Washington, 14 April 1794, John C. Hamilton, ed., The *Works of Alexander Hamilton Comprising His Correspondence, and His Political and Official Writings, Exclusive of the Federalist, Civil and Military* (New York: John F. Trow, 1850-51), 4:531.
758. Samuel Flagg Bemis, *Jay's Treaty: A Study in Commerce and Diplomacy*, (New Haven: Yale University Press, 1962), 284, citing *Secret Journals of Congress*, IV, 185, Oct. 13, 1786.
759. John Jay to Sarah Jay, 15 April 1794, in William Jay, ed., *The Life of John Jay with Selections from his Correspondence and Miscellaneous Papers* (New York: J & J Harper, 1833), 310.
760. U.S. Congress, *Senate Journal*, 3d Cong., 1st sess., April 16, 1794.
761. U.S. Congress, *Senate Journal*, 3d Cong., 1st sess., April 17, 18 and 19, 1794.
762. Joseph J. Ellis, *His Excellency: George Washington* (New York: Vintage Books, 2004), 227.
763. Instructions to John Jay, 6 May 1794, *American State Papers: Foreign Relations*, 1:473.
764. Instructions to John Jay, 6 May 1794, *American State Papers: Foreign Relations*, 1:473.
765. U.S. Congress, *Senate Journal*, 3d Cong., 1st sess., April 28, 1794.
766. Samuel Flagg Bemis, *Jay's Treaty: A Study in Commerce and Diplomacy*, (New Haven: Yale University Press, 1962), 303-11.
767. Samuel Flagg Bemis, *Jay's Treaty: A Study in Commerce and Diplomacy*, (New Haven: Yale University Press, 1962), 325.
768. Treaty of Amity, Commerce, and Navigation, Article I, *United States Statutes at Large*, 8:116.

769. John Jay to Randolph, 19 November 1794, in *American State Papers: Foreign Relations*, 1:503.
770. Treaty of Amity, Commerce, and Navigation, Articles IV, V, VII.
771. Treaty of Amity, Commerce, and Navigation, Article XXV.
772. Treaty of Amity, Commerce, and Navigation, Articles VIII, XV, XVIII: "It is further agreed that whenever any such articles [provisions and other articles not generally contraband] so becoming contraband, according to the existing laws of nations, shall for that reason be seized, the same shall not be confiscated, but the owners thereof shall be speedily and completely indemnified; and the captors, or, in their default, the Government under whose authority they act, shall pay to the masters or owners of such vessels the full value of all such articles, with a reasonable mercantile profit thereon, together with the freight, and also the demurrage incident to such detention," XIX, XXIII-XV, and XVIII; John Jay to Edmund Randolph, 19 November 1794, in *American State Papers: Foreign Relations*, 1:503; *see*, e.g., John Jay to Edmund Randolph, 13 September 1794, in *American State Papers: Foreign Relations*, 1:486.
773. John Jay to Edmund Randolph, 19 November 1794, in *American State Papers: Foreign Relations*, 1:503.
774. Walter Stahr, *John Jay: Founding Father* (New York: Hambledon& Continuum, 2005), 321-333.
775. Stanley Elkins and Eric McKitrick, *The Age of Federalism* (New York: Oxford University Press, 1993), 420; Lyon Gardiner Tyler, ed., *Encyclopedia of Virginia Biography* (New York: Lewis Historical Publishing Co., 1915), 2:87.
776. George Washington to Alexander Hamilton, 3 July 1795, Worthington Chauncey Ford, *The Writings of George Washington* (New York: G.P. Putnam's Sons, 1892), 13:61.
777. George Washington to Alexander Hamilton, 29 July 1795, John C. Hamilton, ed., The *Works of Alexander Hamilton Comprising His Correspondence, and His Political and Official Writings, Exclusive of the Federalist, Civil and Military* (New York: John F. Trow, 1850-51), 6:25-26; George Washington to Edmund Randolph, 29 July 1795, Worthington Chauncey Ford, *The Writings of George Washington* (New York: G.P. Putnam's Sons, 1892), 13:80; George Washington to Selectmen of Boston, 28 July 1795, in Ford, *Writings of George Washington*, 13:75; George Washington to Edmund Randolph, 31 July 1795, in Ford, *Writings of George Washington*, 13:84.
778. Moncure Daniel Conway, *Omitted Chapters of History Disclosed in the Life and Papers of Edmund Randolph* (New York: G.P. Putnam's Sons, 1889), 267.
779. George Washington to Edmund Randolph, 22 July 1795, Worthington Chauncey Ford, *The Writings of George Washington* (New York: G.P. Putnam's Sons, 1892), 13:68-70.
780. Joseph J. Ellis, *American Sphinx: The Character of Thomas Jefferson* (New York: Vintage Books, 1998), 193.
781. Edmund Randolph to George Washington, 29 July 1795, Moncure Daniel Conway, *Omitted Chapters of History Disclosed in the Life and Papers of Edmund Randolph* (New York: G.P. Putnam's Sons, 1889), 269; Edmund Randolph to George Washington, 31, July 1795, John C. Fitzpatrick, ed., The *Writings of George Washington from the Original Manuscript Sources, 1745-1799* (Washington: United States Government Printing Office, 1931-1940), 34:265, n. 81; George Washington to Edmund Randolph, 20 August 1795, Worthington Chauncey Ford, *The Writings of George Washington* (New York: G.P. Putnam's Sons, 1892), 13:90.

782. Timothy Pickering to George Washington, 31 July 1795, Worthington Chauncey Ford, *The Writings of George Washington* (New York: G.P. Putnam's Sons, 1892), 13:86, n. 1.
783. George Washington to Edmund Randolph, 27 September 1795, Worthington Chauncey Ford, *The Writings of George Washington* (New York: G.P. Putnam's Sons, 1892), 13:108; George Washington to Edmund Randolph, 20 August 1795, in Ford, *Writings of George Washington*, 13:90; Octavius Pickering and Charles Wentworth Upham, *The Life of Timothy Pickering* (Boston: Little, Brown, and Company, 1873), 3:218; *See*, e.g., George Washington to Edmund Randolph, 20 August 1795, in Ford, *Writings of George Washington*, 13:90; Stanley Elkins and Eric McKitrick, *The Age of Federalism* (New York: Oxford University Press, 1993), 426; P.V. Daniel, ed.,*A Vindication of Edmund Randolph* (Richmond: Charles H. Wynne, 1855).
784. *See,* e.g., Samuel Eliot Morison and Henry Steele Commager, *Growth of the American Republic,* (New York: Oxford University Press, 1930), tenth printing, 1960, 1:358.
785. Arthur Preston Whitaker, *Spanish-American Frontier: 1783-1795: The Westward Movement and the Spanish Retreat in the Mississippi Valley* (1927: reprint, Gloucester, MA: Peter Smith, 1962), 3-16.
786. Arthur Preston Whitaker, *Spanish-American Frontier: 1783-1795: The Westward Movement and the Spanish Retreat in the Mississippi Valley* (1927: reprint, Gloucester, MA: Peter Smith, 1962), 7-9, 37.
787. George C. Herring, *From Colony to Superpower: U.S. Foreign Relations since 1776* (New York: Oxford University Press, 2008), 22, 34.
788. Arthur Preston Whitaker, *Spanish-American Frontier: 1783-1795: The Westward Movement and the Spanish Retreat in the Mississippi Valley* (1927: reprint, Gloucester, MA: Peter Smith, 1962), 33; Samuel Flagg Bemis, *Pinckney's Treaty: America's Advantage from Europe's Distress, 1783-1800* (New Haven, CT: Yale University Press, 1960), 38.
789. Richard Kluger, *Seizing Destiny: How America Grew from Sea to Shining Sea* (New York: Alfred A. Knopf, 2007), 148-54.
790. Arthur Preston Whitaker, *Spanish-American Frontier: 1783-1795: The Westward Movement and the Spanish Retreat in the Mississippi Valley* (1927: reprint, Gloucester, MA: Peter Smith, 1962), 17, 23.
791. George C. Herring, *From Colony to Superpower: U.S. Foreign Relations since 1776* (Oxford: Oxford University Press, 2008), 38.
792. Arthur Preston Whitaker, *Spanish-American Frontier: 1783-1795: The Westward Movement and the Spanish Retreat in the Mississippi Valley* (1927: reprint, Gloucester, MA: Peter Smith, 1962), 8-9.
793. Arthur Preston Whitaker, *Spanish-American Frontier: 1783-1795: The Westward Movement and the Spanish Retreat in the Mississippi Valley* (1927: reprint, Gloucester, MA: Peter Smith, 1962), 74-75.
794. Frank T. Reuter, *Trials and Triumphs: George Washington's Foreign Policy* (Fort Worth, TX: Texas Christian University Press, 1983), 110-12.
795. Treaty of Paris, 1783; International Treaties and Related Records, 1778-1974; General Records of the United States Government, Record Group 11; National Archives.
796. Arthur Preston Whitaker, *Spanish-American Frontier: 1783-1795: The Westward Movement and the Spanish Retreat in the Mississippi Valley* (1927: reprint, Gloucester, MA: Peter Smith, 1962), 10-11.

797. Arthur Preston Whitaker, *Spanish-American Frontier: 1783-1795: The Westward Movement and the Spanish Retreat in the Mississippi Valley* (1927: reprint, Gloucester, MA: Peter Smith, 1962), 10-11, 16-23.
798. See, e.g., Thomas Jefferson to William Carmichael and William Short, 3 November 1792, *American State Papers: Foreign Relations*, 1:30, 259.
799. George Washington, September 1794, in Charles Cotesworth Pinckney, *Life of General Thomas Pinckney* (Cambridge, MA: Riverside Press, 1895), 126-27; Arthur Preston Whitaker, *Spanish-American Frontier: 1783-1795: The Westward Movement and the Spanish Retreat in the Mississippi Valley* (1927: reprint, Gloucester, MA: Peter Smith, 1962), 92-93.
800. Samuel Flagg Bemis, *Pinckney's Treaty: America's Advantage from Europe's Distress, 1783-1800* (New Haven, CT: Yale University Press, 1960), 110-43,
801. Samuel Flagg Bemis, *Pinckney's Treaty: America's Advantage from Europe's Distress, 1783-1800* (New Haven, CT: Yale University Press, 1960), 11-29.
802. "Free Navigation of the Mississippi," 16 September 1788, John C. Hamilton, ed., The *Works of Alexander Hamilton Comprising His Correspondence, and His Political and Official Writings, Exclusive of the Federalist, Civil and Military* (New York: John F. Trow, 1850-51), 2:473; *see*, e.g., *American State Papers: Foreign Relations*, 1:274, 328, 433-42.
803. Samuel Flagg Bemis, *Pinckney's Treaty: America's Advantage from Europe's Distress, 1783-1800* (New Haven, CT: Yale University Press, 1960), 111, 119 (citing Miró to Espeleta, 27 August 1787, 25 October 1787, in Despatches of the Spanish Governors of Louisiana, 1766-1791, photostatic copy available at the Library of Congress); *see*, e.g., George Washington to Charles Carroll, 1 May 1796, Worthington Chauncey Ford, *The Writings of George Washington* (New York: G.P. Putnam's Sons, 1892), 13:187-88 n. 1; and George Washington "To Henry Lee, 18 June 1786, John C. Fitzpatrick, ed., The *Writings of George Washington from the Original Manuscript Sources, 1745-1799* (Washington: United States Government Printing Office, 1931-1940), 34:459-61; Arthur Preston Whitaker, *Spanish-American Frontier: 1783-1795: The Westward Movement and the Spanish Retreat in the Mississippi Valley* (1927: reprint, Gloucester, MA: Peter Smith, 1962), 15-16.
804. George Washington "To Henry Lee, 18 June 1786, John C. Fitzpatrick, ed., *The Writings of George Washington from the Original Manuscript Sources, 1745-1799* (Washington: United States Government Printing Office, 1931-1940), 34:459-61.
805. Thomas Jefferson to Isaac Shelby, Governor of Kentucky, 29 August 1793, in *American State Papers: Foreign Relations*, 1:455.
806. Isaac Shelby to Thomas Jefferson, 5 October 1793, and Thomas Jefferson to Isaac Shelby, 6 November 1793, in *American State Papers: Foreign Relations*, 1:455; Isaac Shelby to Thomas Jefferson, 13 January 1794, in *American State Papers: Foreign Relations*, 1:455-56; Edmund Randolph to Isaac Shelby, 29 March 1794, in *American State Papers: Foreign Relations*, 1:456.
807. United States Senate Journal, 3rd Cong., 1st sess., May 20, 1794; Thomas Jefferson to John Brown, 1788, in Paul Leicester Ford, *The Writings of Thomas Jefferson* (New York: G.P. Putnam's Sons, 1892-99). 5:17.
808. Samuel Flagg Bemis, *Pinckney's Treaty: America's Advantage from Europe's Distress, 1783-1800* (New Haven, CT: Yale University Press, 1960), 222.
809. Paul Leicester Ford, *The Writings of Thomas Jefferson* (New York: G.P. Putnam's Sons, 1892-99), 6:206; *see* also Samuel Flagg Bemis, *Pinckney's Treaty: America's Advantage from Europe's Distress, 1783-1800* (New Haven, CT: Yale University Press, 1960), 192-94.

810. Frank T. Reuter, *Trials and Triumphs: George Washington's Foreign Policy* (Fort Worth, TX: Texas Christian University Press, 1983), 122.
811. Message from George Washington to the United States Senate, 11 January 1792, in *American State Papers: Foreign Relations*, 1:130-31.
812. *See.*, e.g., Samuel Flagg Bemis, *Pinckney's Treaty: America's Advantage from Europe's Distress, 1783-1800* (New Haven, CT: Yale University Press, 1960), 194-96 (citing Alcudia to Jaudenes and Viar, 9 May 1794, in Spanish Legation, vol. 201; Jaudenes to Randolph, 16 August 1794, in Short Papers, XXVI, 4645, State Department, Notes, Spain).
813. Charles Cotesworth Pinckney, *Life of General Thomas Pinckney* (Cambridge, MA: Riverside Press, 1895), 128; United States Congress, *Senate Executive Journal*, 3rd Cong., 2nd sess., November 21, 1794.
814. George Washington to James Monroe, February 1795, Charles Cotesworth Pinckney, *Life of General Thomas Pinckney* (Cambridge, MA: Riverside Press, 1895), 127.
815. Thomas Jefferson, Paul Leicester Ford, *The Writings of Thomas Jefferson* (New York: G.P. Putnam's Sons, 1892-99), 9:344.
816. Charles Cotesworth Pinckney, *Life of General Thomas Pinckney* (Cambridge, MA: Riverside Press, 1895), 1-25; United States Congress, *Senate Executive Journal*, 3rd Cong., 2nd sess., November 21 and 24, 1794; Paul Leicester Ford, *The Writings of Thomas Jefferson* (New York: G.P. Putnam's Sons, 1892-99), 9:344.
817. Edmund Randolph to Thomas Pinckney, 3 November 1794, Charles Cotesworth Pinckney, *Life of General Thomas Pinckney* (Cambridge, MA: Riverside Press, 1895), 125.
818. The First Coalition against France consisted of Spain, Great Britain, Holland, Austria, and Prussia.
819. Timothy Pitkin, *A Political and Civil History of the United States of America* (New Haven, CT: Howe and Durrie& Peck, 1828), 2:396-97.
820. *See*, e.g., William Short to Edmund Randolph, 9 January 1794, in *American State Papers: Foreign Relations*, 1:442-43, and James Monroe to William Short, 30 May 1795, in *American State Papers: Foreign Relations*, 1:717.
821. See, e.g., James Monroe to William Short, 30 May 1795, in *American State Papers: Foreign Relations*, 1:717.
822. Arthur Preston Whitaker, *Spanish-American Frontier: 1783-1795: The Westward Movement and the Spanish Retreat in the Mississippi Valley* (1927: reprint, Gloucester, MA: Peter Smith, 1962), 148.
823. For a later iteration of the U.S. insistence on their inherent right to navigate the Mississippi, see Thomas Pinckney notes to Don Manuel de Godoy (Prince de la Paz) on a draft of the treaty of San Lorenzo, 25 September 1795, in *American State Papers: Foreign Relations*, 540-41.
824. "II. Secretary of State to William Carmichael, enclosing Outline of Policy, 2 August 1790," Julian P. Boyd, et al., eds., *The Papers of Thomas Jefferson* (Princeton: Princeton University Press, 1950–), 17:111-12; Samuel Flagg Bemis, *Pinckney's Treaty: America's Advantage from Europe's Distress, 1783-1800* (New Haven, CT: Yale University Press, 1960), 130; Charles Cotesworth Pinckney, *Life of General Thomas Pinckney* (Cambridge, MA: Riverside Press, 1895), 130-31; Thomas Pinckney to Prince de la Paz, 23 and 24 October 1795, in *American State Papers: Foreign Relations*, 1:545; Prince de la Paz to Thomas Pinckney, 28 October 1795, in *American State Papers: Foreign Relations*, 1:545; U.S. Congress, *Senate*

Executive Journal, 4th Cong., 1st sess., February 26, 1796; Thomas Pinckney to Edmund Randolph, 21 July 1795, in *American State Papers: Foreign Relations*, 1:534.

825. Prince de la Paz to Thomas Pinckney, 28 October 1795, in *American State Papers: Foreign Relations*, 1:545; Charles Cotesworth Pinckney, *Life of General Thomas Pinckney* (Cambridge, MA: Riverside Press, 1895), 131; U.S. Congress, *Senate Executive Journal*, 4th Cong., 1st sess., February 26, 1796; Thomas Pinckney to Edmund Randolph, 21 July 1795, in *American State Papers: Foreign Relations*, 1:534.

826. Treaty of San Lorenzo, Article I.

827. Treaty of San Lorenzo, Article II.

828. Treaty of San Lorenzo, Article III.

829. Treaty of San Lorenzo, Article IV.

830. David W. Miller, *The Taking of American Indian Lands in the Southeast: A History of Territorial Cessions and Faced Relocations, 1607-1840* (Jefferson, NC: McFarland & Company, 2011), 63.

831. Treaty of San Lorenzo, Articles IV and XXII.

832. Treaty of San Lorenzo, Article IV; Jay's Treaty, Article III; Thomas Pinckney to the Prince de la Paz, 25 September 1795, in *American State Papers: Foreign Relations*, 540.

833. Treaty of San Lorenzo, Article V.

834. *See*, e.g., Thomas Pinckney to the Prince de la Paz, 20 September 1795, in *American State Papers: Foreign Relations*, 1:539Treaty of San Lorenzo, Article XXI.

835. Treaty of San Lorenzo, Article XXII; Summary of Exports, Treasury Department, 28 March 1792, in *American State Papers: Commerce and Navigation*, 1:146; Thomas Pinckney to Edmund Randolph, 28 October 1795, in *American State Papers: Foreign Relations*, 1:546.

836. Treaty of San Lorenzo, Articles VI, VIII.

837. Treaty of San Lorenzo, Articles IX-XVII, XX.

838. U.S. Congress, *Senate Executive Journal*, 4th Cong., 1st sess., February 26 and March 3, 1796; *see*, e.g., Thomas Pinckney to Edmund Randolph, 28 October 1795, in *American State Papers: Foreign Relations*, 1:546; *see* also Thomas Pinckney to Edmund Randolph, 21 July 1795, in *American State Papers: Foreign Relations*, 1:534; George Washington, Farewell Address, 17 September 1796, Worthington Chauncey Ford, *The Writings of George Washington* (New York: G.P. Putnam's Sons, 1892), 13:295-96.

839. Farewell Address, 17 September 1796, Worthington Chauncey Ford, *The Writings of George Washington* (New York: G.P. Putnam's Sons, 1892), 13:295-96.

840. Eugene E. Prussing, *The Estate of George Washington, Deceased* (Boston: Little Brown and Company, 1927), 16.

841. Philander D. Chase, "The Debt Which Must All Pay": Tobias Lear's Diary Account of George Washington's Death, *Pennsylvania Legacies*, Vol. 4, No. 2 (November 2004), 19; Peter R. Henriques, "The Final Struggle between George Washington and the Grim King," *The Virginia Magazine of History and Biography*, Vol. 1107, No. 1, The Private George Washington: A Bicentennial Reconsideration (Winter, 1999), 73-97; Dr. Howard Markel, "December 14, 1799: The Excruciating Final Hours of President George Washington," *PBS News Hour*, December 14, 2014.

842. Gouverneur Morris, "An Oration Upon the Death of General Washington," *Eulogies and Orations on the Life and Death of General George Washington, First President of the United States of America* (Boston: Manning & Loring, 1800), 46.

843. John R. Miller, "The Original American Idol," *The Wall Street Journal,* February 19-20, 2011, A-15.
844. "Thomas Jefferson to Walter Jones, 2 January 1814," J. Jefferson Looney, ed., *The Papers of Thomas Jefferson*, Retirement Series (Princeton: Princeton University Press, 2010), 7:100-04.
845. E. O. Randall, "Washington's Ohio Lands," *Ohio Archaeological and Historical Quarterly*, vol. 19, no. 3, (July 1910), 304-18.

INDEX

B

C

D

E

F

O

P

Q

R

S

Y

ABOUT THE AUTHOR

International lawyer and financier, educator and philanthropist, Cyrus A. Ansary has been a long-term student of the life of George Washington, and his own career fully embodies the entrepreneurial spirit envisioned by our first President for this nation.

Ansary was a member of the Life Guard Society of George Washington's Mount Vernon for three decades. He was also a member of the Woodrow Wilson Council. He chaired the Board of Trustees of American University in Washington, D.C., for about ten years. He managed the first sovereign wealth fund in the world to make transnational equity investments, after which he established his own merchant banking firm and served on multiple corporate and nonprofit boards in Europe, Latin America and the U.S.

A former Marine, Ansary graduated from R.L. Paschal High School in Fort Worth, Texas. He received an economics degree from American University and a law degree from Columbia University. He also studied history at the University of Paris. He lives with his wife Janet Hodges Ansary in suburban Washington, D.C. They are the parents of four children.

cansary@gmail.com

Chock-full of anecdotes told with passion and humor, Cyrus A. Ansary's *Odyssey of High Hopes* is an exquisitely written memoir about a boy's harrowing, captivating, and sometimes funny rollercoaster ride across the slopes of the American dream.

From the dark and crime-infested tenements of South Tehran to the pinnacle of global finance is the inspiring story of a skinny teenager's hell-for-leather determination to rise above poverty and obscurity to secure a coveted American education.

A former Marine and Columbia Law School graduate, Cyrus A. Ansary tells a searing and deeply moving narrative about the struggle for survival in America. Shining a light on the challenges of the young, the memoir is a heartwarming and thought-provoking perspective on their hardships.

What readers are saying:

★★★★★ "If you have ever wondered whether your dreams can come true, this book teaches you to renounce self-doubt, and that human beings can create the life they desire, regardless of age."

★★★★★ "The story is enthralling. Each part begins with a wonderful anecdote or interesting dilemma that the author gets himself into and ends with a thought-inducing epilogue that has the reader thinking 'How can I be like Cyrus?'"

★★★★★ "The powerful message of the book is 'dream high, never lose hope, and never give up.' The author's success made me believe in the power of courage, sacrifice, and determination."

★★★★★ "Every part of the story shows how creative and passionate the author is. A fun and memorable read."

★★★★★ "Anybody who reads this book may find themselves yearning for success or even motivated to reach for the stars!"

Made in the USA
Las Vegas, NV
21 January 2025

9c7380da-19a4-492b-bfb8-58a6853f211fR01